10 **American Foreign Policy and the Politics of Fear**
Threat inflation since 9/11
Edited by A. Trevor Thrall and Jane K. Cramer

11 **Risk, Global Governance and Security**
The other War on Terror
Yee-Kuang Heng and Kenneth McDonagh

12 **Nuclear Weapons and Cooperative Security in the 21st Century**
The new disorder
Stephen J. Cimbala

13 **Political Economy and Grand Strategy**
A neoclassical realist view
Mark R. Brawley

14 **Iran and Nuclear Weapons**
Protracted conflict and proliferation
Saira Khan

15 **US Strategy in Africa**
AFRICOM, terrorism and security challenges
Edited by David J. Francis

16 **Great Powers and Strategic Stability in the 21st Century**
Competing visions of world order
Edited by Graeme P. Herd

Gre   Stability
in the 21st Century

This book addresses the issue of grand strategic stability in the twenty-first century, and examines the role of the key centers of global power – the US, EU, Russia, China and India – in managing contemporary strategic threats.

This edited volume assesses the cooperative and conflictual capacity of Great Powers to manage increasingly interconnected strategic threats (not least, terrorism and political extremism, WMD proliferation, fragile states, regional crises and co   . The con-
tribut   erized by a
predic   te interest-
based   ue that the
operat   ting a new
institu   ·threat specific,   states (not
least   e singular,
collect   of strategic
stabili
Thi   irity, grand
strateg

Graer   in Security
Policy   published
several books, including *Stuarts and Romanovs: The Rise and Fall of a Special
Relationship* (2009), *The Ideological War on Terror: World Wide Strategies
for Counter Terrorism* (2007), *Divided West: European Security and the
Transatlantic Relationship* (2006), *Soft Security Threats and European Security*
(2005), *Security Dynamics of the Former Soviet Bloc* (2003) and *Russia and the
Regions: Strength Through Weakness* (2003).

Routledge global security studies

Series editors: Aaron Karp, Regina Karp and Terry Teriff

1 **Nuclear Proliferation and International Security**
Sverre Lodgaard and Morten Bremer Maerli

2 **Global Insurgency and the Future of Armed Conflict**
Debating fourth-generation warfare
Terry Terriff, Aaron Karp and Regina Karp

3 **Terrorism and Weapons of Mass Destruction**
Responding to the challenge
Edited by Ian Bellany

4 **Globalization and WMD Proliferation**
Edited by James A. Russell and Jim J. Wirtz

5 **Power Shifts, Strategy and War**
Declining states and international conflict
Dong Sun Lee

6 **Energy Security and Global Politics**
The militarization of resource management
Edited by Daniel Moran and James A. Russell

7 **US Nuclear Weapons Policy After the Cold War**
Russians, "rogues" and domestic division
Nick Ritchie

8 **Security and Post-Conflict Reconstruction**
Dealing with fighters in the aftermath of war
Edited by Robert Muggah

9 **Network Centric Warfare and Coalition Operations**
The new military operating systems
Paul T. Mitchell

Great Powers and Strategic Stability in the 21st Century

Competing visions of world order

Edited by Graeme P. Herd

LONDON AND NEW YORK

This book is edited by Graeme P. Herd, with the support of the Geneva Centre for Security Policy

First published 2010
by Routledge
2 Park Square, Milton Park, Abingdon, Oxon OX14 4RN

Simultaneously published in the USA and Canada
by Routledge
270 Madison Ave, New York, NY 10016

Routledge is an imprint of the Taylor & Francis Group, an informa business

Transferred to Digital Printing 2010

© 2010 Selection and editorial matter, Graeme P. Herd; individual
chapters, the contributors

Typeset in Times by Wearset Ltd, Boldon, Tyne and Wear

British Library Cataloguing in Publication Data
A catalogue record for this book is available from the British Library

Library of Congress Cataloging-in-Publication Data
Great Powers and strategic stability in the 21st century: competing visions
of world order/edited by Graeme P. Herd.
p. cm.
1. Security, International. 2. Political stability. 3. Great Powers. 4. World
politics–21st century. I. Herd, Graeme P.
JZ5588.G74 2010
327.1–dc22

2009040023

ISBN10: 0-415-56054-3 (hbk)
ISBN10: 0-415-58579-1 (pbk)
ISBN10: 0-203-86582-0 (ebk)

ISBN13: 978-0-415-56054-2 (hbk)
ISBN13: 978-0-415-58579-8 (pbk)
ISBN13: 978-0-203-86582-8 (ebk)

To the former, current and future participants of the ITC.

Contents

List of illustrations	xiii
List of contributors	xiv
Foreword	xix
AMBASSADOR FRED TANNER	
Acknowledgments	xxi

PART I
Introduction   1

1 **International security, Great Powers and world order**   3
GRAEME P. HERD AND PÁL DUNAY

Introduction 3
Approaches to international relations and the concept of
   security 6
World order paradigms 12
Structure of the book 17

PART II
Strategic threats: nature and evolution   21

2 **Terrorism and extremism**   23
EKATERINA STEPANOVA

Defining terrorism as a security threat 25
Terrorism and extremism: the role of extremist ideologies 27
The origins and periodization of terrorism 29
The evolution of the understanding of terrorism 30
Current trends in terrorism 32
Anti-terrorism at the national level 37
Anti-terrorism at the international level 39

3   Proliferation of weapons of mass destruction   45
GUSTAV LINDSTROM

Introduction 45
The threat of WMD proliferation 45
The challenge of managing WMD proliferation 47
Future trends in WMD proliferation 58
Conclusion 60

4   Regional crisis, conflict and fragile states   65
CATY CLÉMENT

Are fragile states a strategic threat? 65
State fragility, a new threat? 68
Key challenges, obstacles and dilemmas 72
Solutions, future trends and trajectories 77

**5   How energy and climate change may pose a threat to
     sustainable security**   82
TAPANI VAAHTORANTA

The energy–climate era 82
Energy security trends 84
Energy as a security threat 85
Climate change as a security threat 88
Three groups of states on the Kuznets curve 90
Sustainable future 95

**PART III
Centers of global power: strategic priorities and threat
management**   99

6   The United States: leadership beyond unipolarity?   101
MATTHEW RHODES

Introduction 101
Unipolarity 101
The Bush revolution 102
Change under Obama? 107
Conclusion 114

7 **The Russian Federation: striving for multipolarity but missing the consequences**   117

PAVEL K. BAEV

Introduction 117
Foreign-policy thinking and decision-making 118
Russia in/out/about the key international institutions 120
Threat assessment and risk-management 124
Migration, declining population and other human security
*   challenges 130*
Conclusions 131

8 **China as an emergent center of global power**   137

BATES GILL

China: emergent center of global power 137
China's security priorities 138
China's response 145
Current trends and trajectories 150

9 **Global threats and India's quest for strategic space**   154

SIDDHARTH VARADARAJAN

Terrorism and political extremism 159
WMD proliferation 161
Regional crises and fragile states 164
Environmental and energy security 165
Conclusion 167

10 **The EU: facing non-traditional threats in a globalized world**   171

THIERRY TARDY

The EU's foreign and security policy: an aspiration to be a
*   global liberal actor 172*
The EU threat assessment: the prevalence of non-traditional
*   threats 175*
Policy responses and instruments: still focused on crisis
*   management 178*
Europeanization and globalization: the EU as the problem or
*   the solution? 184*
Conclusion 186

PART IV
Conclusions: cooperative and conflictual imperatives   191

11   **Great Powers: towards a "cooperative competitive" future**
     world order paradigm?   193
     GRAEME P. HERD

     Alternative global orders? 197
     2025: towards a globalized interdependent world order? 200
     What's past is prologue? 203

     Bibliography   209
     Index   228

Illustrations

Figures

2.1   Terrorist incidents, fatalities and injuries, 1998–2006   33
2.2   Incidents of Communist/leftist, nationalist and religious
      terrorism   34
2.3   Fatalities of Communist/leftist, nationalist and religious
      terrorism   34
3.1   Chemical and biological terrorist incidents and fatalities,
      1968–2008   46
5.1   Kuznets curve illustrated   91

Table

3.1   Select incidents involving highly enriched uranium and
      plutonium   50

Contributors

Pavel K. Baev is a Senior Researcher at the International Peace Research Institute, Oslo (PRIO). He graduated from the Moscow State University (MA in Political Geography, 1979) and worked in a research institute in the USSR Ministry of Defense. After receiving his PhD in International Relations from the Institute of USA and Canada, Moscow in 1988, he worked at the Institute of Europe, Moscow until October 1992, when he joined PRIO. From 1995–2001 he was a co-editor of *Security Dialogue*, a quarterly policy-oriented journal produced at PRIO, and from 2000–2004 he was head of the Foreign and Security Policies program. He held the NATO Democratic Institutions Fellowship for 1994–1996. He is the author of several books, among them *The Russian Army in a Time of Troubles* (Sage, 1996) and *Russian Energy Policy and Military Power* (Routledge, 2008). His articles on the Russian military posture, Russian energy policy, Russian-European relations, peacekeeping and conflict management in Europe appeared in *Armed Forces & Society*, *Cambridge Review of International Affairs*, *Contemporary Security Policy*, *European Security*, *International Peacekeeping*, *Jane's Intelligence Review*, *The Journal of Peace Research*, *The Journal of Slavic Military Studies*, *Problems of Post-Communism*, *Security Dialogue*, *Security Index*, *Studies in Conflict & Terrorism* and *The World Today*.

Caty Clément heads the Peacebuilding Program and is a resident Faculty Member in Mediation at the Geneva Centre for Security Policy (GCSP). She holds a PhD in International Relations and Comparative Politics, focusing her efforts on conflict and mediation as an academic and a practitioner. Prior to GCSP, Dr. Clément has been a regional expert at the DRC Arms Embargo Panel for the UN Security Council. She concentrates her efforts in Africa, specifically the Great Lakes Region, as seen by her work as Director for the Great Lakes Project for the International Crisis Group. In addition, at the World Bank Fragile States Unit (LICUS), she researched early-warning indicators of state fragility and was a team leader in the Central African Republic on DDR. As an academic, Dr. Clément was a research fellow at Harvard University (the Belfer Center International Security Program and the World Peace Foundation). She was previously a Professor of Political Science at the University of Louvain. Caty Clément wrote a monography on "State Collapse: A Common Causal Pattern?" (University Press of Louvain, 2003) and co-edited a book on *La Belgique et l'Afrique Centrale. De 1960 à nos jours* (GRIP, 2000). Recent publications include "EU Security Sector Reform Mission in the DRC," in *Ten Years of European Security and Defense Policy* (Paris, EU Institute of Security Studies, 2009, pp. 89–117); "Managing Complexity: Political and Managerial Challenges in United Nations Peace Operations" (New York, Geneva Centre for Security Policy and International Peace Institute, July 2009); and "SSR in the DRC," in Hans Born and Albrecht Schnabel, eds., *Security Sector Reform in Challenging Environments* (Geneva, DCAF Year Book 2009, pp. 243–254).

Pál Dunay is Head of the International Security Program (ISP) at the Geneva Centre for Security Policy (GCSP), and Director of its International Training Course in Security Policy (ITC). During 2007 he was also Director of the Hungarian Institute of International Affairs. Between July 2004 and the beginning of 2007 he was Senior Researcher at the Stockholm International Peace Research Institute (SIPRI). Between July 1996 and 2004, he was Course Director of the International Training Course in Security Policy. Before joining the GCSP, Pál Dunay was Assistant and later Associate Professor at the International Law Department of Eötvös Loránd University, Budapest, between 1982 and 1996. During that period he took time off and was Legal Adviser to the Hungarian Delegation to the Conventional Forces in Europe (CFE) talks in 1989–1990 and to the Open Skies negotiations in 1992, respectively. Recent publications include (with Alyson Bailes, Pan Guang and Mikhail Troitsky), "The Shanghai Cooperation Organization" (*SIPRI Policy Paper* 17, May 2007); "The OSCE in Crisis" (*Chaillot Paper* 88, Paris, April 2006).

Bates Gill is Director of SIPRI. Before this, he had the Freeman Chair in China Studies at the Center for Strategic and International Studies in Washington, DC. He has previously held positions at the Brookings Institution, where he was a Senior Fellow in Foreign Policy Studies and the inaugural Director of the Center for Northeast Asian Policy Studies, and at the Center for Nonproliferation Studies of the Monterey Institute of International Studies. He is a Member of the Council on Foreign Relations and the International Institute for Strategic Studies, and has consulted for a number of multinational corporations and government agencies. From 1993–1997, he initiated and led the East Asia Arms Control and Security Project at SIPRI. Dr. Gill has a long record of research and publications on international and regional security issues, particularly regarding arms control, non-proliferation, strategic nuclear relations, peacekeeping and military–technical development. In recent years, this research has broadened to encompass other security-related trends in the post-Cold War world, including multilateral security organizations and the impact of domestic politics and development on the foreign and security policies of states. This work has resulted in several books and more than 120 other publications, which include monographs, chapters, journal articles, essays, magazine columns and opinion pieces. His most recent book, published in February 2009, is entitled *Asia's New Multilateralism: Cooperation, Competition, and the Search for Community* (Columbia University Press), co-edited with Michael Green.

Graeme P. Herd is a resident Faculty Member at the Geneva Centre for Security Policy (GCSP), where he is Co-Director of the International Training Course in Security Policy (ITC). From 2002–2005 he was Professor of Civil–Military Relations at the George C. Marshall European Center for Security Studies, Garmisch-Partenkirchen Germany, where he was also a guest lecturer at the NATO School in Oberammergau. Prior to this, he was a Lecturer in International Relations at both the University of Aberdeen (1997–2002) and Staffordshire University (1994–1997) and a Projects Officer, Department of War Studies, King's College London (1993–1994). Studies in Aberdeen, London and Moscow resulted in a doctoral thesis on the role of Scottish mercenary soldiers in Russian service in the seventeenth century, leading to a book (co-authored with Paul Dukes and Jarmo Kotilaine) entitled *Stuart–Romanov Relations: The Rise and Fall of a Special Relationship* (Dundee University Press, 2009). His articles on Russian, European and transatlantic security issues have appeared in *Armed Forces & Society, Connections: The Quarterly Journal, Cooperation and Conflict, International Politics, IISS Strategic Comments, Journal of Peace Research, Journal of Slavic Military Studies, Political Studies Quarterly, Post-Soviet Affairs, Problems of Post-Communism, Security Dialogue, Security Index* and *The World Today*. Major recent publications include *The Ideological War on Terror: World Wide Strategies for Counter Terrorism* (Routledge, 2007, co-edited with Anne Aldis); *Divided West: European Security and the Transatlantic Relationship* (Blackwells Publishing, 2006, co-authored with Tuomas Forsberg); *Soft Security Threats and European Security* (Routledge, 2005, co-edited with Anne Aldis); *Security Dynamics of the former Soviet Bloc* (RoutledgeCurzon, 2003, co-edited with Jennifer Moroney); *Russia and the Regions: Strength through Weakness* (RoutledgeCurzon, 2003, co-edited with Anne Aldis).

Gustav Lindstrom is Head of the Euro-Atlantic Security Program at the Geneva Centre for Security Policy. He received his doctorate in Policy Analysis from the RAND Graduate School and MA in International Policy Studies from Stanford University. Prior to his tenure at the GCSP, Dr. Lindstrom served as a Senior Research Fellow at the EU Institute for Security Studies. His areas of expertise include European Security and Defence Policy (ESDP), US security policy, homeland security and non-proliferation. Selected publications include: "Enter the EU Battlegroups" (*Chaillot Paper* 97, Paris, EU Institute for Security Studies, February 2007); "The EU's Approach to Homeland Security: Balancing Safety and European Ideals" in *Transforming Homeland Security* (Center for Transatlantic Relations, The Paul H. Nitze School of Advanced International Studies, Johns Hopkins University, Washington, DC,

2006, ed. Esther Brimmer); "Enforcing non-proliferation – The European Union and the 2006 BTWC Review Conference" (*Chaillot Paper* 93, Paris, EU Institute for Security Studies, November 2006, ed.).

Matthew Rhodes is Professor of National Security Studies at the College of International and Security Studies, a part of the George C. Marshall European Center for Security Studies, Garmisch-Partenkirchen, Germany. He was educated at Lawrence University, where he received his BA in Government and German, before completing a PhD in Political Science at the University of Wisconsin-Madison. Before his current employment, he was Assistant Professor of Strategy and International Security at the US Air War College. Rhodes was previously an Assistant Professor of Political Science at Central College in Iowa and a Jan Hus Foundation Academic Mentor at the Department of Politics and European Studies at Palacký University (Olomouc, Czech Republic). His expertise is in US foreign and security policy, national security decision-making, and Central and Southeast European security issues. His recent publications include "A Crisis of Democracy in Southeast Europe," in *Approaching or Avoiding Cooperative Security – The Western Balkans in the Aftermath of the Kosovo Settlement Proposal and the Riga Summit* (September 2007); "National Strategy and Security Sector Reform in Southeast Europe," in *Security Sector Reform in South East Europe – from a Necessary Remedy to a Global Concept* (January 2007); "The U.S. Role in Southeast Europe: In and After the Peace Plans," in *International Peace Plans for the Balkans – A Success?* (September 2006); and "Iran's Nuclear Program: U.S. Options after the Elections," in *Connections* (Summer 2005). He has spoken widely to American and European audiences on the themes of US foreign policy, national security decision-making, and transatlantic relations.

Ekaterina Stepanova heads a research group on unconventional threats at the Center for International Security, Institute of World Economy and International Relations (IMEMO), Moscow. Between 2007 and 2009 she has been on a three-year leave from IMEMO to lead the Armed Conflicts and Conflict Management Program at Stockholm International Peace Research Institute (SIPRI). In the academic year 2009–2010, she is teaching at the European University in Saint Petersburg and Open University of Catalonia, Barcelona. She serves on the editorial boards of the journals *Terrorism and Political Violence* and *Security Index*. The latest of Dr. Stepanova's four monographs is *Terrorism in Asymmetrical Conflict: Ideological and Structural Aspects* (Oxford University Press, 2008), also published in Spanish (Buenos Aires: Ministeria de Defensa, 2009). Her previous book – *The Role of Illicit Drug Business in the Political Economy of Conflicts and Terrorism* (Moscow, 2005) – won the Medal for Young Scientists from the Russian Academy of Sciences. The latest of her co-edited volumes is *Terrorism: Patterns of Internationalization* (Sage, 2009). In 2003 she worked as a Researcher on armed conflict and terrorism at SIPRI, Stockholm, and from 1994–2000 as a Researcher at the Moscow Center of the Carnegie Endowment for International Peace. She has held several Russian research fellowships, was twice a MacArthur Research Fellow (2000 and 2003), and was a MacArthur NGO Fellow at King's College, University of London (1998).

Thierry Tardy has been a Faculty Member at the Geneva Centre for Security Policy (GCSP) since September 2001. He is also an Associate Fellow at the Centre for International Studies and Research (CERI) in Paris. He is Doctor of Political Science (International Relations) from the University of Paris XIII. Prior to joining the GCSP, he was a Researcher at the Foundation for Strategic Research in Paris and Lecturer at the Institut d'Etudes Politiques of Paris, as well as at the War College, Paris. His areas of expertise cover crisis management, security regionalism, the UN and international security, and European security. Recent publications include: *European Security in a Global Context: Internal and External Dynamics* (Routledge, 2009, ed.) and *Gestion de crise, maintien et consolidation de la paix. Acteurs, activités, defies* (Brussels, De Boeck, 2009).

Tapani Vaahtoranta received his PhD from Princeton University in 1990. The topic of his dissertation was the politics of controlling international air pollution. He worked as Research Director of the Finnish Institute of International Affairs (FIIA) from 1990–1991, becoming Director of the Institute in 1991. The Ministry for Foreign Affairs seconded him to the Geneva Centre for Security Policy, where he worked as a Faculty Member from 1998–2001. After returning to Finland, Vaahtoranta worked as Director of the FIIA until 2007. Currently he is the Director of the program on the politics of the environment and resources and Editor-in-Chief of the quarterly *Ulkopolitiikka*, published by the FIIA. He is a Member of the National IPCC Task Force. In 2009 Dr. Vaahtoranta was a public policy scholar in the Environmental Change and Security Program of the Wilson Center in Washington, DC.

Siddharth Varadarajan is the Strategic Affairs Editor of *The Hindu* and one of India's leading foreign policy analysts. A trained economist, he studied at the London School of Economics and Columbia University and taught economics for several years at New York University before joining the *Times of India* in New Delhi as a lead writer. As a journalist, he has reported widely from several conflict zones, including Afghanistan, Iraq, the former Yugoslavia, Nepal and Kashmir, and his commentaries have been published in the *International Herald Tribune, Wall Street Journal, Le Monde Diplomatique* and other publications. In 2005, the United Nations Correspondents Association awarded him the Elizabeth Neuffer Memorial Prize silver medal for a series of articles he wrote on the Iranian nuclear question. In 2007, he was a visiting professor at the Graduate School of Journalism, University of California, Berkeley, and in 2008, a Poynter Fellow at Yale University. His book, *Gujarat: The Making of a Tragedy*, on the anti-Muslim violence in the Indian state of Gujarat, was published by Penguin in 2002. He is currently writing a book on Indo-US relations.

Foreword

The Geneva Centre for Security Policy (GCSP), established in 1995, provides expert training in international security policy to a broad community including diplomats, officers, government officials, civil society representatives, and journalists. In addition, we continue to define, contribute and advance policy research in international peace and security studies. Through fostering cooperative networking with countries, institutions and experts, we have become an established center within the international network of training institutions and, increasingly, the greater "think tank" world. Coupled with these numerous activities at the GCSP, we continue to sustain international interest in our courses given in Geneva and elsewhere around the world.

Our focus is to provide expert training in comprehensive international security policy through a number of specialized courses ranging in duration from three days to eight-and-a-half months. Our most traditional and longest training course is the International Training Course in Security Policy (ITC). The ITC first began in 1986 at the Geneva Graduate Institute of International Studies for mid-career diplomats, military officers and civil servants from foreign, defense and other relevant ministries, and was integrated in 1996 into the newly created GCSP. Since 2006, the course has been opened to a greater number of qualified participants by jointly offering a Master of Advanced Studies (MAS) in International and European Security with the European Institute of the University of Geneva. It is a demanding training course that continues to be well-received and sought after by participants from other fields and other parts of the world. With the widening of the security spectrum and the process of globalization we have witnessed over the years, many of our new participants are arriving from the Middle East, Asia and South Asia, Africa and, more recently, and for the first time, from Latin America. This broad diversity has enriched the knowledge-sharing and open – but professionally guided – exchange of views found within the course.

The year 2010 will mark the fifteenth anniversary of the ITC. Today's courses – with strong diversity among the participants – will benefit from experiencing the variety of views supplied from the comprehensive coverage of international security policy issues provided by both GCSP's resident faculty and its network of accomplished scholars. It is timely that this publication draws upon this accumulated expertise and has been originally inspired by the curriculum offered to the ITC participants. We are committed to supporting knowledge-sharing by making ITC materials available to former and current course participants as well as to the broader community of security policy experts. We believe that this effort will benefit from and contribute to the training and research undertaken in the context of the GCSP courses.

It has been my personal privilege to work at the GCSP and with the ITC in various capacities, not least as the Course Director for the first six ITC course years from 1986. I am confident that this publication will make an important contribution to the debate and understanding of global peace and stability, and the role of organizations and states in risk assessments and the management of the strategic sources of insecurity.

Ambassador Fred Tanner
Director of the Geneva Centre for Security Policy

Acknowledgments

This book is sponsored by the Geneva Centre for Security Policy (GCSP). I would like to thank Ambassador Dr. Fred Tanner, GCSP Director, and Dr. Peter Foot, Academic Dean, for their continuous support and encouragement throughout this project.

The editor is also grateful to Professor Steven Haines and Fabian Grass on the staff of GCSP for their insightful comments on the conclusion, and to Raphael Zaffran and Deborah Huber, two interns at GCSP, for help with the figures and illustrations.

My greatest debt of gratitude is owed to Meghan Lynn who assiduously copyedited the entire volume and whose effective collaboration has been much appreciated. Without her effort this volume would not have seen the light of day.

Graeme P. Herd
Co-Director, International Training Course (ITC) in Security Policy
Geneva Centre for Security Policy
August 31, 2009

Part I

Introduction

1 International security, Great Powers and world order

Graeme P. Herd and Pàl Dunay

Introduction

This volume addresses the issue of strategic stability into the twenty-first century, its nature and likely future evolution. To that end the book identifies the United States, European Union, Russian Federation, People's Republic of China and India as Great Powers. It provides a comparative survey of their approaches to a series of threats that are strategic in nature: environmental change and energy security; terrorism; weapons proliferation; and, fragile states, conflict and regional crises. After highlighting similarities and differences in these Great Power approaches to these strategic threats, we then conclude by considering whether we witness the emergence of a global security agenda based on nascent similarity across national policy agendas. This allows the conclusion to assess the prospects of policy coordination and effective collective action, and so characterize the nature of strategic stability and world order in the twenty-first century.

Great Power status is attained through a combination of self-belief and declaration, as well as bestowed through acknowledgement and recognition by other Great Powers that states with this status have the military and economic capability to play a key role in international affairs, perhaps even to challenge the US's superpower status in the short or medium term.[1] The US National Security Strategy of 17 September 2002 and 16 March 2006 refers to Great Powers – the US, as well as EU, China, India, and Russia – as "centers of global power."[2] A 2008 European Council report on the implementation of the EU's European Security Strategy of 2003 identifies the US as the "key partner for Europe." At the same time, the report notes that the EU has "substantially expanded our relationship with China," "Russia remains an important partner on global issues," and that "there is still room to do more in our relationship with India."[3] The "New National Security Strategy of Russian Federation for the period through 2020" – adopted in May 2009 – notes that, while Russia will seek to build a strategic partnership with the US, the US remains Russia's primary strategic rival. It emphasizes the need to expand partnerships with the EU as well as China, India and Brazil to promote a multipolar world which balances the US.[4] Within its extended neighborhood, India seeks to balance China, Russia and the US in political and hard power terms, and while European norms, concepts and ideas shape Indian behavior, India–EU relations "struggle to gain traction."[5] China seeks to balance India within its neighborhood and the US globally, and to that end improving Russian and EU relations are important.

While exhibiting significantly greater power than others in the international system, there are obvious differences between these five centers. For some, China, India and Russia are understood to be rising powers, while the EU and the US (the old "political West") are in relative decline. Three of the five – Russia, China and the US – are nuclear powers with seats on the UN Security Council (UNSC). India constitutes a non-UNSC nuclear state, while the EU has two nuclear UNSC member-states (France and the United Kingdom). Three of the centers are market-democracies (the EU, India and the US), while two are market-authoritarian (China and Russia).

While "Centers of Global Power" is one way of designating Great Powers, the emergence of new, albeit often weakly institutionalized, frameworks suggests that the aspiration of cooperative international management is present in states whose weight makes their involvement indispensable. The G8 is primarily a Euro-Atlantic grouping, comprising the world's major industrialized democracies: Germany, the UK, Italy, France, Canada, the US and Russia (though its market-democratic credentials are increasingly questioned), with the EU represented and Japan the only member that is not in the Euro-Atlantic area. A broader grouping is represented by the G20 countries, whose geographical and politico-economic composition, by contrast, is much more global in nature than the G8 and reflects a reduced role of Euro-Atlantic states. Another prominent grouping, which began life as a Goldman Sachs marketing tool in 2003, comprises the fast-growing developing countries – Brazil, Russia, India and China – the BRIC states, which were predicted to form a powerful economic grouping that would surpass rich democratic states in the northern hemisphere by 2050, if not sooner.[6] A newer grouping – the "Next Eleven" (or N-11) – is comprised of Bangladesh, Egypt, Indonesia, Iran, Korea, Mexico, Nigeria, Pakistan, Philippines, Turkey and Vietnam. These states were selected as the next set of large population states with rapid growth potential, which could rival BRICs and G7 economies if growth continues.

Will a predictable global order in our century be characterized by a one-world system, an interdependent liberal world order, characterized by interest-based incentives for cooperation which offer functional benefits to all Great Powers, and buttressed by multilateral partnerships in institutions (the UN, G20 and regional variants), regimes (e.g., arms control, climate, trade), shared global norms and strengthened international law? Within the return to the concert of Great Powers system, a division of responsibilities occurs according to resources, expertise and interest.

Alternatively, rather than a new multilateralism and an era of global partnership, will current and emergent Great Powers develop an operational concept of world order that looks to enhance their order-producing managerial role in their near neighborhoods and project power globally through an executive agency constituted by a G14 (consisting of the G7, plus Brazil, Russia, India, China and some of the N-11 states)? Will order be based on material power and the coherence of geopolitical-bloc formation, characterized more by hierarchy and balance of power principles than by interdependence structured around shared interests? If the latter, will Great Powers institutionalize their preferences in ineffective international institutions and organizations and adopt zero-sum thinking with regards to managing sources of insecurity? Do Great Powers want an enlarged role within the existing system, or to change the system itself?

The norms, institutions and regimes represent the *acquis* of the international system through which the decisions are taken, implemented and enforced. It is, however, a challenge for the states that international law does not develop as flexibly as the international system, hence the change of the system (power relations) is only followed by international law with some delay. The centrality of states is apparent in the international system. States are the creators of norms and institutions; adjusting them to changed conditions and terminating them when necessary. Beyond the formal process, their significance is also dependent upon the importance attributed to them by states. If states decide to undermine institutions, readily accepting the violation of norms they themselves have generated, or hollow out international organizations they have established, then norms and institutions fall.

Under the Westphalian international system between the mid-seventeenth and the late-twentieth centuries, the centrality of the state was unchallenged; this is no longer the case.[7] In some circumstances, for example, inter-governmental organizations seek to assume the autonomous management of international affairs. In addition, the influence of non-governmental organizations is considered to be decisive in key areas of current international relations, not least: climate change, support to post-conflict peace-building and development processes, countering terrorism and organized criminality. Even select areas of arms control are among those where states and inter-governmental agencies have to acknowledge and take into account the influence of non-state actors.

Norms, institutions and regimes are mutually linked. Regimes developed to govern and regulate key issue areas in international relations often begin life as soft mechanisms that gradually harden as their normative base (both legally binding and non-binding) is filled with substantive content, and as institutions associated with the regime are established and consolidated. While inter-governmental institutions are entitled to create norms, their "masters" – the states of which they are comprised – identify and define the areas where the organizations may establish norms and the nature of the regulation. When states entitle organizations to create norms, they are in effect giving certain autonomy to them. This freedom is controlled, however, and states can re-assert control when they are not satisfied with their creation, the international organization.

Among the range of normative systems, international law is the best established, as it is the one that most resembles national law as far as the normative structure is concerned.[8] Norms are based on a tri-pillar structure. First, a hypothesis defines the behavior to be regulated, then, a disposition – a "what to do" –

is followed by sanction if the disposition is not respected (i.e., if it is violated). Even though international legal norms broadly follow this structure, they are somewhat special. Critically, in the case of international legal norms, the states that create such norms are also responsible for implementing and enforcing them. States will not agree to norms that they do not want to implement, or introduce sanctions which would endanger their interests and undermine their power. The scope of international legal regulation is widening due to both the growing number of states and the intensity of interaction facilitated by technological development. In addition, international law is created by consensus and its sanctions regime continues to be inherently weak.

This introductory chapter outlines key approaches to understanding international relations and the contested concept of security. To that end, it outlines the three main philosophical approaches to international relations that purport to explain how the world works – realist, liberalist and constructivist – and reviews their claims to constitute the basis of world order. It links these international relations approaches to changing perceptions as to what it is that constitutes "security" and "stability," noting the transition from the classical realist Westphalian state-based conception of security to the wider military and non-military agenda of 1990s. The rise of key non-state actors such as transnational corporations, criminal networks, non-governmental organizations, religious movements and diasporas (to name a few) are best captured by the liberalist tradition. As we shall see, constructivism is a prism through which realist-constructivist or realist-liberalist approaches strive to better understand the role of status, reputation, prestige and identity, for example, in shaping world order based on the use of state-directed military coercive power (realist), as well as state approaches to the utility of international organizations, institutions and regimes (liberalist). The chapter then reviews and assesses a range of contemporary post-Cold War international security paradigms that map relations between key actors and claim to have explanatory power that accounts for world order. This chapter concludes by outlining the structure of the book, identifying the chapters and the key questions addressed within them.

Approaches to international relations and the concept of security

Theories are a set of ideas that are coherent and internally consistent and claim to have some purchase on the nature of the world and how it works. International Relations (IR) Theory, like all theory, is meant to provide a simplified view of a complex subject so as to enable better understanding of it: there is nothing as practical as a good theory; theory is the policy-maker's aid.[9] At its best, theory identifies basic patterns of relations between actors, be they state or non-state, that take place over time and space. Theory claims to be apolitical, but of course theorists cannot divorce themselves from their social, cultural or political background. All theory, therefore, is political. Indeed, the primacy of realism in the Anglo-Saxon-dominated world of the twentieth century was not just a reflection of a perceived reality but also the way policy-makers thought. Theory therefore contributed to shaping the world that it was charged with analyzing. However, good theory minimizes the corrupting influences of prejudice and extreme subjectivity, thus helping objectivity in policy-making. For much of the twentieth century, IR Theory was dominated by two schools of thought – realism and liberalism. More recently, with the end of the Cold War, constructivism has become the third key approach or method of studying international relations.

In the seventeenth century, the international state system took shape, as conceptions of sovereignty and territorial integrity were codified with the Treaty of Westphalia (1648). The rise of nationalism and nation states in the eighteenth and nineteenth centuries was accompanied by attempts by the Great Powers to orchestrate stability in the international system by balance of power/through application of balance of power theory. World War I – with its immense socio-economic, political and military disruption and dislocation – broke the balance of power system and generated the rise of a system based on collective security principles, institutionalized by the League of Nations. However, the failure of the League of Nations with the outbreak of World War II consigned this attempt at containing state aggression and promoting international peace and stability to the "dustbin of history."

In the second half of the twentieth century, during the Cold War (1947–1990), superpower rivalry dominated the international system and had a profound impact on what analysts and policy-makers understood as the fundamental nature of security. Deterrence ("balance of terror") and containment strategies were enacted by the Union of Soviet Socialist Republics (USSR) and the United States of American (USA) and their respective allies in an effort to prevent the hegemony of either side over the course and content of international politics. In this period, perspectives of security were diverse, ranging from countering threats to state sovereignty and territorial integrity, to invoking, directly or indirectly, the notion of threat.

It is against this backdrop that realism became the dominant perspective in international relations – though it hardly constitutes a single theory – and liberalism arose as its chief rival. All realists understand the international system to be anarchic or unstable as there is no consensual jurisdiction or overriding central authority. The anarchic nature of international relations constitutes an autonomous causal force that gives rise to a struggle for power among states. They also agree that states are rational, unitary and formally equal, and constitute the principal actors in international relations – international institutions, non-governmental organizations, multinational corporations, individuals and other sub-state or trans-state actors have little independent influence. As the central actors in international relations, states are rational actors and inherently selfish, defining state interests in strictly material terms. The goal of a state is to maximize its national interest, and the accumulation and exercise of power is the key to understanding international behavior and state motivation. For realists, military power remains the most effective means of ensuring national security and state survival. For this reason, the military distribution of power continues to be essential. Classical realists, most notably Morgenthau, argued that states are aggressive because aggression reflects the fixed and flawed impulses and nature inherent to humans – the psychological predispositions of statesmen drives international relations. Humans want to dominate other humans; so too do states.

By contrast, structural or neo-realism derives from classical realism, but instead of human nature, its focus is predominantly on the international system. How and where power is configured within a unipolar, bipolar or multipolar world determines state behavior, rather than inherently aggressive human nature per se. Within the structural or neo-realist school, systemic pressures are understood to either underpin a status quo through balance of power responses, according to "defensive realists," or a continual struggle for predominance, primacy and hegemony, according to "offensive realists." "Defensive realists" such as Kenneth Waltz[10] and Robert Jervis[11] argue that the logic of the international system tends toward maintaining the status quo and equilibrium via the balance of power, rather than primacy: the opportunity costs of predominance and primacy outweigh the benefits, and cooperation among Great Powers reduces the risks of international anarchy and minimizes the effects of the security dilemma. "Offensive realists," including most notably John Mearsheimer, argue states must either struggle for supremacy, for hegemony – maximize power through expansionist/foreign interventionist behavior – or fail to survive.[12] For most states, regional hegemony is the goal, as global hegemony is hard to establish. Robert Keohane notes that hegemons are able and willing to create and enforce international norms and enjoy decisive economic, technological and military dominance.[13] Thus, Major and Great Powers may go to war against each other if they see an advantage with regards to improving their relative power position. "Offensive realists" argue that the "balance" approach proposed by "defensive realists" does not work because there is no way of knowing what constitutes a safe margin over neighbors, the future intentions and capabilities of potential rival states cannot be predicted, and states that cheat the system to gain more power cannot be stopped.

A third strand of realist thought can also be highlighted. "Neoclassical realism" agrees with "neo-realism" that the distribution of power in the international system constitutes an important independent variable, and with "classical realism" that the role of statesmen and women and the foreign-policy decisions they make constitute a dependent variable and must be taken into account when explaining foreign-policy behavior. Importantly, however, neoclassical realism looks to liberalist thought and adds an intervening variable into the mix: domestic perceptions of the system or the nature of political systems should not be ignored.

Liberalism is a theoretical perspective that rests on the assumption that all humans are rational beings and, as such, they are able to articulate and pursue their interests, understand moral principles and live according to the rule of law. Liberals value individual liberty above all else and believe it is possible to achieve positive interactions and cooperative designs between states. Cooperation is a central feature of all human activity, including international relations, where it occurs within the framework of a series of shared norms and values that build trust over time. States are increasingly interdependent, and as the boundaries between them become more and more permeable, cooperation is promoted and regulated through the spread of democratic institutions, economic liberalization and the growing significance of international institutions and legal norms. Whereas classical realists argue that states curtail international law and confine their focus to technical norms and the management of conflict, liberals attribute more importance to norms and highlight legal regulation as a central element of international relations.

International organizations are the key to trust and confidence-building because they formalize norms and place formal constraints upon state action. A state's use of military tools in achieving goals is important, but so too are political, economic and diplomatic instruments. Consequently, liberals believe that through institutions it is possible to build an international community that is self-policing in its purest form. Although the most obvious example of this is the European Union, permanent international institutions are relatively recent historical phenomena. Until the second half of the eighteenth century, major international conferences addressed emerging strategic issues – notably the Congress of Vienna in 1815, which regulated post-Napoleonic power relations in Europe; the 1878 Berlin Congress that addressed the nationality question in the Balkans, and the 1884–1885 Congo Conference to regulate European trade and colonization in Africa. The first technical organizations appeared in the late-nineteenth century, addressing issues such as measurement, statistics and postal cooperation. The concerns generated by World War I gave impulse to the creation of three major organizations. The League of Nations focused on ethnic minority and human rights. The Permanent Court of International Justice addressed legally binding resolution of interstate disputes. The International Labour Office addressed the rights of workers, reflecting a move to more socially engaged states. The failure of the first and partial failure of the second resulted in an effort to renew and modernize organizations to make them more "heat resistant," which resulted in a web of international institutions – global and regional – designed to cooperatively address financial, trade, health and meteorological issues, as well as matters of intellectual property and industrial development. This web of institutions reflected the anxiety of Europe and North America to avoid at all costs a repeat of the bloody first half of the twentieth century – salvation through cooperative security management was the watchword.

In this new century, liberalists could point to the rise of transnational and non-state actors and the threats they pose to states to underpin their contentions, and not least to explain the "war of terror." Transnational terrorist groups, for example, have no statehood – a concept that is difficult to define, but one that was codified in 1933. Accordingly, it has four components: (a) a permanent population; (b) a defined territory; (c) government; (d) capacity to enter into relations with the other states. Even though sovereignty is a decisive attribute of statehood, it is impossible to practice it without the attributes above. The fact that transnational terrorist groupings do not have to defend these core elements of statehood constitutes an undeniable reality outside of the realm of structural realist thinking. Realist theories are deficient in explaining "war on terror."

Besides the realist and liberal perspectives, international relations can be explained by using constructivist insights about learning and identity construction. The basic view of the constructivist approach, which is not a single school of thought, is that international politics is socially constructed and shaped by different beliefs and cultures. As a result, neither material interests alone, as realists suggest, nor institutions or values, as the liberalists contend, can explain state behavior completely. Constructivism therefore focuses on the role of ideas in shaping our identities and the meaning we give to the world around us. In addition, norms and rules shape international relations. They can be constructed by international organizations and NGOs as much as by states and national values. Material interests, institutions and values matter only if they are made to matter and, in turn often depend on different and partly unconscious psychological mechanisms, as well as on the nature of the interactions between states. In the constructivist paradigm, whether or not to value differences that are deemed to be real is immaterial: they do not matter per se; they are made to matter by the nature of the interpretation placed upon them.

The concept of security itself can be understood as reflecting the concerns of particular states in specific periods as much as it corresponds to any existing reality. Security is a particularly malleable and flexible concept, and a study of security politics reveals as much about the objective nature of stability and instability as about the subjective perceptions of the societies and states that use it. Changes in demography, natural resources and the environment, science and technology, the global economy and globalization, national and international governance and future conflict all impact on the security of individuals, societies, states, regions and the global international system. Although the evolution and impact of these key global trends and dynamics are difficult for the student of international relations to discern, our study of these dynamics will allow us to anticipate and, hopefully, better manage future sources of insecurity and conflict, and so gradually manage the proliferation of sustainable peace globally.

By the late 1970s and 1980s, with the rise of new social movements, such as environmentalism and feminism, and a growing realization of the transformational impact of globalization on state sovereignty and territorial integrity, debates about the boundaries of the subject took place as perceptions of security began to be re-evaluated. The Oil Crisis of 1973 focused attention on energy resources and economic security, whilst the Bhopal (India) chemical plant disaster – 2,000 killed, 200,000 injured – in 1984 and the Chernobyl (Soviet Union) nuclear disaster in 1986 helped promote an awareness of non-military sources of instability. The trans-national impacts of such catastrophes also underpinned the need for co-operative management of these security threats. The 1987 World Commission on Environment and Development (the "Bruntland Report") and the UN Conference on the Environment and Development in Rio in 1992 were evidence that the relationship between poverty, injustice, environmental scarcity and conflict had become accepted, and that this issue was now of greater strategic interest and importance to states.

With the end of the Cold War (1990), the traditional or classical politico-military definition, reinforced by the Cold War era of state defense against the threat of military (nuclear) aggression, was broadened. It was now to include the recognition that states might be threatened by non-military sources of insecurity that could entail non-military responses from official state structures and institutions. In this re-defined and "extended" concept, the military security sector was understood as one – albeit the most important – of five, the other four being the political, economic, societal and environmental security sectors. As a result of the consequences of the changes in the global balance of power after the end of the Cold War, two predominant views of security became apparent and had an influence on policy-makers. One argued for a "narrow" definition of security while the other favored a "wider" agenda. As the decade progressed, the "wide" or "extended" definition was generally accepted as providing the most useful framework through which to understand insecurity in the transformed international system.

"Narrowers" focus on the military aspects of security and have argued that the key element of strategic analysis is the possible use of force. They concede that non-military elements of security may occupy more of the strategists' attention than previously, but ultimately military security should remain the primary focus of analysis as this security sector continued to pose the greatest and most profound and far-reaching threats to states. Security was still to be fundamentally understood as based upon the state, and particularly on the necessity of states to fulfill their raison d'être – survival. Security then concerned the study of the threat, use and control of military force. National security was no longer to be construed in simple Cold War terms – "defense" in which the concepts of deterrence and containment would prevent an invasion by the West or the East, depending on one's perspective in Washington, DC or Moscow.

The "wideners" questioned the primacy of the military element of the security debate.[14] They argued that the focus on territorial integrity of the state and traditional conceptions of sovereignty, in which security encompassed the stability of the core institutions of the state and the integrity of state decision-making structures, ought to be widened to include human, societal, economic and environmental security. Now, security was perceived to mean more than simple military might, but was increasingly understood and measured in terms of the impact and scope of non-military threats on the daily lives of peoples and the integrity of states.

The threat of a "Swine Flu" (Influenza A(H1N1) virus) pandemic in 2009 reinforces the notion that threats can arise from fatal discontinuities, be they induced by natural disaster, violent conflict or unimaginable surprise. Food and water shortage, climate change, nuclear or chemical disasters, financial meltdowns, cyber and terrorist attacks or the disruption of energy supplies: they all create a series of compounded crises and pose threats to the survival of individuals, the stability of societies, states, regions and the international system.[15]

In this realm, the generation of unintended security dilemmas are all-too-apparent: China and India, for example, need increasing energy supplies to drive their economic growth to avoid domestic societal, political and perhaps even military instability. But are these national development paradigms sustainable? Experts argue that:

> The new knowledge that will forever mark this period in human history is the overwhelming scientific evidence that we are over-consuming the planet and accelerating toward ecological catastrophe. The short-term approaches of most ministers of finance and professional economists don't account for how the planet works, or even that the economy exists on a finite planet. Scientists morally committed to protecting the global commons and researching ecological limits to the global economy need much more funding and influence in policy-making.[16]

Martin Rees, a cosmologist, highlights the risks inherent to scientific and technological advancement:

> Science is advancing faster than ever, and on a broader front: bio-, cyber- and nanotechnology all offer exhilarating prospects; so does the exploration of space. But there is a dark side: new science can have unintended consequences; it empowers individuals to perpetrate acts of megaterror; even innocent errors could be catastrophic. The "downside" from twenty-first-century technology could be graver and more intractable than the threat of nuclear devastation that we have faced for decades. And human-induced pressures on the global environment may engender higher risks than the age-old hazards of earthquakes, eruptions, and asteroid impacts.[17]

World order paradigms

The most enduring international relations paradigm – the Cold War (1947–1990) paradigm – dominated the second half of the twentieth century, structured our thinking and understanding of international relations, and embodied classical realist thinking. In this period, superpower rivalry (military–nuclear, economic, ideological–cultural) dominated international relations and shaped the international system, creating a bipolar world. The US and its West European NATO allies (the "First World") constituted one pole. The "political West" confronted the second pole, which consisted of the Union of Soviet Socialist Republics and its Warsaw Treaty Organization, East European allies (the "Second World"). Both these poles competed for influence over the non-aligned, post-colonial and developing states in the Global South (the "Third World"). As the Cold War ended the certainties and stability of this bi-polar world order, it was replaced by a post-Cold War world in which, in dizzying succession, new paradigms attempted to capture best the nature of the new world (dis)order. Let us examine some of the most influential ones.

With the fall of the Berlin Wall in 1989 and the euphoria that accompanied the end of the Cold War, the expectation amongst most scholars, analysts and practitioners was that the newly emergent – in some cases re-emergent – independent states would, in the post-Cold War era, move from authoritarian state-building toward democratizing their political systems, economies and foreign and security policies. As a result, the international system would be characterized by the gradual proliferation of a zone of peace and stability as the threat of armed conflict, use of force, military power and nuclear devastation declined and, ultimately, disappeared.

Francis Fukuyama was the first to suggest that 1989 represented the triumph of market capitalism and liberal democratic ideology over all possible alternatives – he advanced a doctrine of democratic universalism. The ideological dialectic that had shaped the international system, the struggle before 1945 between communism, capitalism and fascism, had been reduced after 1945 to competition between capitalism and communism. In the post-Cold War world, "market-democracy" was set to become the modernization project of choice for all states. The future of the international system was to be characterized by the gradual democratization and consolidation of market-democratic institutions, policies, values and culture. Liberal institutionalism – internationally generated norms, procedures and institutions for the enforcement of mutually agreed legal frameworks – would, ultimately, lead to the replacement of international anarchy with the international rule of law.[18] The adherents of democratization predicted that, as a result, tensions and cleavages within and between the states would gradually diminish, as all undertook a gradual strategic re-orientation westward and reintegrated into a globalized economy. Democratic states shared the same norms and values and consequently enjoyed the efficiency of inter-democratic bargaining and conflict resolution. It was also argued that democratic states choose their wars more wisely than non-democratic states, have larger economies, form stronger alliances, and make better and more consensual decisions. When they do go to war they have higher levels of public support and can count on greater support from their militaries. The accountability and transparency within democratic states and in their oversight of the military reduces corruption in the defense sector and increases public legitimacy.

By 1993, Samuel Huntington, analyzing the same events as Fukuyama, agreed that 1989–1991 represented the demise of the Cold War international system, but offered a radically divergent interpretation of its implications. Huntington argued that, as a consequence of the breakdown of the Cold War order, the future was not one of "democratic peace" and co-operation within a single global system in which the triumph of Western-style modernity was set to create one universal world civilization, but rather one of continual and protracted wars between "civilizational blocs."[19] Understanding the relationship between identity, its construction and the propensity for conflict was the puzzle; the geopolitics of cultural difference the key. According to Huntington, seven civilizations spanned the globe, each at its heart characterized by alternative belief systems and the values they encapsulated – in essence by their cultural identity. Western

Christianity, Slavic Orthodoxy, Islam, Buddhism, Hinduism, Confucianism and "possibly African" civilizations were now unconstrained by rigid bi-polar stability. Where civilizations brushed up against each other, Huntington argued, cultural fault-lines could be identified, and it was along these fault-lines that future conflicts were most likely to occur. Whereas the Cold War paradigm identified typology of states that were "super-power," "client," "neutral," "non-aligned," "gateway," and "domino" in essence, Huntington noted "core states," "cleft countries," "torn countries" and "lone countries" within his civilization paradigm.[20]

Rather than inter-civilizational bloc tension being the driver of insecurity and conflict, Robert D. Kaplan suggests that population increase, urbanization and resource depletion undermine fragile governments across the developing world and so represent a threat to the developed world:

> Future wars will be those of communal survival, aggravated or, in many cases, caused by environmental scarcity. These wars will be sub-national, meaning that it will be hard for states and local governments to protect their own citizens physically. This is how many states will ultimately die. As state power fades – and with it the state's ability to help weaker groups within society, not to mention other states – peoples and cultures around the world will be thrown back upon their own strengths and weaknesses, with fewer equalizing mechanisms to protect them. Whereas the distant future will probably see the emergence of a racially hybrid, globalized man, the coming decades will see us more aware of our differences than of our similarities.[21]

In contrast to Fukuyama's faith in the redemptive power of democracy and democratization, only "hybrid regimes," authoritarian in nature, secured by performance legitimacy, can manage the range of compounded crises that Kaplan identifies.

Increasingly, critiques of international capitalism – which was perceived by many as the cutting-edge of the globalization process – argued that it was a force for oppression, exploitation and injustice, undermining traditional cultures and communities, magnifying income inequalities within and between states, leading to political disintegration, the growth of failed states and, ultimately, the promotion of stateless, decentralized criminal and terrorist networks. "Exclusive globalization," it was argued, was the reality, rather than an "inclusive globalization" process. The "exclusive" nature of globalization supported the closely interdependent triad states, exacerbating divisions between "winners" and non-industrializing "losers" in the globalization process. This outcome – the creation of "20/80" societies in which elites benefited at the expense of the majority of the world's population – was a source of conflict. In short, the markets, multinationals, the International Monetary Fund, World Bank and World Trade Organization – the institutional embodiments of globalization – undermined the role and function of the state (sovereignty and territorial integrity) and, indeed, democracy. A trans-national undercurrent of unease at the perceived destructiveness of globalization emerged.

Thomas Barnett, who studied the impact of globalization upon security and stability, has understood globalization as a dual process, with some states benefiting from "thick globalization" and its attendant sources of stability, and other states being undermined "from thin globalization" and the insecurities that follow. Here it is argued that the "Functioning Core" of the globalized world embodies rule sets, norms and ties that bind it in mutually assured dependence. This "thick globalization" is characterized by network connectivity, financial transactions, liberal media flows and collective security systems that underpin stable governments and populations enjoying rising living standards – notably, between 1980 and 2000 the numbers living in extreme poverty in East Asia have fallen by 60 percent. Open economies lead to interdependence, greater prosperity and decrease the likelihood of insecurity. These states perform well according to the standard indicators – per capita GDP, the UN "Human Development Index," Transparency International's "Corruption Perception Index" and Freedom House's "Freedom in the World" report. By contrast, "thin globalization" allows politically repressive regimes to consolidate, which can be characterized in extreme cases by the prevalence of widespread poverty, corruption, high infant mortality, disease, disenfranchisement, marginalization and massacres. These regions have been called the "Non-Integrated Gap" – they cannot control their borders, they suffer from ethnic and religious conflict and export insecurity – and they constitute a strategic threat environment for the functioning core. Indeed, as four-fifths of the world's oil reserves lies within this "non-integrating gap," the potential for resource wars is high. Seam states such as Greece, Mexico, Brazil, Indonesia and Pakistan lie between the non-integrating gap and the functioning core.[22]

In 2007 Robert Kagan, a leading neo-conservative strategist, offered a neo-realist paradigm for post-Bush US foreign policy. This new "Return of History" paradigm no longer viewed the "political West" as divided, but rather as united in a new bipolar system that pitted market-democratic against a market-authoritarian world order. This paradigm is structured by an intense ideological struggle between two Great Power constellations – the enlarged democratic West that incorporates "New Europe" – and authoritarian capitalism, a "new second world" led by authoritarian capitalist Russia and China, which replace the defeated totalitarian capitalist states of Germany and Japan. Each side now enters a contest for control over resources:

> Until now the liberal West's strategy has been to try to integrate these two powers into the international liberal order, to tame them and make them safe for liberalism. If, instead, China and Russia are going to be sturdy pillars of autocracy over the coming decades, enduring and perhaps even prospering, then they cannot be expected to embrace the West's vision of humanity's inexorable evolution toward democracy and the end of autocratic rule.[23]

Parag Khanna turns our attention to the forgotten "Second World." Rather than the Soviet Union and its allies designated within the Cold War paradigm, Khanna uses the term to refer to what he calls "tipping-point states" that can, in a new century within a "geopolitical marketplace," ally with three dominant and competing "First World" superpowers – the US, Europe and China – and so hold the balance of power.[24] His paradigm suggests a realist world order in which balance of power, hierarchy and zero-sum thinking characterize international relations.

Fareed Zakaria disagrees with both the Kagan and Khanna paradigms, as the former is based on a return to a bipolar world order – a Cold War redux – while the latter ignores the growing roles of Russia, India and Brazil as centers of global power. He argues that the rise of Brazil, Russia and India, as well as China, reflects a seismic shift in global power and attitudes. This process represents the third Great Power shift in modern history – the first being the consolidation and then projection of European power globally in the fifteenth century, and the second the rise of the US at the end of the nineteenth century and the establishment of a *Pax Americana* in the twentieth century. What we are now witnessing, in the third power shift, is not anti-Americanism but a post-American world order driven by "the rise of the rest" – a rich and globalized amalgam of East and West. Though this power shift changes the paradigm of world order, Zakaria's paradigm suggests a strategic calculus based on US accommodation of modernizing states through stakeholder-status in the new order (a greater role in global institutions and, say, in the formulation of rules and regimes) in return for strategic cooperation.[25] However, ethical and normative splits occur between the global North and South: while "no first use," "ecological responsibility," "individual privacy," "democratic governance," "legitimacy" and "responsibility to protect" are emergent norms, they are not universally espoused. General Assembly president Miguel D'Escoto Brockmann of Nicaragua, for example, characterized "R2P" in terms of "redecorated colonialism," reflecting a sense of grievance, resentment and exclusion felt by many developing countries in that Assembly. The assumed normative convergence that underpins the Zakaria paradigm can be and is increasingly questioned.

To what extent and in what ways has the global financial crisis impacted on international security? Niall Fergusson has characterized the crisis as an "axis of upheaval," with unpredictable and unintended geopolitical consequences, as it coincides with the depletion of non-renewable energy sources, a tipping point for global climate change and turbulence associated with a declining world hegemon – the US.[26] Some analysts argue that the crisis does indeed accelerate a power shift toward Asia and a multipolar global order. BRICs, especially China, enjoy a stronger relative global position to the US and Europe, whose standing as a credible model has been weakened. Creditor autocracies now enjoy greater influence over, and independence from, debtor democracies and are less constrained in their behavior. Protectionism, resource nationalism, the continued Balkanization of the Internet and the weakening of core alliances all testify to the reassertion of state control over economies and societies. Such policies risk creating an inward-looking "beggar-thy-neighbor" environment in which zero-sum balance of power logic predominates. If this becomes the predominant trend, challengers to US hegemony may well loosen ties with the political West, but how likely is it that they increase political, security and financial ties between each other, creating a parallel order?

Counter-arguments suggest that the global financial crisis will restructure rather than challenge and overturn the existing order. The G20 meeting in London in April 2009 suggested that Great and rising powers will reform global financial architecture so that it can regulate and supervise global markets in a more participative, transparent and responsive manner: all countries have contributed to the crisis; all will be involved in the solution. Mikhail Gorbachev, the last leader of the Soviet Union, reflected on the G20's location and role within the system of global institutions:

> What is this group: a "global politburo," a "club of the powerful," a proto-type for a world government? How will it interact with the United Nations? I am convinced that no group of countries, even if they account for 90 per cent of the world economy, could supersede or substitute for the United Nations. But clearly, the G20 could claim collective leadership in world affairs if it acts with due respect for the opinions of non-members. The presence in the G20 of countries representing different geographic regions, different levels of development and different cultures is a hopeful sign.[27]

In addition, some have suggested that the financial crisis has a more devastating potential impact on BRIC states than on the US and Europe. Established capitalist societies generally fall further but recover from such crises quicker than autocracies (which suffer less but for longer), with societies more prepared to suffer short-term pain for longer term gain, and elites better able to establish effective regulation.[28] Others note that the US will take a lead in reforming global institutions, so securing its primacy.[29] Moreover, the ability of BRICs and other potential rising powers to balance the US is questioned – Brazil, Russia, India and China have distinctive cultural and historical trajectories, as well as domestic political systems. While they may share uncertainty over US hegemony, they band together to improve their negotiating position with the US rather than balance it.

Structure of the book

Having provided an overview of international security, introducing the reader to classical theories of international relations, security concepts and paradigms, the book now turns to an assessment of the current strategic context. In Part II, threats identified as strategic in nature by the "political West" (EU and US) – terrorism and political extremism, weapons proliferation, failing/failed states and regional crises, and environmental and energy security – are then identified and discussed in terms of their nature, relationship to state, regional and global security, and likely future evolution. In Chapter 2, Ekaterina Stepanova addresses the issue of terrorism and political extremism, Gustav Lindstrom explores WMD proliferation in Chapter 3, and Caty Clément writes on the nature of regional crises, conflict and fragile states for Chapter 4. This part of the book ends with Chapter 5 by Tapani Vaahtoranta, which focuses on environmental and energy security. Each of these contributions is structured in the same way, to allow for ease of comparison. They begin by asking and answering the following questions: Why is the issue in question considered a threat? In what way is the threat understood as strategic in nature? What follows is a brief consideration of the history and evolution of our understanding of the issue, including state-related, international and transnational aspects. Then, the chapters identify the key challenges, obstacles and dilemmas to managing the source of insecurity, and conclude by noting the future trends and trajectories in this sphere.

In Part III we compare-and-contrast Great Power approaches to the strategic threats surveyed in Part II. Matthew Rhodes focuses on the US approach in Chapter 6, noting President Obama's new emphasis and direction after the two Bush administrations. By contrast, Pavel K. Baev, when turning to Russia in Chapter 7, notes more continuity than change in the approach of President Medvedev after the two Putin administrations. Bates Gill then draws our attention to China's understanding and management of these four strategic threats in Chapter 8, while Siddharth Varadarajan addresses India in the same way in Chapter 9 and Thierry Tardy the EU in Chapter 10. These chapters end by identifying current trends and likely future trajectories in the management of these threats.

This allows Part IV of the book to conclude with an assessment of the extent of cooperation and conflict between these Great Powers, and so identify prospects for grand strategic stability through the twenty-first century. Here we compare and contrast Great Power identification and prioritization of the strategic threats, as well as the approaches of Great Powers to managing these threats. This allows us to critically assess the degree of cooperation and conflict in the management of such threats and so identify and define with greater clarity competing visions for world order as the first decade of this new century draws to a close.

Notes

1 Daniel Abebe, "Great Power Politics and the Structure of Foreign Relations Law," *Chicago Journal of International Law* 10, 1 (2009), Barry Buzan, *The United States and the Great Powers: World Politics in the Twenty-First Century* (London: Blackwell Publishers, 2004), pp. 69–71, B. Buzan and O. Waever, *Regions and Powers: The Structure of International Security* (Cambridge: Cambridge Studies in International Relations, 2003), p. 458, David A. Lake, "Regional Security Complexes: A Systems Approach," in *Regional Orders: Building Security in a New World*, eds. D. Lake and P.M. Morgan (University Park: Penn State University Press, 1997), pp. 45–67, John Mearsheimer, *The Tragedy of Great Power Politics* (New York: W.W. Norton, 2001), p. 5, Paul A. Papayoanou, "Great Powers and Regional Orders: Possibilities and Prospects after the Cold War," in *Regional Orders: Building Security in a New World*, eds. D. Lake and P.M. Morgan (University Park: Penn State University Press, 1997), p. 125.

2 The White House, *The National Security Strategy of the United States of America* (2006), *The National Security Strategy of the United States of America* (2002).
3 Council of the European Union, *Report on the Implementation of the European Security Strategy. Providing Security in a Changing World* (2008).
4 The text (in Russian) is available at the Russian Security Council website: www.scrf. gov.ru/documents/99.html.
5 Christophe Jaffrelot and Waheguru Pal Singh Sidhu, "Does Europe Matter to India?," in *European Security in a Global Context: Internal and External Dynamics*, ed. Thierry Tardy (London and New York: Routledge, 2009), p. 193.
6 Goldman Sachs, "Dreaming with BRICs: The Path to 2050," *Global Economics Paper* 99 (2003).
7 Malcolm N. Shaw, *International Law*, 4th edn. (Cambridge: Cambridge University Press, 1997), pp. 36–38.
8 Anthony Carty, *The Decay of International Law? A Reappraisal of the Limits of Legal Imagination in International Affairs* (Manchester: Manchester University Press, 1986), pp. 14–18.
9 Stephen M. Walt, "International Relations: One World, Many Theories," *Foreign Policy* 110, Spring (1998): pp. 29–44.
10 Kenneth Waltz, *Theory of International Relations* (Reading: Addison-Wesley, 1979).
11 Robert Jervis, "Cooperation Under the Security Dilemma," *World Politics* 30 (1977–1978).
12 Mearsheimer, *The Tragedy of Great Power Politics*.
13 Robert O. Keohane, *After Hegemony: Cooperation and Discord in the World Political Economy* (Princeton: Princeton University Press, 1984).
14 B. Buzan, O. Waever and J. de Wilde, *Security: A New Framework of Analysis* (Boulder: Lynne Rienner, 1998).
15 Graeme P. Herd, "International Relations Theory, Catastrophes and the Need for a New Paradigm," in *Potential Global Strategic Catastrophes: Balancing Transnational Responsibilities and Burden-sharing with Sovereignty and Human Dignity*, ed. Nayef R.F. Al-Rodhan (Berlin: LIT, 2009).
16 P.G. Brown and G. Garver, "Don't Fix the Economy – Change It: Sticking with the Model that is Driving Us Toward Ecological Catastrophe Will Eventually Kill Us," *Toronto Star*, 26 December 2008, A59.
17 M.J. Rees, *Our Final Century: Will Civilisation Survive the Twenty-First Century?* (London: Arrow, 2004), p. vii.
18 Francis Fukuyama, "The End of History?," *The National Interest* 16, Summer (1989), F. Fukuyama, *The End of History and the Last Man* (Harmondsworth: Penguin, 1992).
19 Samuel Huntington, "The Clash of Civilizations," *Foreign Affairs* 72, 3 (1993), S. Huntington, *The Clash of Civilizations and the Remaking of World Order* (New York: Simon & Schuster, 1996).
20 Max Bassin, "Civilizations and Their Discontents: Political Geography and Geopolitics in the Huntington Thesis," *Geopolitics* 12 (2007).
21 Robert D. Kaplan, "The Coming Anarchy: How Scarcity, Crime, Overpopulation, Tribalism, and Disease are Rapidly Destroying the Social Fabric of Our Planet," *Atlantic Monthly* 273, (1994), R.D. Kaplan, *The Coming Anarchy: Shattering the Dreams of the Post Cold War* (New York: Random House, 2000).
22 T.P.M. Barnett, *The Pentagon's New Map: War and Peace in the Twenty-First Century* (New York: G.P. Putnam's Sons, 2004).
23 Robert Kagan, "End of Dreams, Return of History: International Rivalry and American Leadership," *Policy Review* 143 (2007).
24 Parag Khanna, The Second World: Empires and Influence in the New Global Order (New York: Random House, 2008).
25 F. Zakaria, *The Post-American World* (New York: W.W. Norton, 2008).

26 Niall Ferguson, "The Axis of Upheaval," *Foreign Policy* March/April (2009).
27 Mikhail Gorbachev, "What Role for the G-20?," *New York Times*, 27 April 2009.
28 Walter Russell Mead, "Only Makes You Stronger," *The New Republic*, 4 February 2009.
29 Stephen and William Wohlforth Brooks, "Spearheading Reform of the World Order: How Washington Should Reform International Institutions," *Foreign Affairs* 88, 2 (2009).

Part II

Strategic threats

Nature and evolution

2   Terrorism and extremism

Ekaterina Stepanova

Terrorism was hardly the primary focus of the international security agenda before the terrorist attacks of 11 September 2001 on US targets. Years later, with other urgent security concerns on the agenda, including those generated by the "war against terrorism" in itself, why is terrorism considered a major security threat? In what way is this threat strategic in nature?

First, in the age of information and mass communications, of critical importance is not just the real scale of armed violence and its direct human and material costs, but also, and increasingly so, its broader destabilizing effect on national, international, human and public security and its ability to affect politics. As demonstrated by 9/11 and the subsequent series of high-profile, mass-casualty terrorist attacks in various parts of the world, it no longer takes hundreds of thousands of battle-related deaths to dramatically affect international security and significantly alter the security agenda at the national and international levels. While the 3,000, mostly civilian, fatalities of 9/11 are by no means comparable to the huge battle-related military and civilian death tolls of major post-World War II wars (such as Korea, Viet Nam or the Iran–Iraq war), the political impact of 9/11 and its repercussions for global security have been comparable with those events. This disproportionately destabilizing, politically manipulative effect is the main hallmark of terrorism and far exceeds its actual damage. The highly asymmetrical nature and effects of terrorism are one of the main explanations for why it is considered to pose a strategic threat for many individual states and societies, and for international security.

Second, although due to the broader destabilizing effects of terrorism measurable parameters alone (incidents, casualties, etc.) do not suffice to show the real scale of the terrorist threat, terrorism has been on the rise even in terms of sheer numbers. In contrast to the downward trend in state-based armed conflicts, the annual totals of which declined by 40 percent since the early 1990s until the 2003 low,[1] overall terrorist activity increased three-fold from 1998 to 2007.[2] The situation has gravely deteriorated as a result of both 9/11 and its spurring effect on international terrorist activity, but also due to the way the post-9/11 "war on terrorism" was conducted: since 2001, terrorism has been most sharply on the rise in those regions – the broader Middle East, especially Iraq, and South Asia, including Afghanistan – that were primary targets of the "war on terrorism."

The rise of terrorism is also part of such broader trends in political violence as (a) the negative dynamics displayed by all forms of one-sided – direct and intentional – violence against civilians since the early 1990s;[3] (b) the relative rise of the role of non-state actors in one-sided violence, in comparison to the relative decline of the role of states.[4] Furthermore, terrorism is unique in its complexity as a "dual" form of violence: terrorism by default involves one-sided violence against civilians, but goes beyond civilians as its immediate targets to serve as a specific, asymmetrical tactic employed by a weaker side in an armed confrontation against a stronger protagonist, usually the state.

Third, do all types and forms of terrorism pose a strategic threat at all levels of security: local, national, regional, global? While terrorism has long been employed both as a standard tactic in many local/regional conflicts and as extreme violence by relatively small and often marginalized radical groups in a state of peace, does "traditional" terrorism pose a strategic threat at the global level? In contrast to familiar types of conflict-related and peacetime terrorism, al-Qaeda, and the evolving violent transnational Islamist networks inspired by al-Qaeda[5] and responsible for a series of major post-9/11 terrorist attacks in Bali, Istanbul, Madrid or London, demonstrated a qualitative upgrade of terrorism to a new phenomenon of global terrorism (also known as superterrorism or macroterrorism). Superterrorism is by definition global in its reach, is not tied to any particular local context, and ultimately pursues existential, non-negotiable, global and in this sense unlimited goals (such as al-Qaeda's goal of challenging the world order). While superterrorism does not replace more traditional forms of terrorism, the phenomenon of al-Qaeda has had a strong demonstrative and inspiring impact on groups pursuing a more limited political agenda by using terrorist means at the more localized level. However, any existing parallels and links between new global terrorism and the continuing, more traditional terrorist activities do not make one conditional upon the other: each type of terrorism retains a significant degree of autonomy, with its own logic and dynamics. Therefore, rather than confronting a fully integrated, universal terrorist network that is spreading from local to global levels, the international community faces a far more difficult challenge: coping with functionally different types and variations of terrorism at different levels, and the complex interrelationship between them.

Fourth, the high strategic importance assigned by developed Western states to transnational Islamist terrorism in particular is underscored by the fact that, while al-Qaeda-type networks operate and train globally, reaching out to both developed and underdeveloped states, most targets of superterrorism have been either located in, or associated with, the developed world. While, for instance, traditional conflict-related terrorism primarily affects regions such as the Middle East or South Asia and has only limited manifestations in Western Europe, such as separatist terrorism in Spain and the UK (Northern Ireland), the new, global Islamist terrorism is particularly well-suited for attacking targets associated with Western democracies. Even though the type of political regime is one of several factors affecting states' vulnerability to terrorism (other factors include the general functionality of the state, the degree of ethno-confessional diversity, identity and cultural factors), democracies have some particular vulnerabilities to terrorist methods. While democratic states ensure a higher level of civil and political rights than other types of political regimes, and give fewer pretexts for political violence, terrorism is the one form of political violence they remain most vulnerable to. Democracies value the lives of their civilians more than other states, and therefore pose particularly lucrative targets of blackmail for terrorists. This vulnerability is a by-product of the essential characteristics of democracy and cannot be "removed." Also, while developed democratic states are less affected by domestic socio-political violence, they may get involved in asymmetrical armed conflicts, military interventions and controversial state-building experiments in other parts of the world, sometimes with little regard for international law or local legitimacy, thus provoking violent resistance, including terrorism directed at "soft" targets associated with the West.

Defining terrorism as a security threat

Confusion stemming from the inability to properly define terrorist threats as distinct from some other security threats cripples the ability of governments, societies and international institutions to accurately identify terrorist threats, fully understand their strategic impact and find effective means to prevent and counter terrorism. This is especially true in view of the post-9/11 "war on terrorism" – an uneasy combination of war-fighting, international peace enforcement and national counter-insurgency campaigns, with some, often secondary, role for counter-terrorism too. In order to explain which specific characteristics of terrorism turn it into a strategic security threat, it is important to define terrorism (a) in relation to other violent security threats and forms of violence, especially the ones it is often confused with; and (b) in relation to a broader notion of political (religious) extremism.

In this chapter, terrorism is defined as the intentional use or threat to use violence against civilians and non-combatants by non-state actors, in order to achieve political goals in asymmetrical confrontation. This definition includes three criteria, a combination of which helps distinguish terrorism from other forms of violence.

The first criterion distinguishes terrorism from plain crime and criminal violence motivated by economic gain – these are terrorists' *political goals* (interpreted very broadly, such a goal may include ideological or religious motivations or be formulated in ideological or religious categories, but always with a political dimension). For terrorist actors, a political goal is an end in itself, rather than a secondary instrument or "cover" for the advancement of other interests (such as the illegal accumulation of wealth, as in the case of organized criminal groups).

While terrorism necessitates a political goal, it is not a goal itself but a tactic; a specific way of using or threatening violence against civilians to achieve that goal. There are terrorist means, rather than terrorist goals: a political goal, including legitimate goals such as national liberation from foreign occupation or colonial rule (freedom-fighting), may be pursued by different tactics employed at the same time and even by the same actors. These tactics may range from military confrontation between armed combatants and terrorist violence to massive non-violent resistance. Thus, the popular "terrorists vs. freedom-fighters" dilemma is misleading, as one does not necessarily exclude the other: "freedom-fighting" is a political goal that can be pursued by a variety of violent and non-violent means and "terrorism" is one of several violent tactics used to advance political goals that may include "freedom-fighting." On the one hand, no political goal, no matter how legitimate it is, can justify the use of terrorism against civilians. On the other hand, the use of terrorist means to achieve a certain political goal does not automatically delegitimize the goal itself: the active use of terrorist means to end French colonial rule in Algeria or the occupation of Palestinian territories does not make these goals less legitimate.

The second criterion – the immediate *target* of violence – distinguishes terrorism from another form of politically motivated violence; namely, insurgent or guerrilla attacks against government military and security forces. In contrast to attacks against government or occupying foreign forces by rebels who presumably enjoy some support of the civilian population, terrorism is specifically directed against civilian population and objects or is intentionally indiscriminate. As the same armed group can use several modes of operation at once, including guerrilla and terrorist tactics, or switch from one tactic to another, the preferred academic term for such groups is "organizations *involved in terrorist activities*," or "*using terrorist means*." Although the "target" criterion is a relative one, considering it is sometimes difficult to identify a target as civilian, prove that civilians were targeted intentionally and distinguish between combatants and non-combatants in a conflict area, this criterion is still an extremely important one. First, in the case of an organized campaign of violence against civilians, it is often not difficult to identify them as the main targets. Second, the target of violence has serious implications from the point of International Humanitarian Law (IHL): rebel attacks against government military and security targets are *not* criminalized internationally (even if they are usually criminalized by national laws), while deliberate attacks against civilians (including terrorist acts), regardless of the character of international or non-international armed conflict, constitute grave violations of the IHL.[6]

While civilians remain the immediate targets and victims of terrorism, they are usually not the end recipients of the terrorists' message. Terrorism is a performance where the use or threat of violence against civilians is specifically "staged" for a more powerful actor – also the terrorists' chief protagonist (usually, *the state* or a group of states) – to watch, and is further meant to blackmail the state and make it do or abstain from doing something. The state as the ultimate recipient of the terrorists' message brings us to the third criterion – the asymmetrical nature of terrorism.[7] Terrorism is a specific tactic of the "weak" (non-state actors) against the conventionally "stronger" side, usually of a higher formal status (the state, group of states, international organization or the international community of states). The asymmetrical nature of terrorism explains the main specifics of this mode of operation: unable to cause major damage to a stronger enemy by conventional means, terrorists opt for causing limited damaged instead, but in such a way that it wreaks maximum havoc and strikes at their opponent's soft spot. Attacks against civilians or non-combatants are needed to serve as a force-multiplier compensating for conventional military weakness, and as a public-relations tool to exercise pressure on state(s) and society(s) at large. This bottom-up asymmetry distinguishes terrorism from other forms of politically motivated violence against civilians: terrorism is not a weapon of the "strong" to be employed against the "weak" – states have other destructive and repressive methods at their disposal to be used against civilians. These methods are often more destructive than terrorism by non-state actors and many such methods employed by states are already criminalized by international law.[8] Nor is terrorism primarily a weapon of the "weak" to be employed against the similarly "weak" (e.g., as in intra- or inter-communal violence).

In asymmetrical armed confrontation between state and non-state actor(s), the "strong" actor does not simply overwhelm the "weak" one – rather, the protagonists differ in their strengths and weaknesses. The asymmetry is two-sided. Anti-system non-state actors at the national and transnational levels cannot match their opponents' main strengths – the states' greater military, political and socio-economic potential (conventional power) and their formal status within the world system where they remain the key formative units. However, violent non-state actors rely on other resources and have their own comparative strengths, such as the high mobilization power of their extremist ideologies reinforced by adaptive structures (organizational forms).

Terrorism and extremism: the role of extremist ideologies

Non-state actors ready to take up arms to oppose a national or international system through terrorist means are by definition more strongly motivated, more ideologically zealous and have higher commitment and stronger resolve than their opponents. In most respects extremist ideologies *are* marginal to the main-stream ideologies, such as market-oriented democracy, moderate nationalism or "national modernism," but they are better tailored for a specific purpose – to serve as a force for mobilization against a more powerful enemy of a higher status.

Extremist ideology is also the main characteristic shared by the broader phenomenon of political, religious and ideological extremism, as well as the narrower phenomenon of militancy which includes, but is not limited to, *terrorism*. The main distinction between "extremism" and "terrorism" is not so much the degree of ideological radicalism, but the preferred methods for action: while "extremism" never excludes violence, it manifests itself through a wide range of means, from political propaganda and religious preaching to a variety of non-violent and violent protest actions. While extremist ideologies may drive and justify armed violence, including terrorism, extremism does not necessarily or automatically lead to terrorism or indeed, to violence. To put it simply, while all terrorists are extremists (as they, at the very least, share extremist ideology), not all extremists are terrorists. Not all extremist violence is terrorism (e.g., right-wing extremism is dominated by violence other than terrorism, such as ethno-confessional vandalism or scuffle provocations), nor do all extremists engage in violent activity in the first place – some professedly extremist organizations (e.g., Hizb-ut-Tahrir in Central Asia) have not resorted to violence, including terrorism, prioritizing propaganda instead.

While ideological extremism does not inadvertently lead to violence, including terrorism, it provides a powerful ideological basis for the latter. However, ideological/religious extremism is not the only condition for the radicalization of extremists into violent actors such as terrorists – radicalization is a gradual process, through which the influence of context-specific social, psychological and cultural factors merge with the impact of political realities re-interpreted in line with an extremist ideology. Nor are terrorist groups necessarily guided by a single extremist ideology. Many are instead driven by more "extremisms" than one: the most common combinations, short of global contexts, include a synthesis of right-wing extremism and religious fundamentalism, nationalism and left-wing radicalism, and more recently, ethno-nationalism and religious, particularly Islamist, extremism.

At the global level, the case of al-Qaeda illustrates the link between transnational extremist ideology and global terrorism. The 9/11 attacks, unprecedented in scale and lethality, were hardly driven by an extremist Islamist ideology alone, but were also shaped by the need to resort to increasingly asymmetrical forms of violence to produce the intended global demonstrative effect, which was no less addressed to the world's Muslims than to Western and world audiences. These "rational" calculations, however, were supported by the most transnationalized, extremist interpretation of the concept of *jihad* (the holy war) to justify mass civilian casualties as long as the "ultimate" target is the "enemy," and as long as citizens of democratic Western states share full responsibility for their governments' policies. The role of extremist ideology is not limited to a mere manipulation of religious-ideological doctrines by terrorist leaders and ideologues and skillfully instrumentalized as a powerful mobilization and communication tool. This extremist ideology is also a genuine reaction to profound socio-political and cultural changes in the Muslim world that are happening under the multiple pressures of modernization, globalization and Westernization, and are perceived by broader segments of elites and the populations in the Muslim regions and diasporas as directed against the global *umma* (Muslim community).

The transnationalized version of Islamist extremism popularized by al-Qaeda has been the only extremist ideology in the late-twentieth–early-twenty-first century to play the role of global anti-system protest ideology – a role that is not currently paralleled by any equally coherent secular protest ideology. What makes this version of Islamist extremism such a powerful anti-system ideology at the transnational level; one that is able to come up with an alternative vision of a global order and inspire enough adepts to promote it with terrorist means? First, it is more than an extremist fringe of a religious current, but a quasi-religious ideology that goes beyond confessional issues and merges political, social and cultural protest with genuine belief in the possibility of an alternative global order – a system based on the direct rule of God. Second, the ultimate agenda and goals are unlimited, and they go beyond the "defence of Muslim lands" and confrontation with the West: "the subject matter … is mankind and [the] sphere of activity is [the] entire universe"; the need "to establish Sovereignty and Authority of God on earth and the true system revealed by God" is considered "enough to declare Jihad."[9] Third, this ideology is not merely internationalist or transnational, but supranational: it does not simply aspire to gain control of existing states, but rejects the very notion of a "nation state," including all existing Muslim states which cannot substitute for the God-sent system of rules. This ideology pretends to exist in another dimension that lies outside the state framework and where people are characterized not by their ethnicity, nationality or citizenship, but by whether they share the faith in one God. Finally, what distinguishes the al-Qaeda-style extremism from radical ideologies of the more localized, socially based and pragmatic movements that combine Islamism with nationalism (such as Hamas or Hizbullah) is that the former is explicitly transnationalized and unlikely to be moderated in principle. The ability of al-Qaeda's ideology to persist and spread as a global reflex or symptom of such fundamental global processes like aggressive globalization, traumatic modernization or Western cultural expansion, make it very adaptive to concrete political/international developments, including the conflicts in Afghanistan, Iraq and Palestine, which provide up-to-date illustrations for the Islamist extremists to support their world view.

The origins and periodization of terrorism

Long before the term "terrorism" emerged in the nineteenth century, a broader notion of "terror" was born in the late-eighteenth century out of the French Revolution; one that originally referred to violent repression by the "revolutionary state" controlled by the radical republicans, the Jacobins. In the nineteenth century, the term started to be used to refer to violent actions, especially political assassinations, by violent actors in opposition to the state (revolutionary, nationalist and national-liberation movements). To distinguish this armed opposition tactic from the broader notion of "terror" and the repressive actions of governments, a special term – "terrorism" – emerged. Remarkably, since the very beginning, the term "terrorism" explicitly referred to politically motivated violence by the actors in *opposition* to the state, i.e., non-state actors.

Use of the term "terrorism" to refer to the tactic of political assassinations by opposition revolutionary groups since the nineteenth century does not mean that similar actions did not take place earlier – in fact, they had been inseparable from political history, at least for the time since formation of the "state."[10] However, the spread of political assassinations directed against state officials in nineteenth-century Europe was unprecedented. The tactic was applied both by individual revolutionaries and groups such as the Italian *carbonari* earlier in the nineteenth century, but the systematic use of "terrorism" as a combination of method, backed by ideology and reinforced by organizational framework, began in the third quarter of the century. While the contemporary notion of terrorism is much broader than its nineteenth-century interpretation (when it was largely reduced to select political assassinations of individual officials), the same term can be applied to both nineteenth and twentieth-to-twenty-first-century terrorism. Terrorism as a form of political violence is a product of modern and contemporary history.

Prior to the mid-nineteenth century, the use of terrorist methods as an asymmetrical, violent "communication" tactic of armed opposition groups was hardly feasible in technological terms. The development of transportation systems such as railways, the invention of dynamite, and especially the spread of the first modern means of communication – the telegraph – created technical and logistical conditions for modern terrorism. Thus, among the main characteristics distinguishing late-nineteenth-century terrorism from the political assassinations preceding it has been its event-setting orientation and public resonance, which depended upon the flow of information through real-time communication.

The first historical peak of terrorism was the period from the end of the nineteenth to the early-twentieth century; times associated primarily with anarchist terrorism in Europe and the United States, revolutionary terrorism in Russia, and the use of terrorist means by national-liberation/anti-colonial movements in Ireland, Poland, the Balkans, India, etc. Despite the historical parallels between revolutionary and nationalist terrorism of the late-nineteenth–early-twentieth period and contemporary terrorism of the left-wing or nationalist bent, there are also multiple distinctions. More generally, the phenomenon – and the notion – of terrorism have gradually expanded since the nineteenth century. From the early-twentieth century, terrorism went beyond selective attacks against political figures and started to target civilians non-selectively and en masse – a pattern that would later become an almost inseparable characteristic of terrorist attacks. The next, post-World War II peak of terrorism was marked by the rise of left-wing terrorism in Europe, Latin America and some other parts of the world after the 1960s, and the wave of anti-colonial/national-liberation terrorism. The latest, current peak of terrorist activity has manifested itself in the late-1990s–2000s, especially after the 9/11 terrorist attacks.

The evolution of the understanding of terrorism

Due to the political, rather than academic, nature and origin of the notion of terrorism, the first interpreters and "students" of terrorism were the revolutionary ideologues and their political opponents. Academic research on terrorism evolved in the twentieth century, especially from the 1970s. Given the high level of politicization of all matters related to terrorism, the definitional aspects remained the most contentious issues. Discussions on definition and typology of terrorism and on the optimal anti-terrorism strategies gained new momentum in the context of the 9/11 attacks and the heavily militarized US-led "war on terrorism." Despite hundreds of existing definitions, the mainstream terrorism research has strongly emphasized the political nature and goals of terrorism, its special "communication" function, with immediate "soft" targets used as victims to generate a broader political message, and the highly context-specific nature of concrete forms and manifestations of terrorism.[11]

With much attention paid to direct manifestations of terrorism, it is only recently that the causes of terrorism started to be systematically addressed by scholars, mostly in the context of critical analysis of the so-called "root causes" approach. In fact, it may be more accurate to refer to different types and levels of causes of terrorism, such as structural, facilitating (accelerator) and motivational causes or explanations at different levels of social structure (individual, group, societal/national and systemic/international levels).[12] One of the most strongly debated issues has been the alleged relationship between poverty (underdevelopment) and terrorism: some of the current research questions the direct or decisive causal effect of poverty on terrorism[13] and emphasizes political conditions, long-standing feelings of indignity and frustration, and lack of political and civil rights as the indicators more directly associated with terrorism. While terrorism can manifest itself everywhere in the world, its roots are most closely associated with areas that are not necessarily the poorest or least developed, but rather the most dramatically affected by incomplete modernization and/or cultural marginalization. Terrorism is not a product of an underdeveloped, traditional society – it is a product of a society undergoing dramatic, painful or failing political, social and economic modernization,[14] and of the frustration associated with the socio-psychological gap between rising expectations and reality (relative deprivation theory).[15] In sum, terrorism is more directly linked to a combination of relative deprivation resulting from "traumatic modernization," perceived or real violations, lack of political and civil rights, and threats to national, (ethno)confessional and cultural identity, rather than to poverty or underdevelopment as such. Much of the current research also stresses the ambiguous relationship between terrorism and the type of political regime (i.e., former authoritarian states undergoing democratization or dysfunctional democracies and weakening or eroding non-democratic regimes tend to create more favorable conditions for terrorism than either consolidated democracies or rigid autocracies do).[16] While the role of failed states as safe havens for terrorist groups is well-acknowledged, the sources of terrorism cannot be reduced to such ungoverned areas alone.

Asymmetric theory of conflict is increasingly applied to the study of terrorism by non-state actors.[17] Some of the latest concepts include focus on the "status," as opposed to just the "power" disparity, and on the "two-way" asymmetry, in which both states and their non-state opponents have their own strengths and weaknesses. The role of ideology in terrorism remains one of the most contentious and understudied themes, with current research dominated by studies of religious, particularly Islamist, extremism.[18] The innovative analysis of organizational forms of terrorism is centered around interpretations of terrorism as network warfare. It builds on (a) organizational network theory,[19] (b) social networks theory as applied to the study of terrorism, especially violent Islamist networks[20] and (c) the focus on organizational features of terrorist groups that are atypical of both networks and hierarchies.[21]

Ideological and organizational patterns merge with psycho-sociological factors to explain mechanisms behind the radicalization of individuals and groups into terrorism and also, more recently, the de-radicalization process.[22] The psycho-sociological school[23] has dominated the research on suicidal terrorism as practiced by both religious and secular groups,[24] but suffers from excessive attention to explanations on the individual level, at the expense of social-group and societal levels of analysis.

While criminological analysis of terrorism helps highlight its sources of funding and form the basis for legal definition and criminal prosecution of terrorist offences, much of it tends to reduce terrorism primarily to a form of "serious crime," de-emphasizes its political nature, overestimates the level of its integration with organized crime, and pays insufficient attention to terrorist financing from legal sources, such as religious donations.[25]

Finally, the rise of superterrorism with unlimited, global goals prompted increasing thought on the possibility of the use of unconventional materials and even weapons of mass destruction (WMD) in terrorism.[26] However, the level of attention received by "WMD terrorism" appears to greatly outmatch the real scale of this threat, often at the expense of attention that could be given to more urgent threats, such as conventional terrorist attacks on critical civilian infrastructure, notably transport, energy, water systems, information and communication networks.

Current trends in terrorism

The two basic trends in the dynamics of terrorism since 1998[27] have been (a) the overall increase of terrorist activity measured in the number of incidents, casualties, active terrorist groups etc.; and (b) the increased lethality of terrorism shown by the rising annual fatality totals and the growing proportion of mass-casualty and suicidal attacks. From 1998 to 2006, the annual total of terrorist incidents increased five-fold (reaching over 6,600 attacks in 2006), while fatalities increased 5.6-fold (over 12,000 in 2006) and injuries were up 2.6-fold (almost 21,000 in 2006); see Figure 2.1.[28] While the interim peak of terrorist activity in 2001 was linked to the 9/11 attacks, since 2003, terrorism owes much of its sharp increase to the conflict in Iraq where it became a standard violent tactic (in 2006, Iraq accounted for 60 percent of terrorist incidents and 79 percent of terrorist fatalities worldwide). Attempts to interpret this high impact of one conflict on overall terrorism dynamics as evidence of an actual decline in terrorism, save for the conflict in Iraq,[29] are flawed, as this dependence is hardly unique: the gradual shift of the center of gravity in terrorist activity from Iraq to Afghanistan, Pakistan and the rest of South Asia in 2007–2008 underscores the

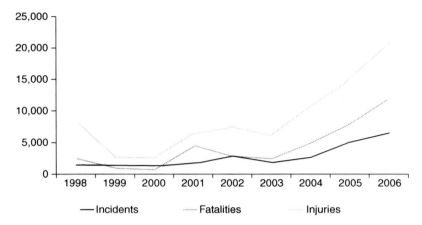

Figure 2.1 Terrorist incidents, fatalities and injuries, 1998–2006 (source: Terrorism Knowledge Base, MIPT, 2007).

decisive role of several major armed conflicts worldwide as contexts for the majority of terrorist activity.

Another major trend is the further internationalization (transnationalization) of terrorism. The main changes here have been qualitative, rather than quantitative. The qualitative upgrade is, for instance, illustrated by the new distinct type and level of terrorism – namely, global terrorism associated with al-Qaeda or al-Qaeda-inspired networks (although this highly transnationalized terrorism is not the dominant type of terrorism worldwide – that role is still played by the more localized, conflict-related terrorism).[30]

In terms of the terrorist groups' dominant ideology and in line with terrorism typology by motivation, as a result of the end of the Cold War and the decline of the radical socialist, communist and other left-wing ideologies, their role as a basis for groups engaged in terrorist activity has decreased. Even as left-wing terrorism in absolute terms has slightly increased since the end of the Cold War, its destabilizing potential and ability to affect politics declined in relation to the rise of nationalist and religious terrorism. Still, the popular claim about the absolute dominance of religious terrorism since the late-1990s is not very accurate, as, from 1998 to 2006, nationalist terrorism not only accounted for most terrorist incidents at the domestic/national level, but also for the bulk of all terrorist incidents – domestic and international combined – worldwide. However, it is religious terrorism that has been the most – and increasingly – lethal, resulting in highest death tolls both at domestic and at international levels (see Figures 2.2–2.3).

In terms of the terrorist group structures, the continuing spread of networks has been increasingly combined with hierarchical elements to form hybrid types of most real-life groups displaying both vertical and horizontal, and formal and informal, links. Increasingly sophisticated information and communication

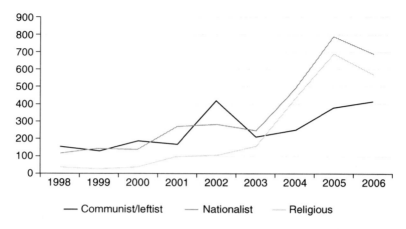

Figure 2.2 Incidents of Communist/leftist, nationalist and religious terrorism.

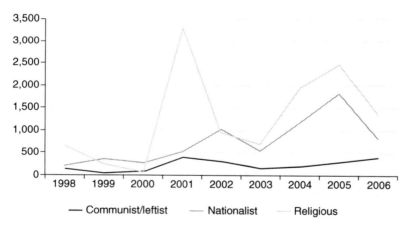

Figure 2.3 Fatalities of Communist/leftist, nationalist and religious terrorism (source: Terrorism Knowledge Base, MIPT, 2007).

capacities of terrorist groups allow them to expand their audience, as well as amplify the message and demonstrative effects of their attacks (despite the otherwise generally standard and not particularly sophisticated technologies, weapons and other materials used by terrorists). The evolution of organizational forms and the upgraded information and communication capacities of terrorist actors have affected their training and recruitment patterns. These have evolved from a more structured and centralized recruitment involving combat training and/or experience, to the more rapid, often voluntary process, which frequently involves online radicalization of individuals or cells. These cells may have a direct link to broader terrorist networks, but may also join a broader movement through less-formal links and, in the case of purely self-generating cells, simply by undertaking "direct action" in the name of the movement.

Growing financial and economic independence of terrorist actors is achieved both by their increasing involvement in criminal activities and by the use of legal financial sources. While the links between terrorism and organized crime have diversified and become stronger since the early 1990s, partly stimulated by declining state support of terrorism, even major recent terrorist acts have been relatively inexpensive, while the financing of most Islamist terrorist groups comes at least as much from legal sources (such as religious donations) as it does from illicit activities.

Traditionally, a basic distinction was made between terrorism at the national and at the international level or, simply, between domestic and international terrorism. That distinction was all too easy to make "on paper," as long as "international terrorism" was "technically" defined as terrorist activity conducted on the territories of more than one state and involving citizens of more than one state. In practice, however, this distinction was never too strict even in the past: systematic terrorist activity was rarely self-sufficient within national borders (notably in terms of logistics and/or internationalist ideology, as in the case of left-wing/anarchist groups).

In the twenty-first century, this distinction has eroded even further:[31] even terrorist groups whose political agenda remained confined to a certain political or national context increasingly internationalized some or most of their logistics, fund-raising, propaganda and even planning activities, often extending them to far-away regions and partly operating from, or being based, abroad.[32] Today there are few terrorist actors that rely on "internal" resources alone. Groups engaged in armed conflicts in very remote locations (e.g., the Maoists during the conflict in Nepal), which have relied primarily on internal resources, have still built ideological links with like-minded movements (e.g., with the Naxalite movement in India) and received some external financial or logistical support. In a peacetime environment, acts of purely internal terrorism are usually limited to isolated attacks by left- or right-wing extremists (e.g., the 1995 Oklahoma City bombing).

The high degree of internationalization of terrorist activities by both communist/leftist groups and, more recently, violent Islamist networks, is not necessarily or primarily driven by pragmatic logistical needs, but also by a progression of their internationalist (transnational) ideologies. For instance, a violent Islamist cell in Europe, comprised of radical Muslims that may be citizens of European states, may have no or limited direct operational guidance, financial or logistical support from the rest of the transnational Islamist movement. However, its terrorist activities may still "qualify" as transnational terrorism as long as they are guided by a universalist, quasi-religious ideology and are carried out in the name of the entire *umma* (Muslim community), e.g., in reaction to Western interventions in Afghanistan, Iraq or elsewhere. This is transnational terrorism, even if it results in casualties primarily among the perpetrators' fellow citizens.

It is important to distinguish between different forms, levels and stages of the gradual erosion of the divide between "international" and "domestic" terrorism.

This erosion may, for instance, be limited to internationalization of some of a terrorist group's activities (such as conducting terrorist acts, or extending logistics and fund-raising activities, abroad). It may also take more advanced forms, ranging from more active interaction between separate groups in different countries to the formation of fully fledged inter-organizational networks or even transnational terrorist networks.[33] As terrorist activity may be internationalized even at localized levels, of primary importance today is not the mechanical distinction between purely "domestic" and "international" terrorism, but the overall level of a group's goals and agenda – local, regional or global.

Before turning to more specific anti-terrorism strategies, it is useful to highlight some of the key challenges in preventing and combating modern terrorism, such as (in declining order of importance):

a   to counter extremist ideologies and neutralize the organizational advantages of terrorist groups;
b   to avoid mistaking anti-terrorism for the "war on terrorism" and highlight the highly specific nature of counter-terrorism as a security activity with the primary goals of prevention, pre-emption and effective disruption of terrorist activity, rather than post hoc coercion, enforcement and retaliation;
c   to find an optimal balance in counter-terrorism between, in declining order of importance: more specific counter-terrorist tasks performed by the intelligence (counter-intelligence) community, more general law-enforcement tasks and, finally, the support role that the military can play in counter-terrorism;
d   to find a balance between functionality and legitimacy of anti-terrorism measures; and,
e   to stimulate political transformation of armed movements – especially the "veto players" (politically and militarily viable and organizationally cohesive groups that enjoy a degree of popular support or are mass-based grassroots movements, such as the Palestinian Hamas or the Lebanese Hizbullah) that have used terrorist means – and their integration in the political/peace process.

Three important reservations should be kept in mind when discussing strategies to prevent and counter terrorism at the national and international levels:

a   The eroding distinction between "domestic" and "international" terrorism implies that counter-terrorist strategies at home and abroad are closely interrelated, and some measures may be equally relevant for preventing and combating terrorism both at the national and at the international levels (while their order of importance may be different).
b   Effective counter-terrorism requires a combination of measures undertaken by different actors, at different levels and within different time frames (from reactive to preventive and from short-term to long-term measures). Short-term preemptive and response measures would hardly have any tangible

effect if they are not part of a comprehensive anti-terrorism strategy that includes mid-term and long-term security, political and other measures.

c   As terrorism is a highly context- and type-specific phenomenon, dealing with different types of terrorism (e.g., according to their motivation typology – religious, nationalist, socio-political) may require significantly nuanced counter-terrorism strategies.

Anti-terrorism at the national level

Still, the following generalizations can be made regarding anti-terrorist measures at the national level (in declining order of urgency, organized into short-term, mid-term and long-term categories):

1   The main focus in anti-terrorism as a distinct security activity should be on the highly specialized, carefully targeted "special operations" conducted by intelligence/counter-intelligence services and aimed, above all, at prevention, pre-emption and pre-emptive disruption of terrorist acts and networks. These operations are completely dependent on resolute government decision-making capacity based on timely, comparative analysis of solid and accurate intelligence (of a strategic, psychological, and particularly tactical type, regarding terrorists' specific plans of action) collected on a permanent basis, both by technical means and from and by human sources (human intelligence, or HUMINT), and with adequate attention paid to open-source means and materials.

2   Next in terms of urgency and importance come the more general prophylactic and preventive measures, such as physical protection measures for the population, buildings and infrastructure, identity checks, etc., conducted primarily by the police/law-enforcement sector.

3   Terrorism crisis-management operations, such as hostage rescue operations, conducted by special counter-terrorism units with support from the military and law enforcement follow suit, supplemented by post hoc consequences management, with an emphasis on civilian victim protection.

4   A range of legal and judicial measures are essential to preserving the balance between functionality and legality (which is crucial if counter-terrorism is not to become counter-productive, i.e., not to produce more terrorism). They range from anti-terrorism legislation to using the civil criminal justice process to prosecute terrorists – strongly preferable to any special military tribunals – even in an internal armed-conflict situation. The role of the judiciary tends to be most effective when it establishes a degree of working cooperation with the "counter-terrorist" security community and, with no significant derogation from the due process of law, adapts some specific procedures to increase the level of professionalism on anti-terrorism matters to make the system more adaptive to anti-terrorism needs and to have some access to the stage of "preliminary" (pre-incident), rather than just post hoc, investigations.[34] Some form of codification of the "terrorism conspiracy"

norm is also required to target terrorists' logistics/financial networks and to open investigations before a terrorist act occurs. In sum, specialization of judicial process (in the form of specialized, but basically normal, legal procedure) and integration/complementarity of intelligence and judicial capabilities are some of the strategies to balance functionality and legality in counter-terrorism.

5   From the mid-term structural perspective, the most effective ways to neutralize and "normalize" structural capabilities of the larger movements that have employed terrorism in the context of a broader armed conflict are (a) to introduce some elements of network organizational design into relevant state security structures (e.g., through more active inter-agency cooperation), try to formalize the informal links, and to turn relatively decentralized hybrid terrorist networks into more formal streamlined hierarchies, making them easier to either talk to or counter; (b) this is best achieved by encouraging both general demilitarization of politics and, more specifically, political transformation of the "mainstream" armed groups – "veto players" (by stimulating them to get increasingly politicized and involved in non-militant activities, and to form distinctive and fully-fledged political wings, rather than merely civilian "front organizations" for fund-raising and propaganda purposes. In turn, these political wings could gradually develop a stake in greater legitimization, develop into or join political parties, and eventually be incorporated into the political process).

While the evolution of a violent non-state group into a legal political party could be extremely painful, may be preceded by or lead to violent splits and intensification of internal and sectarian violence, and maybe even drive more radical factions to actively resort to terrorist means more often (and in an increasingly irrational manner), it is the best way to widen the gap between more moderate leaders and members, which might be demilitarized and included in the political process, and the more radical underground hardliners. This makes the latter easier to isolate, marginalize, de-legitimize and, ultimately, be forced to "freeze" or relocate to other countries (as was the case for many PLO[35] and PFLP[36] off-shoot groups), which facilitates their dissolution or destruction by a combination of specialized and military means.

6   From a mid-term ideological perspective, the hardliners' extremist ideology, especially at the transnational level, is unlikely to be moderated. Still, as shown by the example of violent Islamism, a medium-term strategy centered on countering radical militants by ideological methods – particularly by using Islam in its moderate version against Islamic extremism – may have some modest effect on the radicals' broader support base and may, if not impede, than at least complicate the process of ideological radicalization. Examples include policies encouraging moderate Islamic groups, movements, religious schools, charities and foundations not only in their practical social, humanitarian and reconstruction activities, but also in their political, ideological and religious debates with Islamic radicals on such issues of crit-

ical relevance and importance to anti-terrorism as the concepts of martyr-dom and *jihad*. Of some relevance here are efforts on the part of the moderate Muslim clergy to promote, for instance, the traditional religious/ legal bans on targeting the enemy's women and children (as long as they do not take up arms), as well as on destroying buildings and establishments not directly related to an actual battle, etc.

7   Long-term anti-terrorism measures may range from (a) efforts to address, in the case of conflict-related terrorism, the basic incompatibilities about which the conflict has been fought (be they in the framework of the formal peace process or de facto, even in the absence of such); (b) socio-economic meas-ures aimed at moderating some of the most painful effects of "traumatic" modernization (especially on conflict-torn regions, such as the Gaza Strip); (c) more general efforts aimed at increasing both the general functionality of the state and its political legitimacy and representativeness (such efforts would vary significantly, depending on particular national, historical, cul-tural and other considerations).

Anti-terrorism at the international level

At the international level, the following measures assume critical importance (in declining order of urgency):

1   International cooperation on anti-terrorism (which remains most effective at the bilateral level, but is equally essential at the regional/continental and broader international level) including, in declining order of importance: (a) intelligence cooperation (from exchange of intelligence information to thus far infrequent joint intelligence counterterrorism operations); (b) legal, judi-cial and police cooperation (bilateral and multilateral, with a special empha-sis on Interpol and regional institutional mechanisms), centered on: prosecuting suspected terrorists and people involved in terrorism-related activities (from mutual assistance and exchange of information on criminal matters to joint anti-terrorism investigations) and countering terrorists' logist-ics and financial networks (by no means limited to anti-money-laundering actions, and with at least equal attention given to limiting terrorists' legal sources of funding, as to their financing from criminal and shadow economic sources); (c) political coordination and interaction (particularly in depriving terrorists of political legitimacy, denying them political asylum, and integrat-ing and standardizing, to the full extent possible, international and regional lists of terrorist individuals, groups and entities); (d) military cooperation (from critical infrastructure protection and the use of military resources for terrorism consequences management to CBRN[37]/WMD security and safety measures, in cooperation with other security and civil defense structures).

2   *Physical protection* of citizens, property and businesses abroad.

3   Adoption and active implementation of all international legal instruments against terrorism, both at the UN and at the regional level.

4   Ensuring international transport and communications security.
5   Provision of foreign counter-terrorism (security, technical, legal, immigration) assistance to countries less experienced in these matters, but increasingly affected by terrorist threats.
6   Deprivation of safe-havens for individual terrorists, terrorist groups and networks.
7   International support for peace-building and state-building efforts in post-conflict or weak states as one of the most effective long-term anti-terrorism strategies aimed at preventing the use of these areas as safe-havens for armed groups employing terrorist means and broader transnational terrorist networks (provided that international support is in accordance with the international law and aims at rebuilding functional local state institutions enjoying not only international, but, more importantly, local legitimacy).
8   Effective interaction of counter-terrorism at home and abroad (from countering terrorists' support networks that are usually at least to some extent internationalized, to countering extremist Islamic ideology that has been one of the few characteristics shared by locally based, indigenous organizations of Islamist bent involved in conflict-related terrorist activities and by transnational al-Qaeda-inspired networks).

The future trends and trajectories in the dynamics of terrorism at levels from local to global, and their impact on state and international security and stability, are likely to display patterns of both continuity and change.

If, as noted above, in an era of globalization and modern information and communication technology, growing importance is assumed by the extent of the political and social destabilization caused by armed violence, rather than by the direct physical damage it may cause – i.e., by the degree of asymmetry that it displays, then armed violence is likely to become more asymmetrical. As one of the most asymmetrical forms of political (religious, ideological) violence, and the one for which asymmetrical effect is a key defining criterion, terrorism will be increasingly in demand by non-state actors as a violent tactic in asymmetrical confrontation at different levels.

Speculations can be made about how the main quantitative parameters of terrorism or the regional distribution of terrorism could change. While trends in incidents, casualties, numbers of groups, etc. are likely to show uneven dynamics in the short-to-mid-term, albeit at a higher average level than during the 1990s, the global dynamics of terrorism will heavily depend on major armed conflicts, especially those with external interventions (current examples include Iraq, Afghanistan and Somalia). While at present even terrorism at the local level may be internationalized to some extent, the degree of its transnationalization and the variety of its forms will only increase, and the division between "domestic" and "international" terrorism will become even less relevant.

In terms of ideology and motivation, in the short-to-mid-term, terrorist groups with a dominant religious motivation (often combined with, and reinforced by, socio-cultural protest at the transnational level, and with ethno-nationalist motives at the local/national level) will continue to pose the most serious terrorist threat worldwide. However, in the longer term, depending on structural sociopolitical and socio-economic conditions worldwide, the major comeback of a genuine transnational, secular "post-leftist" protest ideology is quite possible, even as its main violent manifestations may take forms other than terrorism.

In terms of terrorist groups' structure, the continuing spread of network features and hybrid organizational forms will be increasingly reinforced – especially for larger and looser networks – by structural characteristics untypical for either networks or hierarchies. One of the possible examples is effective multilevel coordination through generally formulated strategic guidance, instead of centralized control or consultation mechanisms (first elements of this pattern may be traced in the highly adaptive organizational forms of the al-Qaeda-inspired violent transnational networks).

In terms of means and tactics, terrorists may be more likely to experiment with targets (e.g., by increasingly targeting critical civilian infrastructure) than with weapons and materials, including the unconventional. However, it is the terrorists' extremist ideologies and adaptive organizational forms that will remain the key assets and comparative advantages of such groups in asymmetrical confrontation. Regardless of the developments concerning financial and technical "ways and means" of terrorist activity, no anti-terrorism strategy will be effective unless it challenges ideological extremism and effectively neutralizes organizational advantages of terrorist actors.

Notes

1 According to: Uppsala University Conflict Data Programme (UCDP), *Human Security Brief 2006* (Vancouver: Human Security Centre, 2006).
2 See Figure 2.1.
3 The general trend in the number of campaigns of one-sided violence, including terrorist campaigns, was up from 1989–1999, followed by the very uneven dynamics from 2000 to 2006, albeit at a higher average level than in the previous decade. See Figure 4.1. in "Campaigns of One-Sided Violence, 1989–2006," Andrew Mack and Zoe Nielsen, *Human Security Brief 2007* (Vancouver: Human Security Report Project, 2008), p. 42.
4 See an overview of data on one-sided violence against civilians, authored by the UCDP experts: K. Eck and L. Hultman, "One-Sided Violence against Civilians in War: Insights from New Fatality Data," *Journal of Peace Research* 44, 2 (2007).
5 While this network is still often labeled "al-Qaeda" (or "global Salafi jihad"), at the end of the 2000s the more accurate term is "al-Qaeda-inspired" (or "post-Qaeda") networks. These should not be seen as a single, however loose, organization – rather, as a multi-level network of semi-autonomous groups and self-generating cells in different parts of the world, including the West, that are inspired by the example of the original al-Qaeda and by the same extremist ideology. They share a markedly transnational agenda not tied to any single local/national context and resort to direct violence, mostly in the form of terrorism, in response to what they see as "injustices" and "crimes" against Muslims everywhere, such as interventions in Afghanistan and Iraq. The activities of this global movement are hardly directed from any single "center" – rather, they follow general strategic guidelines formulated by dispersed leaders and ideologues based in many countries.

6 "The Parties to the conflict shall at all times distinguish between the civilian population and combatants, and between civilian objects and military objectives, and accordingly shall direct their operations only against military objectives," "Protocol Additional to the Geneva Conventions of 12 August 1949, and Relating to the Protection of Victims of International Armed Conflicts (Protocol I) (1977)," Article 48. The international law regulating non-international armed conflict (Protocol II) does not prohibit members of rebel forces from using force against government soldiers or property provided that the basic tenets governing such use of force, including refraining from attacks against civilians, are respected.

7 For more detail on the definition and on the asymmetrical nature of terrorism, see E. Stepanova, *Terrorism in Asymmetrical Conflict: Ideological and Structural Aspects* (Oxford: Oxford University Press, 2008).

8 Attacks against civilians and other repressive actions by government forces are excluded from this definition of terrorism. Not only is disproportionate indiscriminate violence or one-sided (intentional) violence against civilians committed by government forces in the context of armed conflict already criminalized by IHL, from the moral point of view these actions by states may be even worse than terrorism by non-state actors, as they undermine the credibility of a state as an actor that has a monopoly on the legitimate use of force. While the need to internationally criminalize violence against civilians committed by states systematically or on a massive scale in a situation short of armed conflict of either an international or non-international nature (and thus not covered by IHL) is still pressing, this is not a sufficient reason to extend the specific notion and tactic of "terrorism" to cover these actions. The "non-state" definition of terrorism used in this chapter does not, however, exclude state support to non-state actors engaged in terrorist activity. Still, in cases where "state support" amounts to or transforms into direct control and strategic guidance over a clandestine group, it makes sense to refer to this group's activities as "covert," "sabotage" or other state-directed operations rather than terrorism as such.

9 S. Qutb, "War, Peace, and Islamic Jihad," in *Contemporary Debates in Islam: An Anthology of Modernist and Fundamentalist Thought*, eds. M. Moaddel and K. Talattof (London: Macmillan, 2000).

10 Sometimes, the term has even been retrospectively applied to violent tactics and campaigns by opposition sects of *sikarios* (first century AD) or *assassins* (eleventh–thirteenth centuries).

11 For more detail on the definition of terrorism, see pages 00–00. For a good review of terrorism research and theories, see Brynjar Lia and Katja Skolberg, "Causes of Terrorism: An Expanded and Updated Review of the Literature" (Kjeller: Norwegian Defence Research Establishment (FFI), 2004); Alex P. Schmid and A.J. Jongman, *Political Terrorism: A New Guide to Actors, Authors, Concepts, Data Bases, Theories, and Literature*, 2nd edn. (New Brunswick: Transaction Publishers, 2005). On definitional aspects, see also Martha Crenshaw, *Terrorism in Context* (University Park: Penn State University Press, 1995); Bruce Hoffman, *Inside Terrorism: From the Iran Hostage Crisis to the World Trade Center Bombing* (New York: Columbia University Press, 1999); Walter Laqueur, *A History of Terrorism*, 5th edn. (New Brunswick: Transaction Publishers, 2007).

12 Tore Bjørgo, ed. *Root Causes of Terrorism: Myths, Reality and Ways Forward* (Abingdon: Routledge, 2005).

13 Alan Krueger and Jitka Maleckova, "Education, Poverty and Terrorism: Is There a Causal Connection?," *The Journal of Economic Perspectives* 17, 4 (2003).

14 On "traumatic modernization," see Piotr Sztompka, *The Sociology of Social Change* (Oxford: Wiley-Blackwell, 1994).

15 T.R. Gurr, *Why Men Rebel*, 4th edn. (Princeton: Center of International Studies, Princeton University Press, 1971); I. Walker and H.J. Smith, *Relative Deprivation: Specification, Development, and Integration* (Cambridge: Cambridge University Press, 2001).

16 See Tanja Ellingsen and Nils Petter Gleditsch, "Democracy and Armed Conflict in the Third World," in *Causes of Conflict in the Third World*, eds. Dan Smith and Ketil Volden (Oslo: International Peace Research Institute (PRIO), 1997).

17 See Stepanova, *Terrorism in Asymmetrical Conflict*; Peter Waldmann, *Terrorismus Und Bürgerkrieg: Der Staat in Bedrängnis* (München: Gerling Akademie Verlag, 2003). Also, see the publications of the Norwegian Defence Research Establishment (FFI) TERRA (Terrorism and Asymmetric Warfare: Emerging Security Challenges after the Cold War) project.

18 John L. Esposito, *Unholy War: Terror in the Name of Islam* (Oxford: Oxford University Press, 2003); Mark Juergensmeyer, *Terror in the Mind of God: The Global Rise of Religious Violence* (Berkeley: University of California Press, 2000); Gilles Kepel, *Jihad: The Trail of Political Islam* (London: I.B. Tauris, 2004).

19 John Arquilla and David F. Ronfeldt, *Networks and Netwars: The Future of Terror, Crime, and Militancy* (Santa Monica: Rand Corporation, 2001); John Arquilla and David F. Ronfeldt, "Netwar Revisited: The Fight for the Future Continues," *Low Intensity Conflict & Law Enforcement* 11, 2 & 3 (2002).

20 Marc Sageman, *Understanding Terror Networks* (Philadelphia: University of Pennsylvania Press, 2004).

21 Renate Mayntz, "Organizational Forms of Terrorism: Hierarchy, Network, or a Type Sui Generis?," in *Max Planck Institute for the Study of Societies Discussion Papers* (Cologne: Max Planck Institute for the Study of Societies, 2004).

22 Omar Ashour, *The De-Radicalization of Jihadists: Transforming Armed Islamist Movements* (Abingdon: Taylor & Francis, 2009); Tore Bjørgo and John Horgan, eds. *Leaving Terrorism Behind: Individual and Collective Disengagement* (Abingdon: Taylor & Francis, 2008); Sageman, *Understanding Terror Networks*.

23 See, for example, John Horgan, *The Psychology of Terrorism* (Frank Cass, 2005).

24 See Ami Pedahzur, *Suicide Terrorism* (Polity, 2004).

25 For more detail, see P. Williams, "Terrorism and Organized Crime: Convergence, Nexus or Transformation?," in *FOA Report on Terrorism*, ed. Gunnar Jervas (Stockholm: Defence Research Establishment, 1998). For a useful discussion, see Louise I. Shelley, "Methods and Motives: Exploring Links Between Transnational Organized Crime & International Terrorism" (Washington, DC: US Department of Justice/National Criminal Justice Reference Service (NCJRS), 2005); Louise I. Shelley and John T. Picarelli, "Methods Not Motives: Implications of the Convergence of International Organized Crime and Terrorism," *Police Practice and Research* 3, 4 (2002).

26 Of the latest studies, see, for example, Magnus Ranstorp and Magnus Normark, eds. *Unconventional Weapons and International Terrorism: Challenges and New Approaches* (Routledge, 2009).

27 All data in this chapter cover the period since 1998 (that is the only period for which complete data on both domestic and international terrorism are available – see note 28).

28 All data-based graphs in this chapter are compiled by the author on the basis of data from the MIPT Terrorism Knowledge Base, compiled by the Memorial Institute for the Prevention of Terrorism (MIPT), www.tkb.org. In 2008, the MIPT Terrorism Knowledge Base was transferred to and is to be integrated into the Global Terrorism Database managed by the National Consortium for the Study of Terrorism and Responses to Terrorism (START) at the University of Maryland, www.start.umd.edu/data/gtd.

29 Mack and Nielsen, *Human Security Brief*, pp. 8–9.

30 For more detail, see page 00–00.

31 For instance, Europol decided to no longer use the distinction between domestic and international terrorism in its analyses.

32 For instance, the Liberation Tigers Tamil Eelam (LTTE), whose political goals do not go beyond intra-state, ethno-political conflict in Sri Lanka, have created one of the most widespread logistics and support networks in the world.

33 For more detail, see Jaideep Saikia and Ekaterina Stepanova, eds. *Terrorism: Patterns of Internationalization* (New Delhi, London, Singapore: SAGE Publications Pvt. Ltd, 2009).
34 For example, the specialized class of French magistrates with long experience in anti-terrorism investigations.
35 PLO – Palestinian Liberation Organization.
36 PFLP – Popular Front for the Liberation of Palestine.
37 CBRN – chemical, biological, radiological and nuclear (materials, security, etc.).

3 Proliferation of weapons of mass destruction

Gustav Lindstrom

Introduction

This chapter examines the threat posed by weapons of mass destruction (WMD) proliferation. It does so by analyzing the nuclear, biological, and chemical dimensions that are frequently subsumed under the "WMD label." In addition, the chapter outlines some of the principal obstacles complicating the management of WMD proliferation, as well as some of the steps that have been taken to address such hurdles. The chapter ends with a brief consideration of future trends in WMD proliferation.

The threat of WMD proliferation

The recognition that WMD proliferation poses a grave challenge to international security goes back to the Cold War. With the advent of the atomic age in 1945, nuclear proliferation received the most attention. In 1963, US President John F. Kennedy observed that "by 1970, unless we are successful, there may be 10 nuclear powers instead of four, and by 1975, 15 or 20.... I regard that as the greatest possible danger and hazard."[1] Although President Kennedy's projections did not materialize, concerns over nuclear proliferation remained. In response, the nuclear Non-Proliferation Treaty (NPT) was opened for signature in 1968 – entering into force in March 1970. In the minds of many, the NPT was instrumental in avoiding the proliferation scenario foreseen by President Kennedy.

Nearly 40 years later, the threat of WMD remains high on the international security agenda. Both the US National Security Strategy and the European Security Strategy identify WMD proliferation as a "key threat" to international security.[2] Diplomatic confrontations between the "West" and countries such as Iran and North Korea serve as reminders of the dangers associated with proliferation and nuclear weapons.

In a post-9/11 world, the perception of the risks associated with WMD proliferation has also changed. Two trends in particular stand out. First, while Western decision-makers continue to place a strong emphasis on curbing WMD proliferation at the state level, there is increasing concern about WMD trickling into the hands of non-state actors. Presently, the possibility that a terrorist group acquires weapons of mass destruction is considered to be among the most frightening scenarios.[3]

According to some academics and officials, the likelihood of a large-scale terrorist attack using weapons of mass destruction is significant. According to Dr. Graham Allison, Director of the Belter Center at Harvard, "if the United States and other governments keep doing what they are doing today, a nuclear terrorist attack on America is more likely than not in the decade ahead."[4] This sentiment was recently echoed by the Commission on the Prevention of WMD Proliferation and Terrorism, which warns that the United States can expect a terrorist attack involving biological weapons within the next five years. Of the two, a biological attack is seen as the more probable given that it involves fewer technical hurdles.[5] While the United States may be perceived as the primary target for such attacks, other countries with strong global interests and international presence may likewise provide an attractive target.

Given these concerns, it is interesting to note that data shows there have been very few terrorist attacks using chemical, biological or nuclear materials. As shown in Figure 3.1, there have been around 70 chemical and biological incidents between 1968 and early 2008. Collectively, these incidents have resulted in slightly more than 60 fatalities – most of them attributable to the 1995 sarin attacks in Tokyo. To date, there is no recorded incident of a nuclear attack by a terrorist group.

In spite of the small number of incidents and fatalities, the *perception* that non-state actors may acquire and use WMD has important implications. While

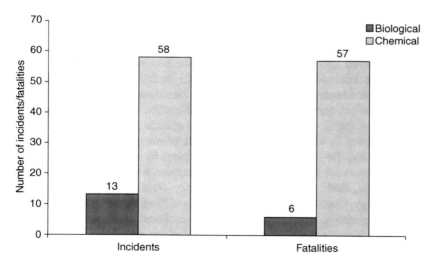

Figure 3.1 Chemical and biological terrorist incidents and fatalities, 1968–2008 (source: MIPT).

Notes
Data for 2008 are as of 7 February 2008. Data for 1968–1997 cover only international incidents. Data for the period 1998–February 2008 cover both domestic and international incidents.

an attack is a low-probability event, it is considered to result in medium-to-high-impacts, demanding attention from policy-makers. Complicating the task of policy-makers is the challenge of finding viable options that may "deter" non-state actors from acquiring or using WMD.

The second trend highlighting a change in the perception of risk is the growing concern that chemical and biological weapons pose a strategic threat to international security. Traditionally, the focus was on nuclear proliferation and nuclear weapons. Presently, worries over a WMD attack by a terrorist group have increased policy-makers' attention to chemical, biological and even radiological threats. Among the three, a biological event is often considered to pose the greatest risk as its consequences could be difficult to detect or rapidly cross borders. The 2003 SARS outbreak provided some indication of the speed at which different countries could be impacted by the spread of a pathogen. Other biological incidents, such as that of the avian influenza, have reinforced concerns over a possible biological attack.

A chemical or radiological attack, on the other hand, is equated more with the use of a "weapon of mass disruption." This is because such attacks are thought to result in few fatalities but produce subsequent large-scale effects. For example, the area impacted by a radiological or "dirty bomb" could be shut down for a long period of time to allow for proper decontamination. Local transport passing through the area as well as businesses would be affected – impacting the local economy. Individuals living in the area might not want to move back until the entire area is fully decontaminated; a process that might be complicated should there be disagreements over what constitutes acceptable levels of decontamination. A similar scenario, but shorter lasting, might occur in the event of a chemical incident or attack.

Taken together, these developments suggest that WMD proliferation remains an important strategic threat for the foreseeable future – even if actual numbers suggest that there have been very few WMD attacks in modern times.

The challenge of managing WMD proliferation

The following section examines the key challenges and obstacles. Given the different characteristics of nuclear, biological and chemical agents, each category is examined separately.

The nuclear dimension

At least three factors complicate the management of nuclear proliferation. First, the nuclear Non-Proliferation Treaty (NPT), which is the principal international treaty against nuclear proliferation, faces mounting internal pressures that are slowly undermining its credibility and legitimacy. A principal dilemma is the growing tension between the objectives spelled out under Articles IV and VI of the NPT. Article IV underscores states' inalienable right to carry out peaceful nuclear activities and is frequently championed by non-nuclear-weapon states aiming to develop a civilian nuclear program. Article VI, on the other hand, calls for nuclear disarmament and for the cessation of the nuclear arms race. It is aimed at the nuclear-weapon states and also serves as a reminder that all State Parties to the NPT have obligations.

While some claim the goals contained in the two articles should be decoupled, the NPT stands on the combined pillars of non-proliferation, disarmament and the peaceful uses of nuclear energy.[6] As such, the two articles form a "bargain" between the nuclear-weapons states and the non-nuclear-weapon states to enable the elimination of nuclear weapons.

The friction caused by Articles IV and VI is particularly noticeable when countries of concern engage in nuclear research or there are suspicions of illegitimate nuclear activities. Presently, several countries believe that Iran is exploiting Article VI to build a civilian nuclear program that would later turn into a military one. The perception that Iran has not been fully transparent regarding its capabilities and intentions adds to such concerns, and leads to mounting pressure for it to abandon its nuclear program. The fact that Iran may benefit from technical cooperation under the auspices of the NPT raises further questions over the treaty's strength. In the event that Iran develops nuclear weapons options while undertaking treaty obligations, a collapse of the NPT is plausible.[7] Certain State Parties also point to other NPT limitations, including a lack of agreement on the type of sanctions that should apply in case of violations, and the "ease" with which a State Party can exit the NPT framework.[8] The case of North Korea's rapid withdrawal from the NPT in early 2003 and the international community's weak response was particularly instructive.[9]

From a different angle, many non-nuclear-weapon states argue that the nuclear-weapon states engage in double standards when they avoid serious commitments to disarm their own stockpiles, as called for under Article VI. An overview of the global stockpile of nuclear weapons shows that, while numbers have dropped over time, there are still thousands of nuclear warheads in the United States and the Russian Federation. The Natural Resources Defense Council estimates that the nuclear stockpile in 2006 was about two-thirds of that in 1968, translating to a reduction of about 12,000 warheads in nearly 40 years – going from 38,000 to 26,000 warheads.[10] While the decrease in the nuclear stockpile is notable, it is important to recognize that the numbers themselves may be misleading. Frequently, it is not possible to determine whether such reductions are "complete, verifiable, and irreversible."[11] The Strategic Offensive Reductions Treaty (SORT) between the United States and the Russian Federation, for instance, lacks acceptable counting rules and corresponding verification procedures.[12]

Some contend that the number of warheads is no longer relevant to gauging disarmament efforts since several nuclear-weapon states are taking steps to modernize their existing stockpiles. Known as "vertical proliferation," examples include the now-defunct US reliable replacement warhead program and the United Kingdom's efforts to update its submarine-launched Trident missiles.

The second factor complicating the management of nuclear proliferation involves the external challenges facing the NPT. An oft-cited example is the

2008 US–India nuclear deal which some fear will further undermine the NPT.[13] Many analysts argue that the deal rewarded India by offering it the benefits of Article IV without demanding that it join the NPT. As a result, other countries will rethink their treaty commitment.[14] There are also concerns over the negative implications the deal could have on international efforts to curb Iran and North Korea's nuclear ambitions.[15] There are further apprehensions that Pakistan and other countries might look for similar nuclear deals, possibly increasing the risks for nuclear proliferation.

Another external challenge facing the NPT and the broad non-proliferation regime is the continued inability to pass other treaties aiming to curb proliferation, such as the Comprehensive Nuclear Test Ban Treaty (CTBT). While the CTBT has been signed by 180 states and ratified by 145, it still needs the ratification of nine specific states before it can enter into force. These include China, the United States and the four states outside the NPT: India, Pakistan, Israel and North Korea. The proposed Fissile Material Cutoff Treaty (FMCT), which was initiated in 1993 with the aim of prohibiting the production of nuclear materials for weapons, is also still far from passing – further weakening global non-proliferation efforts.

The third factor that complicates the management of nuclear proliferation is the growing concern that non-state actors may acquire nuclear materials and know-how. It is believed that a whole range of groups might be interested in pursuing nuclear terrorism, including apocalyptic groups, politico-religious groups, nationalist/separatist groups and single-issue terrorists.[16] Nuclear proliferation from a state actor to a non-state actor is of particular concern as the latter may be more difficult to deter. In addition, non-state actor motivations may be strong and complex, making it difficult to engage with such a group.

The prospect of nuclear terrorism is not new. There have been longstanding concerns that fissile material could be stolen from one of thousands of storage facilities in the former Soviet Union.[17] According to one estimate, there are over 100 scientific/industrial institutions and facilities in the former Soviet Union that maintain nuclear materials, many of which could attract the attention of groups with malicious intentions. Another study estimates there are between 11,000–13,000 nuclear weapons that are considered to be relatively portable, theoretically offering an attractive target for a non-state actor. The majority of these – 8,000 to 10,000 – are located in the Russian Federation.[18]

In fact, in any given year, radioactive materials are stolen or come into illegal possession. In the first six months of 2008 alone, nearly 250 incidents of theft or loss of nuclear or radioactive materials were reported to the International Atomic Energy Agency's illicit trafficking database. While most of these incidents involved small amounts of radioactive material, some encompassed larger amounts and involved either highly enriched uranium (HEU) or plutonium (Pu) which can be used to produce nuclear weapons. Between 1993 and 2007, there were a total of 18 such incidents. In most of these cases – some of which are listed in Table 3.1 – attempts were made to sell the materials across international borders.

Table 3.1 Select incidents involving highly enriched uranium and plutonium

Year	Location	Material involved	Description
1994	St. Petersburg	2.97 kg of HEU	Individual trying to sell stolen material
1994	Munich	363.4 g of Pu	Material seized at Munich airport
1994	Prague	2.73 kg of HEU	Intended for illegal sale, intercepted by police
2006	Tbilisi	79.5 g of HEU	Intended for illegal sale, intercepted by law enforcement

Source: adapted from International Atomic Energy Agency (IAEA) Illicit Trafficking Database (ITDB), available at: www.iaea.org/NewsCenter/Features/RadSources/PDF/fact_figures2007.pdf.

Fortunately, the amount of HEU and Pu intercepted to date is limited. The largest seizure was nearly 3 kg of HEU seized in St. Petersburg (Russian Federation) in 1994. To put this amount in perspective, about 15 kg of HEU is needed to produce a nuclear weapon. With respect to plutonium, roughly 11 kg is needed to create a self-sustaining chain reaction.[19] However, if a shell of reflective material such as beryllium is placed around the plutonium sphere, less than half the amount – roughly 4 kg – would be needed. Thus, even if all the captured HEU and Pu in recent years were combined, it would not be enough to produce a nuclear weapon. This again begs the question: is the risk of nuclear terrorism exaggerated?

In response, analysts and experts point out that there may be risks of a motivated group assembling a crude nuclear explosive using plutonium or uranium. According to one expert, producing a crude nuclear device "would require no greater skill than that required for the production and use of the nerve agent produced by the AUM group and released in the Tokyo underground."[20] It is estimated that such a device would have the explosive power equivalent to 100 tons of trinitrotoluene (TNT).[21]

With respect to accessing nuclear materials, there is also the possibility that groups get their hands on civilian mixed-oxide (MOX) nuclear fuel.[22] There is a growing trade in MOX which is produced in Belgium, France and the United Kingdom and is used to fuel plants in countries such as Germany, Sweden and Switzerland.[23] A terrorist group that is able to steal or illegally access MOX could theoretically remove the plutonium oxide through a chemical process using an ion-exchange column filled with resin.[24] It is thought that a second-year undergraduate should be able to acquire the necessary knowledge needed to separate the plutonium out of the MOX after reading standard reference works and consulting scientific journals.[25]

Besides MOX, groups may exploit weak regulatory controls on accessing radioactive materials. It is presently difficult to achieve effective export controls as there is weak to non-existent regulatory controls in approximately half of the world's countries.[26] Experts also point out that a would-be nuclear terrorist might consider other options for an attack. For example, they might directly target a nuclear plant, a reprocessing site, or spent fuel storage facilities to cause the dispersion of radiation.[27]

A more likely, although vastly less lethal, form of attack resulting from the acquisition of radioactive materials is the use of a radiological dispersal device or "dirty bomb." The materials needed to build a dirty bomb, which is constructed by combining conventional explosives with radioactive material, can be found in most industrialized countries – including plutonium, yttrium, caesium, rubidium, thallium and tritium.[28] Hospitals, research laboratories and selected industries may use or store such materials.

What is being done to curb nuclear proliferation?

Policy-makers have taken several steps at the international level to try to curb nuclear proliferation. For example, an Additional Protocol was added to the safeguards system in 1997 to increase transparency regarding NPT State Parties' nuclear fuel cycle-related activities. The Additional Protocol gives the IAEA authority to carry out on-site inspection measures and to investigate inconsistencies in NPT members' nuclear declarations. While State Parties to the NPT are not obliged to adopt the protocol, they are encouraged to do so. As of October 2008, the Additional Protocol had entered into force in less than half of all NPT State Parties.[29]

To limit possible proliferation from a state to non-state actor, the international community passed UN Security Council Resolution 1540 in April 2004.[30] The resolution obliges UN Member States to "refrain from providing any form of support to non-State actors that attempt to develop, acquire, manufacture, possess, transport, transfer or use nuclear, chemical or biological weapons and their means of delivery."[31] Furthermore, states are to "adopt and enforce appropriate effective laws which prohibit any non-State Actor to manufacture, acquire, possess, develop, transport, or transfer such materials for 'terrorist purposes'."[32]

While UNSCR 1540 reinforces the obligations countries have committed to undertake through their adhesion to the NPT, the Biological Weapons and Toxins Convention (BTWC), and the Chemical Weapons Convention (CWC), have proved difficult to implement. Many countries lack the financial and technical means to keep track of potentially hazardous materials. The dual-use nature of certain products further complicates the task of monitoring the movement and use of certain goods. According to one study which examined nearly 90 states, less than 25 percent had fulfilled the priority obligations contained in UNSCR 1540.[33] While some progress is likely to have been achieved since the 2006 study, the results noted that the regions with the lowest percentage of fulfilled obligations tended to be "trouble spots for the theft and trafficking of WMD including Southeastern Europe, Southeast Asia, and the Middle East."[34]

Parallel to these efforts, some governments are dedicating billions of dollars to secure installations and dismantle weapons of mass destruction in the former Soviet Union. The principal vehicles to achieve these objectives are the

Cooperative Threat Reduction Program and the G8 Global Partnership Against the Spread of Weapons and Materials of Mass Destruction.[35] A host of monitoring and interdiction programs have likewise been initiated, including the Proliferation and Security Initiative (PSI) and the Container Security Initiative (CSI). While these initiatives provide operational means to interdict proliferation, they have certain limitations. For example, CSI covers only specific ports of participating countries, curtailing some of its reach. With respect to PSI, interdiction activities can only be carried out in international waters and may thus be unable to inspect certain cargo. Currently, the PSI focuses on training exercises to facilitate interoperability and international cooperation.

The biological dimension

While nuclear proliferation is considered the most pressing WMD challenge given the lethality of nuclear weapons, the risks posed by biological proliferation frequently come in second place.[36] Exercises carried out at the national level have painted a gloomy picture should there be a biological attack. To illustrate, the 2001 US exercise "Dark Winter," which simulated an outbreak of smallpox, estimated about one million fatalities a few months after the initial outbreak.[37] Another study estimated 95,000 fatalities and 125,000 incapacitated in the event of an anthrax attack in which 50 kg of anthrax is released by an aircraft along a 2 km line upwind of a population centre of half-a-million.[38] While some think that such projections exaggerate the lethality of pathogens, others underline the potential reach of a biological attack – pointing to the 20-to-40 million left dead in the wake of the Spanish influenza outbreak from 1918–1919.

There are four key challenges to curbing biological proliferation. First, the BTWC – the principal norm against biological and toxins proliferation – has far from universal membership. The convention has a substantially lower number of State Parties in comparison to the NPT and the CWC. As of July 2008, there were 162 State Parties, 13 Signatory States that have not ratified the BTWC and 20 Non-Signatory States.[39] While the majority of countries remaining outside the BTWC are unlikely proliferation candidates, they may unknowingly contribute to proliferation in other ways. For example, it is possible that some of these countries are used as "safe havens" by non-state actors – either to prepare or acquire specific pathogens. It is also possible that countries outside the international regime provide inadvertent assistance, for example through transfers that are routed through their territories.

Second, although Article I of the BTWC contains a "catch-all" provision (general purpose criterion) that prohibits the development, production, stockpiling, acquisition or retention of microbial/biological agents or toxins, the convention lacks a verification and compliance regime.[40] As a result, there is no specific body or mechanism to ensure that State Parties follow the guidelines established in the BTWC.[41] Besides weakening the BTWC, the lack of a verification and compliance regime complicates the task of identifying biological proliferation activities or the existence of potential biological weapons programs.

As a result, there have been suspicions of biological weapons programs that could not be investigated in depth. For example, in the 1980s there were allegations of treaty violations, including accusations of a Soviet offensive biological weapons (BW) program after a major anthrax outbreak near Sverdlovsk (currently Ekaterineburg) in 1979.[42] In his book *Biohazard* published in 1999, Dr. Ken Abilek confirmed the existence of a Soviet biological weapons program. Ironically, the program commenced in 1972, the same year the BTWC opened for signature. Dr. Abilek characterized the program – which was still active at the time of his defection in 1992 – as the "largest and most advanced biological warfare establishment in the world."[43] Although maintaining an offensive BW program, which is not allowed under the BTWC, may not necessarily contribute to biological proliferation, it may encourage vertical proliferation as potential holders of offensive BW programs engage in research and development activities to improve the virulence of specific pathogens.

The lack of a compliance mechanism also affects the BTWC by making it more difficult to gauge national implementation of the convention. A 2005 study suggests that less than 50 percent of the State Parties to the BTWC have effective national legislation in place to ensure consistency with the BTWC.[44] This challenge is particularly acute in small or developing states that often lack the resources or capacity to enact legislation that is consistent with the BTWC. Difficulties in adequately controlling and inspecting the flow of dual-use goods and technologies across a nation's borders represents another challenge, especially as trade volumes and flows are increasing in many parts of the world. Ports and other hubs of entry that are not properly monitored may encourage the proliferation of biological agents and equipment.

Third, effective non-proliferation is complicated by the substantial dual-use nature of biological science and biotechnology. Many agents can either have a beneficial or harmful effect depending on their application or combination with other substances. This places a premium on understanding the intent of biological research and development. There may be a fine line between offensive and defensive biological research, which in addition to the dual-use dimension makes it very difficult to identify and address biological proliferation of concern. Under the BTWC, for example, research and development activities for defensive or prophylactic capacity are allowed.

Tackling proliferation in this arena may also be complicated by the inherent need for collaboration among scientists, medical experts and academics to facilitate advances in the field. Sharing research results and methods are often prerequisites for replicating or confirming research results. At the same time, such transparency may also facilitate the spread of know-how to scientists or groups who may have hidden agendas. Finding the adequate balance between openness and secrecy may not always be straightforward. For example, in 2005 an academic article entitled "Analyzing a bioterror attack on the food supply: The case of botulinum toxin in milk" was initially not published for fear that the information might be used for malicious purposes. The article was eventually published as it was deemed that the benefits of upholding academic freedom outweighed the risks of a group attempting to contaminate the milk supply chain.[45] While the article did not directly contribute to proliferation, it was thought that the information might spread know-how on how to carry out a potential attack using biological agents.

A related concern involves the possibility of purchasing certain low-grade pathogens for scientific study. In the early 2000s, it was possible to purchase strains of rickettsiae for US$500 and the salmonella cholera virus for US$150.[46] Similar purchases are still possible today, although stronger precautions are taken to avoid shipments to unauthorized recipients. For example, individuals in academia, government and private industry can purchase a frozen sample of the Influenza A virus (H1N1; strain A/swine/1976/31) for US$300.[47] While precautions are taken to avoid unauthorized shipments, the possibility of misuse raises concerns of accidental proliferation.

Fourth, as is the case with nuclear and radioactive materials, there is some fear that a non-state actor may obtain access to pathogens and/or toxins. There are already several cases of previous attempts, including the 1984 salmonella attack by the Bhagwan Shree Rajneesh sect and the failed attempts of the Aum Shinrikyo cult with botulinum toxin, anthrax, cholera and Q-fever in the early 1990s. As knowledge and know-how spreads, there is concern that other groups may try to create or illegally acquire a pathogen. Already in 2002, scientists demonstrated that it was possible to create a polio virus using DNA segments ordered by mail and genetic information that was publicly available on the Internet.[48] In 2005, scientists reconstructed a virus containing all coding sequences of the 1918 Spanish influenza virus. The publication of the H1N1 genome in the journal *Science* in the same year likewise raised controversy and fears that some might use the information for malicious purposes. With respect to equipment, it is estimated that a biological weapons manufacturing facility may cost around one million dollars – well within the reach of motivated non-state actors.[49]

A terrorist group may also be attracted by the possibility to target the animal or plant kingdom to incur sizeable economic costs to society. They may also be drawn by the possibility that an outbreak in the animal kingdom could eventually spread to humans. Approximately 60 percent of human pathogens are zoonotic, meaning that they originate in animals and may eventually transmit to humans.[50] From a different perspective, over 80 percent of the Center for Disease Control's Prevention Category A potential agents of bioterrorism are zoonotic.[51] From a different vantage point, a non-state actor may try to access dangerous pathogens that are naturally occurring. For example in 1992, members of Aum Shinrikyo unsuccessfully tried to procure samples of the Ebola virus in then-Zaire.[52]

What is being done to curb biological proliferation?

Several initiatives have been taken to limit the scope for biological proliferation.[53] In the area of verification and compliance, several attempts were made to incorporate a verification mechanism under the framework of the BTWC. So far, these efforts have not been successful, as some State Parties have resisted the initiatives. The reasons for such opposition vary, but principally there is fear that a verification system will inadvertently serve to disclose sensitive technical know-how that could make its way into the hands of competitors in other countries.[54] There is also reluctance to open advanced research labs to third parties, and even the pharmaceutical industry has lobbied that inspection or verification mechanisms might disclose commercial patents.

To work around this opposition, the BTWC relies on confidence-building measure (CBM) forms. Each year, BTWC State Parties are obliged to submit a CBM. The CBM forms cover several categories, including a declaration of past activities concerning offensive and/or defensive biological R&D programs. Unfortunately, there has been a historically low CBM response rate. Fewer than one-third of all State Parties have met their CBM obligations.[55] Following the Sixth BTWC Review Conference held in November–December 2006, a small Implementation and Support Unit was set up; one of its core objectives is to enhance the CBM response rate.

There have also been several efforts to increase adherence to the BTWC. For example, starting in 2006, the European Union took the initiative to raise awareness on the importance of attaining BTWC universality and organized regional seminars to encourage non-State Parties to ratify or adhere to the Convention. At the same time, the EU offered implementation assistance to State Parties who needed legal or legislative support with implementing BTWC provisions. In the area of dual use, codes of conduct are used to raise awareness among scientists on ways to limit risks associated with sharing sensitive information, know-how and materials.[56] Additional initiatives include efforts to strengthen biosecurity and biosafety levels in laboratories handling sensitive pathogens.[57]

To complement these efforts, the Australia Group – an informal forum with 40 participant countries and the European Commission – has developed a number of lists covering biological agents, plant pathogens, animal pathogens and dual-use biological equipment. For each list, a number of considerations were taken to identify potential substances of concern. For example, for biological agents, weighed factors include whether an agent has been sought by a country suspected of proliferation, if the agent was developed or used in warfare, if it could be mass produced and whether it is infectious in the aerosol form.

The chemical dimension

Attempts to prohibit the use of chemical weapons date back to the Hague Conventions of 1899 and 1907. In spite of these early efforts, there have been multiple instances of chemical warfare. During World War I, combatants used over 124,000 metric tons of 39 toxic agents, resulting in about one million casualties on all sides. Some 90,000 of these were fatal, with many of the survivors ending up blind or chronically disabled.[58] In modern times, chemical agents have been used in several conflicts: by Italy in its invasion of Ethiopia in 1935–1936; by Japan in the war against China from 1937–1943; by Egypt against Yemen in

1963–1968; and by the United States in Vietnam between 1965 and 1975.[59] More recently, chemical warfare was used during the Iran–Iraq War and by Iraq against the Kurds in Halabja in 1988. Collectively, chemical weapons have produced more casualties than nuclear and biological warfare combined.

With this background in mind, there are five principal challenges to curbing chemical proliferation. First, while the CWC has a large number of adherents – 185 with the inclusion of Lebanon in December 2008 – many State Parties still do not have the rules and regulations needed to implement it. According to the OPCW, as of November 2008, fewer than half (45 percent) of the CWC State Parties have enacted legislation in the required areas.[60] Examples of such areas include appropriate trade regulations and incorporating penal legislation. Some State Parties also do not have a national authority to guide the implementation process at the domestic level.[61] This may be particularly worrisome in countries where weak legislation and oversight may encourage irresponsible handling of chemicals. The implications may be unexpected, including opportunistic dumping of toxic waste. For example, in 2006, five people were killed and over 5,000 were poisoned when a foreign-registered ship discharged several hundred tons of toxic chemicals in Abidjan (Ivory Coast).

Second, although there are continued efforts to dismantle chemicals of concern, there is still a large outstanding stock of chemical weapons. The size of the US and Russian inventories is staggering. For example, the US declared inventory is just shy of 28,000 metric tons.[62] The former Soviet stockpile stands at around 40,000 metric tons of nerve and blister agents.[63] Given the size of these inventories, it is unlikely that the United States and Russia will be able to destroy their quotas by April 2012, which is the final destruction deadline after a five-year extension was granted. The delays are mainly traced to economic, political and environmental challenges relating to the destruction process. Unfortunately, these delays have implications for other State Parties' level of commitment to the CWC.

Third, as is the case for biological agents and toxins, many chemicals have dual-use applications. For example, phosgene can be used as a chlorinating agent in organic chemical reactions or to produce pesticides. It can also be used as a pulmonary or choking agent. Over one million pounds of phosgene is manufactured annually in the United States.[64] The dual-use dilemma also covers so-called "pre-cursor" chemicals which, once combined, can yield a dangerous mixture. To illustrate, the precursor chemicals used to produce the nerve agent tabun – dimethylamine, sodium cyanide and phosphoryl chloride – are all available in the open market.[65] The dual-use dimension of certain chemicals makes it more difficult to stem proliferation efforts as countries or groups may focus on accessing materials that exhibit such characteristics to skirt restrictions. From the perspective of a terrorist group, such chemicals may be particularly attractive as they are simpler to handle than radioactive or biological materials.

Beyond the dual-use challenge, the chemical industry sector is robust and growing. While the vast majority of these industries do not hold the most toxic agents, many handle chemicals that are hazardous. For example, several hundred tons of hydrogen cyanide – a blood agent – is produced annually by US industry. Although the chemical industry does not pose a direct proliferation risk, it may offer opportunities to non-state actors seeking to access specific chemicals. In addition, specific plants could be targeted should it become known that they store toxic chemicals. Accidents in chemical plants, such as the pesticide factory in Bhopal (India) in 1984, demonstrate that the release of specific chemicals can produce thousands of casualties. In the case of Bhopal, the release of methyl iso-cyanate killed approximately 4,000 individuals and injured another 10,000.

As was the case for nuclear materials and biological agents, a fourth challenge is the concern that lethal chemicals may fall into the hands of an individual or group with malicious intent. As implied earlier, the greatest concern here may not be access to traditional chemical weapons such as nerve gas (e.g., soman, tabun and sarin). A more likely scenario is that such groups access or target toxic industrial chemicals (TICs). As a result, efforts focusing solely on the potential proliferation of traditional nerve agents may miss the danger posed by TIC proliferation and targeting.

Fifth, while the CWC has a list categorizing agents according to their lethality, it does not take into account new agents that may be of concern. Moreover, some argue that the "schedules" create loopholes by excluding chemicals that may be employed as non-lethal weapons for law enforcement and domestic riot-control purposes. According to Article II of the CWC, a riot-control agent is defined as a "chemical not listed in a Schedule, which can produce rapidly in humans sensory irritation or disabling physical effects which disappear within a short time following termination of exposure."

As a result, certain chemicals, such as the anesthetic fentanyl used during the Moscow theatre siege in October 2002, are not prohibited by the CWC. In the case of the Moscow theatre siege, the decision by authorities to use the narcotic gas resulted in the death of 129 hostages as well as the perpetrators. There is fear this "loophole" complicates chemical disarmament as states work to develop new generations of non-lethal weapons.[66] Overall, there are multiple types of agents that fall under the general category of non-lethal weapons, including riot-control agents (e.g., adamsite, cholopicrin and bromoacetone), calmatives, malodorants and disabling biochemical agents.[67]

What is being done to curb chemical proliferation?

Several steps have been taken to try to stem chemical proliferation. Among the better known are the efforts undertaken by the Cooperative Threat Reduction Program and the G8 to destroy inventories of chemical weapons in the former Soviet Union. As of October 2007, Western states had allocated 25 percent of the US$2 billion promised under the G8 Global Partnership to destroy Russian chemical stockpiles by 2012.[68]

Under the auspices of the CWC, States Parties are required to make detailed declarations on their activities in the chemical domain. For example, State Parties have to provide information on chemical weapons, chemical weapons storage facilities, chemical weapons destruction facilities, chemical weapons production facilities and facilities used in the past for the development of chemical weapons.[69] To gauge inventories of toxic chemicals, States Parties are also obliged to make declarations relating to toxic industrial chemicals and precursors that are listed in the three schedules of chemicals, including other chemical facilities that produce discrete organic chemicals. Needless to say, the picture provided by these declarations depends on the number of returns obtained, as well as their level of detail. In 2008, 126 State Parties, i.e., 68 percent, provided submissions.[70]

The OPCW also has a verification regime to monitor all chemical-weapons-related activities, including potential proliferation. Since the CWC entered into force in 1997, over 3,500 inspections have been carried out at 195 chemical-weapon-related and approximately 1,100 industrial sites in 81 different countries.[71] While the figures point to an active verification process, there are some indications that the inspections are becoming less intrusive – something that could open the door to would-be cheaters.[72] For example, at the request of certain State Parties, OPCW inspectors cannot use gas chromatograph-mass spectrometers (GC/MS) while conducting an inspection for fears that the GC/MS would reveal chemical manufacturers' trade secrets. Furthermore, sampling and analysis covers only chemical warfare agents and precursors listed in the CWC schedules – potentially allowing proliferators to avoid detection by producing unlisted compounds.[73]

As was the case for nuclear and biological materials, UNSCR 1540 also applies to the chemical dimension and prohibits states from transferring toxic chemicals to non-state actors – effectively reinforcing commitments already undertaken through CWC adhesion. Post-9/11, the OPCW is encouraging CWC State Parties to pass national legislation that also makes the CWC provisions binding on State Parties' citizens and corporations. Under these provisions, penal sanctions would be imposed on violators of the CWC.[74]

Future trends in WMD proliferation

This section briefly identifies three general trends that may have implications for WMD proliferation. For consistency, the trends are broken down into separate categories covering the nuclear, biological and chemical dimensions.

Nuclear trends

While it is difficult to foresee how the NPT might evolve in light of the challenges it is facing, a certain trend in the nuclear arena is a growing demand for nuclear energy. As of October 2008, there were 439 nuclear power reactors operating in 30 countries and the number of new plants under construction is 36.[75] According to one estimate, an additional 162 nuclear plants have been proposed. If this projection goes through, 38 countries would operate nuclear power reactors, including Egypt, Indonesia, Kazakhstan, Turkey and Vietnam. In the

Middle East, Saudi Arabia, Jordan, Kuwait, Syria and the United Arab Emirates have voiced interest in civil nuclear energy.[76]

From a proliferation perspective, the movement toward more nuclear power plants in different parts of the world increases the likelihood that nuclear materials are diverted to produce nuclear weapons. As noted by IAEA Director General Mohammed ElBaradei, "countries that master uranium enrichment and plutonium separation become de facto nuclear weapons capable states" – meaning they can develop nuclear weapons in a short period of time.[77] It is a cause for concern that some of these countries pursue breeder reactors to lower their demand on uranium fuel.[78] A related and likely trend is that some of these aspiring nuclear powers may opt for fourth-generation reactors. The plutonium used in these is "particularly suitable" for producing nuclear weapons.[79]

To address this growing challenge, policy-makers are examining the viability of nuclear fuel banks that are under international control. Under such a system, countries might be less inclined to master the fuel cycle, which is the most complex component of a nuclear energy program. However, the system may not placate those who argue that it goes against the precept embodied in Article IV of the NPT giving countries the right to nuclear research for peaceful purposes. Some analysts predict that more countries will try to develop uranium and enrichment and reprocessing activities to avoid dependence on international suppliers, further complicating the task of curbing nuclear proliferation.[80] Beyond access to sensitive materials such as uranium, there may be a rise in virtual weapon programs which may add a new dimension to nuclear proliferation concerns.[81]

Biological trends

Over the last 30 years, advances in molecular biology, genetics, genomics and proteomics have revolutionized biotechnology.[82] This developmental trend is likely to continue in the foreseeable future. And, while future advances will continue to improve quality of life, some discoveries and applications may encourage the production of new types of biological agents. Unlike previous pathogens, however, future biological agents might be more difficult to detect and counter.

For example, some predict that those aiming to create biological weapons may shift away from micro-organisms that cause infectious disease and focus on bioregulators instead.[83] Bioregulators are a type of natural chemicals found in the human body that control vital functions such as respiration, temperature, mood and the immune response.[84] Tampering with these may cause adverse reactions; for example, the peptides angiotensin and bombesin may be used to increase blood pressure.[85] Administered at high doses or when their molecular structure is modified giving them novel properties, bioregulators can be toxic.[86]

Advances in biotechnology are also likely to facilitate the means for delivering biological agents. Examples of such techniques include viral vectors – currently used to carry out gene therapy – and the use of immunotoxins to target specific cells. Of greater concern, advances may also facilitate the aerosol delivery of biological agents. Already today, advanced processing methods such as "spray-drying" can be used to transform a drug from liquid to a fine powder form that is optimized for aerosolization.[87]

The production of new biological agents may also be possible through advances in genetic engineering. For example, genetic engineering can be used to combine the effects of deadly bacteria, such as anthrax, with bacteria that are prolific and easily enter the human body, such as *Escherichia coli.*[88] Non-state actors have already experimented in this area, with the cult Aum Shinrikyo re-engineering *E. coli* by combining it with botulinum toxin.[89] In the future, advances in synthetic biology may reduce the cost and difficulty associated with genetic engineering, opening the door for genetically engineered pathogens that are vaccine resistant or combine the toxic properties of different organisms.[90]

Chemical trends

In the chemical arena, the advent of nanotechnology is likely to blur the lines between chemistry and biology, especially as it becomes possible to manipulate molecules or individual atoms to produce bio-chemically active agents.[91] The crossover is particularly noticeable when it comes to toxins, bioregulators and their analogues.[92] For these so-called mid-spectrum agents, both the CWC and the BTWC apply but the non-proliferation challenges becoming more and more evident.

For example, given that incapacitating agents are allowed under the CWC for law-enforcement, including domestic riot control, groups and states may exploit this gray area to manufacture bioregulator-based chemical weapons intended to interfere with brain functions.[93] This scenario may become more realistic as new chemical manufacturing methodologies evolve. Over the long term, this may lead to the development of a new generation of psychochemical weapons that may be tailored for specific purposes.[94]

As is the case in the biological field, advances in manufacturing technologies may complicate the task of curbing proliferation. Even before nanotechnology reaches its full potential, advances in manufacturing technologies – such as the development of "microreactors" – may also make it easier to conceal illicit chemical weapons facilities.[95]

Conclusion

WMD proliferation remains an important security challenge. The possibility that a non-state actor acquires and uses WMD is one of the most feared scenarios – even if data suggest that such an incident is a very low probability event.

A principal challenge to the management of proliferation is the pressures facing the principal international treaties aiming to curb WMD proliferation. The NPT, the BTWC and the CWC all face a host of internal and external pressures that complicate effective non-proliferation. Recognizing these challenges, the international community is taking steps to update and strengthen its non-proliferation regimes and tools. The passage of UNSCR 1540, aiming to curb the transfer of WMD from state to non-state actors, represents a good example. And while progress has been made, technological advances and the spread of know-how means that only through continued vigilance and adaptation can non-proliferation efforts remain effective over time.

Notes

1 John F. Kennedy, "News Conference 52," *State Department Auditorium*, 21 March 1963.
2 European Council, "European Security Strategy, 'A Secure Europe in a Better World' " (EU High Representative Dr. Javier Solana, 2003). The White House, "The National Security Strategy of the United States of America" (2006).
3 European Council, "European Security Strategy, 'A Secure Europe in a Better World' "; The White House, "The National Security Strategy of the United States of America."
4 Graham T. Allison, *Nuclear Terrorism – The Ultimate Preventable Catastrophe* (New York: Times Books/Henry Holt, 2004).
5 Bob Graham and Jim Talent, *World At Risk: The Report of the Commission on the Prevention of WMD Proliferation and Terrorism* (New York: Vintage Books, 2008).
6 See, for example, Stephen G. Rademaker, "U.S. Compliance With Article VI of the Non-Proliferation Treaty (NPT)" (paper presented at the Panel Discussion at the Arms Control Association, Carnegie Endowment Building, Washington, DC, February 2005). It can be found online at www.nti.org/e_research/official_docs/dos/dos020305. pdf. See also Michael Rühle, "Enlightenment in the Second Nuclear Age," *International Affairs* 83, 3 (2007).
7 O. Thränert, "Would We Really Miss the Nuclear Nonproliferation Treaty?," *International Journal* (2008).
8 David S. Yost, "Introduction: Thinking About 'Enlightenment' and 'Counter-Enlightenment' in Nuclear Policies," *International Affairs* 83, 3 (2007).
9 Joseph F. Pilat, "The End of the NPT Regime?," *International Affairs* 83, 3 (2007).
10 Sergio Duarte, *Luncheon Address: Making the 2010 NPT Review Conference a Success*, Arms Control Association Annual Meeting: The Nuclear Nonproliferation Treaty at Forty – Addressing Current and Future Challenges (Washington, DC: 2008).
11 P. Sidhu, "Nuclear Proliferation," in *Security Studies: An Introduction*, ed. Paul Williams (London: Taylor & Francis, 2008).
12 Alexei Arbatov and Rose Gottemoeller, "New Presidents, New Agreements? Advancing US–Russian Strategic Arms Control," *Arms Control Today* July/August (2008).
13 See, for example, Joseph Cirincione, "Strategic Collapse: The Failure of the Bush Nuclear Doctrine," *Arms Control Today* November (2008).
14 Pilat, "The End of the NPT Regime?"
15 Michael Krepon, "The US–India Nuclear Deal: Another Wrong Turn in the War on Terror," *The Henry L. Stimson Center* (2006). Available online at: www.stimson.org/pub.cfm?id=283.
16 Charles D. Ferguson and William C. Potter, *The Four Faces of Nuclear Terrorism* (Monterey Institute of International Studies: Center for Nonproliferation Studies, 2004).
17 Allison, *Nuclear Terrorism*.
18 Ferguson and Potter, *The Four Faces of Nuclear Terrorism*.
19 Frank Barnaby, *How to Build a Nuclear Bomb: And Other Weapons of Mass Destruction* (London: Granta Publications, 2003).
20 Barnaby, *How to Build a Nuclear Bomb*, p. 36.

21 Barnaby, *How to Build a Nuclear Bomb.*
22 MOX consists of plutonium oxide mixed with uranium oxide.
23 Barnaby, *How to Build a Nuclear Bomb.*
24 Barnaby, *How to Build a Nuclear Bomb.*
25 Barnaby, *How to Build a Nuclear Bomb.*
26 Ferguson and Potter, *The Four Faces of Nuclear Terrorism.*
27 Ferguson and Potter, *The Four Faces of Nuclear Terrorism.*
28 Gustav Lindstrom, "Protecting the European homeland – the CBR Dimension," *EU-ISS Chaillot Paper* 69 (2004).
29 See the IAEA web page on Safeguards and Verification accessible online at: www.iaea.org/OurWork/SV/Safeguards/sg_protocol.html.
30 In addition, the UN General Assembly adopted the International Convention for the Suppression of Acts of Nuclear Terrorism in 2005.
31 4956th meeting Security Council, "UNSCR 1540" (2004). Accessible at: http://daccessdds.un.org/doc/UNDOC/GEN/N04/328/43/PDF/N0432843.pdf?OpenElement.
32 Security Council, "UNSCR 1540."
33 Peter Crail, "Implementing UN Security Council Resolution 1540: A Risk-Based Approach," *Nonproliferation Review* 13, 2 (2006).
34 Crail, "Implementing UN Security Council Resolution 1540," p. 19. For additional information on UNSCR 1540 and the challenges it faces, see Ben Steyn, "Understanding the Implications of UN Security Council Resolution 1540," *African Security Review* 14, 1 (2005). It is available online at: www.iss.co.za/pubs/ASR/14No1/steyn.pdf.
35 Complementing these efforts is the Global Threat Reduction Initiative launched in May 2004, which aims to secure or repatriate high-risk nuclear and radiological materials and equipment.
36 Biological weapons cause disease through pathogens (e.g., bacteria, viruses and fungi) and toxins that are poisonous compounds. Peter René Lavoy, Scott Douglas Sagan and James J. Wirtz, *Planning the Unthinkable: How New Powers Will Use Nuclear, Biological, and Chemical Weapons* (Ithaca: Cornell University Press, 2000).
37 For more information on exercise Dark Winter, see www.terrorisminfo.mipt.org/video/dark-winter/dark-winter.ppt
38 G.W. Christopher, "Biological warfare: A Historical Perspective," *Journal of the American Medical Association* 278, 5 (1997).
39 Source: The BioWeapons Prevention Project (www.bwpp.org).
40 The international norm against biological weapons includes the 1925 Geneva Protocol, the 1972 Biological and Toxin Weapons Convention and parts of the 1993 Chemical Weapons Convention (relating to toxin weapons).
41 It should be recognized that the BTWC has some overlap with the CWC since some chemicals with biological origins – such as toxins – fall under both conventions.
42 Jean Pascal Zanders and Kathryn Nixdorff, "Enforcing Non-Proliferation: The European Union and the 2006 BTWC Review Conference," *EU-ISS Chaillot Paper* November, 93 (2006).
43 Ken Alibek and Stephen Handelman, *Biohazard* (New York: Random House, 1999), p. x.
44 Treasa Dunworth, Robert J. Mathews and Tim McCormack, "National Implementation of the Biological Weapons Convention," *Journal of Conflict and Security Law* 11, 1 (2006).
45 Lawrence M. Wein and Yifan Liu, "Analyzing a Bioterror Attack on the Food Supply: The Case of Botulinum Toxin in Milk," *Proceedings of the National Academy of Sciences (PNAS)* 102, 28 (2005).
46 Kathleen C. Bailey, "The Biological and Toxin Weapons Threat to the United States" (Fairfax: National Institute for Public Policy, 2001).
47 See the American Type Culture Collection.

48 Lindstrom, "Protecting the European Homeland."
49 Bailey, "The Biological and Toxin Weapons Threat to the United States."
50 Examples of such diseases include Avian influenza, West Nile Fever and Bovine Spongiform Encephalopathy. "Speech by Barry O'Neil, President of the OIE International Committee," *76th General Session of the International Committee, World Organisation for Animal Health*, 30 May 2008. Available at: www.oie.int/fr/session2008/presse-oneill.htm
51 Lonnie J. King, "CDC Agroterrorism and Zoonotic Threat Preparedness Efforts, Statement before the Committee on Homeland Security Subcommittee on Prevention of Nuclear and Biological Attack" (US House of Representatives, 2006).
52 Kyle B. Olson, "Aum Shinrikyo: Once and Future Threat?," *Emerging Infectious Disease* 5, 4 (1999): 513–516.
53 For details, see Zanders and Nixdorff, "Enforcing Non-Proliferation," chapter 3.
54 For an overview of the verification tools available, please see Zanders and Nixdorff, "Enforcing Non-Proliferation."
55 Zanders and Nixdorff, "Enforcing Non-Proliferation."
56 Examples of such codes include the InterAcademy Panel (2005) *Statement on Biosecurity*, the International Centre for Genetic Engineering and Biotechnology (2005), the *Building Blocks for a Code of Conduct for Scientists*, and the International Union of Microbiological Societies (2005) *Code of Ethics for the Prevention of the Misuse of Scientific Knowledge, Research and Resources.*
57 While biosecurity aims to strengthen laboratory containment capacity to avoid accidents or unintentional exposure, biosafety focuses on implementing measures and regulations to prevent the theft, loss, misuse, unauthorized access or diversion of pathogens and toxins.
58 Jonathan Tucker, *War of Nerves: Chemical Warfare from World War I to al-Qaeda* (New York: Pantheon, 2006).
59 Barnaby, *How to Build a Nuclear Bomb.*
60 Peter Boehme, "The Verification Regime of the Chemical Weapons Convention: An Overview," *Chemical Disarmament* 6, 4 (2008).
61 J. Gerard, "The CWC at 10 Years – Partnership, Progress, and the Path Ahead, Statement by the CEO of the American Chemical Council," *OPCW Industry Protection Forum* (2007).
62 www.state.gov/t/isn/rls/fs/64874.htm.
63 Tucker, *War of Nerves.*
64 Chemical profile for phosgene from Scorecard. Available at: www.scorecard.org/chemical-profiles/summary.tcl?edf_substance_id=75-44-5.
65 Barnaby, *How to Build a Nuclear Bomb.*
66 Tucker, *War of Nerves.*
67 Ronald G. Sutherland, "Chemical and Biochemical Non-Lethal Weapons," *SIPRI Policy Paper* 23 (2008).
68 http://g8live.org/2007/10/31/russia-urges-rest-of-foreign-aid-to-destroy-chemical-weapons.
69 Boehme, "The Verification Regime of the Chemical Weapons Convention."
70 Boehme, "The Verification Regime of the Chemical Weapons Convention."
71 OPCW Director-General Chemical Disarmament Ambassador Rogelio Pfirter, "Foreword to the Chemical Disarmament Quarterly," 6, 4 (2008).
72 Tucker, *War of Nerves.*
73 Tucker, *War of Nerves.*
74 Tucker, *War of Nerves.*
75 IAEA Director General Dr. Mohamed ElBaradei, "Statement to the Sixty-Third Regular Session of the United Nations General Assembly" (2008). Available at: www.iaea.org/NewsCenter/Statements/2008/ebsp2008n010.html.
76 Thränert, "Would We Really Miss the Nuclear Nonproliferation Treaty?"

77 ElBaradei, "Statement to the Sixty-Third Regular Session of the United Nations General Assembly."
78 As implied by the name, a breeder reactor produces new fissile or fissionable material at a greater pace than it consumes.
79 Thränert, "Would We Really Miss the Nuclear Nonproliferation Treaty?"
80 Thränert, "Would We Really Miss the Nuclear Nonproliferation Treaty?"
81 Pilat, "The End of the NPT Regime?"
82 Zanders and Nixdorff, "Enforcing Non-Proliferation."
83 Zanders and Nixdorff, "Enforcing Non-Proliferation."
84 Jonathan Tucker, "The Body's Own Bioweapons," *Bulletin of the Atomic Scientists* 64, 1 (2008).
85 For more on future bioweapons, bioregulatory peptides, receptors and new developments in delivery of biological agents, see Malcolm Dando, *The New Biological Weapons: Threat, Proliferation, and Control* (Boulder: Lynne Rienner Publishers, 2001).
86 Tucker, "The Body's Own Bioweapons."
87 Tucker, "The Body's Own Bioweapons."
88 Barnaby, *How to Build a Nuclear Bomb.*
89 Barnaby, *How to Build a Nuclear Bomb.*
90 L. Zoloth and S. Maurer, "Synthesizing Biosecurity," *Bulletin of the Atomic Scientists* 63, 6 (2007).
91 Zanders and Nixdorff, "Enforcing Non-Proliferation."
92 Tucker, "The Body's Own Bioweapons."
93 Tucker, "The Body's Own Bioweapons."
94 Tucker, "The Body's Own Bioweapons."
95 Tucker, *War of Nerves.*

4 Regional crisis, conflict and fragile states

Caty Clément

Are fragile states a strategic threat?

The notion that fragile states constitute a strategic threat to the Global North is fairly recent. In fact, even well into the twentieth century, what are now conceived of as fragile states were still perceived as an opportunity by the strong states of the international system to extend their zone of influence, be it through annexation, or direct, indirect or post-colonial rule. The Global North was made up of few strong states whose boundaries shifted frequently as they integrated or lost territory.

One-sixth of the world's 6.5 billion people live in fragile states whose toxic potential is considerable: although representing only 13 percent of all states, they account for half of the world's civil wars.[1] There is no doubt that fragile states constitute a substantial threat to the international system; they were involved in 77 percent of all international crises of the post-Cold War era.

Failed states share some characteristics, particularly the appalling living conditions suffered by their population, and the enduring character thereof. An average failing state stays that way for about 59 years,[2] while in states emerging from war there is a 50 percent chance that conflict will resume within the following five years.[3] Thirteen years into the Democratic Republic of the Congo (DRC) war, according to International Rescue Committee mortality surveys, death rates today remain well above the regional average with over 1,300 excess deaths on a daily basis. In Liberia, 75 percent of women have been raped at least once and the practice continues unabated.[4]

The conceptual shift from fragile states as "opportunities for influence and expansion," to weak environments that pose "strategic threats" over the past 20 years is the result of a growing concern in the most developed countries for their own human security. The notion of political power as a personal fiefdom has by and large disappeared in the West in favor of "democracy for the people," including their well-being. Although considerable disagreements exist on the root causes and remedies of state failure, the international system and its critics agree that weak states are:

1 a problem
2 for their people as well as for

3   the international system as whole;
4   remedies have often been ineffective, and,
5   something needs to be done.[5]

The contagion effect

Failed states are contagious to their immediate neighbors, but they also have a projection capability that makes them highly poisonous to the international environment.

Regionally

Overall, weak states are more costly to all their neighboring states than they are to themselves. Failed states are extremely costly to their neighbors: the average estimated cost per year of a failing state is at US$276 billion, whereby the lion's share of the financial burden (US$206 billion) falls upon neighboring countries.[6] Keep in mind that the OECD countries' annual aid contribution before the financial crisis reached US$80 billion.

Geographically, poverty, conflict and state fragility often overlap. All failed states but one (North Korea) are located in South East Asia, the Middle East and Africa.[7] Their populations bear the brunt of poverty and conflict.[8] These are also the regions of origin of 75 percent of world's refugee population.[9]

The concentration of fragile states in these regions makes it increasingly difficult for good performers to emerge. The bad neighborhood effect, whereby one failing neighbor substantially increases one's own failure probability, drags entire regions down as warlords, militias and arms circulate across borders. Instability is contagious, but so is poverty: a reduction in a weak state's economic growth rate extends along an 800 km radius.[10]

In Africa, four such bad neighborhoods co-exist, and international observers fear that the four will eventually interlock. From West to East, these bad neighborhoods roughly entail: Côte d'Ivoire–Guinea–Liberia–Sierra Leone, DRC–Rwanda–Uganda–South Sudan, Darfur–Chad–Central African Republic (CAR), and Somalia–Ethiopia–Eritrea. In the Middle East, two clusters live in close proximity: Israel–Palestine–Lebanon–Syria, and Iraq–Kurdish areas–Iran. In Asia, there are at least two more: Indonesia–Timor Leste and Afghanistan–Pakistan.

Internationally

Since 2002, fragile states were recognized as a primary threat within the US National Security Strategy: "America is now threatened less by conquering states than we are by failing ones."[11] Weak states threaten the Global North's safety most notoriously by providing breeding grounds for international terrorists (e.g., al-Qaeda in Afghanistan, Hezbollah in Lebanon) and pirates (e.g., Somalia, South East Asia). They also constitute potential health hazards (e.g., HIV), hosts for criminal networks (e.g., drug production and trafficking), and opportunities for the environmental destruction of forests and water necessary to stall global warming. They are furthermore causes of human flight to the Global North, and are the prime location of burdensome wars, which compound and worsen all of the above. War and its consequences, together with high corruption ratings, are immensely costly to the state itself, its immediate neighborhood, as well as the rest of the world.

Inhospitable living conditions cause brain and muscle drain of legal and illegal migrants toward more secure and developed environments, depleting fragile states of their best and brightest when they need them most. Poor salaries, ongoing insecurity and lack of political voice often render the Global North increasingly attractive to the brightest and strongest in the Global South. The population of failed states, moreover, is usually young and therefore prone to move. There are 200 million international migrants in the world today, and the numbers are increasing: 25 million moved since 2000. "Protection" against immigrants seeking a brighter future in the EU currently costs Europe at least €83 million through its imperfect Frontex system.

One of the least factored-in consequences of failed states is the health hazard they represent. The basic proxy for human well-being – child mortality – is more than five-times higher in failed states than in middle-income countries.[12] In situations with poor living conditions, populations have high incentives to flee the hell holes of the world; with access to facilitated travel means, human flight is not only important, it also reaches distant locations. In the Democratic Republic of the Congo, for instance, the daily death rate is 85 percent higher than that of the Sub-Saharan average. Just 0.4 percent of these deaths are the direct result of violence; the majority is due to malnutrition, dehydration and disease.[13] While some of these diseases can be easily constrained, others cannot. Some of the world's most deadly diseases, such as AIDS (25 million deaths worldwide) and Ebola (1,200 deaths) were born in Africa's Great Lakes region.

Climate change is likely to have devastating consequences for the world's most fragile countries. The Global North – the worst polluter – constitutes a threat to fragile states, which bear the brunt of the consequences of climate change. Climate change, together with deforestation, wildlife destruction or trafficking, artisanal mining, dumping of hazardous substances, and ill or unprotected extraction of nuclear ore are little publicized but are ticking time bombs in the medium term. The world's second lung after the Amazon – Congo's basin – eludes state supervision as concessions continue to be doled out despite a Presidential moratorium.[14] Allegations of actors from European nations dumping toxic, radioactive medical waste into Somali waters have gone unchecked for years. Who will patrol those waters, investigate and file international complaints in the absence of a Somali state?[15]

Weak states have long been breeding grounds for terrorist organizations. Sudan, for instance, has been well-known for hosting two of the world's most notorious terrorists, Carlos and Osama bin Laden. Underground commercial and political actors have become adept at developing extensive cooperation networks allowing them to strike targets far away from their safe havens. Al-Qaeda, an organization curled up in distant Afghanistan, masterminded the bold 9/11 attacks which stunned the world, but terrorists have long trained worldwide. Anti-apartheid's African National Congress, once labeled a terrorist organization, had networks that reached into the rest of Africa (e.g., training camps in Uganda and Tanzania), but also cooperated across continents into Europe, the Middle East and Asia.[16]

Criminal networks have also identified failed states as a commercial opportunity. The use of failed states as informal trading posts for criminal activities recently came to light when, in late February 2009, the son of late President Conte and ten high-ranking security officials were arrested in Guinea for smuggling drugs from Latin America to Europe. Somalia's coast has become the new piracy haven where an initial US$2,000 investment can deliver a US$10 million ransom in a matter of weeks.[17] Trading in human beings, particularly Caucasian women, boomed during the 1990s in the midst of the Balkan crisis, where most of the victims originated. The total profit of trafficking women and girls for the purpose of sexual exploitation is estimated to be a US$32 billion per year business opportunity.[18] Around 95 percent of the global production of hard drugs is estimated to come from failed or fragile states.[19] Columbia, Afghanistan and Myanmar stand out foremost as the poster children. Afghanistan is home to 82 percent of world poppy production; the total value of trade in 2007 amounted to US$4 billion, or 53 percent of the country's GDP.[20]

State fragility, a new threat?

The modern concept of what are referred to as fragile states has actually been a standard fixture of the international system for centuries. In fact, state weakness, pre- or post-Westphalian, was the rule rather than the exception until the mid-twentieth century. Only after World War II did the universal notion emerge that states had obligations toward their citizens to provide peace and security, fair adjudication of societal conflicts and basic social services. It turned the previous patrimonial system – where states were privately owned by individuals and citizens owed obedience to their rulers – upside down. This new international doctrine, whereby states were there to serve the people and as such were also responsible to their inhabitants, constituted a ground-breaking shift from the past.

Half-way through the twentieth century, as state capabilities were taken up a notch, it became clear that certain state capabilities varied considerably and that some states simply could not live up to the new international norm. However, it would take some time before this came to be perceived as an issue to which a global solution needed to be found.

The Cold War's double standards

During the Cold War, fragile states were considered more an opportunity than a threat. It is not that fragile or even collapsed states did not exist, they did: the late 1970s–early 1980s saw Angola, Mozambique, Ethiopia, Chad, Uganda and

Ghana become severely fragile when the first anti-colonial nationalist generation failed.

However, far from being perceived as a human security threat, they were seen by the most powerful states as an opportunity to score points in the Cold War chess game. Loans were handed over as petrodollars were offloaded onto the financial markets. The responsibility to help was still largely driven at a bilateral level, often directed by former colonial powers, or challenged by the two contenders of world order: the Soviet Union and China.

Powerful states from all sides of the ideological spectrum had no qualms about supporting abusive rulers. This includes US support of Pinochet in Chile, Belgo-French propping up of Mobutu in the Congo, Soviet help to Mengistu in Ethiopia and Chinese leniency toward Kim Il-sung in North Korea. The new international paradigm that states were responsible for the welfare of their people was limited to the Northern Hemisphere. That the same should apply to the "Global South" was not yet part of the picture.

The late-1980s negative state

Toward the late-1980s, throughout the course of a series of shocks, conceptions in the developed world amongst security actors, donors and scholars changed with a growing understanding that previous policies had a boomerang or whiplash effect: fragile states came at a cost for the developed world too. The weakness and eventual collapse of the Eastern Bloc brought to the fore a series of issues to which the developed world had in the past turned a blind eye. Indeed, the impact of previous politics brought not one, but a series of crises to the doorstep of the developed world.

- First, the debt crisis started to unfold. When Argentina, the former-Yugoslavia or former-Zaire were no longer able to service their debt, it dawned that the developed world's state fragility color blindness was going to cost it much more than it had bargained for.
- Second, the CNN effect brought viciously abused women and starving children into the living rooms of the developed world.
- Third, the developed world was coming to grips with the scale of the unfolding AIDS pandemic, which had long brewed in Africa's tropical belt and was aggravated by the states' inability to provide a secure environment and basic social services to their citizens.
- Fourth, in Europe, Green parties also came to the political forefront, caring about forest depletion and polluted rivers in distant locations, because at the end of the day, everybody was impacted.
- Fifth, the booming economic years were over for the developed world, which was closing down its mines and eager to keep jobs for its own. Poorly educated immigrants were no longer welcome in the West and had to be kept at bay. A barbed wire fence was built along the US–Mexican border and around Spanish enclaves in Maroko.

As fragile states were becoming an enduring fixture of the international system, the first reaction was to throw the baby (in this case, the state) away with the bath water. Many developing world states did not function, it was argued, because there was too much state, and that had to be reduced. The mid-1980s to mid-1990s thereby saw a drastic reduction in state apparatus: protectionism was bad, trade barriers should drastically diminish if not be suppressed, economies were to be liberalized and administrations shrank.

As opposed to the early twentieth century colonial bilateral approach, and the Cold War's ideological alliances, in the mid-1990s, multilateral institutions (World Bank, UN, NGOs) became more pro-active, engaging heavily in fragile states. If a population was under threat, if individual rights were violated, and the state was unable or unwilling to deal with the situation, a "right of intervention" of other actors of the international community should be considered. Some even suggested a more permanent form of intervention, whereby fragile states would be placed under a statehood learning and oversight process of neo-tutelage.

New century, new era: positive state for all

By the mid-to-late-1990s, the world witnessed some of its worst atrocities: Somalia collapsed, ethnic cleansing went on at Europe's doorstep in former-Yugoslavia, a genocide unfolded in Rwanda, and Africa's First World War erupted in the DRC Congo. The virtues of healthy statehood – its provision of security, basic social services, healthcare, basic infrastructure necessary to nurture economic development and corruption-free ethical institutions – were re-discovered. The 1997 World Bank Development Report focused on the state and the risk of "failed" states. The Report brought the pendulum to the middle: the debate shifted from over-inflated state (a feature of the Cold War) versus skeleton state-building approach in the post-Cold War world to building the "right" kind of state. During James Wolfenson's ten-year rule, the World Bank de facto engaged in politics (although excluded from its mandate) by focusing on "institutions."[21]

Statehood became a positive notion again. The IMF Debt Initiative for Heavily Indebted Poor Countries (HIPIC) initiative and the US Millennium Challenge Accounts were going to support well-performing countries on their way to becoming middle-income countries. The notion of right to intervene, whereby individuals were given primacy over the collective state institution, was replaced by the state-centric Responsibility to Protect. Responsibilities were put squarely on the state, as the prime actor for ensuring the protection of its citizens. This was merely the beginning; the agenda in support of states and state building would truly pick up at the turn of the century.

When terror went global with 9/11, failed states suddenly reached the forefront of the political agenda. A number of countries, including Afghanistan, had fallen between the cracks while not responding to existing development tools. Instead, they remained trapped in a mix of protracted civil war, chronic underdevelopment, a complete absence of the most basic state institutions, which led to extensive population displacement, widespread human rights abuse, and the death and killing of large numbers of civilians – sometimes directly, but overwhelmingly as an indirect consequence.

States could and indeed did fall prey to terrorist and criminal networks. Al-Qaeda, a loose and well-financed Afghanistan-based terrorist organization, reached out across four continents and struck in the United States, Europe, Africa and Asia. Weak and failed states were not only a threat to their own population, but also to global security. Both donors and scholars became engaged in the issue of fragile, weak, shadow, failed or collapsed states in their own right. New tools, new institutional designs and new issues were advocated and (sometimes) embraced.

The international community sought to improve its understanding of fragile states in order to develop an appropriate strategy. Researchers and academics were hired; high-level panels were set up to focus specifically on fragile states. Major changes were advocated in terms of intervention tools (quick disbursement funds, grants versus loans), the nature of the issues falling in the peacebuilding package stretched to include Disarmament, Demobilization and Reintegration (DDR); even parts of Security Sector reform (oversight mechanisms in particular), the promotion of democracy, the implementation of peace agreements and regional solutions were advocated to deal with clusters of fragile states.

To their credit, donors proceeded to their own reality check. They had agreed on a large number of loans which states would most likely never be able to honor. Their procedural requirements were too complicated; weak states became quickly overloaded with demanding structural adjustment policies, burdensome debt service and complicated procedural requirements, particularly when faced with multiple donors. Many of the most successful performing (in economic terms) emerging countries were turning away from the international financial institutions and preferred loans from regular financial institutions.

Competing agendas were developed amongst different donors, but also within the same donor's branches. Development, defense and trade departments of the same donor sometimes pursued competing agendas; as, for instance, in the case of the DRC where EU member states supported a UN arms embargo and favored an EU code of conduct concerning weapons transfers, all the while selling military equipment to the DRC. Donors did not always live up to the transparency, consistency and efficiency standards they imposed on weak states.

This was particularly the case with regard to natural resources and arms as potentially fuelling conflict. Time and time again, violence as a result of the resource curse had devastating consequences for local populations; yet, when activists and observers wanted to impose an obligation of due diligence to commercial operators, they were rebuffed. Similarly, the Small Arms Trade Transparency Barometer repeatedly highlights the discrepancy between some states' promptness to advocate transparency in weak states, while remaining reluctant to disclose information concerning their own activities as the world's largest sellers of small arms.[22]

Multilateral financial institutions also tended to give less to fragile states than they were allowed to and their aid was much more volatile in these states.[23]

Recent data on Ache, for example, shows donor commitments to be more generous in addressing natural disaster than conflict.[24] Multilateral political institutions such as the UN and/or regional institutions increased their financial and physical presence exponentially, often in environments where there was no peace to keep. Deployment of UN uniformed personnel, for instance, surged sixfold over the past decade.[25]

Key challenges, obstacles and dilemmas

Identifying fragile states

As the notion of a universal right to positive statehood became the new international norm, fragile states were no longer perceived as global opportunities, but as threats that had to be dealt with. Weak states became an academic topic in their own right. In 1994, William Zartman published a groundbreaking book, *Collapsed States*, whereby for the first time the issue was clearly identified and labeled to become a field of its own. A new body of researchers emerged, often coming from the field of conflict and negotiation, within which were economists, social and political scientists.

In its infancy, much of the discourse on failed states was conceptual, trying to define what a failed, fragile, weak, phantom or collapsed state was. Eventually, some common understanding seemed to coalesce: fragile states were often conflict prone with little control over their territory; they exhibited flawed and exclusionary institutions; they had poor infrastructure leading to limited delivery of essential social goods; and they were unable to hold the monopoly of violence. In their most acute form, states collapsed, leading to a complete breakdown of public order and social relations.

As they became increasingly complex, definitions entailed various stages, which gave way to an etymologic proliferation including collapsed, weak, fragile, low-income-under-stress, difficult partners, shadow, criminal, quasi-states, etc. Debates emerged that often pitted political scientists against economists. The former, for instance, often equated poor-performing countries with failed states; while the latter contended that poor performers such as Mongolia could in fact be enduring states, while good performers such as Lebanon had dramatically failed. Therefore, not only did political and security dimensions have to be taken into account, but some also argued that the ability of these states to interact with their counterparts at the international level was part of state capacity.

Identifying causes and remedies

By the turn of the century, scholars shifted their attention toward prevention, causes and early-warning indicators of state failure. This sparked an intense debate between economists and political scientists opposing greed (economic demands) to grievance (political dissatisfaction). Eventually, most scholars came to recognize that both were actually intertwined: socio-economic dissatisfaction (need) – particularly when coinciding with identity boundaries – spurred mobilization along primary identities (creed). When the political system is either unwilling or unable to address the original "need," violence tends to ensue. In order to pursue its activities and sustain itself, the resulting rebellion needs to develop strategies to access resources. Failure to achieve its political goals will all-too-often turn a rebellion into a money-making machine (greed).[26]

Notwithstanding the horrific human costs to those living in failed states, preventing failure is likely to be much more cost effective than any peacebuilding or state building attempt. Former Secretary General Kofi Annan argued that "the most pitiful lesson of the past decade has been that prevention of violent conflict is far better, and most cost-effective, than cure."[27] Already, in 1997, the Carnegie Commission on Preventing Deadly Conflict had compared seven major UN interventions in the 1990s and concluded that if the international community had acted preventively, it could have saved itself US$130 billion. Scientific data would then highlight which countries were at risk and the international system would respond accordingly. Soon, early-warning toolkits became all the rage, but within a couple of years they ran into a series of both methodological and political problems.

First, too much data kills data. Scientific findings were used by international donors to develop comprehensive toolkits designed to predict and eventually prevent state failure. However, incorporating ever larger numbers of indicators became a self-defeating process. Toolkits involving over 100 different indicators may well have been very robust, but their use was so cumbersome that often they could not be used for their initial purpose: early-warning.

Second, many early-warning instruments are loaded with readily accessible quantitative data. As a consequence, socio-economic data tend to weigh heavily, while other sectors where quantitative data are scarce or non-existent (e.g., security sector, horizontal inequality, etc.) are simply not integrated. Some variables that qualitative research finds particularly relevant to state fragility have fallen between the cracks and are simply not measured, and therefore are never included in mainstream action plans. Perhaps the most salient examples are horizontal inequality (inequality between social/geographic/religious/linguistic groups) and the role of the elite (bourgeoisie), which was paramount in the Global North state-building process. For both of these factors, no hard indicators exist, therefore they are not measured, not integrated as a cause of fragility in mainstream international institutions, and consequently are seldom part of any action plan.[28]

Third, separating causes from consequences of fragility turned out to be equally painstaking. Large N statistical regressions offer robust correlations, but do not bring much insight with regard to the direction of the causal link. Poverty, for instance, is strongly associated with state failure, but is it a cause, a consequence, or both?

Fourth, an increasing number of well-meaning early-warning indicator operators grew frustrated as a result of political contingencies. At the end of the day, political imperatives of the Global North seemed to prevail over the actual needs of the fragile states. When push came to shove, it was political will in the North rather than scientific data that drove the interventionist agenda. Some countries that have scored poorly on stability indexes and high on early-warning systems have never been considered fragile by their principal donors (e.g., the UK's policy toward Uganda). The 1997 Carnegie Commission on Preventing Deadly Conflict had already highlighted that there was an inverse relationship between the Global North's willingness to intervene and the ease and effectiveness of intervention: support is highest during the conflict as opposed to at the beginning or the end.

Donors were not keen to see their actions dictated by science rather than politics: many ranking instruments could not be published because of their political sensitivity. For example, it took years for the World Bank LICUS team (Low Income Countries Under Stress – the institution's jargon for Fragile States) to be allowed to place the list of countries under their watch in the public domain. The UN operated a similar system, but was never able to publicize it. Researchers in the UK's Department for International Development (DFID) were unable to convince their own politicians that helping Uganda on the grounds of its good performances stood in direct contradiction with the country's poor performance in nearly every aspect of statehood.

Therefore, although many donors initially embraced the idea of predictive toolkits, in a matter of years many shied away from them. One of the most comprehensive tools publicly available today – the State Failure Index, which has the distinct features of integrating both qualitative and quantitative data and being entirely transparent – has been developed by the Global Fund for Peace and is published annually by Foreign Policy. How effective the ranking is as a predictive tool, and to what extent it is actually being used by decision-makers, is not clear.

Strategic threat, strategic response?

Failed states are often caught in a trap of enduring poverty, immense social needs, political instability, protracted violence, population flight and considerable environmental destruction. Not only has the situation not improved (35 countries considered fragile in 1979 are still fragile in 2009), but there is a widening gap between poor performers and the rest of the developing countries (the gap has been widening steadily since the 1970s).[29] Traditional ways to address state failure have not worked and a new system is in order, but shedding old habits has proven an uphill battle. Translating words into action has been a major challenge: "harmonization" of donor action and UN "integration" may look smart on paper, but they are much less straightforward when boiled down to practical implementation. In fact, the inclination to do business as usual has proven such a hard nut to crack that the Organization for Economic Co-operation and Development – Development Assistance Committee (OECD–DAC) decided to track and compare donor pledges and commitments with their actions.

The alter-globalization movement argues that the system has not fundamentally changed: dependency/domination of a handful of strong states is still the rule, although not on a bilateral basis, but through multilateralized international regimes. Resistance to that domination materializes itself, for instance, in the debate on UN Security Council reform, the stalled Doha talks, and opposition to the World Bank's conditionalities.

Some of the fiercest criticism has come from the academic community. The most radical critics contest the very necessity for the international community to keep on supporting fragile states: either politically or financially. Two political analysts in particular have questioned the rationale of saving failing states, which so persistently cost the international community large humanitarian, development and peacekeeping contributions. In two powerful articles, Jeffrey Herbst and Edward Luttwak challenge mainstream policy, arguing that the international community should "Let them [states] Fail," and try to "Give War a Chance."[30] Both authors agree on the underlying problem and recommend a substantial breakaway from current policies.

They raise questions about the soundness of supporting failing states, and wonder whether the international community thereby prolongs the suffering of the populations, instead of letting them collapse and start afresh. Herbst points to the fact that some states may be structured along ill-conceived borders and that separation or redrawing would make more sense than putting them on artificial aid support (e.g., Somaliland's independence from Somalia).

Luttwak draws on findings that wars ending through military victory are considerably shorter and more stable than those that end by means of negotiated settlements. Indeed, negotiated settlements have been twice as likely to fail (+/– 30 percent) than military victories have (+/– 15 percent). Wars that end through peace settlements also tend to last three-times longer than those ending through military victory.[31]

Economists have also severely criticized financial aid flows under its current form. In two other powerful pieces "The Curse of Aid" and "Dead Aid," aid comes under close scrutiny for being ineffective and even counter-productive. As with the "resource curse," whereby wealthy states are relatively weak, a large aid endowment insulates the recipient government from its people and thereby contributes to diminishing democracy. Aid is also accused of impoverishing countries. Between 1970 and 1998 – when aid was at its peak – the number of Africans living in dire poverty has increased from 11 percent to 68 percent.

Jeffrey Sachs in his famous book "The End of Poverty" equally criticized aid for its inability to curb poverty and instability of national institutions. Starting from a similar predicament – that aid results are disappointing – Sachs argues not that aid should stop, but the contrary: that it should be beefed up. Today, Africa receives US$10 billion in aid, but pays US$14 billion to service its debt.[32] Aid's failure is largely the result of insufficient disbursement to the wrong people. The current financial crisis will have a deadly impact on the poorest of world states. According to the IMF, those nations need a rapid influx of US$25 billion in 2009, which the international community is struggling to collect. Compare those figures to the US$150 billion rescue package provided by insurance giant AIG.

Most of the serious pitfalls facing international action in failed states have been known for at least a decade. From the 1997 Carnegie Report on Preventing Deadly Conflict, the 2004 "UN High Level Panel on Threats Challenges and Change," to the 2009 "UN Report on Peacebuilding," some of the same issues have repeatedly been highlighted.

1   The international community acts too late due to cumbersome and inadequate procedures that cause the early recovery window of opportunity to be lost. The fact that fragile states remain in such a condition for two-thirds of a century on average highlights the inadequacy of the current approach. Although most donors set about delivering faster through quick disbursement funds and increases in the number of grants, this is hardly transferred into the field. In the midst of the fighting in Eastern DRC in the Fall of 2008, 3,000 additional UN troops were requested, but none have reached Congolese soil at the time of this writing (June 2009).

2   A common agenda is even difficult to achieve amongst ministers within the same government. Hence, donors are now endorsing the whole-of-government approach to ensure that all ministries (e.g., development, foreign affairs, defense and trade/finance) pursue a single coherent policy agenda in fragile states.

3   There is a lack of coordination between international actors. Therefore, the UN is struggling to implement an integrated approach, particularly in its peace missions, bringing all actors under a single umbrella. However, so far it has often stayed at the leadership level and is still being thwarted by enduring turf fights. The UNDP and the World Bank also tend to be in strong competition with each other. This is particularly evident in the new booming peacebuilding sector – the DDR of former combatants – where organizations have competed for the past few years to set the agenda, administer the funds and even engage in implementation to a certain extent.

4   There is poor cooperation between actors from different fields of activity. Actors functioning in the fields of development, policy and security typically do not interact much, but as the latest Peacebuilding Report highlighted again, there is an urgent need for these communities to develop an integrated approach.

5   Donors apply double standards to themselves and their recipients. Overall, strong and efficient donor countries deliver much less than they pledge, while requiring total transparency and accountability from failed states. With the notable exception of the Nordic countries, most developed nations are still far from providing the targeted 0.7 percent of their GNI to oversee development aid as enshrined in the 2000 Monterrey Consensus. In 2008, total net official development assistance from OECD members rose up to the highest dollar figure ever recorded, US$119.8 billion, but this only represents 0.30 percent of the OECD's combined GNI.[33]

Solutions, future trends and trajectories

The US State Department assesses that failed states will remain a major international threat for the coming 10 to 30 years.[34] There is a global agreement that the current procedures to address state weakness are not working. Therefore, over the past decade new guidelines have being developed calling for an increase in the integration, harmonization, coherence, coordination and complementarity amongst actors, phases and agendas, but are these guidelines actually being implemented?

In 2005, OECD countries agreed to be held accountable for their commitments in the Paris Declaration on Aid Effectiveness. As a first step, the OECD attempted to hold the international community accountable by monitoring its action, although the only sanction in response consisted of naming and shaming. The review has helped to identify some positive developments, but also substantial shortcomings.

In 2007, donors disbursed about 40 percent of their aid to fragile states (which numbered 48). However, most aid flows are very selective and continue to be disbursed according to the political interests of the donors rather than a needs-based approach. In 2007, half of the aid packages directed toward fragile states (20 percent of total ODA) benefited just five countries, with Iraq taking the lion's share. Dependency remains an important issue. About half of fragile states receive the bulk of their aid from no more than three donors. Debt relief typically targets good performers, while debt servicing continues to burden the budgets of fragile states. Moreover, in one-fifth of the overall aid to fragile states packages in 2007, no monetary flux was involved, only debt relief.

Security is increasingly being understood as a crucial issue in fragile states, and the OECD has produced substantial guidelines. Over the past decade, UN blue helmets have increased seven-fold with 110,000 peacekeepers totaling 20 percent of total aid for an annual budget of US$7 billion. However, aid procedures remain cumbersome and ill-adapted to address fragile states. To a large extent, security-sector reform still cannot be included as development aid. Recognizing the importance of the issue, an increasing number of donors have attempted to stretch their security programs to encompass the sphere of development (and therefore aid), for instance by providing water and sanitation to the army.

An encouraging example of providing rapid and flexible support to fragile states has been set by the 2004 Netherlands Stability Fund. The novelty of the Fund's approach lies in the fact that it is demand- rather than supply-driven: it has clearly delinked allocation of resources from ODA (overseas development aid) eligibility. It has successfully applied a whole-of-government approach, receiving strong political support – notably within the parliament – and its budget has doubled between 2004 and 2008 (from €58 to €100 million). However, transferring this system to the international level may take time. Compare its means with that of the Peacebuilding Commission set up at the same time, where pledges accounted for US$221 million, but only US$137 had been received.[35]

In his latest report on peacebuilding, the Secretary General of the UN has developed a list of problems that remain a constant in the documents produced by the international community over the last decade: lack of coordination between donors, a leadership problem within the UN family, financing gaps and numerous calls for additional funding at a time when aid is expected to shrink by 30 percent compared to 2008.[36]

The slow pace at which the international community is adapting its lessons learned may also be a reflection of two more profound and less straightforward issues; an uncertainty about the nature of the states that need to be rebuilt, and the pace at which this should be achieved.

What kind of state?

Failed states force us to reflect on the many assumptions about basic public instruments that the Global North takes for granted, such as property rights, rule of law and democracy. Whereas international donors and organizations some-times see these as basic tools to achieve statehood, alternative societies may have developed different tools to attain similar outcomes. New international powerhouses with different values and historical experience than the Global North are organizing themselves. Calling for a multipolar world, the BRIC (Brazil, Russia, India and China) held their first summit in June 2009.

Helping fragile states only if they first display good behavior in fighting cor-ruption, promoting democracy and human rights may well be an alien concept to some of the newcomers on the world stage. While the Global North is divided between partisans of additional aid and sponsors of "Trade, not Aid," China is one step ahead, developing an international barter economy whereby it develops the infrastructure of fragile states in return for access to natural resources. In 2008, China famously concluded a US$9 billion deal in the Congo (reduced to US$6 billion in 2009) that involved – in a nutshell – the trade of Congolese natu-ral resources for roads and hospitals.

Nowhere is this debate more relevant than for state building, where demo-cracy is often considered to be the silver bullet solution to stabilizing failed states, while the World Bank still argues in its 2009 World Development Report that low tariffs on trade are the recipe for national growth. Just because in the West (US and EU), wealth, low tariffs and trade barriers happen concurrently does not imply a causal link, or the direction of causality. The report does not dwell on the stark oddity characterizing the development of Eastern economies (such as China, India and the four Asian Tigers) that achieved wealth *together* with high tariffs. Although, as Eastern wealth is new, it therefore probably gives a much clearer indication on the direction of the causal link.

The Global North likes to take a high stance, but it does not practice what it preaches. It is, for instance, keen to promote democracy in countries with "unfriendly" autocratic regimes, but it remains timid about the autocracies it is supporting.[37] Sudan is branded by many members of the international community for its support to the Sudanese regime, but little is said about Chad, its neighbor with abysmal socio-economic indicators (e.g., life expectancy at birth is 58 years in Sudan and 51 in Chad, while growth is 10 percent in Sudan and 1 percent in Chad).[38] As explained by one diplomat of the Global North, "What international standards? Chad is our former colonial backyard and that is what matters to us."[39] Overall, the Global North spends 80 percent of their fragile state foreign investments on six countries, and all but one (Pakistan) are important oil exporters.

How to build strong states?

How to do things is perhaps even more difficult than knowing *what* needs to be done. Some, like Jeffrey Sachs, argue for a Big Push; others recommend sequencing (but where does one start?), and still others call for gradualism, as fragile states – it is claimed – have little absorption capacity.

Relatively little attention is devoted to the important distinction between how to *initiate* process (democratization, economic growth, etc.) and how to *sustain* it. In failed states where capacity is low and the need for reconstruction tremendous, reshaping all institutions may be more than a state can stomach, but an initial small-step strategy could end up giving a bigger bang for the buck.

A little institutional change, Dani Rodrik argues, can go a long way to jumpstart growth. The deeper and more extensive institutional reforms that are needed for longer-term development will be easier to implement in an environment of growth rather than stagnation.[40] Perhaps, just like growth, democracy does not need to be implemented as a fully-fledged package, and small institutional arrangements (not necessarily western-type institutions) can go a long way too, but the truth is we just do not know.

Notes

1 Lisa Chauvet, Paul Collier and Anke Hoeffler, "The Cost of Failing States and the Limits of Sovereignty," *WIDER Paper*, February (2007): p. 68, Joseph Hewitt, Jonathan Wikenfeld and Ted Robert Gurr, *Peace and Conflict 2008* (Boulder: Paradigm, 2008), p. 14.
2 Chauvet, Collier and Hoeffler, "The Cost of Failing States and the Limits of Sovereignty."
3 Paul Collier, Anke Hoeffler and Mans Söderbom, "On the Duration of Civil War," *Journal of Peace Research* 41, 3 (2001).
4 Nicolas Kristoff, "After Wars, Mass Rapes Persist," *New York Times*, 20 May 2009.
5 "Fragile States Strategy" (Washington, DC: USAID, 2005), "Ensuring Fragile States Are Not Left Behind" (Paris: OECD–DAC, 2007), "Failed States Index," *Foreign Policy* July (2009), Paul Collier, *The Bottom Billion: Why the Poorest Countries are Failing and What Can Be Done About it* (Oxford: Oxford University Press, 2008), William Easterly, *The White Man's Burden: Why the West's Efforts to Aid the Rest Have Done So Much Ill and So Little Good* (New York: Penguin Books, 2006), Francis Fukuyama, *State-Building: Governance and World Order in the 21st Century* (Cornell: Cornell University Press, 2004), Robert Rotberg, *When States Fail: Causes and Consequences* (Princeton: Princeton University Press, 2004).
6 Chauvet, Collier and Hoeffler, "The Cost of Failing States and the Limits of Sovereignty," Table 2.

7   "The Failed States Index," *Foreign Policy* July/August (2008).
8   Montey Marshall and Benjamin Cole, *Global Report on Conflict, Governance and State Fragility 2008* (George Mason University, 2008), National Intelligence Council, "Global Trends 2025: A Transformed World" (NIC, 2008).
9   "2007 Global Trends: Refugees, Asylum-seekers, Returnees, Internally Displaced and Stateless Persons" (Geneva: UNHCR, 2008).
10 James Murdoch and Todd Sandler, "Civil Wars and Economic Growth: Spatial Dispersion," *American Journal of Political Science* 48 (2004).
11 European Council, "To Serve Europe in a Better World: European Security Strategy" (Brussels 2003), The White House, "The National Security Strategy of the United States of America" (2002), UK Cabinet Office, "Investing in Prevention: An International Strategy to Manage Risks of Instability and Improve Crisis Response," ed. Strategy Unit (2005).
12 "Ensuring Fragile States Are Not Left Behind."
13 "Mortality in the Democratic Republic of the Congo: An Ongoing Crisis" (International Rescue Committee, 2007).
14 Caty Clement, "Agenda for Security, Development and Forest Conflict" (paper presented at the Security, Development and Forest Conflict: A Forum for Action, Brussels, 8–9 February 2006), Greenpeace, "Bassin du Congo, Forets en Sursis" (2007), World Bank, "Frequently Asked Questions," http://web.worldbank.org/WBSITE/ EXTERNAL/COUNTRIES/AFRICAEXT/CONGODEMOCRATICEXTN/0,content MDK:20779255~menuPK:2114031~pagePK:141137~piPK:141127~theSiteP K:349466,00.html.
15 Alex Beam, "The Real Money's in Piracy," *International Herald Tribune*, 21 January 2009.
16 Interviews with former ANC combatants, Kampala and Geneva, 2008.
17 Beam, "The Real Money's in Piracy," G. Luft and A. Korin, "Terrorism Goes to Sea," *Foreign Affairs* November/December (2004).
18 "Global Report on Trafficking in Persons" (Vienna: UNODC, 2009).
19 Chauvet, Collier and Hoeffler, "The Cost of Failing States and the Limits of Sovereignty," p. 17.
20 "World Drug Report" (Vienna: UNODC, 2008).
21 Cynthia J. Arnson and I. William Zartman, *Rethinking the Economics of War: The Intersection of Need, Creed, and Greed* (Baltimore: John Hopkins University Press, 2005).
22 Small Arms Survey, *Small Arms Survey 2009: Shadows of War* (Cambridge: Cambridge University Press, 2009), Table 1.27, pp. 49–50.
23 Victoria Levine and David Dollar, "The Increasing Selectivity of Foreign Aid 1984–2003" (Washington, DC: World Bank, 2004).
24 Small Arms Survey, *Small Arms Survey 2009: Shadows of War*, Figure 8.3, p. 272.
25 Caty Clement and Adam Smith, *Managing Political Complexity: Political and Managerial Challenges in United Nations Peace Operations* (New York: International Peace Institute in collaboration with the Geneva Centre for Security Policy, 2009), p. 2.
26 Paul Collier and Anke Hoeffler, "Greed and Grievance in Civil War," *Oxford Economic Papers* 56, 4 (2004), William Zartman, "Need, Creed, and Greed in Intrastate Conflict," in *Rethinking the Economics of War. The Intersection of Need, Creed, and Greed*, eds. Cynthia J. Arnson and I. William Zartman (Baltimore: John Hopkins University Press, 2005).
27 www.un.org/NewLinks/dpi-2341.pdf
28 Caty Clement, "Failing States, Failing Data: The Case for QCA" (paper presented at the American Political Science Association, Washington, DC, 1 September 2005).
29 www.oecd.org/document/12/0,3343,en_2649_33693550_42113676_1_1_1_1,00. html.

30 Jeffrey Herbst, "Let Them Fail," in *When States Fail*, ed. Robert Rotberg (Princeton: Princeton University Press, 2004), Edward Luttwak, "Give War A Chance," *Foreign Affairs* July (1999).
31 Human Security Report, "War and Peace in the 21st Century" (University of British Columbia, 2005), Monica Toft, "Peace Through Security: Making Negotiated Settlements Stick," *Discussion Paper Harvard University* (2006).
32 Simeon Djankov, Jose Montalvo and Marta Reynal-Querol, "The Curse of Aid," *Journal of Economic Growth* 13, 3 (2006), Dambisa Moyo, *Dead Aid* (London: Penguin, 2009), Jeffrey Sachs, *The End of Poverty* (New York: Penguin, 2005).
33 Five countries exceeded 0.7 percent of GNI: Denmark, Luxembourg, the Netherlands, Norway and Sweden. www.oecd.org/document/35/0,3343,en_2649_34447_42458595 _1_1_1_1,00.html.
34 Bernadette Graves, "Enjeux de Stabilité: Vers l'Emancipation Sécuritaire" (paper presented at the French Ministry of Defence Conference, Paris, 21 January 2009).
35 Stimson Center, "UN Peacebuilding Commission," www.stimson.org/fopo/pdf/UN_ PBC_Fact_Sheet_Jun_07.pdf.
36 United Nations, "Report of the Secretary-General on Peacebuilding in the Immediate Aftermath of Conflict," ed. A/63/881–S/2009/304 (New York, 2009).
37 Thomas Carothers, "How Democracies Emerge: The Sequencing Fallacy," *Journal of Democracy* 18, 1 (2007).
38 *World Bank Development Indicators 2008.*
39 Interview with French Diplomat, November 2008 and Carothers, "How Democracies Emerge."
40 Dani Rodrik, *One Economics, Many Recipes: Globalization, Institutions and Economic Growth* (Princeton: Princeton University Press, 2007).

5 How energy and climate change may pose a threat to sustainable security

Tapani Vaahtoranta

The energy–climate era

We are living in the energy–climate era. It has become evident that global trends in energy supply and consumption and the impact of our reliance on fossil fuels on the climate are unsustainable.[1] Coal, oil and natural gas have long been crucial for the economic well-being of humanity. What is new is the geographical spread of industrial development, which has led to an increase in global demand for energy. Today, there are more main consumers of energy than ever before. At the same time, energy production is concentrating in fewer countries due to peak oil in old producers. Thus there is concern about energy security. Another concern is about the impact of the use of fossil fuels on the global climate. Human-induced climate change is real and its single most important cause is the concentration of carbon dioxide emissions in the atmosphere caused by the combustion of coal, oil and gas.

The global economic crisis does not change the big picture. The increase in energy demand and greenhouse gas emissions is likely to resume when the recession is over.

Energy security and climate change can also have consequences for security. One of the strongest expressions of this concern is the National Security Strategy of the United Kingdom,[2] which observes that the growing global demand for energy is likely to increase competition for energy supplies with potentially serious security implications. The strategy finds it problematic that the supply of oil and gas becomes increasingly concentrated in potentially instable regions. Besides, it also identifies climate change as potentially the greatest challenge to global stability and security, and therefore to national security. It emphasizes that tackling causes of climate change and adapting to its consequences are critical to our future security, as well as to protecting global prosperity and avoiding humanitarian disaster.

But what does it mean that energy and climate change may have implications for security? Any discussion of security also requires a definition of the concept. In particular, one needs to determine whether one is using a broad or narrow understanding of security. The very narrow definition of security focuses on armed conflict. For example, competition for oil has caused inter-state war in the past. Barack Obama, who lived as a child in Jakarta, writes in his book on how Japan – after the attack on Pearl Harbor – moved to take over the Dutch East Indies (today's Indonesia) because of its oil reserves.[3] A number of other wars and violent conflicts in the twentieth century are also attributed to the competition for energy resources.[4] The most recent example of an inter-state war, where oil was a major factor, is Iraq's invasion of Kuwait in 1990. According to a UNEP study, at least 18 violent intrastate conflicts have been fuelled by the exploitation of natural resources since 1990. Oil and natural gas were, or are, present in five of them.[5] Climate change, too, is assumed to have the potential to cause inter-state war. A report to the Pentagon in 2003[6] raised the possibility of abrupt climate change that would create such severe scarcities of resources that they would lead to wars over food, water and energy. There is more recent concern about regional abundance of oil and gas. As the Arctic ice cap melts as a result of global warming, oil and gas reserves in the seabed become accessible. It is feared – especially by the press – that this development, together with the opening up of new sea routes, could trigger new geopolitical competition in the High North and possibly even lead to violent conflict between the coastal states.

However, to draw a parallel between security and the war caused by competition for energy or climate change is impractical for two reasons. First, despite the dire warnings, the likelihood that a struggle to grab energy reserves or climate-induced water scarcity and migration would become a main cause of war seems small.[7] Second, even if energy and climate change did not cause war, they are likely to have other adverse consequences that can be regarded as security threats.

To come to grips with the security implications of energy and climate change, a definition is needed that is broader than inter-state war, but also one that avoids excess expansion of the concept. If the term "security" is broadened too much, there is a danger of labeling any problem as "insecurity."[8] There is also the need to make a distinction between energy security and the implications of energy for security. Any disruption in the supply of energy at an affordable price, for example, is not a threat to national security. Energy may also have security implications other than those that are directly linked to the security of supply. Thus energy and security is at the same time a narrower and broader concept than energy security. Clarity is also needed in discussion about the consequences of climate change. The concept of "climate security" is today used with little agreement as to what the term actually means.

The view adopted here is that the reliance on fossil fuels and climate change may adversely impact on "sustainable security."[9] The concept of sustainable security combines national security, human security and collective security. National security refers to the safety of the state. Both in Europe and the United States, there is considerable concern about the potential national-security implications of dependence on foreign gas and oil. The sea-level rise caused by climate change poses an existential threat to low-lying island nations. The concept of human security draws attention to the well-being and safety of the individual. Climate change may already be killing people, particularly those in poor countries. By using the term "collective security," however, one refers to the entire world. The need to prevent dangerous geopolitical competition for oil and gas or runaway climate change belongs to this category of sustainable security. National security, human security and collective security are intertwined. Measures to strengthen the energy security of one state may have adverse consequences for collective security. A failure to tackle climate change would cause wide-spread human suffering in the developing world, which could result in state failures.

On the following pages, five challenges for sustainable security posed by energy and climate change are discussed. First, the geopolitical implications of energy security are addressed. Second, the concern about hostile policies of energy producers is considered. Third is the implications of the resource curse for weak states, fourth are the difficulties in adapting to the consequences of inevitable climate change and the fifth challenge is the prospect of runaway climate change.

Energy security trends

The concern about the security implications of oil is not new. In the United States, Richard Nixon articulated the goal of energy independence after the Arab countries had proclaimed the oil embargo in 1973. In the aftermath of the Iranian revolution in 1979, Jimmy Carter referred to the intolerable dependence on foreign oil, which he said threatened US economic independence and the very security of the nation. The implications of oil were again high on the agenda during the Persian Gulf War of 1990–1991.

Now, fears of oil shortages are back. This time the cause is not any particular event in the oil-producing Middle East, but the substantial increase in the world's demand for oil. This is the result of the rapid economic growth in populous developing countries, particularly in China and India. China was still self-sufficient in oil in 1993. Today, it imports almost half of its total consumption. India's demand for oil is also increasing rapidly. While in the 1970s North America consumed twice the amount of oil as Asia did, Asian oil consumption has now exceeded that of North America. Although the world is not running out of oil, this rapidly increased demand for it has caused anxiety about energy security in the United Sates and other importing countries.[10]

The International Energy Agency projects[11] that, without major changes, world energy demand will grow 40 percent by 2030, with China and India to account for about half the increase. Oil remains the dominant fuel, although demand for coal is rising faster than demands for other fuels. Oil production has already peaked in some non-Organization of the Petroleum Exporting Countries (OPEC) countries and will peak in most others before 2030. As a consequence, most of the increase in world oil output is expected to come from OPEC countries, with Saudi Arabia remaining the world's largest producer. Production of natural gas is also becoming more concentrated in the most resource-rich countries. About half of current gas production comes from the Middle East. Most of the remaining increase is provided by the former Soviet Union and Africa. Three countries – Russia, Iran and Qatar – hold more than half of the world's gas reserves.

It is the increasing demand caused by the emergence of new main consumers and the fact that the growth in supplies will come from fewer countries than before that have heightened concerns about energy security and its implications for sustainable security. Oil is the main issue in the United States. In Europe, the main anxiety is about natural gas and its dependence on imports from Russia.

Energy as a security threat

Geopolitics of oil and gas

With regard to collective security, the rise of the new big consumers of energy and the concentration of oil and gas reserves in fewer countries have accentuated concerns about the implications of energy. There are two main worries. One is that the dependence of consumers on the same energy reserves leads to dangerous geopolitical competition, and perhaps even war, over access to oil and gas. Also, the more geographically concentrated energy reserves become, the more attention is paid to the stability of energy-rich regions and to the safety of transportation routes.

The American intelligence community[12] regards as likely the following policies of "new" energy players. Russia is believed to be determined to keep Central Asian countries within its sphere in order to control Caspian-area natural gas. China would continue looking for access to oil and gas around the world, and its ties with Saudi Arabia may get stronger. Because of its large oil and gas reserves, Iran may be able to have closer ties with China or Russia. India is assumed to be taking measures to get access to energy in Myanmar, Iran and Central Asia. These developments would constrain the ability of the United States, and Europe, to pursue their interests in these regions and diminish the leverage of the United States, particularly in the Middle East and Central Asia.[13] It has long been the policy of the United States to make sure that it and its allies have access to the energy in the Middle East. This policy is now complicated by the increasing presence of the Asian powers. Looking at the issue from another perspective, the newcomers' growing presence can also be welcomed as a way to balance against the interests and influence of the United States and Europe. But, though these trends imply geopolitical change, there is no necessity that they trigger dangerous competition between Great Powers and become a source of collective insecurity. As Daniel Yergin puts it, "[c]ommercial competition need not turn into national rivalry."[14] It all depends on how Great Powers perceive their interests and manage their relations.

As the world's energy security depends on a smaller number of oil and gas producers, the stability of the regions having the main reserves and the safety of related transportation infrastructure becomes increasingly important. The situation in the Persian Gulf will remain crucial due to its huge reserves. The Strait of Hormuz is particularly important because a large fraction of the world's oil is transported through it. Other strategic choke points are the Suez Canal, the Bosporus Strait, Bab el-Mandeb, the strait that connects the Red Sea and the Gulf of Aden, and the Strait of Malacca. These regional issues have collective security implications if Great Powers decide to use military force to secure the flow of energy, as was the case in the Gulf War.

Much depends on the policies of the United States and China. They rely increasingly on the same oil reserves and compete for influence. On the one hand, there are concerns on both sides about the aims of the other. There are those in the United States who see China as trying to exclude the US and Europe from new oil and gas supplies. Some in Beijing fear that the United States might someday cut China's foreign energy supplies. On the other hand, the United States and China share an interest in supporting stable global energy production at an affordable price. It is in the interest of both countries to maintain stability in the Middle East and to secure the transportation routes. The key is to build on these common interests to avoid zero-sum thinking and engage China in the global energy economy.[15] In fact, China's resource policy may already be becoming a more cooperative and market-based one.[16]

Political leverage

While "collective security" refers to several countries or the international community as a whole, the focus of national security is on the key interests of individual states. With regard to energy, the main issue is the dependence of the importer on the producer and the possibility that the producer uses this asymmetrical relationship to carry out policies that are detrimental to the security interests of the importer. This concern has been particularly widespread in the United States. Oil revenues are seen in Washington to have emboldened the anti-American rulers of Venezuela and Iran, and Russia is often claimed to use its gas supplies as a political weapon. The paradox is that the US and other energy importers finance these "dangerous regimes" by buying their oil and gas.[17]

The root cause of the concern is that energy revenues not only enrich producers but also seem to make many of them more authoritarian and hostile. This is the petropolitics thesis, which has been popularized by Thomas Friedman.[18] According to the thesis, there is a correlation between the price of energy and democracy. The higher the price, the more democracy is eroded in "petrolist" states, and the more assertive their foreign policies become. The explanation is that when the price of oil and gas are high, energy-rich regimes do not have to tax their citizens and, consequently, do not have to listen to them. Energy wealth also gives these regimes the possibility of patronage spending, which dampens pressures for democratization. In their foreign policies, petrolist states tend to become increasingly self-assertive, not caring about what others say or think about them. It is this domestic political development, and its impact on foreign policy behavior, that generate many of the security fears of importers.

In Europe, the concern is about Russia. Europe buys a quarter of its gas from Russia and Europe's demand for gas is increasing. One cause of the worry is that Russia may not be able to provide all the gas that Europe needs. There is also the concern that Russia uses Europe's gas dependence to pursue its political interests.

Few would deny that Moscow's quest for regaining its Great Power status is based on its energy reserves, and that in order to secure the future demand for its gas, Russia aims to control transit routes and buy upstream Central Asian gas and downstream assets in Europe.[19] It is more difficult to determine, however, to what extent Russia is using its energy as a means to increase its political influence in the post-Soviet space[20] or to submit the foreign policies of European governments to Russian interests.[21] Some of Russia's measures – and the measures of its state-owned energy companies – seem to have clear political motives. Cutting oil supplies to the Czech Republic one day after Prague had signed an agreement with the United States regarding the stationing of an anti-missile radar station on its territory is one example. But the economic motive also plays a role in Russian behavior. Why should Russia sell gas to Ukraine at a cheaper price than to EU member countries? Whatever the relative importance of the different motives of Russian policy on energy, the key issue is that, due to its recent heavy-handed treatment of Ukraine and Georgia, as well as its authoritarian development, Europeans find it more difficult to trust reassurances from Russia that it is pursuing purely economic interests.

Current low-energy prices are hoped to impact on the development and behavior of petrolist states, but high prices are likely to return once the recession is over. Thus the solution to the problem posed by Russia or Venezuela is not the inevitable impoverishment and subsequent democratization and pacification of these countries. Rather, the solution is to reduce the dependence on problematic producers and to create more symmetrical relationships with them. As an example, on the website of the White House, the Obama administration sets as its goal curbing US dependence on foreign oil. In Europe, the focus is on diversifying energy supplies as a means to reducing dependence on Russia. One way of accomplishing this is to build pipelines that bypass Russia. The Baku–Tblisi–Ceyhan pipeline already transports Central Asian oil through Azerbaijan, Georgia and Turkey. The Nabucco pipeline, if built, would transport natural gas through Turkey to Europe. A more far-reaching plan is to diversify the EU's energy supply by increasing the use of renewable energy, such as the solar power to be generated in the North African desert. However, there is no immediate way of reducing Europe's gas dependence on Russia.

Resource curse

While the regimes in petrolist states can use energy revenues to promote social stability and increase national power, the problem in many poor energy-producing countries is that the abundance of oil and gas and energy revenues does not improve the social and economic conditions of their people. Paul Collier calls this phenomenon the "natural resource trap," which is also one of his four main reasons why poor countries are not able to get out of poverty.[22] A common feature in these countries – namely their dependence on energy and other natural resource exports – tends to undermine other export sectors of the economy, leading to a malfunctioning democracy. In low-income countries with weak governance, this "resource curse" tends to result in the misuse of opportunities and so they fail to grow. Human security is at stake, particularly because poverty makes a country prone to civil war.[23] If the resource curse leads to violent conflict or state failure in developing countries, it can also have wider implications for collective security.

The way to manage this problem is to improve national governance. A stronger and more accountable government helps to ensure that energy resources are used to promote positive societal development and human security. Particularly important is the improvement of transparency about the use of energy revenues.

In this case, too, China is an issue. Attention has been paid to the implications for problematic regimes engaged by China in its search for energy, especially the one in Sudan. The concern is that without China's support for the Sudanese government and China's policy of non-involvement in the domestic affairs of the host governments, the regime in Khartoum would not survive and the killing in Darfur might come to an end. The Chinese are also accused of undercutting Western efforts to force the Angolan government to introduce political reforms. While China's influence is limited in Angola since Chinese Sinopec is just one of the foreign oil companies doing business there, China's role and responsibility in Sudan is bigger. However, and although the jury is still out on the topic, China seems to be changing its policy and it may also be becoming more willing to put pressure on the Sudanese government.[24]

Climate change as a security threat

Climate change emerged as a major international issue at the end of the 1980s due to heat waves and drought, and led to the creation of the International Panel on Climate Change (IPCC) and the first international climate treaty in 1992. It drew more attention again as a result of the heat wave in Europe in 2003 and Hurricane Katrina in the United States in 2005. After the Fourth Assessment Report of the IPCC,[25] there is no longer doubt that human-induced climate change is happening, and that immediate, large-scale mitigation is required to prevent climate change from getting beyond the reach of human action. Regardless of the potential success in reducing emissions, some climate change is inevitable due to the presence of greenhouse gases (GHGs) already in the atmosphere, and because of ongoing energy consumption and emissions that continue to increase. Thus, there is need to both mitigate emissions and adapt to the consequences of climate change.

Our understanding of climate change has evolved quickly. The direct physical consequences of climate change are rather well-known. Besides heat waves, climate change also causes scarcity of natural resources, such as fresh water and arable land, and low-lying coastal flooding. The more the temperature increases, the more severe these direct consequences are projected to become. The Stern Review added economic considerations to the view of scientists by arguing that the cost of the measures taken now to mitigate climate change will be manageable, but lack of action adds to the risk of severe economic consequences in the future. In any case, new energy technologies and changes in human behavior are needed to sufficiently curb energy use and GHG emissions.

A more recent development is the growing sense that climate change is also a security issue. In 2007, the UN Security Council debated climate change for the first time, with several countries agreeing there is a link between global warming and security. The UN General Assembly adopted a draft resolution in May 2009, saying that it was "deeply concerned" that the adverse impacts of climate change could have possible security implications.[26] The European Union sees climate change as a "threat multiplier" which includes "political and security risks that directly affect European interests."[27] Scientists are calling on governments to take actions in averting "catastrophic"[28] and "dangerous and irreversible"[29] climate change. In addition to the UK National Security Strategy, the Annual Threat Assessment by the American Intelligence Community states that, although climate change is not traditionally viewed as a threat to US national security, it could threaten domestic stability in some states and it affects lives, property and other security interests in the United States.[30]

Climate change does not only directly impact on security, for example by producing stronger storms, but it is also suggested that global warming may pose a more traditional security threat. Many see climate change as one of the drivers of the Darfur conflict, and it is warned that the melting of the ice cap in the Arctic is creating competition for hydrocarbons that may lead to "armed brinkmanship" among the coastal states.[31] Symptoms of this concern about "climate war" include a study which states that there have been significant correlations between war frequencies and temperature changes in the past.[32] This concern is an example of the potential consequences of the consequences[33] of climate change. While human action causes climate change that has direct physical consequences, the societal consequences of these consequences are shaped by the human reaction to the physical changes.

The security consequences of climate change are still more potential than real. However, it is evident that the direct consequences of climate change can pose a threat to human security. The heat wave in 2003 in France and Central Europe killed 35,000 elderly people. Even though we do not know for sure whether this was caused by global warming, the temperature of 2003 is projected to be the *average* summer temperature in Europe in 2040. More recently, wildfires killed over 200 people in Australia in February 2009. According to some scientists, global warming likely contributed to the record heat wave that fueled the disaster. Diseases, storms and other direct consequences of climate change also pose threats to human life. Notably, it is estimated that five million years of life were lost in the world in 2000 because of climate-change-caused deaths. However, climate change is not the main killer; 30 million years of life were lost due to alcohol, tobacco caused the loss of 50 million years of life, and the main killer – childhood and maternal malnutrition – caused the loss of 200 millions of years of life.[34] The situation is likely to change. The World Health Organization, for example, has predicted that the number of deaths linked to climate change would exceed 300,000 a year by 2030.[35] The Global Humanitarian Forum estimates in its report of 2009 that the number of deaths could be nearly twice this number by 2030.[36]

As to the consequences of consequences, climate change will exacerbate the scarcity of natural resources and ecosystem services, which, in turn, may lead to competition for scarce resources and cause people to migrate to other regions and countries. Both such consequences may contribute to armed conflict. Climate change may also weaken state institutions and their ability to prevent violent conflict.[37] Nevertheless, climate change is unlikely to be the sole cause of armed conflict. Its effects will be felt in association with socio-economic factors and much depends on the ability of the state to manage the consequences of climate change. Research to date has failed to find any significant statistical association between resource scarcity and civil war,[38] but this linkage may become more visible when the global temperature rises. A common understanding is that climate-induced conflicts are most likely in the poorest countries.

There is also the possibility that, instead of the projected gradual warming, increasing emissions take the planet beyond its tipping points and cause an abrupt change of climate. However, scientists who share concern about the implications of human-induced climate change do not have any consensus on whether the global environment is nearing such thresholds at which climate change would suddenly become unstoppable.[39] It is at least equally as difficult to agree on the exact security consequences of runaway climate change since "nonlinear climate change will produce nonlinear political events."[40]

Three groups of states on the Kuznets curve

To manage the security implications of climate change, both mitigation and adaptation are necessary. The point here is that the political challenges posed by such management depend on the level of economic development. The view is illustrated in Figure 5.1.

The figure is based on the *IPAT* equation, according to which adverse environmental impact (I) is the result of the size of population (P), affluence (A) and the technologies (T) used to transform natural resources into economic well-being. Both the number of humans and their affluence have rapidly increased since the beginning of the industrial era. In 1800, there were about one billion people. Since then the world's population has grown to over six billion. By 2050 there will be more than nine billion people on earth. Affluence has increased even more rapidly. The GDP of the global economy is today about 70 times bigger than 200 years ago. The third factor is the technology that causes humanity to rely on fossil fuels as its main energy source. To produce and sustain the current level of affluence, primary energy use has increased 35-fold from

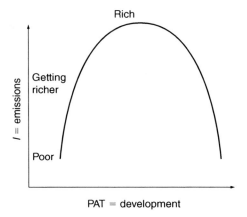

Figure 5.1 Kuznets curve illustrated.

1800–2000.[41] The *IPAT* equation illustrates the importance of technological development for the mitigation of climate change. Without new energy technologies and low-carbon growth, it is difficult to see how emissions can be cut to avoid abrupt climate change.

The idea of the environmental Kuznets curve is that the adverse environmental impact does not remain the same at all levels of economic development. According to its optimistic assumption, reducing adverse environmental impact, for example by cutting emissions, is possible as a result of further economic and technological development. The logic is as follows. Prior to industrial development, the human impact on the environment is local rather than regional or global. When economic development takes off, little weight is given at first to environmental consequences, since the main focus is on economic gain and satisfying basic needs. As a result, environmental degradation tends to increase with the first phases of industrialization. Population also grows rapidly due to a decreasing rate of mortality. But after a certain level of development has been reached, and physical needs have been met, an interest in a clean environment is likely to emerge, and reversing the trend of environmental damage should become possible. Affluent people have the willingness to protect the environment, as well as the financial and technological means to do it. At the same time, the subsequent decline in fertility completes the demographic transition and leads to a slowdown of population growth.

The way the industrialized world has first caused and then solved many of its environmental problems, like the acid rain caused by sulfur and nitrogen emissions, conforms to the Kuznets curve. The key question now is whether this change for the better will also happen in the case of greenhouse gas emissions, and whether it will happen fast enough to avoid runaway climate change.

Managing the security implications of climate change poses a difficult challenge because greenhouse gas emissions are the very product of the industrial era; its population and economic growth and the use of fossil fuels. Major changes in these fields are difficult to achieve quickly, making the mitigation of climate change a much more demanding task than, for example, the prevention of ozone depletion. The task is made even more difficult by the fact that states are at different levels of industrial development and, consequently, have different responsibilities for current and future greenhouse gas emissions, different economic interests and abilities to tackle the problem, and different adaptation capabilities. Although there is agreement about the need to act on climate change, it is more difficult to agree on who should do what. There are three main groups of states: rich industrialized nations, emerging economies that are getting more affluent and poor developing countries. Each group represents a particular challenge. Poor countries will have difficulties in adapting to the consequences of climate change; curbing climate change does not succeed if emerging economies do not start mitigating the growth of their emissions; and developed countries, having caused the current climate change, should be able to guide humanity out of the predicament.

Poor countries and the challenge of adaptation

Ugandan President Yoweri Museveni once said that "climate change is an act of aggression by the rich against the poor."[42] He had good reasons for being unhappy about climate change, which is caused by other states but will hit least-developed countries the hardest. Due to their dependence on rain-fed agriculture for livelihood and their weak ability to adapt to the consequences of global warming, climate change is becoming a problem-amplifier in poor countries, making their existing problems more difficult to solve and perhaps even contributing to violent conflict.

Adapting to changing climatic conditions has always played a role in the developing world, but the rate and scope of change caused by climate change will be so great that the capacity of poor countries to adapt will be seriously tested. Africa may be the hardest hit. The IPCC projects[43] that tens of millions of Africans will be exposed to increased water stress, agricultural production will be severely compromised in many African countries, sea-level rise will affect low-lying coastal areas with large populations, and arid and semi-arid areas will increase. Climate change may also interact with socio-economic and political factors and aggravate the conditions that cause social tension and conflict. A joint paper by the EU Commission and the Secretary-General/High Representative[44] summarizes the common understanding of the potential causal linkage between climate change and armed conflict, and repeats the assumption that Africa is particularly vulnerable because of its multiple stresses and low adaptive capacity. According to the EU, climate change is expected to increase the scarcity of resources in many parts of Africa and, as a consequence, migration is likely to intensify in areas under strong demographic pressure. If these changes take place in countries with governments that are unable or unwilling to meet the needs of their populations, or to provide protection in the face of climate change-induced hardship, the outcome can be frustration, tension between ethnic and religious groups, and destabilization of countries and entire regions.

Resource scarcity in poor countries is a critical issue. The pie metaphor provides a useful illustration of the challenge. In many poor countries the pie is already too small. Rapid population growth is aggravating the problem by increasing the number of people eating the pie. Although there has been no global population explosion, the population of the developing world is still growing rapidly. The world population is expected to increase by 50 percent by the middle of this century, with 95 percent of that growth occurring in poor countries. Climate change is a problem-amplifier since it will increase resource scarcities and therefore threatens to reduce the size of the pie even further.

The frustration of the Ugandan president is understandable since there is no easy way out. Poverty reduction would strengthen the ability of the least-developed countries to adapt to climate change. However, despite all the international effort, the poor countries are still poor, and climate change is making it even harder to reach the Millennium Development Goals.[45] The question is, how can poverty be reduced without the economic growth that causes more greenhouse gas emissions?[46] If low-carbon growth is not made possible, poor countries would follow the development pattern of the industrialized world and emerging economies, which would make it even more difficult to curb climate change. To achieve growth that reduces poverty and does not damage the global climate, poor countries need financial and technological assistance. But giving massive new aid is difficult, especially while the developed world is in recession.

Emerging economies and the challenge of mitigation

The challenge posed by emerging economies is mitigation. Although countries like China and India start experiencing the negative impacts of climate change as the temperature keeps increasing, their top priority is continuous economic growth to further reduce poverty. A member of the Indian delegation to the UN climate conference in Bonn in April 2009 said that India will not take on binding emission reduction commitments: "It is morally wrong for us to agree to reduce when 40 per cent of Indians do not have access to electricity."[47]

Emerging economies have been growing fast, and China is the country that has managed to raise more people out of poverty than any other country in the world. This is not good news for climate-change mitigation, however, since China's greenhouse gas emissions have rapidly increased at the same time. Although developed countries are responsible for most industrial emissions thus far, the rest of the world already emits half of GHGs. The Chinese themselves recognize the message of the Kuznets curve when they acknowledge that China is on the upward curve of industrialization and therefore its demand for energy will grow. Such growth is partly attributable to the fact that China is nine-times less energy efficient than Japan.

Their big populations make the situation in emerging economies different from that of many developed countries. Even if the average Indian or Chinese causes much less GHGs than the average American or European, China and India's share of global emissions is significant and growing rapidly due to their large populations. According to some estimates, China is already the biggest source of carbon dioxide emissions. India, too, is among the main emitters. It has been calculated that, soon after 2025, cumulative carbon dioxide emissions from the South would exceed those from the North. Thus, even if developed nations eliminated all of their emissions immediately, cumulative emissions from the rest of the world are estimated to be adequate for pushing us over the threshold of dangerous climate change.[48]

Obviously, it is insufficient to only "hope you won't make the same mistakes we made," as Hillary Clinton told her hosts on her first visit to China as Secretary of State.[49] What is needed is to find means to persuade China and other emerging economies to start limiting their emissions. The task is different from that of assisting poor countries. It is possible in the developed world to suggest giving massive economic aid to poor countries to strengthen their capacities to adapt to climate change. It is politically more difficult to claim that industrialized countries should help China and India move to the low-carbon phase of development. The reason is the growing number of rich people in emerging economies and the fact that their increasing emissions are linked to their growing power and the move toward a multipolar world. More reciprocity is necessary between industrialized nations and emerging economies than between the rich and poor countries.

Rich countries and the challenge of transition

Europe, the United States and Japan have gone through industrialization, become affluent service economies, and are responsible for the bulk of the industrial greenhouse gases now in the atmosphere. Besides their moral responsibility for climate change, they also have reasons for being concerned about its impact. With regard to Europe, global warming will make Southern Europe hotter and drier. The indirect consequences of climate change are also cause for concern. As a result of the impact of climate change on Africa and the Middle East, migratory pressure on Europe is expected to increase, and Europe's energy supplies may be disturbed. Still, Europe will be better equipped to adapt to these consequences than many other parts of the world. Essentially, the aim of the European Union is to play the leadership role in post-2012 diplomacy and be an example for the rest of the world in showing the way to a low-carbon economy.

Europe's climate-change policy can be explained with the help of the Kuznets curve. Europe has reached the stage in its development where it has the willingness to start cutting the emissions that cause global warming. Europe also has the money and technological means to reach the reduction targets. However, Europe will not be able to prevent runaway climate change by just cutting its own emissions. Due to the size of its population and the growth of other economies, Europe's share of the global emissions is just 14 percent and declining.

Now that the US policy on global warming has changed, the whole industrialized world is planning to make deep cuts in its emissions. By reaching its targets, the industrialized world would show that the transition to low-carbon and low-emission growth is possible. But this is no longer sufficient. Industrialized nations still face the challenge of finding ways to move emerging economies onto a low-carbon path and help poor countries adapt to climate change.

Sustainable future

Our current way of using energy is unsustainable. Fossil fuel reserves are finite and climate change is becoming more severe. Competition for oil and gas and the adverse consequences of high energy revenues pose threats to sustainable security. So does global warming, particularly with regard to runaway climate change. Good governance is needed both at the national and international level to minimize the adverse impacts of energy and climate change, and to avert armed conflicts. The only long-term solution is the decarbonization of the world's energy sources. The global economic crisis offers an opportunity for change. If the ensuing recovery is built on the development of clean technologies, and if states agree to cut their emissions, the worst predictions should not come true. In this respect, much depends on the United States and China. Their leaders must be able to guide humanity onto the downward part of the Kuznets curve.

Notes

1 International Energy Agency, "World Energy Outlook 2008: Executive Summary" (Paris: OECD/IEA, 2008), p. 3.
2 "The National Security Strategy of the United Kingdom: Security in an Interdependent World" (Cabinet Office, 2008), pp. 18–19.
3 Barack Obama, *The Audacity of Hope: Thoughts on Reclaiming the American Dream* (New York: Three Rivers Press, 2006), p. 272.
4 Arthur M. Westing, "Environmental Factors in Strategic Policy and Action: An Overview," in *Global Resources and International Conflict: Environmental Factors in Strategic Policy and Action*, ed. Arthur M. Westing (Oxford: Oxford University Press, 1986), p. 12.
5 UNEP, "From Conflict to Peacebuilding – the Role of Natural Resources and the Environment" (United Nations Environment Program, 2009), pp. 8–11.
6 Peter Schwartz and Doug Randall, "An Abrupt Climate Change Scenario and Its Implications for United States National Security" (Global Business Network, 2003).
7 For this argument, see David G. Victor, "What Resource Wars?," *The National Interest Online* November/December, 92 (2007).
8 Nils Petter Gleditsch, "Environmental Change, Security, and Conflict," in *Leashing the Dogs of War: Conflict Management in a Divided World*, eds. Chester A. Crocker, Fen Osler Hampson and Pamela R. Aall (Washington, DC: US Institute of Peace Press, 2007), p. 178.
9 Gayle Smith, "In Search of Sustainable Security," in *The Sustainable Security Series* (Center for American Progress, 2008).
10 Daniel Yergin, "Ensuring Energy Security," *Foreign Affairs* 85, 2 (2006): pp. 3–6.
11 International Energy Agency, "World Energy Outlook 2009", Executive Summary (Paris: OECD/IEA, 2009), p. 4.

12 National Intelligence Council, "Global Trends 2025: A Transformed World" (NIC, 2008), p. 51. Available at: www.dni.gov/nic/NIC_2025_project.html.
13 Council on Foreign Relations, "Task Force Report, National Security Consequences of U.S. Oil Dependency" (2006), pp. 26–27.
14 Daniel Yergin, "Energy under Stress," in *The Global Politics of Energy*, eds. Kurt M. Campbell and Jonathon Price (Washington, DC: The Aspen Institute, 2008), p. 40.
15 See, for example, Council on Foreign Relations, "National Security Consequences of U.S. Oil Dependency," p. 56.
16 Victor, "What Resource Wars?," pp. 2–3.
17 Richard G. Lugar, "Raise the Gas Tax: A Revenue-Neutral Way to Treat Our Oil Addiction," *Washington Post*, 1 February 2009.
18 Thomas L. Friedman, *Hot, Flat, and Crowded* (New York: Farrar, Straus & Giroux, 2008), pp. 93–104.
19 Angela Stent, "An Energy Superpower? Russia and Europe," in *The Global Politics of Energy*, eds. Kurt M. Campbell and Jonathon Price (Washington, DC: The Aspen Institute, 2008), pp. 77–79.
20 Keith C. Smith, "Russia and European Security: Divide and Dominate" (Center for Strategic and International Studies, 2008).
21 Stent, "An Energy Superpower?," p. 81.
22 Paul Collier, *The Bottom Billion: Why the Poorest Countries are Failing and What Can Be Done About it* (Oxford: Oxford University Press, 2008), pp. 38–52.
23 Collier, *The Bottom Billion*, pp. 20–21.
24 Henry Lee and Dan Shalmon, "Searching for Oil: China's Oil Strategies in Africa," in *China into Africa: Trade, Aid, and Influence*, ed. Robert I. Rotberg (Washington, DC: Brookings Institution Press, 2008), pp. 109–136. Also, Lydia Polgreen, "As Chinese Investments in Africa Drop, Hope Sinks," *The New York Times*, 25 March 2009.
25 According to the Fourth Assessment Report, warming of the climate is unequivocal and most of the observed increase in global average temperatures since the mid-twentieth century is very likely due to the observed increase in anthropogenic GHG concentrations. The Report also warned that anthropogenic warming could lead to some impacts that are abrupt or irreversible, depending upon the rate and magnitude of the climate change. Available at: www.ipcc.ch/ipccreports/assessments-reports.htm
26 Available at: www.un.org/ga/search/view_doc.asp?symbol=a%2F63%2FL.8%2FRev.1&Lang=E
27 Paper from the High Representative and the European Commission to the European Council, "Climate Change and International Security" (S113/08, 2008), p. 2.
28 Dan Glaister and James Randerson, "Act on Climate Change, Top Scientists Warn US," *Guardian*, 30 May 2008.
29 Ian Sample, "Climate Change: Carbon Capture from Power Stations Must Start Soon, Say Scientists," *Guardian*, 10 June 2008.
30 Dennis C. Blair, "Annual Threat Assessment of the Intelligence Community for the Senate Select Committee on Intelligence" (National Intelligence Council, 2009), pp. 41–43.
31 Scott G. Borgerson, "Arctic Meltdown: The Economic and Security Implications of Global Warming," *Foreign Affairs* 85, 2 (2008): pp. 63–77.
32 David D. Zhang *et al.*, "Global Climate Change, War, and Population Decline in Recent Human History," *Proceedings of the National Academy of Sciences (PNAS)* 104, 49 (2007): pp. 19214–19219.
33 Dan Smith and Janani Vivekananda, "A Climate of Conflict: The Links Between Climate Change, Peace and War," *International Alert* (2007): p. 3.
34 John P. Holdren, "Science and Technology for Sustainable Well-Being," *Science* 319, 5862 (2008): p. 425.

35 John Podesta and Peter Ogden, "Security Implications of Climate Scenario 1: Expected Climate Change over the Next Thirty Years," in *Climatic Cataclysm: The Foreign Policy and National Security Implications of Climate Change*, ed. Kurt M. Campbell (Washington, DC: Brookings Institution Press, 2008), p. 107.

36 The report is available at: www.ghf-ge.org/programmes/human_impact_report/index.cfm.

37 The special issue of *Political Geography* 26 (August 2007) contains analysis of the linkage between climate change and violent conflict.

38 Halvard Buhaug, Nils Petter Gleditsch and Ole Magnus Theisen, "Implications of Climate Change for Armed Conflict," *Paper Presented to World Bank Workshop on Social Dimensions of Climate Change* (2009).

39 Andrew C. Revkin, "Among Climate Scientists, A Dispute over 'Tipping Points'," *New York Times*, 28 March 2009.

40 Leon Fuerth, "Security Implications of Climate Scenario 2: Severe Climate Change over the Next Thirty Years," in *Climatic Cataclysm: The Foreign Policy and National Security Implications of Climate Change*, ed. Kurt M. Campbell (Washington, DC: Brookings Institution Press, 2008), p. 135.

41 Nebojsa Nakicenovic, *The Changing World: Energy, Climate and Social Futures* (Vienna: IIASA Conference '07 on Global Development, 2007), Podcast presentation. See also, John McNeill, *Something New Under the Sun: An Environmental History of the Twentieth-Century World* (London: Penguin Books, 2000), pp. 3–17.

42 Cited in Nick Mabey, "Delivering Climate Security: International Security Responses to a Climate Changed World," *The Royal United Services Institute for Defence and Security Studies, Whitehall Paper*, 69 (2008): p. 59.

43 The International Panel on Climate Change, "Climate Change 2007: Synthesis Report. Summary for Policymakers" (Valencia: IPCC, 2007), p. 11.

44 Paper from the High Representative and the European Commission to the European Council, "Climate Change and International Security," pp. 3–5.

45 There are eight Millennium Development Goals: eradicate poverty and hunger, achieve universal primary education, promote gender equality and empower women, reduce child mortality, improve maternal health, combat HIV/AIDS, malaria and other diseases, ensure environmental sustainability, and develop a Global Partnership for Development – that should be achieved by 2015. They are drawn from the Millennium Declaration that was adopted during the UN Millennium Summit in 2000.

46 Vinca LaFleur, Nigel Purvis and Abigail Jones, "Double Jeopardy: What the Climate Crisis Means for the Poor," *Brookings Blum Roundtable Report*, 5 (2008).

47 Rama Lakshmi, "India Rejects Calls For Emission Cuts," *Washington Post*, 13 April 2009.

48 David Wheeler and Kevin Ummel, "Another Inconvenient Truth: A Carbon-Intensive South Faces Environmental Disaster, No Matter What the North Does," *Center for Global Development Working Paper*, 134 (2007).

49 Mark Landler, "In China, Clinton Focuses on Climate Change," *New York Times*, 21 February 2009.

Part III

Centers of global power

Strategic priorities and threat management

6   The United States

Leadership beyond unipolarity?

*Matthew Rhodes**

chapter 3

Introduction

The United States emerged from the Cold War with a nearly unprecedented share of global power. However, the internal consensus that primacy renders robust American leadership essential to world order has extended to neither prioritization of threats nor choice of means to confront them. President Bill Clinton sought to manage globalization but was criticized for diversion into "social work."[1] More recently, President George W. Bush pursued an assertive Global War on Terror, but left office widely viewed a failure. His successor Barack Obama has promised a new course that reverses past mistakes, but the depth of global recession and looming pitfalls for his agenda leave its achievements and durability suspect as well.

More so than for many decades, the United States' ability to achieve its major goals and maintain its central influence in international affairs will require political acumen, outside support and simple good luck. If we accept the US as "indispensible" but insufficient[2] for mobilizing action to address the major strategic challenges of the new century, other centers of power – as well as smaller states – retain a stake in its success.

Unipolarity

In 1990, journalist Charles Krauthammer famously proclaimed America's "unipolar moment," a time frame he later extended to an "era."[3] The most systematic academic spokesmen for the case, William Wohlforth and Stephen Brooks, attributed the historical uniqueness of America's position to its lead across all the usual measures of power simultaneously.[4]

The rehearsal of indicators has become familiar but remains instructive. In the year 2000, US military spending of $300 billion was five-times greater than that of its nearest competitor (Russia), and equal to the budgets of the next 15–20 countries combined. America's wide qualitative edge in global mobility and precision weaponry had proven decisive in conflicts from the Persian Gulf to the Balkans and underlay its capacity to "command the commons" of global air and sea-lanes.[5] With annual GDP of $12 trillion, the American economy comprised more than one-quarter of global output, enjoyed faster growth than Europe or Japan, and led in development and application of information technologies. Additional factors such as long-standing constitutional democracy, ubiquitous popular culture, and leading positions in key international institutions provided unmatched reserves of so-called "soft power."[6]

Moreover, contrary to the expectations of international relations theory, America's persistent predominance into the new millennium failed to spark more than token counter-balancing among its most plausible rivals. Geopolitical distance, an essentially benign hegemony and the sheer hopelessness of catch-up all seemed to mitigate opposition to "Mr. Big."[7]

Within this context, scholars of various stripes remained cautious about unipolarity's durability and offered contending prescriptions for long-term US strategy. Realist proposals ranged from restraint and selective engagement[8] to offshore balancing[9] to blocking the rise of competitors.[10] Liberals advocated "democratic peace"[11] or new institutional order.[12] Constructivists promoted norms of human rights[13] and the unity of the West.[14]

Meanwhile, in the realm of practical politics, unipolarity lent itself to the impression that America faced no immediate threats. Bill Clinton's election to the presidency in 1992 over the more experienced incumbent George H.W. Bush succeeded in part because traditional high politics seemed to have receded in importance.

Coming to identify globalization as "the central reality of our time," the Clinton administration took its main foreign task to be managing the turbulence created by that phenomenon's advance; important to sustaining both America's domestic growth and to progressively enlarge the circle of stable democracies.[15] In practice, this entailed immersion in formerly low political matters such as internal regime "transitions," transnational organized crime, humanitarian disasters and regional financial crises. Over the longer term, potential threats from other Great Powers or even mid-size "rogue states" would diminish further as market forces pressed them to embrace the norms of modern liberalism or face stagnation and decline.

The administration's instruments of choice for such work were typically multilateral. These included conclusion of new trade agreements such as North American Free Trade Association (NAFTA) and establishment of the World Trade Organization. They also included work through intergovernmental organizations, including the United Nations but often others such as the International Monetary Fund (IMF) or North Atlantic Treaty Organization (NATO), in which America enjoyed greatest influence.

The Bush revolution[16]

World-view and threat perception

Presidential candidate George W. Bush started with an even lower profile on foreign policy. As a former oil executive and then-governor of Texas, Bush had substantial dealings in energy and trans-border issues with Mexico. Otherwise, he lacked extensive experience or strong prior positioning with regard to international affairs.

Although Bush may have held few detailed opinions, he evinced a gut-level instinct for what has been called "ABC – anything but Clinton." Working with campaign advisors such as Condoleezza Rice, he refined this inclination as a desire to return to a more realist approach. Such a policy would emphasize no-nonsense relations with other Great Powers (including emerging "strategic competitors" such as China) rather than internal problems in the periphery, getting the military out of humanitarian nation-building and back to deterrence and war-fighting, and preventing international organizations and agreements of dubious value or legitimacy from constraining America's sovereign freedom of action.[17] Perhaps better than anything else, Bush's "un-signing" of the Kyoto Protocol on climate change during his first months in office would symbolize these latter commitments.

The terrorist attacks that killed 3,000 people in and around the World Trade Center in New York and the Pentagon near Washington, DC in September 2001 shocked America and the world. They reinforced some aspects of the Bush administration's prior policy approach, but radically changed others. Most fundamentally, the attacks ended the perception of American security as unchallenged.

After 9/11, terrorists – particularly those of "global reach" such as al-Qaeda – were elevated from a secondary nuisance to the primary threat to America and international order. Relatedly, weak, failed and rogue states that provided resources, sanctuary or breeding grounds for terror and extremism displaced rival Great Powers as the political units of greatest concern. Finally, the potential "nexus" between terrorism and weapons of mass destruction represented the most chilling culmination of these dangers. Should determined terrorists obtain a nuclear bomb or other device, perhaps with the aid of a rogue state, the resulting death and destruction would dwarf the effects of 9/11.

Strategic response

Having identified these threats, the administration launched an integrated set of initiatives against them. Its strategy's centerpiece was the War on Terror. While the term sometimes encompasses the administration's response as a whole, here it refers specifically to the most direct, immediate efforts against terrorists, their sponsors and weapons proliferation.

Two sub-elements within this pillar generated greatest debate. One was the notion of "preemption" first described by President Bush in a speech at West Point military academy in the summer of 2002, and included in the National Security Strategy document issued that fall. The President argued that the cata-strophic nature of weapons of mass destruction and the inherent difficulties in monitoring or deterring shadowy non-state actors forced the US to broaden its conception of self-defense. It had to be prepared to take military or other deci-sive action against emerging threats even before they fully developed.

The other was "enhanced" methods of intelligence gathering. Successful preemptive action requires timely information concerning terrorists' plans. Accordingly, the administration authorized a range of measures such as coercive interrogation, extraordinary rendition, the special detention camp at Guantanamo Bay and expanded monitoring of electronic communications.

Meanwhile, a second pillar – the Freedom Agenda – represented the administration's longer-term antidote to terrorism. Influenced by the arguments of scholars such as Bernard Lewis and the findings of the 2002 UN Arab Development Report, the administration took terrorism's underlying root cause to be the lack of political voice or economic opportunity within the Middle East and other parts of the world.[18] The resulting frustrations render vulnerability to diversion into extremist beliefs, sometimes with the encouragement of the same corrupt, authoritarian rulers responsible for the lack of opportunity in the first place. The spread of "effective democracy" (systems that couple free and fair elections with good governance, the rule of law and minority rights) and market-based economic growth would allow people in such countries to channel their energies into constructive improvements rather than violence.[19]

The final pillar, transformation, aimed to reorient national institutions and international relationships that were still largely legacies of the Cold War. Building on pre-9/11 efforts at the Pentagon, the military and other national security institutions were to become leaner and more flexible by adopting networked information technology (including for missile defense) and entrepreneurial, private business-style practices.[20] Likewise, America's international partnerships were to become less static and fixed on formal alliances such as NATO. Preference would be given instead to varied bilateral relations and situation-dependent "coalitions of the willing"; in implicit criticism of Clinton's work through NATO in the Balkans, Secretary of Defense Donald Rumsfeld insisted there would be no "war by committee" and that henceforth the "mission would determine the coalition" rather than the reverse. In the immediate post-9/11 context at least, this was also seen as an opportunity for improved cooperation with non-democratic states, including powers such as Russia and China, who shared concern about terrorism.

All these elements came together most directly with Iraq. Citing the dangers of Iraqi President Saddam Hussein's alleged links with terrorists and efforts to develop weapons of mass destruction, in March 2003 President Bush ordered American military forces to lead a coalition to remove Hussein from power. A broader hope was that this act would both deter other rogue states from pursuing WMD and create a model democracy that would trigger demand for change across the region as a whole.

The initial intervention succeeded in toppling Hussein's rule in three weeks. However, the follow-on stabilization phase proved much longer and more difficult, as multiple violent insurgencies kept Iraq as the War on Terror's "central front." A "surge" of additional forces in early 2007 brought belated signs of progress while keeping 140,000 US troops in the country through 2008.

Evaluation

By the Bush administration's final years in office, its strategic response was widely deemed a failure at home as well as abroad. In 2007 former National Security Advisor Zbigniew Brzezinski assigned the Bush team's handling of foreign affairs an "F,"[21] while 91 percent of a more balanced spectrum of experts assembled by the journal *Foreign Policy* believed the world was becoming more dangerous for the US under Bush's watch.[22] Public approval for President Bush's job performance finished around 25 percent, with three-quarters of Americans specifically hoping their next president would take a different approach to foreign policy.[23]

Case for success

Of course, as in art, achievement in politics and international relations is not always recognized in its own time. The post-World War II administration of President Harry Truman also left office with low popularity, only to win widespread praise for its initiatives in hindsight.

Although it remains a minority view, a serious case can be made for a similarly more appreciative re-assessment of Bush's security policy.[24] First and most importantly, no major terrorist attack occurred in the United States after 9/11. Second, financial controls and the killing or capture of dozens of al-Qaeda's top operatives severely degraded the network's operational capabilities. Third, Libya's termination of its nuclear weapons program and exposure of the Pakistan-based A.Q. Khan network after the Iraq intervention represented significant breakthroughs for non-proliferation. Fourth, even as US relations soured with prominent parts of Europe, they reached new highs with Asia-Pacific countries such as Japan, Australia and India; indeed, steps toward strategic partnership with the latter in particular could prove to be among President Bush's most enduring achievements. Finally, specific rationales and means aside, removing the Taliban and Saddam Hussein from power ended two of the world's most repressive regimes and provided opportunity for the people of Afghanistan and Iraq to build better lives. The less-direct diplomatic support of the administration also bolstered mid-decade "color revolutions" against corruption and fraud in Georgia, Ukraine, Kyrgyzstan and Lebanon.

Critiques

Taken as a whole, then, the case for success is substantial. However, the following counter-arguments continue to drive the greater skepticism.

First, critical cost–benefit analysis finds often partial or fragile benefits outweighed by extraordinary negative costs. Focusing just on Iraq, *direct* costs begin with the deaths of more than 4,000 American service members and perhaps 100,000 Iraqis. They continue to include financial outlays projected to reach at least $1.2 trillion.[25] Likewise, *indirect* costs include the sharp decline in global attitudes toward the US, tremendous strain on the American military and unintended consequences such as the strengthened regional position of Iran. Finally, *opportunity* costs – alternative actions not taken or even conceived because of the overriding focus on Iraq – may count the failure of the US to head off deteriorating conditions in Afghanistan, genocide in Darfur or crisis in the global economy.

Second, whatever the wisdom of Bush presidential policy on paper, even some sympathetic observers complain procedural dysfunction harmed its implementation in practice. Iraq is again the prime example, but also on other matters the domineering personalities of Vice President Dick Cheney and Secretary of Defense Donald Rumsfeld, and/or a greater than usual emphasis on personal and political fidelity over functional expertise in next-tier appointments are blamed for having marginalized input from career professionals, undermined interagency coordination and circumvented Congressional oversight.[26] Weak advance planning as well as slowness to recognize and adjust to emerging problems were typical results.[27]

Third, the most fundamental charges fault the Bush policies as not only excessively costly or poorly implemented, but flawed in their very conception. To begin with, the label "War on Terror" arguably overemphasized military means, unduly glorified terrorist criminals as warriors, and counterproductively lumped together diverse issues and groups as a single unified enemy.[28]

The emphasis on light deployment, high-tech weaponry and private contractors in the administration's initial approach to transformation is also seen to have proved poorly suited for the stability operations in Afghanistan and Iraq.[29] The preference for flexible coalitions of the willing may also have underestimated the greater legitimacy and more reliable, politically sustainable support that can flow from working through formal organizations.

Finally, critics accuse the administration's Freedom Agenda of being hypocritical and/or naive. Some democracy advocates argue the Bush team did little of practical consequence to back up its rhetorical commitments in this area.[30] Others detected "double standards" in the contrast between the condemnations of political restrictions in some non-democracies (such as Iran) and the relative silence and even support for others (such as Pakistan or Saudi Arabia). Meanwhile, still others saw the administration's intelligence methods in particular as casting doubt on America's own democratic credentials.[31]

As for naiveté, critics, prominently including traditional realists, argue that freedom must develop internally within other countries and that outsiders like the US lack effective tools for accelerating that process. Attempts to do so are likely only to lead to instability or empowerment of extremists, as illustrated by the victory of Hamas in the 2006 Palestinian elections. Likewise, the rhetoric of spreading freedom may needlessly alienate and threaten potential non-democratic partners, whose cooperation is needed against terrorism, proliferation or other serious matters.

Cumulatively, the administration's perceived shortcomings sparked a new wave of US declinism. Despite a shift toward greater pragmatism and a less confrontational tone in its second term, its policies were blamed for eroding the foundations of power it inherited.[32] Even before the implosion of US financial markets in fall 2008, analysts began speaking of a "post-American world."[33] The US intelligence community itself forecast that multipolarity would become a fact of life within a decade and a half.[34]

The deepening downturn intensified these views. From spring 2007 to fall 2008, the US economy lost nearly half its stock market value, a quarter of household net worth and more than five million jobs. The freeze-up of credit markets following the collapse of the Lehman Brothers investment firm in September 2008 pushed the US government to extend hundreds of billions of dollars in emergency government funds to prevent the rapid dissolution of other financial institutions. After receiving smaller amounts of aid, two of the country's three major automakers – General Motors and Chrysler – would fall into bankruptcy by late spring 2009. Given the degree of global interdependence, the broader repercussions of this downturn will include overall contraction of the world economy in 2009 for the first time since World War II. Recovery in 2010 and beyond looks slow and uncertain.

Thus, while German Finance Minister Peer Steinbrück's comment that the onset of the crisis marked the end of the US as a "financial superpower" seems at best premature, the downturn could accelerate the relative shift of economic weight toward China and other emerging economic powers over the medium to longer-term. In regard to soft power, the crisis has already tempered America's "reputation for success,"[35] as well as the general attractiveness of the liberal "Anglo-Saxon" model of capitalism espoused by it for decades. In the words of Chinese Vice Premier Wang Qishan, "The teachers now have some problems."[36]

Simultaneously, the crisis could undermine US capacity for international leadership via two concomitant effects. First, increased concerns for domestic public welfare within the US itself, as well as its major international interlocutors, could politically crowd-out efforts to address problems elsewhere. Second, the negative fiscal impacts of the crisis are likely to reduce resources available for security initiatives. With forecast trillion-dollar deficits over the next few years, defense budgets may struggle simply to keep pace with inflation. This would widen an emerging gap with both existing procurement programs and expected operational demands.[37]

Change under Obama?

For present purposes, whether negative judgments of the Bush legacy are justified matters less than the fact that America's new President and his top advisors largely share them. Indeed, it was precisely within that context that a victorious Barack Obama promised a "new dawn of American leadership" on election night in November 2008.

Like many new leaders, Obama seeks to revive American strength and influence by reversing the perceived failings of his predecessor. While less frequently linked to international relations theory, his emergent policy shows elements of continuity with the Bush as well as earlier Clinton approaches. It also entails notable departures in both substance and process.

Economy–energy nexus

In terms of substance, most significant is the emergence of the global financial crisis as the number one *security* issue for the new administration.[38] As journalist Thomas Friedman put it, this is "Obama's 9/11."[39]

Especially noteworthy is not simply the ascendance of these issues to the top of the agenda (also the case for most *other* governments), but the way Obama has sought to address them. A centerpiece has been an effort for coordinated stimulus among the world's major economies. Within this context, much like Bush's administration defined the potential linkage between terrorism and WMD as America's greatest danger, Obama's has identified the connection between the current economic downturn and an accelerated "green energy" transition as the nation's greatest need and opportunity.

As down-payment on a broader decade-long project, $80 billion (10 percent) of the stimulus package approved by Congress for 2009–2010 is slated for spending on things such as improved insulation in public buildings, high-speed rail and "smart" electricity grids. Economically, the investment is intended both to generate employment now and to improve efficiency and competiveness over the longer term.

At the same time, the changes should bring cuts in US greenhouse gas emissions and boost the standing of the US at UN talks on a successor to Kyoto to be finalized in Copenhagen at the end of 2009. Additional measures in this regard have included authorizing the Environmental Protection Agency to regulate carbon dioxide, and backing Congressional legislation for a carbon cap-and-trade system.

A further side benefit may result from the reduced wealth transfer to often authoritarian, sometimes hostile regimes of energy-exporting countries who have used past windfalls to strengthen their grip on power, support extremists or destabilize their neighborhoods.[40]

Revamping counter-terror

Meanwhile, terrorism also remains a top-tier concern, even as the new administration signals departures from the manner of opposing it. During the election campaign, Obama explicitly affirmed that he viewed counter-terror efforts as a "war." However, since his inauguration the phrase "Global War on Terror" has dropped into official disuse, a fact that "speaks for itself," as Secretary of State Clinton has remarked.

Beyond this change, Obama has repudiated the prior administration's most controversial intelligence methods. Rejecting a "false choice between our security and our values," on his first full day in office Obama signed executive orders to close Guantanamo Bay prison within one year, forbid the operation of secret prisons elsewhere and restrict all government agencies to the interrogation techniques approved in the US Army Manual.

He has further sought to reduce hostility and distrust toward America within the Muslim world through high-profile acts of public diplomacy. An early interview with Al Arabiya television and speeches in Ankara and Cairo sought to communicate cultural understanding and respect.

A parallel shift comes in geographic focus. Obama opposed intervention in Iraq, Bush's "central front" against terror, from the start. Also, within his first month as President, he announced a withdrawal of US combat troops from the country by August 2010. In the absence of a contrary request from the Iraqi government, remaining non-combat forces would depart by the end of 2011.

Meanwhile operational drawdown in Iraq has opened the way for new initiatives to both the East and West. To the East, this means elevated attention to deteriorating conditions in Afghanistan and Pakistan considered as a whole. Even as the security situation in Iraq improved in 2008, attacks and deaths rose on both sides of the porous "AfPak" border. Most worryingly, persistent frustration with corruption and slow development progress under the Karzai government in the former has become matched or overtaken by fear that the spread of Taliban influence in the latter could bring the collapse of the post-Musharaff political order.

To deal with those trends, the administration has appointed Richard Holbrooke as special envoy for both countries, named General Stanley McChrystal as the new commander of US and NATO forces in Afghanistan, and announced the dispatch of an additional 21,000 US troops as part of a new strategy to improve public security and security force training in Afghanistan. Along with raising the level of bilateral economic assistance for Afghanistan to $2.8 billion for 2010, it has targeted $7.5 billion of such aid for Pakistan over the coming five years.

To the West, this has meant high-level engagement to restore some hope for an Israeli–Palestinian peace process. Here President Obama has appointed another special envoy, former Senator George Mitchell.

Grand bargains in counter-proliferation

Concerning counter-proliferation, the new administration has both embraced the goal of a nuclear-weapons-free world and signaled openness to exploring interim "grand bargains" with the key countries of Russia and Iran.[41]

As a first step, the administration has offered to open broad direct dialogue with Iran. Indeed, President Obama's March 2009 video message to the leaders and people of the country further exemplified his regional public diplomacy and may implicitly have rejected the policy options of preemption and regime change.[42] The notional bargain here would involve Iranian acceptance of verifiable limits on its nuclear enrichment program and support for regional terrorist groups (including those in neighboring Iraq and Afghanistan) in exchange for guarantees of its security, economic benefits such as the lifting of sanctions and admittance to the WTO and some type of recognition of its role as a regional power.

Vice President Joe Biden called for a similar "reset" in relations with Russia at the Munich Security Conference in early 2009. While the administration resists the notion of a quid pro quo, implicit terms of exchange might be the indefinite postponement of Bush administration plans for missile defense sites in Poland and the Czech Republic (perhaps necessary in any case with the no-confidence vote in the latter's government in March 2009) and efforts to fast-track NATO membership for Ukraine and Georgia, in exchange for Russian support for tougher diplomacy against Iran's nuclear program (that obviates the need for missile defense) and for NATO efforts in Afghanistan. An equally important result for both sides would be a negotiated successor to the Strategic Arms Reduction Treaty (START) arms control treaty, which expires at the end of 2009. Such a bilateral agreement could set the stage for broader disarmament and a strengthened Treaty on the Non-Proliferation of Nuclear Weapons-regime. As a step toward these goals, the Joint Understanding framework document signed by Obama and his Russian counterpart Dmitry Medvedev at their Moscow summit in July envisions reductions in strategic warheads to slightly more than 1,500 per side.

Fragile regions and states

Policy regarding weak, fragile and failing states has also seen shifts in focus. In the context of the global financial crisis, many developing and transition states in particular are facing intensified stress from sudden drops in foreign investment, trade and remittances. The need to prevent vulnerable economies from being pushed further toward weak or failed state status justified the US$100 billion contribution to increased drawing rights for the IMF, as well as administration plans to double bilateral foreign aid by 2012.

However, compared to the prior administration, Obama's seems to have lowered attention to weak states as a source of terrorism. To be sure, the administration's warnings about the dangers of state failure in Pakistan or Afghanistan have focused on the threatened re-emergence of terrorist safe havens there. In other places such as Somalia, however, the problem of piracy seems to have assumed greater urgency. Regarding neighboring Mexico, fears have focused on the spike in narco-violence and spread of swine flu.[43]

This shift has been accompanied by a similar step back from democracy-promotion as a centerpiece of policy toward fragile states. In its place, Obama aides have suggested "dignity promotion," focused more on meeting people's basic material needs.[44]

Redeeming process

As the Obama team links its predecessor's errors in policy substance to short-comings in process, it has also committed itself to changes in the latter. To begin with, it has pledged to replace the past "culture of secrecy" with openness and transparency.[45] Within the executive branch, this entails streamlining document declassification procedures as well as strengthening conflict of interest restrictions for political appointees. The administration has also pledged bipartisan partnership with Congress via faithful implementation of existing legislation, forthcoming response to requests for testimony or information, and proactive prior consultation, including through monthly meetings with a new Consultative Group of key Congressional leaders. Finally, the administration plans to engage the broader public more actively in foreign policy matters, employing many of the Internet-based techniques it used with great effect in its election campaign.

Second, the phrases "team of rivals" and "czarism" describe the new administration's approach to filling top policy posts. The frequently invoked former label originally referred to the manner in which Abraham Lincoln, President during the American Civil War, appointed a Cabinet of highly accomplished men who had been his leading political opponents rather than friends and loyalists; Lincoln's self-confidence as a leader enabled him to co-opt the talents of accomplished, independent figures.[46] The contemporary version manifests itself above all in the appointment of former Senator and First Lady Hillary Clinton, who very nearly bested Obama for the Democratic Party's presidential nomination, as Secretary of State. Other examples include naming former NATO Supreme Allied Commander James Jones, who had appeared at a campaign event with Obama's Republican opponent John McCain, as National Security Advisor, and asking Robert Gates, Secretary of Defense in Bush's last two years, to remain in that post.

The latter term "czarism" refers here not to historical Russian absolutism but rather idiomatically to someone appointed outside of regular bureaucratic channels to manage a key policy issue. In addition to the previously noted cases of George Mitchell and Richard Holbrooke, important examples here have included Dennis Ross for Iran-related issues and James Brennan as Deputy National Security Advisor for counter-terrorism and homeland security.

Rebalancing a strategy toolkit seen as disproportionately militarized represents another goal for the new administration. While more than a question of money, under President Bush annual defense spending topped $600 billion, doubling in nominal terms and increasing 60 percent with adjustment for inflation. This further widened the resource gap between the Pentagon and other departments involved in foreign affairs. A telling illustration is the fact that the number of troops in military marching bands exceeds that of career Foreign Service Officers within the State Department.[47] Echoing prior statements by Secretary of Defense Gates, Secretary of State Clinton testified at her Senate confirmation hearing that raising the profile of the second and third "Ds" within the trinity of security policy – "defense, diplomacy, and development" – would be a major priority. As initial steps, the State Department's proposed aid and operations budget for the fiscal year 2010 received a 10 percent increase to $52 billion, with planned further growth to $69 billion by 2014. State will also initiate a Quadrennial Diplomacy and Development Review parallel to the Pentagon's established four-year planning practice. These measures should complement

moves by Secretary Gates to adjust defense planning itself with increased attention to counterinsurgency and stability operations.[48]

Finally, as both a desired side-effect and means of achieving substantive
goals, Obama links renewed US leadership to revitalized multilateralism. In a
formulation Obama first used in his summer 2008 speech in Berlin, part of the
administration's efforts will focus on "strengthening alliances by asking
America's partners to do more." For NATO and other European states in particular, this has meant being asked to contribute additional troops or other resources
to the mission in Afghanistan, as well as to accept former prisoners released from
Guantanamo. The frequency of visits to Europe by Obama as well as by senior
officials such as Vice President Biden (three times each in the administration's
first six month) is offered as testimony to the priority of relationships there.[49]

Meanwhile, additional effort will go to formalizing ties with emerging economic centers via the G20, and forging a "more effective framework in Asia that
goes beyond bilateral agreements, occasional summits, and ad hoc arrangements."[50] Although as yet undefined, such an initiative would presumably seek
to embed relations with China in particular within a broader regional context.
Pending such an effort, the administration has introduced a Cabinet-level
"US–China Strategic and Economic Dialogue," broadening a finance-focused
process begun under President Bush.

Secretary of State Clinton summed up these initiatives as an effort to "lead by
inducing greater cooperation among a greater number of actors ... tilting the balance away from a multipolar to a multi-partner world."[51]

Evaluation

Even more so than description, assessment of the Obama strategy necessarily
remains provisional. Much may be riding on its ultimate success, but even at this
early stage, a number of potential pitfalls can be seen as in the way.

The first source of difficulty is the sheer scope and ambition of Obama's
agenda. Obama and other officials argue circumstances leave them no choice.
However, the experience of past presidencies counsels for concentrating on a
smaller set of clear priorities. Trying to accomplish major breakthroughs on multiple fronts at once can simply dissipate political capital so thinly that little
progress can be made on any of them. Especially in conjunction with equally
grand domestic goals such as overhauling healthcare, the new administration's
international initiatives clearly risk this fate.

The administration's procedural reforms may exacerbate the challenge of an
overfull agenda. On the one hand, moves toward greater openness may simply
serve to simply slow decision-making further and provide multiple opportunities
for opponents to block changes from the status quo. Opposition even by fellow
Democrats in Congress to funding the closure of Guantanamo – if that involves
the transfer of detainees to the US – has been an example.

On the other hand, announced commitments to principle may simply raise
expectations that later go unmet. The invocation of an ethics waiver for the

appointment of Raytheon vice president William Lynn as Deputy Secretary of Defense is an early case in point. Continued legal arguments for the indefinite preventive detention of suspected terrorists and withholding of release of photographs of past detainee abuse could do the same.

In addition, whatever their virtues separately, the combination of "rivals" and "czars" in policy may work at cross-purposes. Rather than streamlining process, the proliferation of special envoys and coordinators could simply blur lines of authority as well as undercut the input and stature of formally more senior officials.[52]

The perishability of international good-will presents another factor. Given the widespread antipathy toward Bush, a certain "Obamamania" greeted his successor's election. However, as with its everyday analogues, the pertinent question is not whether Obama's global honeymoon will end, but how. Whether hopeful excitement yields to embittered disappointment or mature, appreciative partnership will be determined both by how well the new President lives up to others' expectations, as well as how they, in turn, respond to his appeals for cooperation.

While some external partners worry the new administration may too readily set aside concern for democratic principles in pursuit of agreements with authoritarian regimes, here the dismissive initial reactions to its specific proposals bode most ill. Iranian leaders first demanded Obama apologize for past US actions prior to any talks and later blamed Western leaders for post-election demonstrations in their country. Perhaps less expectedly, tepid support also came from continental Europe for Obama's G20 calls for coordinated reflation. Czech Prime Minister Miroslav Topolanek, whose country held the EU presidency, condemned this approach as a "road to hell." Other leaders such as German Chancellor Angela Merkel expressed their skepticism less colorfully but with equal adamance. Meanwhile, the response to calls for increased International Security Assistance Force commitments was mostly limited to small, short-term deployments to assist with summer elections. Indian leaders bluntly rejected binding carbon emissions targets during a visit by Secretary Clinton in July. A continued dearth of tangible progress for such initiatives could revive doubts about the value of soft power and multilateralism.[53]

A final challenge is the tyranny of events. Dramatic new developments, such as a spectacular terrorist act blamed on softened policies, could quickly undermine Obama's political support. Former Vice President Cheney in particular has already warned changes by the new administration leave the country "less safe." Likewise, sudden deterioration in areas not envisioned as priorities could deflect the administration from deliberate strategy to reactive crisis management. Lastly, reversal of the cautious hopes that the financial and economic crisis had reached bottom by mid-2009 might effectively close Obama's window of opportunity for a successful presidency or even a second term in office.

The challenge of developing effective security strategy would then fall to yet another administration, probably under even more challenging circumstances.

Conclusion

None of the pitfalls described above are inevitable. However, cumulatively they illustrate the difficulties the current as well as future administrations face in shoring up US leadership in the cause of world strategic stability. Addressing the daunting list of global challenges will be exceedingly difficult, even with energetic and wise US engagement. The absence of such engagement need not lead to the nightmare scenarios of global anarchy or a new Dark Ages,[54] but it would make dystopian world order more likely.

However, two oft-cited historical observations may allow for conclusion on a note of cautious optimism. In the late nineteenth century, German Chancellor Otto von Bismarck, the leading statesman and strategist of his age, remarked that only God's "special providence" could explain the otherwise undeserved resilience of "drunks, fools, and the United States of America." During World War II, British Prime Minister Winston Churchill praised Americans' reliability to "do the right thing, after they've exhausted all the alternatives."

Perpetual reliance on divine assistance would make a dubious strategy, and the severity of threats may not abide endless policy experimentation. Thus, the United States may not remain the unipolar colossus imagined in the recent past. Still, it remains plausible, if not preordained, that America will retain sufficient power and find a sufficiently attractive formula to lead against the challenges of our time as well.

Notes

* The views expressed in this chapter are those of the author and do not reflect the official policy or position of the George C. Marshall European Center for Security Studies, the Department of Defense, or the US Government.

1 M. Mandelbaum, "Foreign Policy as Social Work," *Foreign Affairs* 75, 1 (1996).

2 L. Gelb, *Power Rules: How Common Sense Can Rescue American Foreign Policy* (New York: HarperCollins, 2009), pp. 114–119, B. Scowcroft, "The Dispensable Nation?," *National Interest* 90 (2007).

3 C. Krauthammer, *The Unipolar Moment – Foreign Affairs: America and the World* (New York: Macmillan, 1990), C. Krauthammer, "The Unipolar Moment Revisited," *National Interest* 70 (2002).

4 S. Brooks and W. Wohlforth, "American Primacy in Perspective," *Foreign Affairs* 81, 4 (2002), W. Wohlforth, "The Stability of a Unipolar World," *International Security* 24, 1 (1999).

5 B. Posen, "Command of the Commons: The Military Foundations of U.S. Hegemony," *International Security* 28, 1 (2003).

6 J. Nye, *Soft Power: The Means to Success in World Politics* (New York: Public Affairs, 2004).

7 J. Joffe, "Who's Afraid of Mr. Big?," *National Interest* 64 (2001).

8 R. Art, *A Grand Strategy for America* (Cornell: Cornell, 2003), E. Gholz, Daryl G. Press and Harvey M. Sapolsky, "Come Home America: A Strategy of Restraint in the Face of Temptation," *International Security* 21 (1997).

9 C. Layne, "From Preponderance to Offshore Balancing: America's Future Grand Strategy," *International Security* 22, 1 (1997).

10 John Mearsheimer, *The Tragedy of Great Power Politics* (New York: W.W. Norton, 2001).

11 B. Russet, *Grasping the Democratic Peace: Principles for a Post-Cold War World* (Princeton: Princeton University Press, 1993).

12 G.J. Ikenberry, *After Victory: Institutions, Strategic Restraint, and the Rebuilding of Order after Major Wars* (Princeton: Princeton University Press, 2001).

13 M. Finnemore, *National Interests in International Society* (Ithaca: Cornell University Press, 1996).

14 S. Huntington, *The Clash of Civilizations and the Remaking of World Order* (New York: Simon & Schuster, 1996).

15 S. Berger, "A Foreign Policy for the Global Age," *Foreign Affairs* 79 (2000), W. Clinton, *A National Security Strategy of Engagement and Enlargement* (1994), W. Clinton, "State of the Nation Address," 27 January 2000.

16 The subtitle of I. Daalder and J. Lindsay, *America Unbound: The Bush Revolution in Foreign Policy* (Washington, DC: Brookings, 2003). Other authors found greater continuity with historical US policy: J.L. Gaddis, *Surprise, Security, and the American Experience* (Cambridge: Harvard University Press, 2004), R. Kagan, *Dangerous Nation: America's Place in the World from its Earliest Days to the Dawn of the Twentieth Century* (New York: Knopf, 2006).

17 J. Mann, *Rise of the Vulcans: The History of Bush's War Cabinet* (New York: Penguin, 2004), C. Rice, "Promoting the National Interest," *Foreign Affairs* 76, 1 (2000).

18 B. Lewis, *What Went Wrong? Western Impact and Middle Eastern Response* (New York: Oxford University Press, 2002).

19 G.W. Bush, "Second Inaugural Address," 20 January 2005.

20 C. Rice, "Transformational Diplomacy," *Speech at Georgetown University*, 18 January 2006, D. Rumsfeld, "Transforming the Military," *Foreign Affairs* 85, 6 (2002).

21 Z. Brzezinski, *Second Chance: Three Presidents and the Crisis of American Superpower* (New York: Basic Books, 2007).

22 "Terrorism Index," *Foreign Policy*, September/October (2007): p. 62.

23 "Poll, November," *NBC/Wall Street Journal* 2007.

24 T. Lynch and R. Singh, *After Bush: The Case for Continuity in American Foreign Policy* (Cambridge: Cambridge University Press, 2008).

25 P. Orszag, "Estimated Costs of U.S. Operations in Iraq and Afghanistan and of Other Activities Related to the War on Terrorism," *Statement of the Director of the Congressional Budget Office*, 24 October 2007, J. Stiglitz and L. Bilmes, *The Three Trillion Dollar War: The True Cost of the Iraq Conflict* (New York: W.W. Norton, 2008).

26 B. Gellman, *Angler: The Cheney Vice-Presidency* (New York: Penguin, 2008), B. Graham, *By His Own Rules: The Ambitions, Successes, and Ultimate Failures of Donald Rumsfeld* (New York: Public Affairs, 2009).

27 J. Dobbins, "Who Lost Iraq? Lessons from the Debacle," *Foreign Affairs* 86, 5 (2007), N. Ornstein and T. Mann, "When Congress Checks Out," *Foreign Affairs* 85, 6 (2006), T. Ricks, *Fiasco: The American Military Adventure in Iraq* (New York: Penguin, 2006), B. Woodward, *State of Denial: Bush at War, Part III* (New York: Simon and Schuster, 2006).

28 P. Gordon, *Winning the Right War: The Path to Security for America and the World* (New York: Times Books, 2007).

29 M. Gordon and B. Trainor, *Cobra II: The Inside Story of the Invasion and Occupation of Iraq* (New York: Pantheon, 2006), H.R. McMaster, "Learning from Contemporary Conflicts to Prepare for Future War," *Orbis* 52, 4 (2008).

30 T. Carothers, "The Democracy Crusade Myth," *National Interest* 90 (2007).

31 J. Mayer, *The Dark Side: The Inside Story of How the War on Terror Turned Into a War on American Ideals* (New York: Doubleday, 2008).

32 R. Pape, "Empire Falls," *National Interest* 99 (2009).

33 F. Zakaria, *The Post-American World* (New York: W.W. Norton, 2008).

34 National Intelligence Council, "Global Trends 2025: A Transformed World" (NIC, 2008).

35 Gelb, *Power Rules*.
36 R. Altman, "The Great Crash 2008," *Foreign Affairs* 88, 1 (2009): p. 11.
37 A. Cordesman, "A Poisoned Chalice? The Crisis in National Security Planning, Programming, and Budgeting," *CSIS Report* (2008), A. Michta, "Double or Nothing," *National Interest* 93 (2008).
38 Dennis C. Blair, "Annual Threat Assessment of the Intelligence Community for the Senate Select Committee on Intelligence" (National Intelligence Council, 2009).
39 T. Friedman, "Win, win, win, win, win ...," *New York Times*, 27 December 2008.
40 R. Lugar, "The New Energy Realists," *National Interest* 80 (2006), T. Friedman, "The First Law of Petropolitics," *Foreign Policy* May/June (2006).
41 R. Hutchings and F. Kempe, "The Global Grand Bargain," *Foreign Policy* webposting (2008).
42 R. Cohen, "From Tehran to Tel Aviv," *New York Times*, 23 March 2009.
43 Joint Forces *Command, The Joint Operating Environment: Challenges and Implications for the Future Force* (Suffolk: United States Joint Forces Command, Center for Joint Futures, 2008).
44 S. Ackerman, "The Obama Doctrine," *American Prospect* 19, 4 (2008).
45 The White House, "Foreign Policy Agenda," webposting 2009.
46 D. Kearns Goodwin, *Team of Rivals: the Political Genius of Abraham Lincoln* (New York: Simon and Schuster, 2005).
47 J.A. Holmes, "Where are the Civilians?," *Foreign Affairs* 88, 1 (2009).
48 R. Gates, "A Balanced Strategy," *Foreign Affairs* 88, 1 (2009).
49 I. Daalder, *Speech to Security and Defence Agenda*, 6 June 2009.
50 The White House, "Foreign Policy Agenda."
51 H. Clinton, "Address at the Council on Foreign Relations" (15 July 2009).
52 D. Rothkopf, "A Thousand Envoys Bloom," *National Interest* 101 (2009).
53 G. Rachman, "Europe Spurns the Beloved Obama," *Financial Times*, 30 March 2009, G. Rachman, "Obama and the Limits of Soft Power," *Financial Times*, 1 June 2009.
54 N. Ferguson, "A World Without Power," *Foreign Policy* 143 (2004), Gelb, *Power Rules*, M. Mandelbaum, *The Case for Goliath: How America Acts as the World's Government in the Twenty-First Century* (New York: Public Affairs, 2005).

7 The Russian Federation

Striving for multipolarity but missing the consequences

Pavel K. Baev

Introduction

Russian foreign policy in the first decade of the twenty-first century has been driven by two mutually reinforcing ambitions: to assert its status as one of the "Great Powers" in the world arena, and to ensure that global affairs are run by several powers of equal rank. Despite the often-proclaimed Russian adherence to political pragmatism, these ambitions have never been based on a rational assessment of its national interests and capabilities for advancing them. The dominant perception is that by the merits of its unique history and vast territory, Russia is entitled to "Great Power" rank and that a world order controlled by a group of major powers is a more natural and fair arrangement than a unipolar world – or, for that matter, a globalized non-polar world.

The global economic crisis, which arrived in Russia in the second half of 2008 and ravaged it with greater force than it did most Western countries, or petro-states, or other "emerging markets," has profoundly affected its self-perception and world-view. The proud feeling of being a "rising power" with every right to demand respect from declining peers has suddenly changed into a sinking feeling accentuated by reflections on the collapse of the USSR not quite 20 years ago. Foreign policy has accordingly evolved into an unstable combination of residual self-assertiveness, desperate rescue measures and hesitant steps toward re-launching cooperation with the West. As the crisis continues to unfold, there are few reasons to expect the emergence of a more coherent course at the start of the new decade.

By examining Russian foreign policy in the context of its patterns of managing key external risks and challenges, this chapter aims to arrive at reasonably informed guesses about its further evolution. It starts with a general evaluation of the main traits of thinking and decision-making mechanisms in Russian foreign policy, before moving to an overview of Russia's interactions with the central international organizations and regimes. Then, one-by-one, Russian assessments of, and defenses against, the major strategic threats are examined. The conclusion speculates about the sustainability of Russia's current course.

Foreign-policy thinking and decision-making

One distinct and perhaps defining feature of Russian foreign policy in the current decade has been the extreme centralization and even personification of the process of setting the priorities and guidelines, which has naturally emanated from the type of regime built by former president Vladimir Putin.[1] Foreign Minister Sergei Lavrov is an experienced professional, but his role is limited to implementing orders that are prepared by a narrow circle of Putin's trusted aides, who have little trust in the Foreign Ministry's recommendations, and even less in independent expertise. With the promotion of Dmitri Medvedev to the pivotal presidential post, this extra-small and hermetically sealed mechanism of decision-making has not changed very much, as Putin has maintained essential controls and relies on personal networks in his position of prime minister.

From the very start of his "reign," Putin persistently emphasized the pragmatic and non-ideological nature of his state-centered course, and Medvedev now diligently follows this line. In reality, however, the character of Russian foreign policy has resembled more of a mixture of mercantilism, particularly energy-related (conceptualized as "energy security"), and a progressively escalating ambition to restore Russia's "greatness," often metaphorically portrayed as "rising from the knees." This perception of "rising power" was based on the strong economic growth that started in 1999 – after a devastating sovereign default in August 1998 – and lasted until mid-2008, so that the gross domestic product (GDP) increased by nearly twice.[2] The sharp break in this trend, which had been officially projected to continue until 2020, has deflated this seriously exaggerated self-assessment, although so far a more realistic one has not emerged.

In parallel with the process of personal-power aggrandizement, resentment over Western reluctance to recognize Russia's special rights and "privileged interests" (the term coined by Medvedev), which could be interpreted as envy and Russo-phobia, was growing.[3] Putin objected to lessons in democracy taught by a "kind but stern gentleman in cork helmet" and armed with a "missile stick," which probably fit well with the anti-colonial discourse exploited by many "third world" populists, but was rather odd coming from the leader of Russia, a state which had built and successfully defended a vast empire.[4] This resentment was conceptualized as a principled rejection of a "unipolar" world, where the collective West was allegedly able to advance its interests under the guise of "values." This proposition is expressly omitted in the Foreign Policy Concept (which also does not mention Russia's status as a "Great Power"), but just a month after its approval, Medvedev formulated five principles of Russian foreign policy, and the second one asserts that:

> the world should be multi-polar. A single-pole world is unacceptable. Domination is something we cannot allow. We cannot accept a world order in which one country makes all the decisions, even as serious and influential a country as the United States of America. Such a world is unstable and threatened by conflict.[5]

There is a distinct reference to anti-Americanism in this "principle," and this sort of "contrarianism" was certainly a very useful foreign-policy tool in the second half of this decade; but, with the arrival of the Obama administration, Moscow had to cut down on the US-bashing due to the world-wide popularity of the new President, who demonstrated a readiness to "reset" relations with Russia.[6] What is perhaps even more problematic to this vision, as several Russian experts pointed out, is the historical experience of European "multipolar" systems that tend to correct complex power balances through wars.[7] The world is definitely undergoing a profound reconfiguration, but Russia cannot take its privileged position for granted in any post-crisis constellation.

The key question here is about the nature, distribution and capacity for mobilization of state power, and the views in Moscow on that crucial matter are quite ambivalent. The traditional "Soviet-realist" school of thought, which asserts that military power remains the indispensable instrument of policy and the ultimate determinant of global competition, is still quite influential. Putin proclaimed the commitment to build up Russia's military might on multiple occasions, particularly emphasizing the priority of upgrading the strategic deterrence arsenal. In actuality, he consistently channeled the bulk of defense expenditures toward force maintenance and personnel, paying scant attention to modernization, perhaps being wary of building combat-capable armed forces that would be able to advance their own political agenda.[8] Even switching to tough security rhetoric after the famous "Munich speech," Putin refrained from any experiments with the use of force, so the last two years of his "reign" – when hostilities in Chechnya remained low-intensity and Russian military bases were withdrawn from Georgia – were in fact the most peaceful period in Russia's post-Soviet history. That trend was broken in August 2008 by the Russian–Georgian war, which momentarily turned Russia into a "revisionist" power, but Medvedev took pains in convincing each and every Western partner to "turn the page" and return to "business as usual."[9]

If the "securitization" of foreign policy has been more rhetorical than real, the centrality of energy matters in Putin's world-view and daily schedule is beyond doubt. The fusion of Russia's external agenda and gas strategy has reached such a degree that it is impossible to establish whether its foreign policy serves *Gazprom*'s interests or *Gazprom* is an instrument for restoring Russia's "greatness." What is undoubtedly clear is that the unprecedented rise of prosperity and political stability in Russia during Putin's "era" was secured by the steady increase of oil and gas export revenues due to the breathtaking run of world oil prices since 1999.[10] Seeking to harvest maximum financial and political dividend from this god-sent position of "energy strength," Moscow also entertained some ideas about diversification, for instance, placing a premium on developing nano-technologies. These pretensions were cut short by the steep fall in oil prices in the second half of 2008, which served to shatter Putin's prediction that "the era of cheap hydrocarbons is over" and reveal the fragility of Russia's state power.

Russia in/out/about the key international institutions

Moscow has consistently proclaimed its commitment to advance international cooperation by working constructively in various inter-state organizations, and Medvedev – while pointedly underscoring his training as a lawyer – has even further increased the emphasis on upholding international law. Russia's record of international engagements, however, is quite mixed, and the organizations it has created itself in the post-Soviet space, including the Collective Security Treaty Organization (CSTO), are notoriously ineffectual. It is the Shanghai Cooperation Organization (SCO), which brings together Russia and China and four Central Asian states (except for the particularly neutral Turkmenistan), which has attracted the most attention, but its functions are limited to organizing problem-free summits.[11]

The UN Security Council

The UN is typically presented by Moscow as the depositary of international law, and the privilege of being a permanent member of the UN Security Council (UNSC) is of extremely high value as irrefutable proof of Russia's "Great Power" status. At the same time, Russia is not particularly active in various UN agencies and branches, and while formally declaring support for reforming the UNSC (backing Germany's claim for permanent membership in particular), it actually keeps blocking most proposals seeking to ensure the exclusivity of its privileges. Moscow prefers not to block resolutions by using its "veto" right, but also seeks to reduce to a minimum the practice of applying international sanctions. So, in many cases – from Sudan's protracted atrocities in Darfur to North Korea's testing of long-range ballistic missiles in April 2008 – Russia's "moderate" position prevented the UN SC from adopting forceful resolutions that might have implied justification for pro-active measures.[12]

In Moscow's view, the main prerogative of the UNSC is the capacity to authorize the use of force against the most blatant violators of international law. The condition that it cannot be done without Russia's consent is seen as a crucial "security guarantee" against any "encroachments" into its sphere of influence, for instance in support of a "color revolution." Insisting that no non-regional organization could legitimately make a decision on intervening in a conflict situation, Moscow maintains that the NATO operation against Yugoslavia in 1999, as well as the US invasion into Iraq in 2003, constitutes a breach of the most fundamental provisions of international law.[13] A related issue is the recognition of Kosovo's independence by the USA and many European states, which is seen as a violation of UN resolutions confirming Yugoslavian/Serbian territorial integrity.[14] Alleging that this mistake has opened a "Pandora's box" of secessionist troubles, Moscow also maintains that its own recognition of Abkhazia and South Ossetia as independent states in August 2008 is irreversible, so the only solution to these formally separate but in fact implicitly related problems is to "draw the line" and re-confirm the basic principles anew.

Another important matter where the UNSC plays a central role is nuclear non-proliferation, specifically regarding the Russian position on the Iranian nuclear program. Russia maintains that Iran has the right to develop nuclear research and technology, and has constructed the Bushehr nuclear power plant (not yet operational as of mid-2009); it also insists that the International Atomic Energy Agency (IAEA) has discovered many irregularities in the implementation of the uranium-enrichment program – but no evidence of its military character. Moscow has agreed to introduce symbolic, UN-approved sanctions against Iran, but remains adamant that only political dialogue could bring a solution, even offering to build an international uranium-enrichment facility on Russian territory (Angarsk), meanwhile indicating that a strict IAEA supervision over Iranian nuclear facilities would be a satisfactory option.[15]

The G8/G20

During the time of protracted economic disaster and political turmoil in the 1990s, Russia saw the invitation to join the exclusive "club" of G7 as a major foreign policy achievement and confirmation of its rank as one of the leading world powers. President Putin sought to build on that achievement, despite a growing and irritating campaign to expel Russia from this "club" because of the non-democratic character of his regime. Russia's chairmanship of the G8 in 2006 and the opportunity to preside over the Strelna summit was supposed to be the crowning moment of Putin's "reign," but in fact, and despite its perfect organization, it brought disappointingly few dividends.[16] While domestic affairs in Russia were never a topic for discussions in the "club," Putin could not avoid the uncomfortable feeling of being an outsider who cannot – and was not expected to – make a contribution to the key matters on the agenda, from global poverty to the Middle East quandary.

The devastating deepening of the global economic crisis since the second half of 2008 made it imperative to expand the "club" to the G20 format, and Moscow welcomed this transformation despite the obvious devaluation of its own status.[17] Medvedev made a particular display out of preparing Russia's position for the London G20 summit, but his performance there was far from impressive.[18] He discovered that Russia is quite isolated in this not-small crowd, and that the main axis of cooperation–competition was taking shape around the bilateral US–China relations, while Russia was quite marginal vis-à-vis this "Big Two."[19] The carefully cultivated "strategic partnership" with China turned out to be largely irrelevant, and the agenda for re-launched dialogue with the US has turned out to be very limited.

The problem was not just that Russia was not able to connect with the European *troika* in any meaningful way (except for on energy issues), or that its participation in the Asia-Pacific Economic Cooperation (APEC) generated few useful ties, or that the BRIC (Brazil, Russia, India, China) group ceased making any practical sense as the states were pushed apart by the crisis-driven forces. The main part of the problem was that Medvedev had nothing to say about a possible way out of the crisis because Russian economic doctrine – oriented toward distributing massive oil revenues and consolidating state control over key industries – had inevitably lost coherence with the arrival of "unplanned" crises, even if economic debates in Moscow became quite lively.

Economic fora

One remarkable feature of Russia's international profile is its very low level of engagement with economic organizations, which goes against the trend of increasing openness of its economy, and answers neither to its permanent need of foreign direct investment, nor its high dependency upon export revenues. Russia is not included in the G7 of finance ministers, neither is it a member of the Organization for Economic Cooperation and Development (OECD), though the "roadmap" for its accession was approved by the Council in November 2007 when Poland lifted its objections against the application initially submitted in mid-1996.[20]

The main obstacle on this road, however, is Russia's deadlocked attempt to join the World Trade Organization (WTO), which started back in mid-1993 with the establishment of the Working Party on accession and was identified by President Putin as one of the key foreign-policy goals.[21] Nevertheless, in August 2008 Russia cancelled several domestic regulations aimed at ensuring compliance with the accession requirements, and in February 2009 Putin even expressed sarcastic gratitude to the European Commission delegation for preventing Russia from joining the WTO.[22] In the situation of deepening economic crisis, it indeed makes little sense for Russia to tie its own hands against the introduction of protectionist measures that are creeping back into trade policy of many countries, even between the EU member states. In spring 2009, both the EU leaders and President Obama encouraged Medvedev to make the final effort in the accession process but Medvedev and Putin opted instead for a collective entry with Belarus and Kazakhstan (as one yet-to-be-formed custom union), which effectively meant postponing the issue into the indefinite future. Moscow still saw the cancellation of the Jackson–Vanik Amendment (1974) as the litmus test for US readiness to move forward in the economic area, but the US Congress is yet to take this long-overdue decision.[23]

Of particular importance for Russia are the organizations focused on energy matters, but here again it is not involved in the work of the International Energy Agency (IAE), and is not a member of the Organization of Petroleum Exporting Countries (OPEC). Saudi Arabia and other major producers have persistently invited Russia to join OPEC, but Moscow is quite satisfied with its observer status and sees no good reason to tie its hands with the quota system. At the same time, Russia's own ideas about establishing an organization of natural-gas-exporting countries, often called a "gas OPEC," remain ambivalent and have not advanced beyond loose coordination with Iran and Qatar.[24] The focal point of institutional–economic controversies, as far as Russia is concerned, is not the stalled accession to the WTO, which is paralyzed by irreconcilable differences, but the Energy Charter, which Medvedev seeks to replace with a new "conceptual approach" to energy security, albeit with little success.

European "architecture"

Ever since Mikhail Gorbachev advocated the construction of an "all-European house," Russia has been most intensely involved in various European institutions, but in the second half of this decade it has become increasingly opposed to their patterns of work and plans for transformation. The most acute conflict has ripened within Russia's relation to the North Atlantic Treaty Organization (NATO), which Moscow refuses to recognize as the main pillar of the European security system and generally perceives as a functionally and ideologically anti-Russian entity. President Yeltsin was bitterly opposed to NATO enlargement in the 1990s, but it was the prospect of setting Georgia and Ukraine on a "fast track" to membership that Moscow was determined to block by all available means.[25]

Moscow appeared very keen in 2007–2008 to restore the priority of military–security problems in Europe, protesting forcefully against the US plan to deploy strategic defense assets in Poland and the Czech Republic, and executing various "counter-measures," from the withdrawal from the Conventional Forces in Europe (CFE) Treaty to the announced (and then cancelled) deployment of *Iskander* tactical missiles in the Kaliningrad region. In 2009, although the agitation about a "new Cold War" has subsided, Russia's underlying and irreducible tensions with European political institutions remain. Each session of the Council of Europe involves a quarrel on Russia's non-compliance with its obligations; Moscow is expressly dissatisfied with the work of the Organization for Cooperation and Security in Europe (OSCE); and the prospects for negotiating a new Partnership and Cooperation Agreement (PCA) between Russia and the EU are clearly not good.[26]

These "Russian issues" are in fact spinning around the central problem of values, as Moscow not only refuses to discuss its policy of curtailing the democratic process, but is irritated by the methods of observing elections and establishing their fairness, and is particularly irked by Western support for "regime change" by means of "color revolutions." Seeking to cut short all discussions on "values," Medvedev advanced a proposal to build a new treaty-based super-structure that would unite various European institutions and redress their incoherence and malfunctioning areas.[27] The content of this proposal was elaborated in a draft treaty presented by Medvedev in November 2009, and despite its narrow focus on setting a mechanism for consultations about perceived threats, various European politicians expressed readiness in working on it. However, thew unmistakable goal of undermining NATO's central position makes this proposal unacceptable for most European states, and the suggestion to hold a special Organization for Security and Cooperation in Europe (OSCE) summit turned out to be a non-starter.[28] The turmoil and uncertainty brought by the as-yet immeasurable crisis make a poor background for entertaining grand political designs, and it is entirely possible that Russia itself, with its poor record of managing domestic discontent and vast potential for trouble-making, might emerge as the major challenge for European security.

Threat assessment and risk-management

It is the National Security Strategy that is supposed to identify the sources of threat to Russia, but the document approved in May 2009 – after several rounds of revisions – contains a lengthy and undifferentiated list of "negative impacts" on Russia's national interests, starting from "possible recurrence of unilateral power policies" to "improvement of forms of unlawful activities in cybernetic and biologic spheres" [sic.] and the deficit of fresh water.[29] The Foreign Policy Concept approved in July 2008 is also rather imprecise in this task.[30] The relevant passage reads as follows:

> new challenges and threats (first of all, international terrorism, narcotraffic, organized crime, spread of weapons of mass destruction and means of their delivery, regional conflicts, demographic problems, global poverty, including energy poverty, as well as illegal migration and climate change) are global problems that require adequate response of the entire international community and solidarity efforts to overcome them. The ecological factor is playing an increasingly important role, the problem of prevention of and counteracting infectious diseases is becoming evermore urgent.

Prioritization of these challenges appears to be rather haphazard but they can still be classified into five main groups.

Terrorism

Russia encountered the threat of terrorism earlier than the US and Europe, and the two deadly blasts in Moscow in September 1999 (still not conclusively investigated) signified in essence the same psychological and political watershed as the one commonly marked with the numerals "9/11." The struggle against terrorism became the central security task during Putin's first presidential term and it shaped many key features of the political regime that emerged in Russia in the first half of this decade.[31] In 2002–2004, Moscow saw more deadly terrorist attacks, including suicide bombings, than any other capital in the world, but since 2005 the intensity of this campaign has sharply subsided. The lifting of the special "counter-terrorist operation" regime in Chechnya in April 2009 confirmed that the Russian leadership had good reasons to declare that victory in this particular "War on Terror" has indeed been achieved, but the bomb that derailed the Nevsky Express train in November 2009 showed that the threat of terrorism remained acute.

Its is exactly here that significant differences between the counter-terrorist campaign in Russia and the US-led struggle against terrorism can be found: the latter is global in nature, while in Russia all significant terrorist attacks have been related to the local war in Chechnya that spilled over into Dagestan, Ingushetia and some other parts of the North Caucasus.[32] Despite serious reservations in the West about Russia's conduct of combat operations and enforcement of "constitutional order" in Chechnya, cooperation in the area of counter-terrorism between Russia and US, as well as NATO, did develop productively in 2001–2005. Moscow attached high importance to disrupting international networks that were sustaining the rebels in Chechnya and considered the US and NATO operations in Afghanistan to be a useful effort aimed at resolving the crucial task of denying the terrorists the most significant "safe haven."

Since 2006, however, Russia's contribution to further developing this cooperation has gradually diminished as the terrorist threat inside the country began to recede, so the Federal Security Service (FSB) found it opportune to take charge over this "struggle" through the newly-created National Antiterrorist Committee (NAK).[33] The way Moscow sought to assume leadership in deterring "color revolutions" – first of all in Central Asia – was particularly unhelpful for implementing a common agenda, because its counter-revolutionary strategy both defined and treated opponents of ruling regimes as extremists and terrorists.[34] This made the task of coining a common and broadly-acceptable definition of terrorism, which is a contested issue at the best of times, into a completely deadlocked exercise, so the lists of organizations involved in or financing international terrorism compiled by the US, the EU and Russia had perhaps only al-Qaeda in common. Moscow, for that matter, has few reservations against maintaining normal political dialogue with Hamas and sees no grounds whatsoever for shunning Iran and Syria as states that sponsor terrorism. In general, the struggle against terrorism – as an area where the West needs Russian cooperation but Russia needs little in return – is perceived by Moscow as an interesting element of the global agenda. As Russia can also make a valuable contribution to this field, it can therefore be open to bargaining while expecting rewards of an "asymmetric" character.

Regional conflicts and failed states

Russia's experience with local conflicts associated with fragile states is vast, very recent and completely different from the lessons learned by the US, NATO and key European states. The main reference point for the notion of a "failed state" for Moscow is not Somalia, but the collapse of the USSR in late 1991, in which the Russian leadership was the main accomplice but perceives it now, in hindsight, as "the major geopolitical catastrophe of the century."[35] That massive breakdown was, astonishingly, peaceful overall, but still produced a chain of violent local clashes – from Transdniestria to Tajikistan – escalating into civil wars, in which Russia had to take on the responsibility of mediator and peace-enforcer.[36]

The West, much preoccupied with the Balkan wars, was generally content to let Moscow experiment with its peace operations, controversial as they were. By the mid-1990s, hostilities in all post-Soviet "hot spots" had been terminated, but only in Tajikistan was a genuine peace accord achieved, while in most other cases ceasefires monitored by Russian peacekeepers (except for Nagorno Karabakh) fixed outcomes that were unacceptable for at least one party to the "frozen conflicts." Russia's ability to project power and influence was deeply undermined in the second half of the 1990s by the war in Chechnya, which required a massive concentration of military effort and still forced Moscow to accept a humiliating defeat. The Second Chechen war was conducted under Putin's leadership with even more brutal determination and was brought to an end through installing a despotic and barely controllable regime of Ramzan Kadyrov.[37]

In the second half of this decade, Russia employed economic instruments (that were not available in the 1990s) as the key means of conflict management in its neighborhood, seeking to maximize a particular kind of "soft power" derived from its support for "enlightened authoritarian" regimes from Belarus to Turkmenistan. The only exception in this picture of "benevolent dominance" was Georgia. Here, a strong impulse toward democratization provided by the so-called "rose revolution" of late 2003 interplayed with a pronounced desire to undo the disastrous results of the secessionist wars of the early 1990s, and with a desperate urge to join NATO – to form a particularly complex knot of tensions.[38] The sudden escalation of smoldering hostilities in South Ossetia into a full-blown war in early August 2008 was fairly predictable and entirely preventable, yet the ill-conceived forceful move by Georgia granted Russia an opportunity to score an impressive military victory, which did not involve political consequences that would have made Moscow regret the decision to recognize the independence of Abkhazia and South Ossetia.[39]

Russia's angry demarche against NATO's exercises in Georgia in May 2009 confirmed that risks of a new confrontation in this "hot spot" remain dangerously high, and while Georgia constitutes a special case, the resonance from this epicenter goes far. Afghanistan, for that matter, is perceived by Moscow less like a regional conflict in dangerous vicinity to Central Asia, but more like a bargaining chip in the geopolitical game with the US and NATO. Another regional conflict toward which Russia seeks to increase its profile primarily for geopolitical reasons – and thus takes a less than truly constructive position – is Sudan.[40] Sending combat ships from the Baltic and Pacific Fleets to patrol the Gulf of Aden, Moscow aims not so much at making a contribution to the struggle against piracy, but more toward demonstrating its ability to project naval power.[41] Deepening economic crisis could and most probably will take more states to the brink of failure, and Russia quite possibly will look for opportunities to take advantage of these misfortunes, while humanitarian considerations are of little consequence in this opportunism.

Nuclear non-proliferation and WMD

Russia attaches great importance to maintaining a principled stance on nuclear non-proliferation, seeing it as a means not only to advance its international reputation but also to safeguard its highly valued privilege as a legal owner of nuclear weapons. Moscow can claim credit for two significant achievements in upholding the NPT regime in the turbulent period after the collapse of the USSR. The first one is guaranteeing that the colossal Soviet nuclear arsenal was not divided between the newly-independent states but stayed concentrated under Russian control, which involved complicated negotiations and some pro-active steps, like transporting all tactical nuclear weapons from Ukraine to Russia without asking permission. The second achievement is taking all necessary precautions for securing storages of nuclear weapons and materiel so that none of the alarmist predictions of terrorist groups or "rogue states" getting access to "nuclear suitcase-bombs" or fissile materials has come true.[42]

Moscow consistently presents its engagement in strategic arms control as Russia's unique contribution to strengthening the non-proliferation regime, and fulfillment of its commitment in the Nuclear Non-Proliferation Treaty (NPT) on reducing the legitimate nuclear arsenals. In fact, the real value of this process for Russia has always been more in line with maintaining a crucially important dialogue with the US on equal footing, so the Bush administration was bitterly criticized by Moscow not only for abandoning the Anti-Ballistic Missile (ABM) Treaty in 2001 and advancing plans for the deployment of elements of strategic defense system in Europe, but also for neglecting negotiations on relevant matters, so that the whole system of strategic arms control deteriorated to a dangerous degree.[43] With the arrival of the Obama administration, the revival of arms-control talks aimed at replacing the Strategic Arms Reduction Treaty (START-I, expired on 5 December 2009) has become one of the key elements in "re-setting" US–Russia relations.[44] Moscow is very keen to establish new binding limits for nuclear warheads and delivery systems that would fit well with the natural shrinking of its inventory of weapons and thus consolidate the notion of a "strategic parity" with the US; it has, however, serious issues with responding to President Barack Obama's initiative on setting the goal of total elimination of nuclear weapons.[45] The dominant strategic perception is that Russia is highly vulnerable to a wide range of conventional and unconventional security threats – including from NATO – that could be deterred and countered only by reliance on nuclear weapons. Therefore, Russia believes that the aim of abolishing this ultimate nuclear security guarantee is plain nonsense.

Russia's position on the two most urgent problems in the non-proliferation area – the advancement of nuclear programs in Iran and North Korea – remains legally solid in the sense that Moscow insists on ensuring the peaceful character of these programs, but in fact it is rather ambivalent in the case of the former and passive in the latter. Russia duly condemned the nuclear test and missile launches in North Korea in May 2009, but in the course of protracted international management of this crisis it has shown readiness to grant leadership to China instead, and has not tried to influence Beijing's position despite the obviously close vicinity of North Korean nuclear facilities to Vladivostok, the capital of the Russian Far East. As for Iran, one key point for Moscow has been the completion of the Bushehr nuclear power plant (scheduled to start producing electricity in March 2010, after many delays), which is seen as a pilot project for several potential contracts in the Middle East. The central point in Russia's position, however, is the unacceptability of a "military solution" – including even indirect threats – stretched further to include a presumed inefficiency of sanctions; a stance which in fact amounts to sheltering Iran from the pressure of the US. What makes this legally impeccable position rather dubious is the firm (even if rarely expressed) conviction in Moscow that no amount of incentives offered by Western negotiators would suffice to convince Tehran to terminate its uranium-enrichment program. The National Security Strategy asserts with certainty that "the risk of increasing the number of states possessing nuclear weapons will grow," and Russia is apparently prepared to live with this risk, while assuming that a nuclear-armed Iran would remain a stable and rational neighbor.

One particular issue related to the non-proliferation agenda is the management of a large amount of nuclear waste, including decommissioned weapons, that Russia was only able to accomplish during the hard times in the early 1990s, with the help of US through the Cooperative Threat Reduction (CTR) program, also known as the Nunn–Lugar initiative (after US Senators Sam Nunn and Richard Lugar, who sponsored the key legislation in 1991). The CTR program has been hugely successful, for instance by securing the deactivation of over 7,500 warheads, and its funding has continued at an average level of about US$450 million through the 2000s, while the Obama administration allocated US$400 million in the FY 2010 military budget. The Russian authorities, however, have been slow in providing corresponding funding for treating various kinds of nuclear waste, and the current financial crisis may result in further delays in implementing the relevant projects, particularly in the Kola Peninsula, where the total costs of eliminating the potential sources of nuclear contamination are estimated at €2 billion.[46]

Russia also faces difficulties in meeting the commitment to destroy all its stockpiles of chemical weapons by the end of 2012, as required by the Organization for the Prohibition of Chemical Weapons (OPCW). Moscow signed the Convention on Prohibition of Development, Production, Stockpiling and Use of Chemical Weapons in 1993 and ratified it in 1997, declaring an arsenal of 40,000 tons of chemical weapons, of which 30 percent were destroyed by March 2009. Despite contributions from many Western states, the construction of chemical weapons destruction plants at Pochep and Shchuchye was delayed, so another extension of the deadline might be necessary.[47] The situation with biological weapons arouses less concern, and despite the lack of security during the closure of many Soviet labs in the early 1990s, no incidents comparable with the anthrax leak in Sverdlovsk in 1979 were registered.[48] Overall, the vast Soviet system of preparedness for chemical and biological warfare has been partly dismantled and partly deteriorated to such a degree in fact that an industrial accident or an epidemic outbreak today represents a hard-to-meet challenge.

Climate change and environment

Russia's most significant contribution to the global campaign for reducing "dangerous anthropogenic interference" (as described in the UN Convention on Climate Change) is ratification of the Kyoto Protocol in November 2004. President Putin took the decision against objections from the Ministry of Industry and Energy and the Russian Academy of Sciences, which focused respectively on the potential negative impact of the Kyoto regime on Russia's economy and on the insufficient evidence of the causal connection between the growing emissions of greenhouse gases and global warming.[49] The EU had advocated strongly for that decision, since Russia's ratification paved the way for the Kyoto Protocol to legally enter into force in February 2005. Putin, therefore, granted his consent in exchange for the EU supporting Russia's accession to the WTO, which was pursued as a major foreign policy goal at that time.

The basic calculation behind Putin's decision was that the protracted recession of the 1990s created a situation where actual greenhouse-gas emissions in Russia in the mid-2000s were considerably lower than in 1990 (which is the key reference point in the Kyoto Protocol), so for many years to come there would be no need to worry about enforcing emissions reductions, while Moscow might even engage in a commercially beneficial trade in quotas. Fast growth of Russian industry through most of the 2000s put those calculations in doubt, and as of mid-2008 for instance, Russia was the fourth largest emitter of carbon dioxide from power generation.[50] The main cause of that dubious achievement was colossal waste in energy transportation and consumption, so, soon after he assumed power, President Medvedev signed a decree on increasing energy efficiency by establishing the goal of "reducing by at least 40 per cent the amount of energy used to produce the country's gross domestic product by 2020, as compared to 2007."[51] The main instrument for achieving this goal was the gradual increase of regulated domestic prices on energy and gas, a scheme which in fact suited the interests of *Gazprom* far more than it promoted energy-saving technologies. The controversy around this Soviet-style directive was short-lived, as the deep industrial contraction in early 2009 forced the government to abandon the plan for raising tariffs, so the intentions concerning energy efficiency were reduced to a figure of speech.

The scale of the problems related to the environment can be deduced from Medvedev's assessment that "40 million of our citizens live in substandard environmental conditions. Of these, one million are forced to live in areas with dangerous levels of pollution."[52] The legacy of Soviet industrialization is indeed extremely difficult to transform in accordance with modern EU standards of ecological protection, which are increasingly used as a reference point. The profound industrial decline of the 1990s resulted in a significant reduction of many sources of pollution, but in the period of sharp growth up to mid-2008, such giants as *Norilsk Nickel*, for instance, were reluctant to invest in profit-reducing "clean" technologies. Thus, from 75 million tons of dangerous industrial waste produced in 2007, only 18 percent was duly treated. Correcting Medvedev's estimates, the

Audit Chamber established that one-sixth of Russia's territory – with a population of 60 million people – was ecologically problematic.[53] What is particularly disturbing in this context is the common practice of exploiting the results of ecological monitoring for the hostile take-over of various industrial assets; the saga of the *Sakhalin*-II project, where an international consortium led by *Shell* was forced to sell controlling interest to *Gazprom*, is typical in this respect.[54]

Migration, declining population and other human security challenges

The scope and intensity of various challenges related to human security – from illegal migration to drugs and AIDS – have reached alarming proportions in Russia, and President Putin, in his first address to the parliament, declared that "population decline threatens the survival of our nation." He returned to this issue in the 2006 address, and Dmitri Medvedev made this "perilous problem" one of the key topics in his presidential campaign, arguing that "measured by life expectancy Russia is 100th in the world and by life expectancy for men, 134th."[55] Much positive spin was placed on the slight improvement of vital statistics in early 2008, but the arrival of the crisis has inevitably eliminated all the micro-achievements.[56] It is quite obvious that the strong emphasis on stimulating families toward the second child was politically motivated in order to shape Medvedev's image as a "family-friendly" president, while Russia's real problem of abnormally high mortality was barely addressed; for that matter, the number of deaths in the first half of 2008 was higher than in the corresponding period of 2007.[57]

Russia's population has been shrinking for a long time, with the average rate of 0.4 percent in the 2000s, but it was only since the middle of the decade that the labor force has started to contract. The economic boom of Putin's "era" created an expanding demand on the labor market, and that generated a strong inflow of migration – entirely necessary given Russia's demographic situation – but also generated a lot of social tensions. While migrants from other newly-independent states, and particularly Central Asia, were eager to take low-paid jobs that were not attractive for the "locals" – primarily in construction – resentment against the former compatriots took such ugly forms as the pogrom in Kondopoga, Kareila, or the explosion in the Cherkizovsky market, Moscow (both in August 2006). Political sensitivity about the problem of migration made it all but impossible to adapt legislation that would have regulated the import of labor. In consequence, much of the human trafficking and exploitation of *Gastarbeiter* remained illegal, leading to the criminalization of migrant communities and a rise of skinhead violence, often under-reported.[58] The sharp rise of unemployment in the course of economic recession increased the pressure on labor migrants for whom returning home, for instance to the desperately poor Tajikistan, was not an option.[59]

The high level of mortality is caused by many factors, but besides traditional alcoholism and violent death, the spread of infectious diseases is increasingly important. Reflecting upon this problem, Putin decided to make "the fight against infectious diseases" one of the three key themes for the G8 Strelna summit.[60] However, as it turned out, Russia – except for presiding over various meetings – had little to contribute to this matter. Russia is certainly very exposed to the risks of global pandemics, like the H1N1 influenza virus ("swine flu") in 2009, but the main problem is that entirely insufficient resources are directed toward checking the spread of HIV/AIDS and antibiotics-resistant tuberculosis. Both diseases have far greater consequences for Russian society and economy than the authorities are prepared to acknowledge, and this denial is rooted in the highly ambivalent policy regarding sexual minorities in the HIV/AIDS case, and in the manifest reluctance to invest efforts in improving the horrible conditions in prisons, which are the main network for the spread of tuberculosis.[61] A massive aggravating factor in the spread of both diseases is the steady increase in drug addiction, notably heroin, which is flowing in from Afghanistan. The Federal Service for Control over Trafficking of Narcotics (*Gosnarkokontrol*) was deeply involved in "clan wars" between several law-enforcement agencies in the last year of Putin's presidency, and is neither able nor interested in waging an efficient "war on drugs" in the period of deepening economic crisis.[62] The particular attention paid to healthcare in the National Security Strategy approved in May 2009 will hardly be translated into a sustained priority in resource allocation.

Conclusions

The evolution of views among the Russian political elite and within Russian society regarding transformation of the world system and Russia's place in it was sharply broken by the devastating impact of the economic crisis. As a result, the steady strengthening of expectations for assuming the "natural" role as one of the key players in a "multipolar world" has given way to disorientation not dissimilar to the one accompanying the collapse of the USSR. It was not the turn of economic fortunes per se that has caused this reluctant devaluation of ambitions, but rather the exposure to a bundle of inter-connected problems; perhaps the most obvious being the demographic decline, which had remained camouflaged in the years of petro-prosperity. Through the frustration of wasted efforts, a sobering recognition is emerging that a Russia which is not able to secure a life expectancy of 60 years for its men or produce a sufficient cohort for military draft cannot project much influence in global affairs.

Like many – perhaps even most – countries ambushed by the crisis, Russia is consumed with the current affairs of its management, but in its political class, which is more corrupt and cynical than its Western counterparts, a conviction is growing that the post-Cold War model of globalization shaped by US domination and based on Western norms and values is breaking down. Little can be foreseen about the post-crisis world order, and the newly-set G20 does not constitute a convincing framework for global governance, but Moscow expects that tougher competition and less-binding cooperation would be the features of inter-state relations in the 2010s. In a sense, the pronounced strengthening of the economic role of the state, which is forced to assume key regulatory functions in the financial system and expand its presence in many crisis-affected sectors, fits into the state-centric political philosophy that underpins Russia's often inconsistent foreign policy maneuvering. What is more important, however, is that the very particular model of quasi-democratic and hyper-centralized system of power based on a symbiosis between top bureaucracy and big business – a model that Moscow saw as an alternative to the hypocritical Western "liberal democracy" on a par with the Chinese "market Communism" – has shown high vulnerability and perhaps non-sustainability. Little consolation, therefore, can be found in the revival of states as the central actors in the global system and the retreat of various non-state agents, including NGOs, as Russia's own state has yet again arrived at a dead-end where the rigid political regime constitutes an obstacle for economic rehabilitation.

Moscow declares adherence to, and positions itself as a staunch upholder of, international law, but in fact Russia consistently aims at reducing the prescriptive power of rules adopted by inter-state organizations and minimizing their enforcement mechanisms. Russia would then be secure from any unwanted external interference but retain sufficient freedom of maneuver for selective power projection, like in the war with Georgia. Focusing primarily on traditional *Realpolitik* risks of inter-state competition, Moscow pays little attention to, and underestimates its own vulnerability to, non-traditional security challenges – from climate change to corruption and crime. Russia has developed a habit of ushering transformation of the global system, which might indeed accelerate due to the profound crisis at the end of the second post-Cold War decade, but it is not building a new position of strength and so could find itself among the losers.

Notes

1 Two solid sources on Putin's system of power are Richard Sakwa, *Putin: Russia's Choice*, 2nd edn. (London: Routledge 2007); Lilia Shevtsova, *Russia – Lost in Transition: The Yeltsin and Putin Legacies* (Washington, DC: CEIP, 2007); also useful is Dale Herspring, ed. *Putin's Russia: Past Imperfect, Future Uncertain*, 3rd edn. (London: Rowman & Littlefield, 2006); my analysis here draws on findings and conclusions from Pavel Baev, *Russian Energy Policy and Military Power: Putin's Quest for Greatness* (London: Routledge, 2008).
2 The goal of "doubling the GDP" was one of Putin's best-known economic guidelines; see Sergei Shelin, "The Bubble of Doubling the GDP [in Russian]," *Gazeta.ru*, 4 February 2009.
3 Ghia Nodia, "The Wounds of Lost Empire," *Journal of Democracy* 20, 2 (2009).
4 On Putin's political vocabulary, see Fedor Lukyanov, "Sarcasm and Tiredness [in Russian]," *Gazeta.ru*, 1 November 2007. For brilliant examinations of how Russia "was able to resist the onslaught of Europe" in the course of its unique history, see Marshall T. Poe, *The Russian Moment in World History* (Princeton: Princeton University Press, 2003). Dominic Lieven, *Empire: The Russian Empire and Its Rivals* (New Haven: Yale University Press, 2000) is perhaps the best source on Russian imperialism.
5 The English version of the transcript of the interview for Russian TV channels on 31 August 2008 is available on the presidential website: http://president.kremlin.ru/eng/speeches/2008/08/31/1850_type82912type82916_206003.shtml.

6 On the imperative to limit Putin's instrumental use of anti-Americanism in Medvedev's foreign policy, see Pavel Baev, "Medvedev Fingers the "Reset Button" but Preaches Anti-Americanism," *Eurasia Daily Monitor*, 23 March 2009; Nikolai Zlobin, "The Window is Open [in Russian]," *Rossiiskaya gazeta*, 18 March 2009.

7 Vladislav Inozemtsev, "Dreams About a Multi-Polar World [in Russian]," *Nezavisimaya gazeta*, 18 September 2008; Aleksandr Konovalov, "The World Should Not Be Multi-Polar [in Russian]," *Nezavisimaya gazeta*, 16 September 2008.

8 The real scale of degradation of Russian armed forces by the end of Putin's presidency is analyzed in the report prepared by Boris Nemtsov and Vladimir Milov, *"Putin:Itogi* [Putin: The Results] – Independent expert report," *Novaya gazeta* 2008.

9 One balanced analysis of that war is Roy Allison, "Russia Resurgent? Moscow's Campaign to 'Coerce Georgia To Peace'," *International Affairs* 84, 6 (2008); on Medvedev's efforts, see Aleksei Arbatov, "International Security After the Caucasian Crisis [in Russian]," *Polit.ru*, 17 October 2008.

10 Marshall Goldman, *Petrostate: Putin, Power, and the New Russia* (Oxford: Oxford University Press, 2008) made a thorough evaluation of the central role of Russia's energy sector right before the turn of economic fortunes.

11 Alyson Bailes *et al.*, "The Shanghai Cooperation Organization," *SIPRI Policy Paper* 17 (2007).

12 On the Russian veto that blocked the Western efforts to impose UN sanctions against Zimbabwe in July 2008, see "The Return of Mr Nyet," *The Economist*, 17 July 2008.

13 Spring 2009 saw a new round of debates in Russia on the ten-year-old conflict; see Aleksandr Sharavin, "Demonstrative Application of Allied Force [in Russian]," *Nezavisimoe voennoe obozrenie* (2009).

14 Fedor Lukyanov, "After the War of Ambitions [in Russian]," *Gazeta.ru*, 19 February 2009.

15 On the Russian assessments of the Iranian nuclear prospects, see Igor Ivanov, "What Could Be Offered To Tehran? [in Russian]," *Vremya novostei*, 29 May 2009; on the Angarsk project, see Anton Khlopkov, "The Angarsk Project: Enrichment vs Proliferation," *Security Index* 85, 3 (2008).

16 Andrei Illarionov, former economic adviser to Putin, argued that Russia did not meet the basic criteria of G7 membership: Andrei Illarionov, "On the Eve of the Summit: The Death of the G8 [in Russian]," *Vedomosti*, 18 April 2006. A useful preview of the Strelna summit is Vladimir Orlov and Miriam Fugfugosh, "The G8 Strelna Summit and Russia's National Power," *The Washington Quarterly* 29, 3 (2006). My analysis is in Pavel Baev, "Leading in the Concert of Great Powers: Lessons from Russia's G8 Chairmanship," in *The Multilateral Dimension in Russian Foreign Policy*, eds. Elana Wilson Rowe and Stina Torjesen (London: Routledge, 2008).

17 The proposal for expanding the format was already pioneered by Canadian Prime Minister Paul Martin in 2004; see Johannes Lynn and Colin Bradford, "The Irrelevant G8 Summit in St. Petersburg," in *Global Economics Paper* (The Brookings Institution, 2006).

18 The proposals (marked by quite distinctive anti-Americanism) were displayed on the presidential website but found little reflection in the approved documents: http://president.kremlin.ru/eng/text/docs/2009/03/213995.shtml.

19 Fedor Lukyanov, "The Legend About the Big Two [in Russian]," *Gazeta.ru*, 26 February 2009.

20 Sergei Lavrov, "Russia and the OECD," *Wall Street Journal*, 25 April 2007.

21 It is remarkable that the content of debates on the costs and benefits of Russia joining the WTO has not changed much since the early 2000s; see for instance Katinka Barysch *et al.*, *Russia and the WTO* (London: CER, 2002).

22 Andrei Kolesnikov, "Flying Pucks [in Russian]," *Kommersant*, 7 February 2009.

23 Several reports and position papers were prepared by US think tanks in early 2009 on "resetting" relations with Russia, including the WTO issue; see, for instance, Anders

Åslund and Andrew Kuchins, "Pressing "Reset Button" on US–Russia Relations," in *Policy Brief* (Washington: CSIS, 2009). On the Jackson–Vanik Amendment, see Stephen Sestanovich, "Cold War Leftovers," *International Herald Tribune*, 19 May 2009.

24 V.I. Revenkov and V.I. Feigun, " 'Gas OPEC' or other forms of cooperation? [in Russian]," *Russia in Global Affairs* 4 (2007).

25 Literature on NATO–Russia relations is vast and often biased; one useful overview is Hannes Adomeit, "Inside or Outside? Russia's Policies Towards NATO," in *The Multilateral Dimension in Russian Foreign Policy*, eds. Elana Wilson Rowe and Stina Torjesen (London: Routledge, 2008). A midstream Russian position is Sergei Karaganov, "About Russia–NATO and more [in Russian]," *Rossiiskaya gazeta*, 26 March 2008.

26 Sharp and balanced analysis of Russia–EU relations is Arkady Moshes, "EU–Russia Relations: Unfortunate Continuity," *European Issues (Foundation Robert Shuman)* 126 (2009). On the OSCE troubles, see Arkady Dubnov, "OSCE as a Battlefield [in Russian]," *Russia in Global Affairs* 4 (2008).

27 The idea was first put forward in Medvedev's public speech in Berlin on 5 June 2008 and then elaborated at a world policy conference in Evian on 9 October 2008; Foreign Minister Lavrov, summing up the results of 2008, argued that the "security architecture" was fragmented and inadequate to current tasks; an English version of his statement is available on the Foreign Ministry website at: www.mid.ru/brp_4.nsf/english?OpenView&Start=1.145.

28 Arkady Dubnov, "NATO Has No Trust in Russian Architects of European Security [in Russian]," *Vremya novostei*, 5 December 2008.

29 The text (in Russian) is available at the Security Council website: www.scrf.gov.ru/documents/99.html; one sharp comment is Aleksandr Golts, "Landscape After the Battle [in Russian]," *Ezhednevny zhurnal*, 20 May 2009.

30 English translation of the Concept is available at the Foreign Ministry website: www.mid.ru/ns-osndoc.nsf/osndd.

31 For my more elaborate analysis of this impact, see Pavel Baev, "Instrumentalizing Counter-Terrorism for Regime Consolidation in Putin's Russia," *Studies in Conflict & Terrorism* 27, 4 (2004).

32 One good source on this difference is E. Stepanova, *Terrorism in Asymmetrical Conflict: Ideological and Structural Aspects* (Oxford: Oxford University Press, 2008). James Hughes, *Chechnya: From Nationalism to Jihad* (Philadelphia: University of Pennsylvania Press, 2007) is useful on Chechnya.

33 In spring 2009, the NAK prepared a concept for countering terrorism, which is yet to be adopted and is not presented on its rather primitive website: http://nak.fsb.ru.

34 I examined this fusion of counter-terrorism and counter-revolution in Pavel Baev, "Turning Counter-Terrorism into Counter-Revolution: Russia Focuses on Kazakhstan and Engages Turkmenistan," *European Security* 15, 1 (2006).

35 Putin made this much-cited assessment in the annual report to the parliament on 25 April 2005; for a sound reading, see Dmitri Trenin, "Reading Russian Right," in *Policy Brief* (Washington, DC: CEIP, 2005).

36 Christoph Zürcher, *The Post-Soviet Wars: Rebellion, Ethnic Conflict, and Nationhood in the Caucasus* (New York: New York University Press, 2007).

37 In the vast literature on Chechnya, Anatol Lieven, *Chechnya: Tombstone of Russian Power* (New Haven: Yale University Press, 1998) is probably the best account of the first war, while Matthew Evangelista, *The Chechen Wars: Will Russia Go the Way of the Soviet Union?* (Washington, DC: Brookings Institution, 2002) examines the path into the second one, and Richard Sakwa, ed. *Chechnya: From Past to Future* (London: Anthem Press, 2005) is also useful.

38 Dov Lynch, "Why Georgia matters," *Chaillot Paper* 86 (2006).

39 Allison, "Russia Resurgent? Moscow's Campaign to 'Coerce Georgia to Peace'."

40 Ekaterina Kuznetsova, "Double Standards Russian-Style [in Russian]," *Nezavisimaya gazeta*, 17 March 2009.
41 Aleksandr Ryabushev, "Anti-Pirate Cruise of Neustrashimy [in Russian]," *Nezavisimoe voennoe obozrenie*, 13 February 2009.
42 A useful collection of analyses of relevant issues by top Russian experts is Aleksei Arbatov and Vladimir Dvorkin, eds. *Nuclear Weapons After the Cold War* (Moscow: Carnegie Center, 2008).
43 See, for instance, Anatoly Diakov and Evgeny Miasnikov, "Post-2009 SOA Control in Russia and the United States: Room for a compromise?," *Security Index* 86, 1 (2008). A highly useful collection of data and commentary is gathered at the blog "Russian Strategic Nuclear Forces" edited by Pavel Podvig at Stanford University: http://russianforces.org.
44 Aleksei Arbatov and Rose Gottemoeller, "New Presidents, New Agreements? Advancing US–Russian Strategic Arms Control," *Arms Control Today* July/August (2008).
45 Evgeny Grigoryev, "From Gorbachev to Obama; New US President Tries to Harvest Political Dividend from the Illusion of Nuclear-Free World [in Russian]," *Nezavisimaya gazeta*, 20 April 2009.
46 Very useful information on the nuclear problem is accumulated at the Bellona Foundation website; see for instance, Anna Kireeva, "Russia Spurs Ahead Environmental Overhaul of Decrepit Northern Fleet Bases," *Bellona News*, 12 January 2009.
47 On the opening of the Shchuchye plant in May 2009, see Clifford J. Levy, "In Siberia, the Death Knell of a Complex Holding a Deadly Stockpile," *International Herald Tribune*, 26 May 2009.
48 The USSR signed and ratified the Biological Weapons Convention in 1975, so the development of weaponized bio-substances in the *Biopreparat* agency was revealed only after 1991; on the poor security at the Pokrov lab, see Bob Graham, "Bioterrorism – A Preventable Catastrophe," *Boston Globe*, 18 December 2008.
49 Andrei Illarionov, Putin's economic adviser, was the most vociferous critic of the Kyoto Protocol: Andrei Illarionov, "Global Darkening: Absurd Goals, Expensive Decisions, Falsified Arguments in the Fight Against Climate Warming [in Russian]," *Izvestia*, 30 March 2005.
50 China has advanced to the top of that list, followed by the US and India; see "China Passes US, Leads World in Power Sector Carbon Emissions," *Center for Global Development*, 27 August 2008.
51 The text is available at: www.kremlin.ru/eng/text/news/2008/06/202099.shtml.
52 That meeting on "Improving Environmental and Energy Efficiency in the Russian Economy" was held in June 2008, right before the first hit of the economic crisis. See: www.kremlin.ru/eng/speeches/2008/06/03/2225_type82912type82913_202070.shtml.
53 Aleksandra Koshkina, "The Audit Chamber Evaluated the Waste [in Russian]," *Gazeta*, 22 May 2009.
54 Marshall Goldman, "The Russian Power Play on Oil, Natural Gas Reserves," *Boston Globe*, 23 August 2008.
55 That session of the Presidential Council for Implementing Priority National Projects and Demographic Policy in March 2007 can, in retrospect, be seen as the start of his rise to the presidential nomination. See: www.kremlin.ru/eng/speeches/2007/03/07/1944_type82913type82917_119295.shtml.
56 Anatoly Vishnevsky, Director of the Institute for Demography, argued that the increase in the number of births in 2008 would be followed by a deep and sustained decline; see Aleksandra Samarina and Ada Gorbacheva, "The Demographic Pit [in Russian]," *Nezavisimaya gazeta*, 6 March 2009.
57 Solid analysis of the politics of Russia's demographic problems can be found in Graeme Herd and Gagik Sargsyan, "Debating Russian Demographic Security: Current Trends and Future Trajectories," *Security Index* 82, 2 (2007).

58 Lidya Grafova, "Migrants Must Become Legal! [in Russian]," *Novaya gazeta*, 13 November 2008.
59 Russian trade unions demanded a complete ban on the import of labor and the government contemplated the proposal for helping repatriations; see Ivan Rodin, "The Government Contemplates the Rights of Migrants [in Russian]," *Nezavisimaya gazeta*, 2 February 2009.
60 Putin's statement on that, as well as on the relevant meetings of the working groups, is available on the summit website: http://en.g8russia.ru/agenda.
61 On the HIV/AIDS policy, see Celeste Wallander, "The Politics of Russia's HIV/AIDS Policy," in *HIV/AIDS in Russia and Eurasi*, ed. Judyth L. Twigg (London: Palgrave Macmillan, 2007). On the economics of a flu pandemic, see Sergei Guriev and Oleg Tsivinsky, "Ratio Economica: The Economics of Plague [in Russian]," *Vedomosti*, 12 May 2009.
62 The head of *Gosnarkokontrol*, Viktor Cherkesov, revealed some of the "ideology" behind that "internecine war" in an article published in *Kommersant*: Viktor Cherkesov, "We Cannot Allow the Warriors to Become Traders [in Russian]," *Kommersant*, 9 October 2007. My reflections are in Pavel Baev, "Infighting Among Putin's Siloviki Escalates to a 'Clan War'," *Eurasia Daily Monitor*, 11 October 2007.

8 China as an emergent center of global power

Bates Gill

China: emergent center of global power

It seems hard to believe today, but not so long ago the prestigious journal *Foreign Affairs* published a serious article entitled, "Does China Matter?"[1] Such a question was still worthy of debate in the late-1990s, but now it is almost universally recognized that China does indeed matter, given its growing weight in global affairs, and its increasing ability – for better or for worse – to shape the future world order.

Numbers alone readily attest to China's emerging status as a global power center. China has the world's largest population, largest standing army, second largest military expenditures, the third or fourth largest nuclear weapons arsenal and is one of five veto-wielding permanent members of the United Nations Security Council. It has had the fastest-growing economy over the past 30 years and is currently the world's third largest economy with the largest foreign currency reserves. It is the largest importer of iron ore, aluminum and paper, the second greatest consumer of oil, and the largest emitter of greenhouse gases. China has the world's largest number of mobile telephone and Internet users, Chinese is the dominant language for content on the worldwide web, and China is the third-largest patent-filer after the United States and Japan. Over the past 25 years, China has lifted some 200 million or more persons from poverty – one of the most rapid and remarkable socioeconomic transformations in history. The statistics go on and on.

But China has also attained its status through other, less tangible, though nevertheless important, channels of influence and power. China today has an active and growing diplomatic presence across the globe, and increasingly takes part in a full range of multilateral governmental and nongovernmental organizations, including those concerned with global order and stability. Chinese enterprises and entrepreneurs can be found from the world's capitalist capitals, to the most remote parts of the globe and everywhere in between, and all are seeking profit and shareholder value. Chinese overseas direct investment is expanding exponentially, from a mere US$2.7 billion in 2003 to an expected US$100 billion-plus in 2009.[2] Since 2004, the Chinese government has established more than 300 Confucius Institutes – typically based at universities to promote the study of

Chinese language, culture and history – in more than 80 countries, with ambitious plans to add hundreds more in the years to come.[3] China sent some 180,000 students to study abroad in 2008, and accepted some 190,000 students from 188 countries and regions to study in China.[4] Chinese official development aid and other forms of governmental assistance in the developing world are rapidly growing. Chinese contributions to United Nations peacekeeping forces have increased by 20-fold since the late-1990s.

In short, there is little doubt that China deserves recognition as an emerging center of global power, but this point only raises more questions about *how* China will exercise its growing power and influence to shape the future world order. In particular, an analysis of China raises important questions that are central to this volume. What are the Chinese perceptions about the major challenges to Chinese security and world order, especially those identified as strategic in nature by the "political West," such as terrorism, failing states and regional instabilities, proliferation of weapons of mass destruction (WMD), and environmental and energy security? What policies are being made by the Chinese government in response to these challenges? To what extent will Chinese policy look to the pillars of a more liberalized world order – more open borders, global and regional institutions, multilateral regimes and international law – to help cope with these challenges? What will China's future approach to shaping global order look like?[5]

To shed some light on these questions, this chapter will first provide an overview of Chinese security challenges and priorities as perceived by Beijing. With these in mind, the chapter will then discuss the principal policy actions that have been taken by Beijing in response to these challenges, including the extent to which Beijing's security decisions are shaped by globalization and international organizations, regimes and law. The chapter will conclude by looking at current and likely future trajectories for China's approach to important security threats and global order and its implications.

China's security priorities

The vast majority of Chinese strategists and policy-makers would probably give differing priorities than those in the West to such challenges as terrorism, failing states and regional instabilities, proliferation of WMD, and environmental and energy security. However, while these issues did not traditionally receive a great deal of attention in recent decades in China, their salience has quickly increased over this period, with some issues – such as energy and environmental security – gaining ground faster than others. The growing importance of these issues in Chinese strategic thinking is likely to continue, but in most cases will still fall short of the weight they receive on the list of security priorities as seen by the West.

Why is this the case? The principal reason for this likely continuing mismatch lies, understandably, in how Chinese leaders and strategists view their own security environment. Simplistically speaking, they are more concerned with what they see as more immediate and readily-identifiable "domestic" or "internal" threats to Chinese sovereignty, territorial integrity, leadership legitimacy and stability, than they are with the kinds of "global" challenges identified by the West. From a Chinese perspective, the principal security concerns for China would include pro-independence movements in places such as Taiwan, Tibet and Xinjiang, domestic socioeconomic development and stability, and attempts by "outside forces" to undermine China's cohesion at home, interfere in its internal affairs and contain China's aspirations as a rising power. To the degree that the global challenges highlighted in this volume – such as terrorism, failing states and regional instabilities, proliferation of WMD, and environmental and energy security – clearly impact on these core Chinese sovereignty, stability and security concerns, then they are more likely to gain in prominence and priority in China.

Sovereignty, territorial integrity and domestic stability

In the most authoritative document outlining Chinese security thinking – the biannual Chinese defense white paper – we learn that, at a strategic global level, Beijing is cautiously optimistic and believes that "[p]eace and development remain the principal themes of the times, and the pursuit of peace, development and cooperation has become an irresistible trend of the times." However, at the same time, the white paper recognizes that "global challenges are on the increase, and new security threats keep emerging."[6] This understanding is based on the strategic assessment that:

> Economic globalization and world multi-polarization are gaining momentum ... progress toward industrialization and informationization throughout the globe is accelerating and economic cooperation is in full swing, leading to increasing economic interdependence, inter-connectivity and interactivity among countries. ... In addition, factors conducive to maintaining peace and containing war are on the rise, and the common interests of countries in the security field have increased, and their willingness to cooperate is enhanced, thereby keeping low the risk of worldwide, all-out and large-scale wars for a relatively long period of time.[7]

The white paper also notes that in spite of uncertainties in the Asia-Pacific region, including "conflicting claims over territorial and maritime rights," an increase in US "strategic attention to and input in the Asia-Pacific region," and problems of "terrorism, separatist and extremist forces" and "non-traditional security issues," it finds that the "Asia-Pacific security situation is stable on the whole."[8]

When turning specifically to China's security situation, the white paper finds that "China's security situation has improved steadily" owing to its modernization, increase in overall national strength and improvements in the country's capability to uphold national security. But, despite this good news overall, the white paper stresses that China confronts "long-term, complicated and diverse threats and challenges." The white paper spells out these problems clearly:

> Issues of existence security and development security, traditional security threats and non-traditional security threats, and domestic security and international security, are interwoven and interactive. China is faced with the superiority of the developed countries in economy, science and technology, as well as military affairs. It also faces strategic maneuvers and containment from the outside while having to face disruption and sabotage by separatist and hostile forces from the inside. Being in a stage of economic and social transition, China is encountering many new circumstances and new issues in maintaining social stability. Separatist forces working for "Taiwan independence," "East Turkistan independence" and "Tibet independence" pose threats to China's unity and security. Damages caused by non-traditional security threats like terrorism, natural disasters, economic insecurity, and information insecurity are on the rise. Impact of uncertainties and destabilizing factors in China's outside security environment on national security and development is growing. In particular, the United States continues to sell arms to Taiwan in violation of the principles established in the three Sino-U.S. joint communiques, causing serious harm to Sino-U.S. relations as well as peace and stability across the Taiwan Straits.[9]

Emergent new security challenges

While concerns about China's domestic security will remain paramount, the country's increasing engagement and integration with a globalizing world has meant that global security challenges increasingly have an impact on China's domestic situation. As noted above, the Chinese defense white paper recognizes increasing problems for China caused by "non-traditional security threats like terrorism, natural disasters, economic insecurity, and information insecurity." Importantly, the white paper also sees a strengthening "interwoven and interactive" linkage between "uncertainties and destabilizing factors in China's outside security environment" on the one hand and "national security and development" on the other. As such, while of secondary importance compared to the domestic concerns described above, global, non-traditional security issues have been in recent years accorded greater and greater weight in Chinese deliberations about national security.[10]

For example, let us consider the four issue areas examined by this volume: terrorism, failing states and regional instabilities, proliferation of WMD, and environmental and energy security. Of these, environmental and energy security has probably gained the greatest new attention and priority in China in recent years because of its increasing relevance to matters of domestic stability. On this issue, China faces a strategic dilemma. On the one hand, Chinese leaders at the national level see continued economic growth not only as central to the country's strategic ambitions to regain Great Power status, but also as at the core of an unspoken, but tacitly understood, "social compact" between China's leaders and its people: in return for continued prosperity and economic opportunity, Chinese one-party rule can retain its claim to legitimate leadership of the country.

But, on the other hand, to make good on this compact, Chinese leaders must continue to stoke the engines of economic growth – it is widely understood among Chinese leaders that growth should be maintained at 7 or 8 percent annually – in spite of the attendant challenges of energy and environmental security that inevitably arise. Under these circumstances, China has become increasingly reliant on foreign sources of energy to fuel its economic trajectory. This dependence will only increase over the foreseeable future as the country seeks to diversify its energy mix and respond to growing demand – especially in the transport, industrial and power-generation sectors – for natural gas and refined petroleum products.

As the Chinese white paper on energy clearly notes:

> Energy security is a global issue. Every country has the right to rationally utilize energy resources for its own development, and the overwhelming majority of countries could not enjoy energy security without international cooperation. To realize a steady and orderly development of the world economy, it is necessary to promote economic globalization to develop in a direction featuring balance, universal benefit and win–win, and it is necessary for the international community to foster a new concept of energy security characterized by mutual benefit and cooperation, diversified development and coordinated guarantee.
>
> [...]
>
> Safeguarding world peace and regional stability is the prerequisite for global energy security. The international community should work collaboratively to maintain stability in oil producing and exporting countries, especially those in the Middle East, to ensure the security of international energy transport routes and avoid geopolitical conflicts that affect the world's energy supply. The various countries should settle disputes and resolve contradictions through dialogue and consultation. Energy issues should not be politicized, and triggering antagonism as well as the use of force should be avoided.[11]

To put it another way, accessing reliable, stable and affordable supplies of energy will be a critical factor in assuring continued growth, development and domestic stability. Moreover, Chinese leaders recognize that China's more active presence in energy markets abroad, to include political and economic relationships with such countries as Iran and Sudan, often creates diplomatic problems for Beijing's ties with key Western governments. China's approach to meeting its energy needs also has an impact on its domestic environmental situation: China's continued heavy reliance on domestic, high-sulfur sources of coal – the country meets about 75 to 80 percent of its energy needs through exploitation of its own vast coal reserves – contributes massively to the heavy air-pollution so commonly found in China's industrialized and urbanized areas.

Environmentally speaking, China's unprecedented economic growth has led to worsening ecological conditions for the country's people, its public health and its landscape: lowered water tables, deforestation, desertification, poisoned waterways and agricultural areas, and polluted air. Moreover, the situation also has a detrimental impact on China's economy and international image. Some studies suggest that ongoing environmental degradation and pollution could cost the Chinese economy between 8 and 12 percent of GDP annually; in 2005, the Vice Minister of China's Environmental Protection Agency stated, "the [economic] miracle will end soon because the environment can no longer keep pace." In turn, this situation has also become a catalyst for unrest, civil disturbances and rioting in localities in China where environmental degradation threatens lives and livelihoods.[12]

In recent years, concern within China about terrorism and political extremism has also increased. This increased concern has partly been a result of the far higher prominence this issue is given by other major actors in the international system, such as the United States, especially since the September 2001 attacks on US soil. But here, again, China's concern appears to be largely associated with how extremist networks outside of China may affect questions of Chinese sovereignty, territorial integrity and stability rather than with terrorism at a global level.

In particular, Beijing claims it faces its own domestic terrorist challenge in the form of violent acts perpetrated by identified pro-independence Uighur groups – such as the Eastern Turkestan Islamic Movement (ETIM), the East Turkestan Liberation Organization and the World Uighur Youth Congress – in China's far northwestern region of Xinjiang. Among other incidents, Beijing points to bombings and loss of life in Urumqi and Beijing in the 1990s, the apprehension of Uighur Chinese nationals in Afghanistan during the US-led invasion of the country in 2001, the January 2007 raid of a suspected ETIM holdout on the China–Afghan border, a foiled skyjacking in March 2008, the attack killing 16 police in Xinjiang by two armed men just before the 2008 Beijing Olympics, as well as other incidents, as evidence of the domestic terrorist challenge it faces. The ethnic violence that flared between Han Chinese and Uighurs in the summer of 2009, especially in Urumqi, only fueled further tensions and suspicions in China about terrorist activity and violent pro-independence extremism. In turn, this will likely deepen the linkage Chinese strategists and policy-makers see between the global challenge of terrorism and political extremism and China's domestic stability concerns.

China's concern with WMD proliferation has likewise undergone a change over the past two decades. In terms of priorities, however, it too ranks below the major domestic challenges China faces, and is probably also seen as less of a problem than potential threats posed by energy and environmental security, or by terrorism and political extremism. Nevertheless, WMD non-proliferation has increased in profile and salience within the Chinese security agenda, especially when compared to 20 years ago – China did not even join the Nuclear Non-Proliferation Treaty (NPT) until 1992.

But, even as WMD proliferation is taken more seriously by Beijing, the problem has been largely perceived as one that does not necessarily affect China directly, and hence has not been accorded as high a priority as other challenges. It is true that China has signed on to all the major international arms control and non-proliferation treaties, and has put in place most of the necessary domestic policy decisions, regulatory frameworks and enforcement mechanisms commensurate with those commitments. Beijing has also worked more closely in recent years with major international partners to address proliferation concerns in places such as Iran and North Korea. There are a range of good explanations for these choices and China's stronger interest and action with regard to arms control and non-proliferation.[13]

By and large, however, these decisions by Beijing appear to have been taken with an eye to burnishing China's reputation and in response to pressures and inducements by the United States. Beijing seems far more reluctant to impose tough measures on would-be proliferators, either unilaterally or multilaterally, as a means to addressing emergent WMD proliferation threats. China's unwillingness to support stricter United Nations sanctions on Iran, for example, in spite of mounting evidence of Iran's long-term nuclear ambitions, is a case in point. There remains within some parts of China's strategic and political elite a lingering ambivalence toward WMD proliferation, with many believing non-proliferation is a hypocritical ploy of more powerful countries, particularly in the West, to assure that weaker countries stay that way, while the strong continue to build up their nuclear and conventional arsenals.

The one case of WMD proliferation toward which China has given very high priority is North Korea. The reasons behind Beijing's far more active engagement to stem WMD proliferation on the Korean peninsula are complex, but here too – and as is the case with the other three strategic security challenges discussed in this section – Beijing's concern seems primarily driven by more narrow Chinese domestic concerns than with a concern about addressing a global strategic challenge per se.

At the heart of China's approach to Pyongyang's WMD aspirations is Beijing's concern for avoiding at all costs a rapid political or social change in North Korea, such as regime collapse – be it through sanctions or warfare or by Pyongyang's own actions – which, in Beijing's view, could have enormous negative effects on China. Among these negatives would be the potential large-scale and destabilizing refugee flows into China's northeast, the loss of a quasi-allied buffer state, the prospect of American and American-allied forces in northern Korea near the Chinese border and the possibility of a unified Korean peninsula allied with the United States. As North Korea continued its pursuit of nuclear weapons and tensions rose on the Korean peninsula, China – reluctantly at first – became more engaged with regional partners to address the problem, primarily through hosting and seeking resolution through the Six Party Talks in the early-to-mid-2000s.

In prioritizing the four strategic challenges discussed here, the problems of failed states and regional instability would probably come last on Beijing's list. Two important reasons stand out for this view, and both can be related to Beijing's overriding concern with domestic security. The first is more practical: for most of the past two decades, China's immediate periphery and the country's domestic stability were not urgently threatened by the specter of failed states and regional instabilities. Rather, quite the opposite was the case, as East Asia since the end of the Cold War has gone through a remarkable period of dynamic economic development, considerable political stability and a near-absence of major armed conflict.

A second reason is based on principle. By and large, Beijing is reluctant to proactively address issues concerning failed or failing states, or matters of regional instability, owing to its longstanding principle of non-interference in the internal affairs of states. As a developing world state with a colonialized past, and as a country which was subjected to invasion and occupation by imperial powers, China has – since its founding as the People's Republic in 1949 – stood for the rights of sovereign states to carry out their own business within their own borders, free from coercion, hegemony and intervention from outside forces. Beijing also has its own self-interested reasons for standing by this principle, as it vehemently opposes efforts by outside powers to meddle in what it deems to be strictly Chinese domestic affairs, such as relations with Taiwan or the status of minorities in places such as Tibet and Xinjiang.

All that said, Beijing has taken steps in recent years to demonstrate some greater concern with the stability of certain states, and has taken quiet steps to "intervene" diplomatically and economically with the aim of shaping outcomes more in China's favor. This slight change in Chinese thinking has arisen in part because of the greater incidence of internal turmoil and potential state failure in critical countries on China's border – such as Afghanistan, Myanmar, North Korea and Pakistan. Another reason behind China's changed thinking on this issue is the country's deepening engagement in a globalizing world, such that regional instabilities once considered far beyond Chinese borders are now being felt at home. Nevertheless, we are only now seeing the beginnings of a debate among Chinese strategists and policy-makers on how China, as an emergent power with growing global and regional interests, should more flexibly interpret its traditional principle of non-interference.[14]

In sum, since the late-1990s and early-2000s, Beijing has given increasing priority to the four strategic challenges highlighted in this volume. However, it is important to recognize and understand the principal prism through which Beijing sees these challenges – that of domestic sovereignty, territorial integrity, social stability and political legitimacy. As, and when, such challenges as terrorism, failing states and regional instabilities, proliferation of WMD, and environmental and energy security have a greater bearing on matters of Chinese domestic sovereignty, stability and security concerns, those global issues rise in importance to China. Beijing has begun to see such a pattern in recent years, and has started to adjust its foreign policy and strategic thinking accordingly.

China's response

Having reviewed Chinese perceptions of its security environment, the chapter now turns to discussing the principal policy actions Beijing has taken in response to the four strategic security challenges highlighted in this volume. This section will focus in particular on the extent to which Beijing's policies regarding these challenges are shaped by globalization and engagement with international organizations, regimes and law.

Three broad points serve to introduce and frame this part of the discussion. First, as noted above, China's deepening integration into a more globalized world has surely had an impact on shaping Chinese perceptions of, and policy responses to, its security environment. With its burgeoning economic, trade and investment activities leading the way, China has become more and more intensely integrated into world affairs, and has an increasing stake in security and stability in more and more places around the globe. As one of the world's major actors in, and beneficiaries of, globalization, Chinese leaders, strategists, business people and other elites are all the more acutely aware of how global challenges can have an impact on Chinese interests; especially its core interests related to sovereignty and domestic stability. As noted above, China's growing global interests mean that such strategic challenges as energy security and terrorism – issues which were not even given a particularly high priority until the late-1990s – are now given increasing attention, both at home and as part of Beijing's international diplomacy.

Second, China has long stressed the importance of key international organizations and international law as the most appropriate instruments through which problems of global and regional security should be mediated. As a developing world state with a self-proclaimed perception of itself as a relatively weak and formerly victimized player in the international system, China insists the world should look to international institutions such as the United Nations and its Charter as the fairest, most legitimate and most "democratic" means to addressing problems between and among states. China puts forward this view of a more "democratic world order" in opposition to what it sees as the hegemonic, unilateralist and "bullying" tendencies of other major states in the international system (without typically naming names, Beijing is usually referring to the United States in this context). Beijing will typically oppose efforts by a single state or small group of states to forcefully impose their interests on others without first building a broader regional or international consensus to do so, preferably expressed in the form of political support or express mandates from the appropriately authorized international organization. If anything, China is probably more "conservative" on this score – being reluctant to reform current institutions or precipitously create new, more proactively effective ones – compared to members of the Western bloc of countries.

Third, over the past 10 to 15 years China has dramatically increased both the quantity and quality of its international engagement with a range of multilateral institutions concerned with security issues. China has become more active as a member of the United Nations Security Council, supporting all the United Nations Security Council resolutions in opposition to terrorism and WMD proliferation, and in signing on to nearly all the major arms control and non-proliferation treaties, agreements and regimes. In addition, China has taken a more active role in a host of emergent multilateral channels to address the challenges of energy and environmental security, and become a more active participant in a wide range of multilateral bodies concerned with regional security; even working to initiate new groupings. These include the Association of Southeast Asian Nations (ASEAN) Regional Forum (ARF), the Asia Pacific Economic Cooperation (APEC) forum, the Shanghai Cooperation Organization (SCO), the Six Party Talks on Korean peninsula security, the ASEAN +3 process, and the East Asia Summit.[15]

Terrorism and political extremism

Over the past decade, China has increasingly looked to international organizations and other foreign relationships to address the threats it perceives from terrorism and political extremism. As noted above, this is especially true to the extent that Beijing can draw a link between terrorism and political extremism abroad and what it deems to be terrorist activity within its own borders.

Since the mid-to-late-1990s, China has made stemming the "three evils" of terrorism, separatism and extremism a central official goal of its activities within the "Shanghai Five," an informal grouping of China and four of its bordering Central Asian states, Kazakhstan, Kyrgyzstan, Russia and Turkmenistan, and within the Shanghai Cooperation Organization (SCO), which was formally established in 2001 (the SCO consists of the Shanghai Five countries plus Uzbekistan; at the time of this writing, the SCO also has four observer participants: Afghanistan, India, Iran and Pakistan). With the formal establishment of the SCO, the group also issued the Shanghai Convention on the Fight against Terrorism, Separatism and Extremism, which commits SCO member countries to cooperate in combating terrorism along their common borders. Such cooperation has included joint anti-terrorism exercises conducted by military and paramilitary forces of SCO countries. The Convention also led to the establishment in 2002 of the Regional Anti-Terrorism Structure in Tashkent, Uzbekistan, as a permanent agency of the SCO.[16]

In addition, in 2001 and 2002, following the terrorist attacks against the United States in September 2001, China, along with the United States, Afghanistan and Kyrgyzstan, succeeded in listing the East Turkestan Islamic Movement (ETIM) as a "terrorist organization" with the United Nations under United Nations Security Council Resolutions 1267 and 1390. China has also signed on to the relevant United Nations Security Council (UNSC) resolutions to combat terrorism, such as UNSC Resolutions 1368 and 1540, as well as United Nations conventions against terrorism. Furthermore, China has signed formal agreements and carries out regular consultations with neighbors and other partners to cooperate in combating terrorism. For example, in November 2002 at the summit between the ASEAN and China, the parties issued the "Joint Declaration of ASEAN and China on Cooperation in the Field of Non-Traditional Security Issues," in which counter-terrorism is listed as a priority area for cooperation. China is also cooperating with neighbors under the rubric of the ASEAN +3 process (joining the ten nations of ASEAN with China, Japan and South Korea) to include regular consultations of the ASEAN ministers responsible for transnational crime issues with their counterparts from Beijing, Tokyo and Seoul. China also joined its partners in the ARF in 2002 to issue the ARF Statement on Measures Against Terrorist Financing (including freezing of terrorist assets, information exchanges and technical assistance). Also in 2002, China joined its ARF partners in establishing a regular, working-level consultation among ARF members on the issue of counter-terrorism and transnational crime.[17]

China has worked with the United States to have ETIM officially recognized by Washington as a terrorist organization, and has cooperated with the US in sharing limited intelligence information and by taking part in the US-led Container Security Initiative (CSI), which seeks to prevent the shipment of WMD from foreign ports to US shores.[18] In the run-up to the 2008 Beijing Olympics, Chinese authorities sought and received various forms of advice and support from other governments to prevent terrorist incidents during the international games.

Failing states and regional instabilities

Owing to China's traditionally strict interpretation of noninterference, the country has typically been reluctant to intervene politically (let alone militarily) to address problems arising from failing states or regional instabilities. As a permanent member of the UNSC, Beijing only very cautiously invokes the authority of the United Nations to intervene in the internal affairs of sovereign states.

However, when there is a broad international consensus for action, and/or when Chinese national interests are more directly threatened, Beijing will support a response from the United Nations to address security concerns emanating from within states, or to deal with regional instabilities. The best example of this relates to United Nations actions in response to North Korea's nuclear ambitions. Beijing has supported increasingly tough financial and trade sanctions on Pyongyang in response to North Korea's nuclear and missile tests since 2006. China also gave its support within the United Nations for action against Afghanistan following the September 2001 terrorist attacks against the United States. China's approach to developments further afield – such as in Sudan and Iran – also exhibit some greater willingness to work with other major powers to address regional security problems.

At the same time, however, Beijing vetoed UNSC resolutions in 2008 intended to bring greater pressure on the governments in Myanmar and Zimbabwe. In addition, while China is one of the leading economic investors in Afghanistan, it has shown little interest beyond diplomatic support to contribute directly to the stabilization of Afghanistan or to take a more active role in assuring the longer-term stability of Pakistan.

One of the most interesting developments for China in recent years in relation to failing states and regional instabilities is its dramatic increase in contributions to United Nations peacekeeping operations. Until the late-1990s, China typically contributed between 50 and 100 military observers to United Nations missions in such places as the Golan Heights and along the Iraq–Kuwait border. However, as of early 2009, China increased its contributions by more than 20-fold: as of June 2009, China had 2,153 troops, police and observers serving in 10 out of 19 missions. At that time, China was the largest contributor to United Nations peacekeeping operations among the Permanent Five members of the UNSC.[19] China is most active as a contributor of troops to missions in Africa, including its contribution of more than 300 troops to the joint United Nations–African Union deployment in Darfur (UNAMID), and an additional 400-plus troops in southern Sudan (UNMIS). China also contributes personnel to United Nations peacekeeping missions in Haiti, Western Sahara, Democratic Republic of the Congo, Lebanon, Liberia, Timor-Leste, Cote d'Ivoire and with the United Nations Truce Supervision Organization (UNTSO) in the Middle East.[20]

Proliferation of WMD

Since the early-to-mid-1990s, China has been an increasingly constructive contributor to international efforts to stem the proliferation of WMD. China joined the NPT in 1992, and supported the treaty's indefinite extension in 1995. China also signed and ratified the Chemical Weapons Convention in 1993, and signed (but has not yet ratified) the Comprehensive Test Ban Treaty in 1996, and has been a de facto adherent of the treaty (along with other signatory nuclear weapons states France, Russia, the United Kingdom and the United States) by not testing nuclear weapons since that time. China joined a range of other multilateral non-proliferation mechanisms such as the Zangger Committee and the Nuclear Suppliers Group, and has entered into a number of bilateral agreements with the United States – such as agreeing to halt new nuclear cooperation with Iran – going beyond its multilateral commitments.[21]

At the same time, however, China has shown its reluctance in some cases to fully impose the will of the international community to prevent would-be proliferators from achieving their objectives. For example, while showing a willingness to sanction North Korea for its nuclear activities and missile tests, and also hosting the Six Party talks to broker a diplomatic solution to denuclearize the Korean peninsula, Beijing was nevertheless unwilling to allow what it saw as harsh measures by the United Nations or other international actors to bring North Korea into compliance with its non-proliferation obligations. Similarly, Beijing has only allowed for limited penalties and reprimands by the United Nations against Iran, in spite of increasingly concerned reports on the part of the International Atomic Energy Agency (IAEA) about Iran's nuclear programs.

Rather than acting unilaterally or with a handful of like-minded states, Beijing will continue to favor the existing international network of non-proliferation treaties and agreements as what it views as the best available means to prevent the proliferation of WMD, while also allowing for legitimate access to advanced technologies by developing world states. As China's most recent white paper on arms control, disarmament and non-proliferation states:

> The issue of non-proliferation should be dealt with by political and diplomatic means within the framework of international law. The existing international legal system on arms control, disarmament and non-proliferation should be maintained, further strengthened and improved. The legitimate rights and interests of all countries as regards the peaceful use of science and technology should be guaranteed and the role of the UN and other multilateral organizations be brought into full play.[22]

Environmental and energy security

As noted above, China has increasingly recognized the importance of environmental and energy issues to its domestic security situation and how it is viewed internationally. As a result, since the early-to-mid-2000s, it has put in place a more active and constructive set of policies to engage the international community on these issues. It appears to be clearer than ever to Chinese leaders and policy analysts that China must seek to engage international partners and find solutions to its energy- and environmental-related challenges more intensively.

China, along with the United States – even as the two largest emitters of carbon gasses – failed to ratify the Kyoto Protocol. However, Beijing has increased other forms of international engagement on environmental and energy issues. These include taking part in both multilateral and bilateral mechanisms and dialogues, and establishing national-level regulatory frameworks conducive to foreign cooperation and investments in environmental- and energy-related infrastructure and technologies. As the Chinese white paper on energy issues notes, "China's development cannot be achieved without cooperation with the rest of the world" and "with accelerating economic globalization, China has forged increasingly closer ties with the outside world in the field of energy."[23]

At the global level, China is an observer of the Energy Charter and takes part in the International Energy Forum and World Energy Conference. China has shown a particular interest in working within regional multilateral initiatives on energy issues. For example, China engages itself in the energy-related working groups of APEC, the ASEAN +3 Energy Cooperation group, and the Asia-Pacific Partnership for Clean Development and Climate. Bilaterally, China has opened a number of dialogue and technical cooperation mechanisms with a number of key partners – including the European Union, Japan, Russia, the Organization of Petroleum Exporting Countries (OPEC) and the United States – to discuss and develop policy responses on exploration, responsible energy consumption, technological solutions, renewable energy and environmental protection. Beijing and Washington, for example, have launched plans to establish a national-level clean energy research center in China.

Looking ahead, Beijing has formally called upon the international community to establish new mechanisms for promoting energy security and clean development through the intensification of cooperation in energy exploration and utilization, setting up a cooperative system to develop and popularize energy and environmental technologies, and avoiding the politicization of energy and environmental issues.[24] In spite of this official rhetoric, much of the world will focus its attention on China's role and contributions in the run-up to and during the Conference of Parties meeting for the United Nations Framework Climate Change Convention in Copenhagen in December 2009. For a more effective "Copenhagen Protocol" to emerge from the meeting, and to realize a sustainable long-term stabilization of greenhouse gas emissions, China must make a serious and proactive commitment to reduce its emissions.

Current trends and trajectories

From this brief overview of Chinese security priorities and policy responses, we see that the four global security challenges highlighted in this volume are steadily gaining greater and greater attention from Beijing. There is now expanding common ground between China and other major powers to cooperate bilaterally and multilaterally to address these concerns, and that trend is likely to continue in the years ahead.

However, it is also clear that Beijing will be constrained in many ways from taking a highly active or high-profile position on some or all of these issues. Conversely, other major powers will have their own interests and concerns which may limit their willingness to fully engage with China. Among the many important factors at play, three in particular will be critical in shaping the dynamics between China and other major powers on these issues.

The first and perhaps most important relates to China's domestic situation. A more engaged and proactive China on the international scene, and one prepared to address the four global security issues highlighted in this volume, will be strongly determined by the country's ability to maintain domestic stability and steadily build its capacity to meet the economic and social needs of its citizens in an accountable and responsive way. On the one hand, as global security challenges – such as energy and environmental security, or terrorism and political extremism – come to affect China's domestic security situation, Beijing will be all the more intensely committed to address such problems in cooperation with international partners. On the other hand, a China that is plagued by mounting domestic instabilities – or incapable of meeting the rising expectations of its people – could become a far more suspicious, inward-looking and far less cooperative partner on the international scene. This will be a delicate and difficult balance in the coming years, and will deeply affect how China chooses to engage internationally.

Second, in part because of the first point, it appears more likely in the near-to-medium term that Beijing will devote most of its economic, political and diplomatic energies toward regional, rather than global, aspirations. China finds itself in a more favorable economic and diplomatic position within its nearby region, particularly vis-à-vis Northeast, East and Southeast Asia, and while the country is still likely to profess a relatively low-profile approach, it seems likely that in these regions China will seek more of a "leadership" role. Thus, efforts to gain greater Chinese participation and constructive contributions to tackle critical security challenges should look first to engaging China within its own region. While China will certainly need to be engaged to resolve security challenges at a global level, and those efforts need to continue, international partners should also recognize that China will have both a greater political will and substantive capacity to make contributions regionally.

Finally, the willingness of international partners to work with China at either a global or regional level will also be shaped by perceptions of China as a rising power. That is, choices made in Beijing about how it chooses to exercise its growing influence and might will in turn either strengthen or undermine the willingness of others to work with China. For example, the rapid military build-up that has accompanied China's economic rise has sparked considerable worry by some who view it as part of an aggressive Chinese design to remake East Asia and the globe. Many concerns also accompany China's growing role as a provider of "no-strings-attached" overseas development aid, or as a supporter of regimes in such places as Sudan or Myanmar. Still others voice concern that Beijing merely seeks to gain fully from the benefits of the international system, with increasing options to diverge from the current world order if it should choose to do so.

These critical factors and other important developments should lead us to expect a China in the future that will be increasingly sensitive to and willing to constructively engage in the agenda of the emergent global security concerns highlighted in this volume. But interested parties should not have overly high expectations. China's contributions are unlikely to be hasty or proactive, and Beijing will rarely take the lead within global organizations to forge consensus, generate reform or catalyze forward-leaning thinking and action. These points are not merely the view of outside observers, but are also well understood in Beijing. As stated by one of China's most prominent experts in international affairs:

> At present, China is a rising power, and it will incur more and more criticism. We need to be aware that this is an inevitable phenomenon during the course of moving forward and respond by employing moderation, being level-headed, and not publicizing it, and thus the pressure will be somewhat less. If you only read Chinese newspapers and web sites, you may feel that the entire Western media is commenting on or slandering China. Actually, if you observe the Western media carefully, you may discover that China is not at the center of various controversies or disputes. The present is, as far as China is concerned, a rare period of strategic opportunity. We must actively avoid becoming embroiled in the central maelstrom of world politics and concentrate on managing our own affairs well.[25]

In sum, China has made encouraging progress along a path toward becoming a more "responsible stakeholder" and engaging constructively with international partners to meet the global challenges of the twenty-first century. However, far more can and should be done, though this will be neither quick nor easy. All partners interested in engaging China more deeply in addressing the key strategic challenges of the twenty-first century should expect an often frustrating process of "two steps forward, one step back."[26]

Notes

1 Gerald Segal, "Does China Matter?," *Foreign Affairs* September–October (1999). An edited volume was later published that revisited the question in 2005; the book's authors expressed a strong consensus view that China had indeed emerged as a far more important player in world affairs, but that the question of its role and relative weight should still be debated vigorously. See Barry Buzan and Rosemary Foot, eds. *Does China Matter? A Reassessment* (London: Routledge, 2004).
2 "Outbound Investment Unlikely to Outstrip FDI," *China Daily*, 2 July 2009.
3 This information is drawn from www.confuciusinstitute.net/college/index4Cache.htm and "China to Host Second Confucius Institute Conference," *Xinhua*, 6 December 2007.
4 "More Chinese Students Study Abroad," *China.org*, 15 June 2009. "Foreign Student Quota to Expand," *China Daily*, 29 July 2008.
5 Among the many studies since the late-1990s that have examined these questions, see in particular Alastair Iain Johnston, *Social States: China in International Institutions* (Princeton: Princeton University Press, 2008), Ann Kent, *Beyond Compliance: China, International Organizations, and Global Security* (Stanford: Stanford University Press, 2007), Bates Gill, *Rising Star: China's New Security Diplomacy* (Washington, DC: Brookings Institution Press, 2007), Avery Goldstein, *Rising to the Challenge: China's Grand Strategy and International Security* (Stanford: Stanford University Press, 2005), David M. Lampton, ed. *The Making of Chinese Foreign and Security Policy in the Era of Reform* (Stanford: Stanford University Press, 2001), Elizabeth Economy and Michel Oksenberg, *China Joins the World: Progress and Prospects* (New York: Council on Foreign Relations, 1998), Andrew Nathan and Robert S. Ross, *The Great Wall and the Empty Fortress: China's Search for Security* (New York: W.W. Norton and Co., 1997).
6 Quotes from the Chinese defense white paper are from "China's National Defense in 2008" (Beijing: Information Office of the State Council of the People's Republic of China, 2009).
7 "China's National Defense in 2008."
8 "China's National Defense in 2008."
9 "China's National Defense in 2008."
10 Quotes in this paragraph are from "China's National Defense in 2008."
11 "China's Energy Conditions and Policies" (Beijing: State Council Information Office, 2007).
12 The quote from Pan Yue, as well as an extensive and detailed critique of China's environmental challenges, is found in Elizabeth Economy, "The Great Leap Backward?," *Foreign Affairs* September/October (2007). See also Elizabeth Economy and Kenneth Lieberthal, "Scorched Earth: Will Environmental Risks in China Overwhelm its Opportunities?," *Harvard Business Review* June (2007).
13 On the evolution of China's non-proliferation policies, see Gill, *Rising Star*, Evan S. Medeiros, *Reluctant Restraint: The Evolution of China's Nonproliferation and Practices 1980–2004* (Stanford: Stanford University Press, 2007), especially chapter 3.

14 On China's evolving approach to sovereignty, intervention and non-interference, see Allen Carlson, *Unifying China, Integrating with the World: Securing Chinese Sovereignty in the Reform Era* (Stanford: Stanford University Press, 2005), Gill, *Rising Star*, especially chapter 4.

15 On China's approach to multilateral institutions and the development of an Asian security community, see Wu Xinbo, "Chinese Perspectives on Building an East Asian Community in the 21st Century," in *Asia's New Multilateralism: Cooperation, Conflict, and the Search for Community*, eds. Michael J. Green and Bates Gill (New York: Columbia University Press, 2009).

16 The English-language website for the Regional Anti-Terrorism Structure is: www. ecrats.com/en.

17 On ASEAN–China cooperation in this area, see the ASEAN website, www.aseansec. org/14396.htm and Guo Xinning, *Anti-Terrorism, Maritime Security, and ASEAN–China Cooperation: A Chinese Perspective* (Singapore: Institute of Southeast Asian Studies, 2005).

18 For a detailed summary and analysis of US–China cooperation in counter-terrorism and Chinese policies related to terrorism, see Shirley A. Kan, "U.S.–China Counter-terrorism Cooperation: Issues for U.S. Policy," *Congressional Research Service* 7 May (2009).

19 Data on Chinese peacekeeping contributions are drawn from the website of the United Nations Department of Peacekeeping Operations: www.un.org/Depts/dpko/dpko/contributors.

20 For a more detailed analysis of Chinese peacekeeping activity, see Bates Gill and Chin-hao Huang, "China's Expanding Role in Peacekeeping: Prospects and Policy Implications," *IPRI Policy Paper* 25 (Stockholm: Stockholm International Peace Research Institute, 2009), "China's Growing Role in UN Peacekeeping" (Brussels: International Crisis Group, 2009).

21 Medeiros, *Reluctant Restraint*.

22 "China's Endeavors for Arms Control, Disarmament, and Non-proliferation" (Beijing: State Council Information Office, 2005).

23 "China's Energy Conditions and Policies."

24 "China's Energy Conditions and Policies."

25 Zhao Lingmin, *Optimistic View of Sino-US Relations – Exclusive Interview With Professor Wang Jisi, Dean of the School of International Studies at Peking University* (2008). Translated from Chinese and appearing in http://snuffysmithsblog.blogspot. com/2008/11/chinas-foremost-america-watcher-on.html.

26 On engaging China more effectively to become a more "responsible stakeholder" in world affairs, see, for example, Bates Gill and Michael Schiffer, "A Rising China's Rising Responsibilities," in *Powers and Principles: International Leadership in a Shrinking World*, eds. Michael Schiffer and David Shorr (Lanham: Lexington Books, 2009).

9 Global threats and India's quest for strategic space

Siddharth Varadarajan

One of the characteristics of the post-post-Cold War world order is the progressively rapid transition from one seemingly steady equilibrium to the next. Each successive order proclaims its own set of norms, hierarchy of threats and opportunities, and preference for certain instruments over others, only to generate new forms of instability and crisis. The post-1990 "unipolar" moment[1] wedded the United States' immediate strategic aim of preventing the re-emergence of a new global rival[2] with the re-tasking of anachronistic institutions like the United Nations Security Council (UNSC) and NATO.[3] Well-established legal norms on the use of force and non-interference, which survived their frequent violation by the two Superpowers during the Cold War, gave way to the doctrines of pre-emption, humanitarian intervention and the "responsibility to protect."[4] Concerns about the nuclear arsenal and doctrines of the US, Russia and other "official" nuclear weapon states – a staple of Cold War-era discourse on arms control – were transformed into generalized fears about the proliferation of weapons of mass destruction (WMD) by "rogue states" and, later, non-state actors. Terrorism, which countries like India were quietly condemned to suffer throughout much of the 1990s, got elevated to the status of a "global war" once the US found itself on the receiving end of devastating attacks in Dar es Salaam, Nairobi and, most tragically, in New York City in 2001.

The multilateralist "unipolar" order, which began with Operation Desert Storm in 1990 and the imposition of sanctions and "no flight zones," reached its apogee with the 1999 NATO-led attack on Yugoslavia during the Clinton administration. This order ran aground soon after when Old Europe joined hands with Russia and China to begin seeking an end to the UN-imposed sanctions on Saddam Hussein's Iraq. What followed, eventually, was the US-led invasion of that country in 2003, though Washington was forced to rethink the doctrines of pre-emptive war and regime change, as well as its preferred instrument of unilateralism, in the face of the post-war challenges it faced in Iraq.

Confronted by the limits of American power, George W. Bush, in his second term as president, tried to effect a course correction. The National Security Strategy of 2002 had always spoken of the need for cooperation between the Great Powers. True, it also remained focused on preventing the rise of peer competitors, but Bush and his advisors quickly grasped that the most effective way to prevent the emergence of a challenger might well be to induce cooperative behavior between the US and other rising poles of the world system. Gaddis argues Bush correctly surmised from the first flush of global support for the US war on Afghanistan after 9/11 that Great Powers "prefer management of the international system by a single hegemon as long as it is a relatively benign one," and one that is able to associate its power with "universal principles."[5] The Iraq War and its aftermath – like the exposure of torture at Abu Ghraib – had destroyed America's ability to portray its power as benign and its conduct as representative of common values. A fresh pitch for managerial rights to the international system had to be mounted. The Bush administration did this by forging issue-specific, US-driven coalitions with both mid-sized and major powers – Russia, China, India, Indonesia, Japan, South Korea, Australia, Brazil and Europe – to push for solutions to challenges as diverse as energy security, the North Korean and Iranian nuclear issues, free trade and climate change. It is not a coincidence that the strategic partnership with India – one that was centered around the Indian desire to rid its nuclear energy sector of sanctions, and the American desire to cultivate a rising power as a market for military and civilian goods and services, and as a potential outsourcer of hegemonic power in Asia – crystallized precisely in this post-Iraq War period.[6] India had heralded its arrival on the world stage in 1998 by conducting a series of nuclear tests and attaining a high rate of economic growth despite the sanctions that were imposed on it by the US and a number of countries. President Bill Clinton began the process of engagement with India soon after, but it was the Bush administration that saw an opportunity to manage New Delhi's "peaceful rise" and ensure that it acts like a "responsible stakeholder."[7] Pushing through an exception for India from the restrictive guidelines of the Nuclear Suppliers Group (NSG) – the 46-nation cartel whose rules prohibit the sale of nuclear equipment and fuel to countries that are not party to the Nuclear Non-Proliferation Treaty (NPT) – may well have been the last triumph of American unilateralism. But the effort would not have succeeded without the strong backing of Russia and France, both of whom had compelling economic and strategic reasons for opening the doors of nuclear commerce for New Delhi.

Toward the end of his second term, Bush better understood what the rise of China had done to the world but failed to build a constructive relationship with Beijing because he was more interested in hedging against, rather than engaging with, Chinese power. As for Russia, his administration was never able to come to grips with what the re-rise of Moscow under the presidency of Vladimir Putin meant for the international system. The abrogation of the Anti-Ballistic Missile Treaty in 2001 and the aggressive promotion of missile defense, including the proposed location of early-warning radars on the territories of Poland and the Czech Republic, reduced Washington's leverage in Moscow at a time when it was most needed.

Had the US been willing to engage in good old-fashioned dialogue and diplomacy to deal with real and perceived challenges to its interests that emanated from Iran, North Korea, Syria and the breakdown of world trade talks and the growth of terrorism, this inability to forge genuinely cooperative Great Power relationships might not have mattered. The combination of these two mistakes, however, would prove costly as coalition-based solutions which initially seemed within grasp started slipping away. The most dramatic demonstration of this problem came with the 2006 nuclear test by North Korea. When Washington scrapped the Agreed Framework in 2002, the assumption was that China and Russia would work closely with the US to ensure Pyongyang did not go nuclear, but that did not happen. As in the case of Iran, Beijing and Moscow remained suspicious of US motivations and wary of the consequences of escalating the punitive measures they had already reluctantly agreed to at the Security Council. In both cases, the US found itself unable to "punish" the willful defiance of its demands by the North Koreans and Iranians. The presidency of Barack Obama is likely to see a fresh and more purposeful attempt to reconcile the American wariness of potential peer competitors with the urgent, practical need to cooperate with them. Bush's failure to do so was ironic because nobody understood the tension between political cooperation and strategic competition better than his Secretary of State – Condoleezza Rice. For those tempted to argue that the fundamental challenge facing the international community, in the wake of Iraq, was how to tame American power, Dr. Rice sought to drive home a picture of world order in which "new threats" like terrorism, the proliferation of weapons of mass destruction and pandemics posed a common danger to all countries, big or small. In this narrative, every challenge to the interests of the US and its allies was represented as a global threat. The Iranian uranium enrichment issue, for example, which was more a product of unresolved tensions between Washington and Tehran and the fragility of the wider Middle East Peace Process, and which needed to be resolved within that framework, got repackaged as a problem of imminent nuclearization.

In a major speech to the United Nations General Assembly on the occasion of the UN's sixtieth anniversary in 2005, the US Secretary of State claimed that the emergence of new threats had shifted "the very terrain of international politics … beneath our feet."[8] In the old world – starting from 1945 and presumably ending with the demise of the Soviet Union – "the most serious threats to peace and security emerged between states and were largely defined by their borders." Today, however, "the greatest threats we face emerge within states and melt through their borders – transnational threats like terrorism and weapons proliferation, pandemic disease and trafficking in human beings." In a highly influential newspaper article later that year, she made the link between these threats, and the need for a new concert of powers, more explicit. "For the first time since the Peace of Westphalia in 1648, the prospect of violent conflict between Great Powers is becoming ever more unthinkable," she wrote:

> Major states are increasingly competing in peace, not preparing for war. To advance this remarkable trend, the United States is transforming our partnerships with nations such as Japan and Russia, with the European Union, and especially with China and India. Together we are building a more lasting and durable form of global stability: a balance of power that favors freedom.[9]

It is not difficult to see in the writings of President Obama's foreign policy advisors a sympathetic echo of the very same concepts.[10] Nor does it take much effort to locate in the discourse and policies of the Clinton administration the lineage of a similar approach. In other words, what appears at first glance to be three different and even contrasting approaches to world power, from Clinton to Bush and now Obama, actually forms part of a continuum where the stated priorities (protection of Kuwaitis or Kosovars, terrorism and WMDs, Iraq and AfPak) and instruments (sanctions or war, unilateralism or coalitions of the willing or multilateralism) are periodically reordered without changing the essence of the *longue durée* of hegemonic strategy.

And yet, the fact remains that this strategy has not really succeeded in enforcing hegemony, which is why the international system has been in a state of flux since 1990. The main reason the United States has been unable to stabilize a world order is that it has never fully taken into account the underlying changes in the relative distribution of global economic and political power, nor has it pushed for the institutions of global governance to reflect these changes. The consequences of this failure have, in turn, been magnified by the attempt to "globalize" the reach of military power, coalitions and alliances that lack the credibility and ability to deliver stable, benign outcomes. What we have, as a result, is the worst of all possible worlds: the United States and its allies continue to have the ability to disrupt existing structures of order across all continents but not enough power to impose an effective, alternative order. Gaddis's single hegemon, it turns out, has no clothes.

As a country that finds itself excluded from the main circuits of global decision-making, India welcomed the recognition it appeared to be receiving in the Bush–Rice scheme of things. Ever since the end of the Cold War and especially after India openly proclaimed its nuclear weapons status, Indian strategic thinkers have argued that the world is "multipolar" or "polycentric."[11] This thesis was not so much intended to undermine America's "unipolar" status as to advance the claim that the world could no longer afford to ignore India's legitimate aspirations. Though India carved out a niche for itself as a leader of the developing and nonaligned world during the Cold World, the Indian strategic community is not in the least bit sentimental about the passing of the old order. Indeed, insofar as the major global institutional structures continued to reflect the relative distribution of power as it obtained in 1945, the need to push for a new order is seen as an urgent necessity. But if Indian analysts agree on the necessity for change, cleavages exist on the question of what the contours of the new order should be and how India should exercise its power once it gets a seat at the global high table. Indian analysts can all agree that the country must be made a permanent member of the UNSC, but which way should India vote if confronted with the demand for more sanctions on Iran or Sudan? Or with a resolution asking the prosecutor of the International Criminal Court to open an investigation into war crimes committed by Israel during its invasion of Gaza in December 2008–January 2009? The Indian vote in favor of a September 2005 International Atomic Energy Agency resolution finding Iran in non-compliance of its safeguards obligations proved to be highly controversial within the country, especially after evidence emerged that the US had leaned on India and warned that an abstention would jeopardize the passage of the Indo-US nuclear deal through Congress.

Another issue that divides the Indian strategic community is the choice and combination of instruments India should utilize to help bring a more representative world order into being. On one side is the American offer, stated explicitly in March 2005, to help further India's global ambitions. "The Administration has made a fundamental judgment that the future of this region as a whole is simply vital to the future of the United States," a senior State Department official told reporters in a detailed briefing on South Asia. "Its goal is to help India become a major world power in the twenty-first century. We understand fully the implications, including military implications, of that statement."[12] To Indian analysts, it is obvious that this offer comes bundled with the expectation that New Delhi would work closely with Washington on a wide range of global issues and threats. On the other side, questions have been raised about the extent to which the US and India share strategic interests, and whether New Delhi might damage its relations with Beijing and especially Moscow by drawing too close to Washington. Even on an issue like terrorism, for example, there are well-known divergences, with the US reluctant to accept India's contention that the Pakistani military is part of the "AfPak" problem and not part of the solution. And although the Indo-US nuclear agreement of 2005 narrowed the gap between the two sides on an issue that had been a serious bilateral irritant since the mid-1970s, major differences remain on the Comprehensive Test Ban Treaty (CTBT) and India's right to access enrichment and reprocessing technology and items from the international market.

Although Indian diplomats have demonstrated a considerable degree of comfort with the idea that the four threats that are the subject of this volume – terrorism, WMD proliferation, environmental and energy security, and fragile and failed states – pose a grave danger to the international community, policy-makers do not consider these to be in any way an exhaustive list of the challenges confronting the country. For the Indian strategic community and the wider political community that takes a keen interest in foreign policy and international political economy, the discourse about "new threats" is problematic because it assumes the "old threats" to world order have either vanished or become less critical. In reality, the old threats have become more virulent and pose an even more fundamental challenge to the international system than their newer strains. Consider this list: the tendency for powerful countries to use force against smaller countries under one pretext or another; the nuclear arms race, which is now leading to ballistic missile defense, the weaponization of outer space as well as the search for smaller, "usable" nukes; the refusal to solve outstanding conflicts, especially in the Middle East, which is a major contributing factor to terrorism; the persistence of exclusion and poverty, which give rise to derivative "threats" like human-trafficking and global pandemics and financial instability and trade protectionism.

Although India's analysis of the nature of global threats and the approach that they require differs from the Great Powers paradigm, it has adopted an eclectic approach that seeks to increase its strategic space while striving for specific outcomes – especially on terrorism, climate change and energy – that more directly contribute to enhancing the country's security interests.

Terrorism and political extremism

In official Indian discourse, terrorism and extremism in all its manifestations – territorial separatism (as in the North-Eastern states of Assam, Manipur, Tripura and Nagaland), Islamic extremism (whether fused with separatism as in Jammu and Kashmir, or with some vague notion of "global jihad," as manifested in a growing number of urban bomb blasts) and left-wing extremism – is seen as the most important and immediate threat to the country's national security. Among these forms, it is left-wing extremism that is often cited as the "gravest internal security threat."[13]

Despite this prioritization, Indian domestic efforts to deal with the problem of terrorism have lacked coherence. Sloppy police work, poor forensics and intelligence-gathering have combined with draconian laws and impunity for the security forces to create a situation where terrorist crimes are rarely solved or successfully prosecuted. At the international level, Indian efforts have focused on three fronts: getting the world to put pressure on Pakistan to abandon its policy of sheltering anti-India terrorists; demanding enforcement of UN Security Council anti-terrorism resolutions like 1267 so that terrorists known to be targeting India are sanctioned by the Taliban and al-Qaeda Sanctions Committee;[14] and getting the United Nations to adopt a comprehensive convention on terrorism. The last initiative, arguably more of symbolic rather than practical significance, has floundered because of the Arab–Israeli dispute over the right of the occupied people of Palestine to wage an armed struggle against their occupiers. On Pakistan, however, India, after years of frustration at the West's lack of interest, has finally begun to make some headway.

When the separatist insurgency started in Kashmir in 1990, the US and most Western countries refused to accept India's contention that Pakistan was actively involved in arming and training militants. Instead, Washington seized on a number of well-established instances of gross human rights violations by the Indian security forces in the state to criticize New Delhi and push for a negotiated solution to the status of the disputed territory with American mediation. When India claimed to have found evidence linking Pakistan's intelligence agency, the Inter-Service Intelligence, to the serial bomb blasts that rocked Bombay in 1993, the US took notice but failed to exert the kind of pressure on Islamabad that India wanted it to. A noticeable change in the US approach came about in 1999, when Pakistani soldiers took advantage of Indian seasonal redeployments in the Kargil area and crossed the Line of Control dividing the two countries.[15] India fought back and vacated the aggression, but the war ended only when President Bill Clinton extracted from Nawaz Sharif, Pakistan's Prime Minister at the time, a commitment that Islamabad would henceforth respect the sanctity of the Line of Control.[16] A more dramatic shift in American attitudes occurred after 9/11. Prior to the terrorist attacks on the World Trade Center and the Pentagon, India, along with Iran and Russia, had been a key backer of the anti-Taliban Northern Alliance. Once it became clear that the US had decided to militarily retaliate against the Taliban regime in Afghanistan, India offered Washington the use of its territory for any offensive action. Since 2001, India and the US have actively shared intelligence, the most celebrated example of that being the cooperation between the FBI and Indian investigators in the wake of the November 2008 Mumbai terrorist attacks.[17]

Where, then, does the Indian strategic community stand on the threat posed to global security by terrorism and on the means required to deal with this threat? The picture is confused. There is a great deal of satisfaction at the fact that the US has finally been forced to recognize the threat posed to its national security by the AfPak region, but there is also fear that domestic political pressure will force President Obama to withdraw US forces before the Taliban and al-Qaeda (TAQ) have been fully defeated and the new, hopefully democratic, regime in Afghanistan has managed to secure and stabilize itself. Even though it has reservations about using its own military against suspected terrorist camps in neighboring countries and has condemned the Israeli offensives against Lebanon and the Gaza Strip in 2006 and 2009, the Indian establishment has not wavered in its support for the US military effort in Afghanistan. Indeed, India sees the "wobble" that is so evident in the British and American press on the question of the Afghan war as fodder for hardliners within the Pakistani military establishment who argue that Islamabad should preserve its "strategic assets" – the Taliban – so it can be in a position to capture power if and when the US eventually pulls out. Dealing with the threat of terror, therefore, requires forcing a course correction on the Pakistani military, which created and sustained a number of terrorist groups over the years as a force multiplier against India and Afghanistan and against mass-based political parties within its own territory.

From the 1990s, nothing has rankled the Indian establishment more than the perceived double standards of the West on the question of terror. As long as Pakistan-based terrorist groups were bombing Indian cities and killing Indian citizens, the US and Europe did not seem particularly concerned. The events of 9/11 changed matters somewhat, but even now Indian policy-makers believe the US does not consider a group like the Lashkar-e-Tayyaba – accused of the November 2008 terrorist attacks in Mumbai – to be as much of a threat to America as the TAQ, despite the fact that these groups are known to share personnel, intelligence, targeting and Methods of Operation, and to form what US Secretary of State Hillary Clinton aptly called a "syndicate of terrorism."[18]

An interesting footnote to this discussion is that India, despite enjoying close strategic ties with Israel and relying on Israeli military technology for a range of anti-terrorist tasks, continues to rebuff Tel Aviv's request that groups like Hizbollah and Hamas be declared illegal under Indian law. Though some may be tempted here to accuse India of a double standard, the fact remains that the Indian government has traditionally been a strong backer of the Palestinian right to self-determination and has consistently resisted efforts to brand the Palestinian resistance as "terrorist." However, this has not prevented India from criticizing Hamas for its rocket attacks on Israeli civilians. New Delhi has also sought to highlight the organizational and ideological links between the active anti-India terrorist groups from Pakistan, and Islamic extremists active in Chechnya, Uzbekistan and China. Though the Indian government has not pursued a close political relationship with the Shanghai Cooperation Organization (SCO), partly in deference to US reservations about the "exclusivist" nature of the regional grouping, it has participated in the activities and exercises of the SCO's Regional Anti-Terrorist Structure.

To sum up, India has sought to use America's belated recognition of the threat posed to global security by terrorism, especially in the AfPak region, to push for a change in US policy toward Pakistan. Just how important a goal this is for the Indian establishment can be seen from its continuing support for US operations in Afghanistan, despite the fact that this is likely to lead to the long-term military presence of an outside power in South Asia. At the same time, India has not hesitated to cooperate with other global and regional powers like Russia, China and Iran in pursuit of a balanced, durable settlement in Afghanistan.

WMD proliferation

As India has moved from being a target of international non-proliferation efforts to a sought-after ally in the drive to prevent the further spread of nuclear weapons, its position on the proliferation of weapons of mass destruction is clear and categorical: India does not wish to see any other country in its extended neighborhood or elsewhere acquire this capability.[19] The dilemma for policy-makers however, has been how to translate this into a set of priorities and policies at the global level, especially when there are those who believe the only way to prevent further proliferation is by the use of pre-emptive war or even sanctions; two approaches India has traditionally tended to oppose. The problem was perhaps best summed up by a former US ambassador to India, Robert Blackwill:

> If I can be blunt, it is my impression that although India very much wants Iran not to acquire nuclear weapons, if it faces a binary choice of either that or an American military attack on Iran, it would choose to try to deal with a nuclear Iran, without the attack.[20]

A more fundamental contradiction stemming from India's traditional opposition to the NPT (the principal international treaty aimed at preventing more countries from acquiring nuclear weapons) as discriminatory was partially resolved in 2008 when the NSG unanimously decided to grant India a waiver from its rules prohibiting nuclear sales to countries that did not accept full-scope safeguards. The decision primarily sprang from commercial and *realpolitik* considerations, but was also based on the assessment of the international community that India's possession of nuclear weapons did not pose a proliferation risk. In exchange, India pledged to observe its moratorium on nuclear testing, help negotiate a Fissile Material Cut-off Treaty, and separate its military and civilian nuclear facilities, with the latter being placed under IAEA supervision. The IAEA's Director General, who strongly backed the India exception, acknowledged the concerns some countries had but said the international non-proliferation system would be strengthened with India inside the regime rather than outside.[21]

India's nuclear weapons program had its origins in the technology choices made by the country as early as the 1950s, but it was only after the first Chinese test of a nuclear device at Lop Nor in Tibet in 1964 that Indian scientists began serious work on nuclear weapons.[22] India was an active participant in the negotiating process leading up to the NPT in 1968 but declared its intention not to sign-on because of the arbitrary and discriminatory nature of the 1967 cut-off date for a de facto nuclear weapon state to have tested an explosive device.[23] Six years later, India conducted its first nuclear explosive test, though it self-consciously characterized the event at Pokhran in 1974 as a "peaceful nuclear explosion."

Although India thereby became the first "proliferator" of the NPT era, its diffidence in proclaiming its own intention to weaponize allowed the international community to maintain the fiction that the Indians could still be persuaded – or prevented – from attaining full-fledged nuclear weapons status. And yet, there was little sense of urgency. The US introduced a national embargo on nuclear sales to India but the Nuclear Suppliers Group, which was set up at the urging of Washington, did not impose such a ban at the multilateral level. It was only after the Cold War ended that the US got the NSG to adopt full-scope safeguards as a necessary criterion for nuclear exports.

Throughout the 1980s and 1990s, India said it had only peaceful nuclear intentions and sought to play a role in international forums as an advocate of nuclear disarmament. It backed the UN General Assembly decision to seek the International Court of Justice's advisory opinion on the legality of the use or threat of use of nuclear weapons and was an early sponsor of the Comprehensive Test Ban Treaty. When the CTBT negotiations began in earnest at Geneva, India quickly realized that the US, China and other powers were keen to use the treaty as a way of shutting the door on India's nuclear option. India had yet to weaponize its nuclear technology and it was felt that if the CTBT's entry into force were made conditional on its ratification by 45 potential nuclear capable nations, including India (the so-called Annex II countries), this might force the country to give up its "right" to test. The US-inspired strategy backfired. Instead of remaining confined forever to the halfway house of nuclear ambiguity, the Indian government chose to test in May 1998. Having tested its weapons however, it promptly declared a moratorium and added that it would not stand in the way of the CTBT entering into force.[24] The implication was that if all other Annex II countries came on board, so would India. The US Senate's refusal to ratify the CTBT in 1999 effectively derailed the international momentum that was building and gave the Indian side some respite. During the Bush years, all other arms-control initiatives floundered, including the proposed Fissile Material Cut-off Treaty, but now that President Obama is re-emphasizing the importance of these treaties in the context of global non-proliferation efforts, it is useful to see where India will stand.

Although India has resisted adopting a moratorium on the domestic production of fissile material, it has no serious objections to the efforts underway at the Conference on Disarmament to negotiate a verifiable FMCT. India will, however, insist on its clauses being non-discriminatory. Any attempt to distinguish between the five states whose possession of nuclear weapons is permitted by the

NPT and a country like India would clearly not be acceptable. The CTBT, however, will present India with greater difficulties, not least because of the controversy raging within its scientific community over the degree to which its 1998 tests – especially of the one thermonuclear device – were actually a success.[25] Indian policy-makers hope Obama will not manage to secure the two-thirds backing he needs in the Senate to ratify the CTBT. However, if the US does ratify the treaty, Chinese ratification is a foregone conclusion and the world would then expect India (and then Pakistan) to come on board fairly soon. Over the past few years, India has begun to distance itself from its earlier promise of "not standing in the way," questioning the extent to which the CTBT is a genuine disarmament instrument or not. "India has been a consistent votary of a CTBT but did not sign the CTBT as it eventually emerged because it was not explicitly linked to the goal of nuclear disarmament," said Shyam Saran, the Indian Prime Minister's special envoy on nuclear issues, in a talk at a Washington think tank in March 2009. "For India, this was crucial since it was not acceptable to legitimize, in any way, a permanent division between nuclear weapon states and non-nuclear weapon states."[26] Is the latest Indian stand a holding position given the uncertainty of US ratification? Or is it a lever with which to ensure Obama seriously pursues his proposal for a nuclear-free world, an outcome India is still officially committed to although many in the Indian strategic community would question the benefit of universal disarmament? At any rate, it is hard to imagine India wanting to remain outside the CTBT because it would like to initiate a new round of testing at some point in the future. If the US or China were to test again, it is almost certain that the Indian nuclear and defense establishments would press for additional tests; but, so long as the moratorium holds, India is unlikely to be the first to break it.

As with terrorism, India's views on non-proliferation have also been conditioned by what has happened in its own neighborhood. It is an open secret that China had a proliferation relationship with Pakistan in the 1980s and that the US administration turned a blind eye toward this because of the role Islamabad was playing in the anti-Soviet mujahideen insurgency in Afghanistan. India has also been vocal about the proliferation risks Pakistan poses in the context of revelations about the manner in which its top nuclear scientist, A.Q. Khan, had sold nuclear blueprints to Libya, North Korea and Iran. Despite this, however, it has refused to join the US-led Proliferation Security Initiative which seeks to interdict suspicious shipping on the high seas. India's reservations are linked to the 2005 amended protocol to the Convention for the Suppression of Unlawful Acts Against the Safety of Maritime Navigation, which introduced an NPT/Non-NPT distinction for the shipping of nuclear materials on the high seas. India's stand once again underlines its unwillingness to sign up to global non-proliferation instruments that are discriminatory.

On Iran, India was a reluctant recruit to the US-led push to declare that country in violation of its safeguards agreement at the September 2005 meeting of the IAEA Board of Governors. This reluctance was captured by the official explanation of the vote that India provided, in which it essentially argued that Iran was not in violation and that the IAEA remained the best forum for resolving any doubts about the peaceful nature of the Iranian nuclear program. Since India is not a member of the Security Council, or even of ad hoc coalitions like the P5+1, it has remained a passive observer of the Iran issue. The country has implemented the limited sanctions imposed on Tehran by the UN, but is unlikely to agree to implement any unilaterally imposed embargoes, such as the ban on gasoline sales being discussed in Washington.

Regional crises and fragile states

Despite the fact that India's periphery is ringed by states in various degrees of fragility, this is seen by Indian policy-makers as the manifestation of a South Asian problem requiring a South Asian solution, rather than a global problem calling for the involvement of global players. The only exception is Pakistan, where India appreciates the US role to the extent that it undermines the Pakistani state's ability and willingness to use terrorism as an instrument of military policy; but even there, as Prime Minister Singh recently articulated, India and Pakistan need to establish peace on their own terms lest foreign powers become permanently involved in the region. "Unless we talk directly to Pakistan, we will have to rely on third parties to do so," he told Parliament in July 2009.

> I submit to this august House that this particular route has very severe limitations as to its effectiveness and for the longer term view of what South Asia should be, the growing involvement of foreign powers in the affairs of South Asia is not something to our liking. I say, therefore, with strength and conviction that dialogue and engagement is the best way forward.[27]

Part of the reason for India's sanguine approach to the prospect of being ringed by failed states is the relative success of its new South Asian policy. It successfully brought an end to the Nepal civil war, quietly assisted the Sri Lankans to finish their war against the Liberation Tigers of Tamil Eelam, and has the best of relations with Bangladesh after a brief but significant bout of military-led cleansing of the political system in that country brought Sheikh Hasina back to power with a thumping majority. India increasingly sees the challenge of managing its neighborhood as an economic rather than security-centric problem, and has begun focusing on improving physical connectivity and enhancing trade and investment flows across South Asia. Indian officials have managed a certain level of coordination with the US in Nepal and Bangladesh. And though New Delhi keeps a close watch on China's growing economic ties with Sri Lanka and Nepal, it is reasonably secure about its status as the most important power in the subcontinent.

As for failed and fragile states elsewhere in the world, especially those convulsed by civil war and conflict, India has shown a great willingness to commit itself to UN-led peacekeeping and peace-building initiatives. In the past decade, Indian peacekeepers have served in the Democratic Republic of Congo, Liberia, Sierra Leone, Lebanon and elsewhere, sometimes sustaining casualties.

The second pillar of Indian policy toward fragile states outside its neighborhood is economic: part of the legacy of non-alignment means joining hands with other major developing countries like Brazil and South Africa to ensure a fairer deal for the least developed. India has also emerged as an increasingly important source of foreign aid, especially aid embedded in appropriate technologies. This approach fits well with the growing internationalization of Indian big business, which sees huge opportunities from investing in, and selling to, Africa.

Although India paid lip service to the Bush-era notion of a coalition of democracies, it has stuck to its conservative position on non-intervention and non-interference in the internal affairs of countries, and generally refrained from sitting in judgment on the nature of regimes, let alone tying its economic relations to whatever normative preferences it might have. Thus, India has rejected the idea that the only way to deal with Myanmar or Zimbabwe is with sanctions.

Environmental and energy security

On climate change, India has been an active participant in all the UN conferences and articulated a position that emphasizes the historical burden that the unequal exploitation of the global atmospheric commons by the advanced industrialized countries has placed on the world, and which requires the West to drastically cut its greenhouse gas emissions in order to make room for developing countries. "It is India's view that the planetary atmospheric space is a common resource of humanity and each citizen of the globe has an equal entitlement to that space."[28] The official Indian assessment of the problem and its solution runs as follows:

> Climate Change is taking place not due to the current level of GHG (Greenhouse Gas) emissions, but as a result of the cumulative impact of accumulated GHGs in the planetary atmosphere.... The accumulated stock of GHGs in the atmosphere is mainly the result of carbon-based industrial activity in developed countries over the past two centuries and more. It is for this reason that the UNFCCC (UN Framework Convention on Climate Change) stipulates deep and significant cuts in the emissions of the industrialized countries as fulfillment of their historic responsibility. Secondly, the UNFCCC [and Kyoto Protocol] do not require developing countries to take on any commitments on reducing their GHG emissions."[29]

Having said that, India has committed itself to not allowing its per capita GHG emissions to exceed the average per capita emissions of the developed countries, which effectively puts a cap on its future emissions, although strictly speaking provides no legally binding target. It also announced, in the run up to the UN's December 2009 climate change summit in Copenhagen, its intention of reducing the carbon intensity of the country's growth by 20–25 percent by 2020. India's stand is driven by two primary considerations. First, its own annual per capita CO_2 emissions, at 1.1 tons, are much less than the 20 tons the US emits or the 10-ton Organization for Economic Co-operation and Development average. Even if the large Indian population is taken into account, India is the source of only 4 percent of total global emissions compared to the US and China, each of which are responsible for a 16 percent share. Second, India has already begun paying the price of climate change, despite not being responsible for the global warming that has occurred over the past few decades. The Indian government estimates that the country already spends over 2 percent of its GDP on adaptation to cope with the high degree of climate variability that is now in evidence. For India, therefore, the question of adaptation to climate change that is already taking place should also be the focus of global environmental security initiatives, and not just GHG reduction and mitigation.

The Indian position puts it in direct conflict with the US, Europe and other advanced industrial countries, but allows it to take the lead in forging a developing-country consensus at international fora, with the G77 and Brazil, South Africa and China (as part of the so-called BASIC countries).

Linked to climate change is the question of energy security, which has emerged in recent years as a major preoccupation for India. More than one-third of India's energy needs are met by oil, and 70 percent of its national requirement is imported. India also imports coal and liquified natural gas (LNG), and has toyed with the idea of building gas pipelines from Myanmar, Iran and Turkmenistan to feed its growing demand for energy. India has sought to pursue its energy security along three distinct tracks. First, it is giving a decisive push to the development of nuclear energy, which today accounts for around 2 percent of electricity generated. The official plan of raising that figure to 20 percent by 2020 may be too ambitious, but already plans have been drawn with Russia and France for the construction of half-a-dozen 1,000-MW light water reactors. At the same time, the lifting of the NSG embargo means the lack of domestic uranium will no longer be a constraint on the expansion of India's indigenous pressurized heavy water reactor and fast breeder programs. The second energy security track India has followed is the acquisition of equity oil around the world. Indian public and private sector companies have acquired, invested in or actively prospected for hydrocarbon assets as far afield as Russia's Sakhalin Island, Cuba, Venezuela, Iran, Nigeria and Angola, sometimes in alliance with other major oil consuming countries like China.[30] The third track is maritime security, an increasing priority for Indian policymakers given the volume of energy flows on the high seas and the growth of piracy in crucial water ways. For a country rediscovering its maritime imperatives after two centuries of colonial rule and half a century of underdevelopment, India believes the oceans around it provide an opportunity not just for the projection of its power but for the forging of wider, non-exclusivist collective security arrangements that the Asian region currently lacks. As Shivshankar Menon, who was India's top diplomat until his retirement in August 2009, put it:

The IEA (International Energy Agency) estimates that global energy demand will grow by at least 45% between 2006 and 2030, and that half that increase will come from India and China. We are both at an energy intensive phase of our development. Between 1990 and 2003, oil consumption in India and China grew by 7% on average, against 0.8% in the rest of the world. By 2050 India could be the largest importer of oil in the world. Thus both India and China face a "Hormuz dilemma." For China this is compounded by a "Malacca dilemma" as well.

My question is therefore: if energy and trade flows and security are the issues, why not begin discussing collective security arrangements among the major powers concerned? Is it not time that we began a discussion among concerned states of a maritime system minimizing the risks of interstate conflict and neutralizing threats from pirates, smugglers, terrorists, and proliferators? India's concerns in the north-west Indian Ocean and China's vulnerabilities in the north-east Indian Ocean cannot be solved by military means alone. The issue is not limited just to the Indian Ocean but indeed is one of security of these flows in areas and seas which affect the choke points.

These arrangements should deal with transnational issues such as piracy, crime and natural disasters. Now that Asian states and powers have evolved the capabilities and demonstrated the will to deal with these questions, it is time that a structured discussion among them and the major littorals took place.[31]

Conclusion

Although India has often been accused of lacking a coherent national security strategy, and even a strategic culture, the manner in which it has responded to the threats and opportunities posed by the changing nature of world order is neither incoherent nor irrational. If one were to identify a common thread in the Indian approach to the international system, it is the quest for strategic space. If strategy, to paraphrase and extend Liddell Hart's classic definition, is the art of distributing and applying national power through military and non-military means to fulfill the ends of policy, India has effectively used its nuclear status, its high growth rate, its soft power, its democratic credentials and other attributes of comprehensive national power to create a situation within the international system where its rise has generally been welcomed by all the Great Powers except, possibly, China, and where its core security interests cannot easily be violated or ignored.

Of the four challenges examined in this volume, India clearly regards terrorism and environmental and energy security to be the most important. The proliferation of WMD and the failure of fragile and vulnerable states are also matters of concern, but mainly to the extent that these impact directly on Indian security. There are other priorities for India, though: maritime security, reform of the UN and its Security Council that includes a permanent seat for India, a fair and equitable international trading regime, the creation of Asian security and economic architecture, global financial stability and the pursuit of development. On all of these issues, India is discovering the value of a multi-vector foreign policy. Its strategic partnership with the United States, particularly during the Bush era, delivered certain benefits such as an end to India's nuclear isolation, but it did this at a cost.

India failed to pay equal priority to the strengthening of relations with Great Powers like Russia and China, which had reservations about the geopolitical motives of Washington in reaching out to New Delhi. It also allowed its relations with Iran and the Arab world to stagnate. In the years ahead, managing the unrealistic expectations that the United States may have will be a major strategic challenge for India, as will be the task of managing the triangular relationship between itself, the US and China. Directly taking on the arguments of Robert Kaplan, who suggested the US could act as a "sea-based balancer" and "honest broker" between India and China as the two Asian giants rub against each other in the Indian Ocean and littoral,[32] a former Indian foreign secretary has said neither Delhi nor Beijing would favor the US playing such a role:

> Which major power would not like to play the role of balancer, given the chance? It is cheaper and easier and leaves the real work to the powers being balanced. For a superpower that is refocusing on Asia but finding the landscape considerably changed while she was preoccupied with Iraq and Afghanistan, this would naturally be an attractive option. But is it likely that two emerging states like India and China, with old traditions of state-craft, would allow themselves to remain the objects of someone else's policy, no matter how elegantly expressed? I think not.
>
> Instead, what is suggested is a real concert of Asian powers, including the USA which has a major maritime presence and interests in Asia, to deal with issues of maritime security in all of Asia's oceans. As Asia becomes more integrated from Suez to the Pacific, none of Asia's seas or oceans can be considered in isolation. This would be a major cooperative endeavour, and a test of Asian statesmanship.[33]

As a rising power, India is not preoccupied with peer competitors and is wary of getting ensnared in rivalry between the Great Powers. The Indian conception of a stable world order, at the end of the day, is one that is based on cooperation driven by shared interests and common perceptions about where the principal threats and challenges to security lie. Such a framework will still allow for the pursuit of national interests by individual countries, so long as the temptation to think of power in zero-sum terms is kept firmly at bay.

Notes

1 Michael Mastanduno, "Preserving the Unipolar Moment: Realist Theories and U.S. Grand Strategy after the Cold War," *International Security* 21, 4 (1997), Christopher Layne, "The Unipolar Illusion: Why New Great Powers Will Rise," *International Security* 17, 4 (1993).

2 The Pentagon's 18 February 1992 draft of the Defense Planning Guidance for the Fiscal Years 1994–1999 stated:

> Our first objective is to prevent the re-emergence of a new rival. This is a dominant consideration underlying the new regional defense strategy and requires that we endeavor to prevent any hostile power from dominating a region whose resources would, under consolidated control, be sufficient to generate global

power. These regions include Western Europe, East Asia, the territory of the former Soviet Union, and Southwest Asia.... There are three additional aspects to this objective: First the US must show the leadership necessary to establish and protect a new order that holds the promise of convincing potential competitors that they need not aspire to a greater role or pursue a more aggressive posture to protect their legitimate interests. Second, in the non-defense areas, we must account sufficiently for the interests of the advanced industrial nations to discourage them from challenging our leadership or seeking to overturn the established political and economic order. Finally, we must maintain the mechanisms for deterring potential competitors from even aspiring to a larger regional or global role.

("Pentagon's Plan: 'Prevent the Re-Emergence of a New Rival',"
New York Times, 8 March 1992)

3 Siddharth Varadarajan, "Ruses for War: Nato's New Strategic Concept," *Times of India*, 10 May 1999. For a Russian perspective on the "hegemonic" significance of Nato's expansion eastward, see Irina Kobrinskaya, "Russia: Facing the Facts," in *Enlarging NATO: The National Debates*, eds. Gale A. Mattox and Arthur R. Rachwald (Boulder: Lynne Rienner, 2001). Though committed to the expansion of the Cold War-era military alliance at an early stage, President Clinton and his advisors acknowledged the danger of drawing new dividing lines in Europe through their "Partnership for Peace" initiative. See James M. Goldgeier, "NATO Expansion: The Anatomy of a Decision," in *The Domestic Sources of American Foreign Policy: Insights and Evidence*, eds. Eugene R. Wittkopf and James M. McCormick (Lanham: Rowman and Littlefield, 2007).
4 Carlo Focarelli, "The Responsibility to Protect Doctrine and Humanitarian Intervention: Too Many Ambiguities for a Working Doctrine," *Journal of Conflict and Security Law* 13, 2 (2008).
5 John Lewis Gaddis, "A Grand Strategy of Transformation," *Foreign Policy* (2002). See also Robert J. Lieber, *The American Era: Power and Strategy for the 21st Century* (Cambridge: Cambridge University Press, 2005), pp. 43–46.
6 Siddharth Varadarajan, "America, India and the Outsourcing of Imperial Overreach," *The Hindu*, 13 July 2005.
7 Xenia Dormandy, "Is India, or Will It Be, a Responsible International Stakeholder?," *The Washington Quarterly* 30, 3 (2007). Ever since Robert Zoellick introduced the phrase "responsible stakeholder," the question Professor Dormandy asks is normally reserved for China.
8 Address of Secretary of State Condoleezza Rice at the 60th United Nations General Assembly, 17 September 2005: www.un.org/webcast/ga/60/statements/usa050917eng.pdf.
9 Condoleezza Rice, "The Promise of Democratic Peace," *Washington Post*, 11 December 2005.
10 G. John Ikenberry and Anne-Marie Slaughter, *Forging a World of Liberty Under Law, U.S. National Security in the 21st Century*, Princeton Project on National Security Final Report (Princeton: Princeton University Press, 2008). Available at: www.princeton.edu/~ppns/report.html. Professor Slaughter heads the Policy Planning Division of the State Department in the Obama administration.
11 See, for example, K. Subrahmanyam, *Shedding Shibboleths: India's Evolving Strategic Outlook* (New Delhi: Wordsmiths, 2005).
12 Background Briefing by Administration Officials On U.S.–South Asia Relations, Washington, DC, 25 March 2005. Transcript available at: http://statelists.state.gov/scripts/wa.exe?A2=ind0503d&L=dospress&P=1831.
13 See, for example, the speech by Prime Minister Manmohan Singh on 15 September 2009. "PM's Address at the DGPs and IGPs Conference – 2009": http://pmindia.nic.in/lspeech.asp?id=822.

14 A special Security Council committee created by Resolution 1267 (1999) is meant to oversee the implementation of an assets freeze, travel ban and arms embargo by all countries on individuals and organizations associated with the Taliban, Osama Bin Laden and al-Qaeda. Over the years, India has successfully campaigned to have groups like the Lashkar-e-Tayyaba and Jaish-e-Mohammed, as well as some of their leaders, sanctioned by the 1267 committee.

15 See J.N. Dixit, *India–Pakistan in War and Peace* (New Delhi: Books Today, 2002).

16 Bruce Riedel, *American Diplomacy and the 1999 Kargil Summit at Blair House* (Philadelphia: Center for the Advanced Study of India, University of Pennsylvania, 2002).

17 Jay Solomon and Siobhan Gorman, "Pakistan, India and U.S. Begin Sharing Intelligence," *Wall Street Journal*, 22 May 2009.

18 "Pakistan Must Tackle Terror At All Levels," *The Hindu*, 20 July 2009.

19 Chidanand Rajghatta, "No Difference with US on Iran: Manmohan," *Times of India*, 16 September 2005.

20 Speech of Ambassador Robert Blackwill to IISS–Citi India Global Forum in New Delhi, April 2008. www.iiss.org/conferences/iiss-citi-india-global-forum/igf-plenary-sessions-2008/fourth-plenary-session-india-and-the-great-powers/fourth-plenary-session-ambassador-robert-blackwill.

21 Siddharth Varadarajan, "As Pakistan Hails 'Precedent,' Other IAEA Members Express Doubts, Fears," *The Hindu*, 2 August 2008.

22 For comprehensive accounts of the history and evolution of the Indian nuclear program, see Itty Abraham, *The Making of the Indian Bomb: Science, Secrecy and the Post-Colonial State* (London: Zed Books, 1998), George Perkovich, *India's Nuclear Bomb* (Berkeley: University of California Press, 2002).

23 For a detailed description of India's negotiating stance at the Geneva Disarmament Conference, see Ashok Kapur, *India's Nuclear Option: Atomic Diplomacy and Decision Making* (New York: Praeger, 1976).

24 Since the treaty can only enter into force if India also signs it, this promise was widely seen as a statement of India's willingness to become a party to the CTBT. "India Will Not Obstruct CTBT Coming To Force, Says Jaswant," *Rediff.com*, 9 February 1999.

25 K. Santhanam and Ashok Parthasarathi, "Pokhran-II Thermonuclear Test, a Failure," *The Hindu*, 17 September 2009. See also Siddharth Varadarajan, "Fizzle Claim For Thermonuclear Test Refuted," *The Hindu*, 27 August 2009, and R. Ramachandram, "Why There is no Case for Further Nuclear Tests," *The Hindu*, 25 September 2009.

26 Shyam Saran, "Indo-US Civil Nuclear Agreement: Expectations and Consequences," *Address by Special Envoy to the Prime Minister*, 23 March 2009.

27 "PM's Statement in Lok Sabha on the Debate on the PM's Recent Visit's Abroad on July 29, 2009": http://pmindia.nic.in/lspeech.asp?id=805.

28 Ministry of External Affairs, "The Road to Copenhagen: India's Position on Climate Change Issues" (New Delhi: Public Diplomacy Division, 2009).

29 Ministry of External Affairs, "The Road to Copenhagen."

30 Siddharth Varadarajan, "India Casting a Wide Net in its Hunt for Energy," *International Herald Tribune*, 25 January 2006.

31 Shivshankar Menon, *Maritime Imperatives of Indian Foreign Policy* (New Delhi: National Maritime Foundation, 2009).

32 Robert D. Kaplan, "Center Stage for the 21st Century: Power Plays in the Indian Ocean," *Foreign Affairs* March/April (2009).

33 Menon, *Maritime Imperatives of Indian Foreign Policy*.

10 The EU

Facing non-traditional threats in a globalized world

Thierry Tardy[1]

The evolution of the EU in the political and security domains, combined with general long-term perspectives toward a multipolar system, have led to its placement in the category of potential poles of that system. Together with the US, China, India and Russia, it is no longer France or the UK that is presented as a future power, but instead the European Union of 27 states (most likely more than 30 in 15 or 20 years). Such a typology is welcome for European-integration advocates insofar as it shows that the EU is perceived and accepted as a potential, if not an existing power, which is comparable to other powers such as the US or China.

On the other hand, this label raises questions as to the kind of power the EU is said to become. Fundamentally, the EU is a civilian, normative actor that has recently embraced a more robust conception of power that includes a military dimension. Theoretically, as the Maastricht Treaty put it, the EU is supposed to define for itself a "common defence policy, which might in time lead to a common defence." Some Member States may indeed want to see the EU becoming a power in the sense that the US or China is, and realists would even argue this is what is expected from any actor aspiring to play a political role on a global scale.[2]

In reality, though, the EU has not yet become a power in the sense that states can be. It has remained a soft power; one that is comfortable with neither the notion of strategic culture nor the use of force it might entail. Furthermore, the majority of states or policy-makers in the EU would most likely be of the view that if the EU does increasingly resemble a state and should further develop its foreign and security policy, it is nevertheless not supposed to become a power comparable to the US or China.

Indeed, the idea that the EU is *sui generis* (the only example of its kind) implies that it plays in a different league, intentionally. Such differences are limitations to any comparative analysis between the EU and traditional powers, especially if such analysis is made on the basis of traditional criteria of power (military capability, use of force, strong and coherent decision-making processes, etc.). The same limitations apply to the qualification of the EU as a "center of global power."

In this context, this chapter addresses the issue of how the EU understands and manages what it identifies as threats to its security in a globalized world.

By doing so, the chapter aims to highlight the liberal approach of the EU in the security domain, which makes it a specific actor. The EU has indeed developed a widened conception of both security and the notion of threat, and consequently a security policy that is reflective of this post-modern vision.

At the same time, the chapter intends to stress the gap between what is reality and what is EU rhetoric or potential. The EU aspires to be a fully-fledged security actor that thinks and acts in an open-minded and effective manner, but it is also constrained by a series of political and technical factors that play down its overall ambitions. In particular, while the EU has proved itself to be open to the realities posed by non-traditional threats such as organized crime or climate change, its security policy has remained largely focused on the more traditional field of crisis management. As far as non-traditional threats are concerned, EU levels of resources, state policy coordination and actual delivery are still far from what tackling these threats would require.

The chapter first looks at the development of the EU's foreign and security policies and how the organization has, over a period of 15 years, turned into a security actor. This is followed by a proposed overview of the threats either already faced by the EU, or perceived as potentially harmful. Third, policy responses and instruments of the EU are analyzed, with a distinction between the general approach to crisis management and the response to non-traditional threats. Finally, the chapter examines the relationship between globalization and development of the EU security policy.

The EU's foreign and security policy: an aspiration to be a global liberal actor

The European Community was created in the late-1950s as the result of a highly political project: creating institutions and links that would encourage states to cooperate and build a security community, rather than let the security dilemmas and inherent inter-states zero-sum games prevail. By nature, the very project of European integration was – and still is, to a large extent – aimed at overcoming geopolitics in Europe. The European Community in the wake of World War II and the European Union after the end of the Cold War were largely built on the idea that the Westphalian system, based on states, territories and frontiers, had to be transcended. As Cooper puts it, the Treaty of Rome is "a conscious and successful attempt to go beyond the nation state," while "modern Europe was born with the peace of Westphalia."[3]

In hindsight, the European integration process proved to be a powerful conflict-prevention mechanism. War has indeed become obsolete among EC/EU members. The whole process was also embedded in liberal thinking, i.e., in the belief in liberal democracy, free-market economy and good governance, as well as in the prevalence of pacific dispute settlement over the use of force. The European Community was then characterized as a civilian power,[4] which was also a way to stress that, in a Cold War environment dominated by power politics, the EC was a rather weak political actor on the international scene.

EU ambitions from Maastricht to Saint-Malo

The European Community started to develop for itself a foreign and security policy with the end of the Cold War and the major evolutions it carried for Europe. Institutionally, a Common Foreign and Security Policy (CFSP) was defined in the 1991 Maastricht Treaty, which also transformed the European Community into the European Union. With this, the EU wants to assert itself as a liberal or normative power that stresses the importance of norms and multilateralism as pillars of interstate interaction, and one that promotes principles such as rule of law, liberal democracy, human rights and good governance.[5] Beyond these principles, the EU also intends to become a political actor, influencing world politics through foreign policy action.

However, in reality, the Yugoslav conflicts of the 1990s, and the inability of the EU to provide a coherent and coordinated response, illustrated the difficulty in transcending national agendas and giving substance to the newly defined CFSP.[6] The EU inertia was further illustrated in the Kosovo case, where the EU did try to take initiatives, but was sidelined when the military operation became the preferred option.

This succession of missed opportunities led to a new effort to empower the EU in the security domain with the birth – at the December 1998 Franco-British Saint-Malo Summit – of the European Security and Defence Policy (ESDP) as an integral part of CFSP. The Saint-Malo final declaration stated: "The European Union needs to be in a position to play its full role on the international stage," and, "To this end, the Union must have the capacity for autonomous action, backed up by credible military forces, the means to decide to use them and a readiness to do so, in order to respond to international crises."[7] The Summit led to a series of decisions aimed at making ESDP concrete, namely through the establishment of permanent political and military institutions and the definition of military and civilian Capabilities Headline Goals. In practice, the military capabilities that are put in place within the framework of ESDP are supposed to be used in relatively low-intensity military operations. What the EU is aspiring to be able to do is crisis-management operations, defined as "humanitarian and rescue tasks, peacekeeping tasks, and the use of combat forces in crisis management, including peacemaking." This level of ambition tends to downplay the aspiration of the EU to "play its full role on the international scene." In the late-1990s, the objective for the EU was to do the type of operations that NATO was then running in Bosnia-Herzegovina in the post-Dayton phase, or in Kosovo in the post-"Allied Force" operation. There was, at the same time, no consensus to go beyond robust crisis-management, which is already a political and operational challenge in itself. The decade to follow would confirm this relatively low-ambition approach, with the EU deploying its first crisis-management operations. As of 2009, 16 of the 22 ESDP operations are of a civilian nature, while only three military operations were deployed in a relatively non-permissive environment (Artemis in the Democratic Republic of the Congo (DRC) in 2003; EUFOR DRC in 2006; EUFOR Chad/Central African Republic [CAR] in 2008/2009).

Notwithstanding the nature of EU-led operations, the 22 operations run by the EU fundamentally changed the nature of the debate about the role of the EU in security governance. They showed that the EU was capable of going beyond the rhetoric of being a security actor by actually becoming present on the ground. This evolution also challenged the notion that the EU was a civilian power, and raised the issue of the impact of militarization on the normative/civilian dimension of the EU.

These questions are nurtured by the assumption that a military dimension would inevitably alter the EU's conception of its role, in the sense that it would change its vision of what it can do, and subsequently shape its interests differently. The EU would then move away from its civilian, normative, liberal status to become a self-interested actor, capable of resorting to force to serve objectives that were previously not even considered. An alternative interpretation is that of an EU conception of power that would be distinct from the traditional approach as defined by political realists.[8] Because the EU does not resemble other security actors and is built on values and liberal thinking, it would be able to combine soft and hard power so as to behave on the international scene more as a force for good than as any form of hegemon. It is also argued that as long as EU-led military operations are confined to peacekeeping, even if they are robust, they will not fundamentally alter the civilian nature of the EU.[9]

The EU, between Venus and Mars

The aspiration of the EU to play a role on the international scene is further conceptualized through the December 2003 *European Security Strategy* (ESS).[10] The whole document reflects a general intention of the EU to take its part in global security governance, as any other key actor would. It starts by stating that the European Union is "inevitably a global player," and as such, "should be ready to share in the responsibility for global security and in building a better world."[11] This being said, the EU aspiration to be a fully-fledged security actor raises the question about propensity and capacity to resort to force whenever a situation is perceived as requiring it. The EU stance in this respect is ambiguous, and reflects the difficulty an institution faces in theorizing what still falls within the prerogatives of states.

On the one hand, the ESS aims at presenting the EU as an institution that can possibly resort to coercion if need be. Referring to "military activities" as an instrument for crisis management, "robust intervention" when necessary, or a "price to be paid" for countries that have "placed themselves outside the bounds of international society," the ESS intends to give credibility to the concept of "effective multilateralism," which implies the necessity to have functioning international organizations, but also the readiness "to act when their rules are broken." By the same token, mandates of some EU-led operations – those that are created on the basis of a UN Security Council (UNSC) Chapter VII resolution – are relatively explicit about the possible use of force. Also, documents such as the EU paper submitted to the UN-mandated High-Level Panel on

Threats, Challenges and Change,[12] or the EU Strategy against weapons of mass destruction (WMD) proliferation,[13] make clear reference to coercion or military intervention, should it prove necessary to enforce accepted rules. In a way, such commitments are a response to Kagan's argument that Europe "is turning away from power," and that "Europe's military weakness has produced a perfectly understandable aversion to the exercise of military power."[14]

On the other hand, the ESS falls short of using the term "use of force" and remains ambiguous on how robustly or coercively the EU could act. The notion of "effective multilateralism" may necessitate a robust response in cases where the "rules are broken," but what this means is not specified. This ambiguity is confirmed in the 2008 report on the implementation of the ESS,[15] which refers to the concept of "responsibility to protect" and to the fact that "Sovereign governments must take responsibility for the consequences of their actions," or to the "need for additional measures in support of the UN" if the Iranian program advances, but without ever being clear on the actual possibility of resorting to force.

Such ambiguity questions the nature of the EU as a security actor and the kind of strategic culture it is supposed to develop. Two issues come into play here. One is the meaning of strategic culture for an entity that by nature is not a state. Another is the extent to which the EU can pretend to be a security actor if it is reluctant to contemplate the use of force as a policy option. For some, this timidity reflects a general weakness of the EU, which results from the inability of its Member States to overcome national divergences as well as from their unwillingness to empower the EU.[16] For others, the reluctance to approach the use of force, while any security actor would, is the result of a deliberate choice and leads back to the liberal approach and the preference for inclusion over confrontation.[17] Because the EU is a hybrid institution, its approach to strategy and power should match its hybrid nature,[18] which pushes it to develop its own strategy, "between the two extremes of Venus and Mars."[19]

The EU threat assessment: the prevalence of non-traditional threats

The "raison d'être" of a security actor

The identification of security threats is consubstantial with existing as a security actor. The EU thus started to think about the kind of threats it could face while defining itself as an entity playing a role in world affairs, and therefore susceptible to being threatened. In this process, the question of whether the EU as such, rather than its Member States, could be the object of a threat was raised. What is at stake here is whether an institution can become a referent object of security. A related question became whether the EU would identify for itself threats that would not otherwise be considered threats for a given Member State.

No systematic assessment of security threats to the EU had been done prior to the adoption of the *European Security Strategy* (ESS) in 2003. Up to that date, threats to the EU were by and large the threats that EU Member States were identifying for themselves. In the same vein, threats to the values promoted by the EU were also perceived as threats to the EU itself.

The ESS makes the distinction between global challenges and threats. Global challenges characterize general features of the international system that may be the sources of threats. They are globalization, conflicts, poverty/underdevelopment, disease, global warming and energy dependence.

As for threats, having noted the improbability of large-scale aggression against any Member State, the ESS characterizes the "new threats" to Europe as being "more diverse, less visible and less predictable." Five key threats are identified: terrorism, proliferation of weapons of mass destruction, regional conflicts, state failure and organized crime. First, terrorism is presented as a "growing strategic threat to the whole of Europe," which is both a target and a base for terrorism. The link is established between the "most recent wave of terrorism" and "violent religious extremism." Second, WMD proliferation is described as "potentially the greatest threat" to European security, with the "most frightening scenario" being the acquisition by terrorist groups of WMD. Third, regional conflicts, among others the ones in Kashmir or Africa, and therefore not just the ones taking place in Europe or in its vicinity, are presented as directly or indirectly threatening European interests, *inter alia* through their connection with terrorism, state failure, organized crime and even the demand for WMD. Fourth, state failure is dangerous for Europe because of the associated threats it leads to, with organized crime and terrorism cited as the most obvious. Finally, organized crime is an internal threat that has many external ramifications (cross-border trafficking in drugs, women, illegal migrants and weapons), including those that can have links with terrorism. The strategy also defines three strategic objectives for the EU: addressing threats, building security in the EU neighborhood and building an international order based on "effective multilateralism."

The 2008 report on the implementation of the ESS[20] confirms the existence of these five threats, and adds three: cyber security as a "new economic, political and military weapon"; energy security – or rather energy dependence – with a declining European production of oil and gas and therefore an increasing dependence on external producers; and climate change, described as a "threat multiplier" in line with the March 2008 document on the same issue.[21]

The EU does not distinguish between first- and second-order threats. However, the three "new" threats introduced in the 2008 implementation report are clearly not given the same attention as the five ones initially identified. Among these five ones, terrorism and WMD proliferation also seem to be given priority over the others.

Through this threat-assessment exercise, the EU reveals a widened conception of security and of the concept of threat.[22] While taking its distance from the traditional approach to security, the EU acknowledges the multi-layered dimension of security as well as its general evolution, encapsulated in the security and development nexus, the interweaving of internal and external security, recognition of the role of non-state actors, or the admission of an increased vulnerability of the EU as a result of globalization. Furthermore, with the exception of regional conflicts, all other key threats are non-traditional in the sense that they are not of a military nature and they do not necessarily emanate from state actors. For the EU and its Member States, the threat is no longer external, state-based and materialized through the use of military force. It can come from a group of individuals operating within the European space and resorting to non-traditional means of attacking European interests and values.

Russia and the traditional nature of threats

One should note, however, that threat perceptions in EU countries were slightly altered following the August 2008 Russia–Georgia war. For at least some European states, the analysis according to which threats to Europe and European states are no longer state-based and military needs to be reviewed, as Russia exemplifies a traditional threat that has to be integrated in any threat-assessment exercise. Countries such as Poland, Estonia or Sweden have publicly expressed concerns about the resurgence of a Russian threat at the frontiers of the EU. In Latvia, a report released prior to the Russia–Georgia conflict was already placing Russia on a list of "major security threats" to the Baltic state.[23]

A clear distinction is usually not made between a threat from Russia that would take a traditional form – or, in the extreme case, a cross-border military action – and a threat that would materialize through energy or cyber-attack, but there is a feeling in neighboring countries that Russia challenges the establishment of a security community in Europe. For European North Atlantic Treaty Organization (NATO) members, this "new" fear leads to the need to reassert NATO as the principal security guarantor of Europe.

One can see a dichotomy here between the security of the EU and the narrative it develops on one hand, and that of its Member States on the other. For the EU, Russia is not presented as a threat, at least not in the traditional, i.e., territorial and military, sense. The 2008 report on the implementation of the ESS mentions Russia seven times, but it never insinuates that Russia could constitute a threat to the EU. Under the heading "Energy Security," the document notes in a neutral way that energy is a "major factor in EU–Russia relations." The wording is more direct when referring to the Russia–Georgia conflict, as the report states that, "Our relations with Russia have deteriorated over the conflict with Georgia," and that "the EU expects Russia to honour its commitments in a way that will restore the necessary confidence." It is also mentioned that, "our partnership should be based on respect for common values, notably human rights, democracy, and rule of law, and market economic principles as well as on common interests and objectives."[24] The strong vocabulary used by some EU countries is not taken up in the official EU documents.

Policy responses and instruments: still focused on crisis management

The CFSP and ESDP are aimed at enabling the EU to play a role as a security actor, participating in world security governance. Consequently, the identification of policies and instruments that the EU has come up with to tackle security threats should presumably be done by looking at these intergovernmental, second-pillar activities. At the same time, CFSP and ESDP policies and instruments reflect a relatively narrow conception of security that tends to focus on politico-military issues with a short-term perspective. Although this approach is crucial, it cannot pretend to provide a response to the broad security challenges the EU is faced with. This *problématique* leads to the role of the European Commission and its implication in areas that – according to a wide conception of security – also contribute to the maintenance of international peace and security. The CFSP/ESDP and Commission's policies are conceptually distinct but also offer high potential for complementarity. In practice, however, the two-track approach has prevailed, with CFSP and ESDP most often separate from European Commission activities, and even competing in some areas.

Furthermore, while the EU threat assessment is wide-ranging and invites the EU to respond with an equally wide array of policies and instruments, the management of crises through ESDP has remained the main focus of EU attention over the last ten years, to the detriment of other areas of strategic importance.

Crisis management: central but how relevant for tackling the "new threats?"

CFSP and ESDP are the principal instruments of the EU security policy. Following the definition of ESDP in the late 1990s, a crisis management political–military structure was put in place to allow for its implementation. Four bodies were initially created within the Secretariat of the Council: a Political and Security Committee (PSC), a Military Committee, a Military Staff and a Committee for the Civilian Aspects of Crisis Management (CIVCOM). The subsequent development of ESDP then led to creation of the European Defence Agency (EDA) in 2004; a civil–military cell as well as an operation center were also established in 2005/2006 within the EU Military Staff, in response to the need to be able to plan and conduct small-scale crisis-management operations autonomously (i.e., without resorting to NATO assets or calling on states). In 2007–2008, the civilian crisis-management structure was developed through the establishment of a Civilian Planning and Conduct Capability (CPCC) to plan and conduct all ESDP civilian operations. It was followed in 2009 by the establishment of the Crisis Management and Planning Directorate (CMPD), that merged DG VIII (defense issues) and DG IX (civilian crisis management) strategic planning functions.

Insofar as capabilities are concerned, a first military "Headline Goal" was defined in 1999, according to which "Member States must be able, by 2003, to deploy within 60 days and sustain for at least one year military forces of up to

50,000–60,000 persons capable of the full range of Petersberg tasks."[25] This Headline Goal was declared to be met in May 2003, although "limited and constrained by recognised shortfalls."[26] Subsequently, a new Headline Goal was defined in 2004 ("Headline Goal 2010"), with a shift from a quantitative approach – with the corps-level target – to a more qualitative approach through the "Battlegroup" concept. Capabilities were simultaneously developed in the civilian sphere. Four "priority areas" were initially identified: police, rule of law, civil administration and civil protection. A broader civilian Headline Goal was then adopted in December 2004, to be met in 2008. It enlarged the scope of EU operations to Security Sector Reform (SSR) and Disarmament, Demobilization and Reintegration (DDR) processes. The Headline Goal 2008 was declared to be completed and is now replaced by the new civilian Headline Goal 2010.

As already noted, the EU has launched and run 22 ESDP operations since 2003, among which six were of a military nature (Concordia in Macedonia in 2003; Artemis in the DRC in 2003; Althea in Bosnia-Herzegovina as of 2004; EUFOR DRC in 2006; EUFOR Chad/CAR in 2008/09; and EU NAVFOR Atalanta in the Gulf of Aden as of December 2008). The 16 civilian missions took place in Europe (Bosnia-Herzegovina, Macedonia, Kosovo, Georgia), Africa (DRC, Darfur, Guinea-Bissau), Asia (Indonesia, Afghanistan), and in the Middle East (Palestinian Territories, Iraq), and implemented various mandates dealing with ceasefire-agreements monitoring, police training, rule of law, SSR or support to good governance.

These operations have demonstrated a certain capacity of the EU in the area of crisis management, at a time when all actors in this field, such as the UN, NATO or the Organization for Security and Cooperation in Europe (OSCE), encounter difficulties. The six military operations have proved to be successful, although the EU was never really tested in these operations, nor did it ever deploy troops for a long period of time in unstable environments. Insofar as the civilian operations are concerned, they enabled the EU to be present in post-conflict environments and to develop a peace-building capacity. Yet, these operations have also remained limited in scope and duration, and quite a few of them eventually achieved very little on the ground (for example, the two operations in the Palestinian territories, or the SSR and police missions in the DRC).

This being said, the development of ESDP and the creation of the first EU-led operations beg the question of whether ESDP, which was introduced as a response to the post-Cold War turbulences and their consequences for Europe, actually provides answers to the threats the EU has identified for itself. The link between ESDP and the two threats of regional conflicts and state failure is rather easy to establish. On the other hand, the extent to which ESDP makes the EU better prepared to fight terrorism, organized crime or climate change is less obvious. The ESS included "support for third countries in combating terrorism" as a potential cause for ESDP missions,[27] a link confirmed in the Lisbon Treaty, which stated that all ESDP tasks "may contribute to the fight against terrorism, including by supporting third countries in combating terrorism in their territories."[28] Work was also carried out on the CFSP/ESDP contribution to the fight against terrorism. ESDP operations aiming to prevent the occurrence of failed states and regional conflicts are presented as making "a considerable contribution to long term actions for the prevention of terrorism."[29] In addition to prevention, ESDP can contribute to the fight against terrorism through protection (of key civilian targets among others), and consequence management.

Notwithstanding this, the relative narrowness of ESDP makes it difficult to reconcile with the wide-ranging needs of a counter-terrorism policy. This was confirmed with the release of the EU Counter-Terrorism Strategy in 2005,[30] which promotes a holistic approach based on four dimensions (prevent, protect, pursue, respond) that go well beyond the remit of ESDP and the second pillar. The same critique applies when looking at WMD proliferation and organized crime, and *a fortiori* when energy security, climate change and the cyber threat are taken into consideration.

What role for the Commission in tackling threats?

In this debate, the European Commission offers a different picture of the way the EU tackles threats to its security. First and foremost, the very fact that the European Commission comes into play in the definition and implementation of a wide-ranging security policy for the EU is illustrative of the evolution of both the concept of security and of the EU itself. The European Commission is not, *prima facie*, a security actor, and has developed an institutional culture that is not necessarily open to a role in this area. In this context, the implication of the Commission in the security field has been the result of the widening of the security agenda and the interweaving of development and security. If, as the ESS puts it, "security is a precondition of development,"[31] and development is an instrument for crisis management and conflict prevention,[32] then all development-related Commission activities are indirectly falling within a broader security agenda. In general terms, through activities such as humanitarian assistance, development aid, economic cooperation or support to good governance, programs of the European Commission directly or indirectly address state fragility and the root causes of instability, which may lead to the development of regional conflicts, organized crime or terrorism.[33] By the same token, policies such as the European Neighbourhood Policy (ENP) or the newly defined Union for the Mediterranean are part of an inclusive "conflict prevention through partnership" approach.

In the more narrowly defined field of crisis management, the European Commission is mainly active through the financing of security-related programs that are implemented by other international organizations or by non-governmental organizations (NGOs).[34] In Africa, the EU finances crisis-management activities through its African Peace Facility[35] (from the European Development Fund), which has been used to finance African Union (AU) operations in Burundi, Darfur, the Comoros and Somalia, as well as the Economic Community of Central African States (ECCAS) operation in the CAR, among others.[36] Capacity-building programs of the AU and sub-regional organizations have also benefited from AFP funding. On a broader level, the 'Instrument for Stability' aims to provide technical and financial assistance, including support for diplomatic efforts, and the establishment of interim administrations, good governance, rule of law and security-sector reform to countries confronted with a crisis situation.[37] Other crisis-management-related activities, such as humanitarian assistance or SSR and DDR programs, are financed by European Commission agencies or funds (ECHO; European Development Fund).

This multi-actor and multi-dimensional approach is supposed to reflect the holistic policy of the EU in the field of crisis management, and also its adaptation to the width of contemporary security threats. However, this aspiration has also raised the issue of coordination between these different instruments, and of overall EU policy coherence. In the civilian crisis-management area, the fact that both the Commission (first pillar) and the Council secretariat (second pillar) are involved in policy-making and implementation of sometimes very similar programs once again raises the issue of cross-pillar coherence and EU visibility. Within the ESDP, coordination between military and civilian crisis-management has also been a challenge. The simultaneous presence in Bosnia-Herzegovina of a military operation (Althea), an ESDP civilian operation (EU Police Mission) and of the Commission through longer-term recovery programs, provides an illustration of this compartmentalization.

Looking at the issue of coherence and visibility, a European Commission communication stated that, "Unsatisfactory co-ordination between different actors and policies means that the EU loses potential leverage internationally, both politically and economically."[38] In the crisis-management field, the need for greater coordination has led to the concept of "comprehensive planning," which is defined as a "systematic approach designed to address the need for effective intra-pillar and inter-pillar co-ordination of activity by all relevant EU actors in crisis management planning," and one that is aimed at the "development and delivery of a coordinated and coherent response to a crisis on the basis of an all-inclusive analysis of the situation, in particular where more than one EU instrument is engaged."[39] This is also the logic that has led to the end of the three-pillar structure and creation of the position of High Representative for Foreign Affairs and Security Policy by the Lisbon Treaty. In practice, though, it remains to be seen how institutional overhaul can help overcome cultural differences.

The EU and the new threats

In comparison with EU crisis-management policies and achievements, its response to the so-called new threats is far less developed and institutionalized. Terrorism and WMD proliferation have led to the adoption of strategies that combine long-term policies and shorter-term actions, strategies that are supposed to involve a wide range of actors. The 2005 Counter-Terrorism Strategy, adopted after the London attacks of July 2005, defines four pillars of EU action to "combat terrorism globally while respecting human rights."[40] The first pillar is to "prevent people turning to terrorism by tackling the factors which can lead to radicalization, in Europe and internationally"; second, to "protect citizens and infrastructure, including through improved security of borders"; third to "pursue terrorists, to impede planning, travel and communications, to disrupt support networks and to cut off funding"; fourth to respond, i.e., to be able to "manage the consequences of a terrorist attack." The document states that "Member States have the primary responsibility for combating terrorism," but that the EU can "add value in four main ways": by strengthening national capabilities, facilitating European cooperation, developing collective capability and promoting international partnership. The EU clearly keeps its distance from the US "War on Terror" approach, by focusing on root causes and long-term actions as opposed to military activities. The strategy leads to the EU Action Plan on combating terrorism, which takes up the four above-mentioned pillars and lays out more specific policy actions. These documents are complemented by a series of decisions, such as adoption of the European Arrest Warrant, the creation of the position of EU Counter-Terrorism Coordinator, or the strengthening of the EU law-enforcement organization the European Police Office and other border-control instruments. The fight against terrorism is supposed to be a cross-pillar activity, with the European Commission and the Member States acting toward the establishment of an area of Freedom, Security and Justice.

Yet, the policy suffers from diverging national perceptions and a general reluctance of EU Member States to transfer responsibility to the EU. Overall, the fight against terrorism remains a state prerogative and no integration has really taken place.[41] It follows a relatively poor implementation of agreed measures and a lack of financial and human resources. The 2008 report on the implementation of the ESS addresses terrorism and organized crime together. The document praises the achievements since 2003, but also recommends renewed coordination efforts in the fields of "handling a major terrorist incident," curbing terrorist financing and information sharing, and countering radicalization and recruitment. The report also stresses that "national action is central" in the fight against terrorism, and that "progress has been slow and incomplete" in the areas of "coordination, transparency and flexibility [...] across different agencies, at national and European levels."[42] At the policy level, terrorism is addressed in conjunction with organized crime under the framework of the 2004 Hague Programme, a wide-ranging action plan dealing with terrorism, organized crime, migration management, visa policies, asylum, privacy and security, and criminal justice.[43]

The fight against WMD proliferation has also led to a Strategy and Action Plan, both adopted in 2003. The EU Strategy against WMD proliferation defines the EU objective as, "to prevent, deter, halt and, where possible, eliminate proliferation programmes of concern worldwide."[44] To do so, the EU wants to rely on "effective multilateralism," the promotion of a stable international and regional environment, and close cooperation with key partners. Furthermore, the instruments at the disposal of the EU are: multilateral treaties and verification mechanisms, national and internationally coordinated export controls, cooperative threat reduction programs, political and economic levers, interdiction of illegal procurement activities, and, "as a last resort, coercive measures in accordance with the UN Charter." The strategy lists a series of measures aimed at strengthening the efficacy of these instruments. The 2008 report on the implementation of the ESS places WMD proliferation at the top of the list of security threats, and states that the risk of WMD proliferation has increased over the last five years. It mentions Iran as a "growing source of concern,"[45] and describes the "development of a nuclear programme capability" in Iran as a "threat to EU security that cannot be accepted,"[46] but falls short of alluding to any coercive measure. Here, again, the overall EU policy is hampered by differences in national perceptions toward the reality of the threat, and by limited intelligence-sharing. In the case of Iran, the hypothetical resort to force by the EU itself – should Iran reach full nuclear military capability – is also difficult to envisage, both politically and practically. As in other domains, the EU promotes a cooperative and inclusive approach that distinguishes itself from the US policy, but seems ill-equipped or powerless when faced with determined offenders.[47] The EU policy has also tended to remain state-focused, with the risks of illicit trafficking from non-state actors – as stated in UNSC Resolution 1540 (2004) – only recently being taken into account.

The three threats inserted in the 2008 report on the ESS implementation – cyber security, energy security and climate change – have led to the definition of specific policies at the EU level only recently, and no instrument has yet been created to tackle them. The extent to which these threats have been "securitized" – i.e., whether or not they have moved away from the strictly political or economic areas to become security issues or threats – is debatable. Their inclusion into the EU security policy discourse may have started the process of securitization, yet in terms of policy this has not so far led to any substantive development.

Information society security is dealt with at the EU level by the European Network and Information Security Agency, which is mandated to give advice and recommendations to the European Commission and Member States, raise awareness on information society security, and facilitate communication between EU institutions, Member States and the private sector. There is also an EU Strategy for a Secure Information Society that tackles security challenges for the information society through "specific network and information security measures, the regulatory framework for electronic communications, and the fight against cybercrime."[48] However, cybercrime has so far been mainly considered as a criminal activity motivated by profit; neither the political dimension of the threat nor the state as a potential target – as Estonia was in 2007 – have been addressed in earnest.

By the same token, energy security and climate change have only recently appeared on the EU agenda as security issues, and the extent to which they are indeed threats to the EU is not established with absolute clarity. The two themes are closely interrelated and have been addressed by the EU concomitantly. In March 2007 the European Council issued an "Integrated climate and energy policy," which defined, on the basis of the Commission's "energy and climate change package," the "20–20–20 climate change commitments" (encompassing a 20 percent reduction in greenhouse gas emissions, a 20 percent share of renewable energy and a 20 percent saving in energy demand by 2020).[49] The issue of climate change was also introduced as a threat to international and eventually European security: climate change is presented as a "threat multiplier which exacerbates existing trends, tensions and instability," and which carries "political and security risks that directly affect European interests."[50] In response, the December 2008 European Council adopted the "climate and energy package," which endorsed the "20–20–20" targets and, despite being significantly scaled down by Member States and amended to please the industrial sector,[51] nonetheless places the EU in the lead when it comes to the fight against climate change.

However, the connection between climate change and the security of the EU is not straightforward. The March 2008 document establishes a link between climate change and international security, but the short-term impact on the EU is not clearly established, apart from the fact that climate change will affect areas that are of key importance for Europe (politically, economically or due to migration). By the same token, the security considerations were not central to the discussions around the "climate and energy package."

In parallel, the European Commission introduced its Energy Security and Solidarity Action Plan, which is aimed at responding to the precariousness of Europe's energy supply security and supporting the "20–20–20" commitments. Five areas of action in need of particular attention are identified in order to limit EU energy dependence in the future: infrastructure needs and the diversification of energy supplies; external energy relations; oil and gas stocks and crisis-response mechanisms; energy efficiency; and making the best use of the EU's indigenous energy resources.[52] The need for a coordinated policy was reasserted with the new episode of the Russia–Ukraine gas supply crisis of early 2009. However, the ability of EU Member States to think and act collectively in this field – and fully integrate the issue into their security policy – has yet to be seen, especially with Russia doing well to divide EU countries and making bilateral deals. Furthermore, the very idea that EU Member States are indeed in favor of a common energy policy is not given, as for some of them a common policy would play against national interests.[53] Consequently, energy dependence has not translated into a truly European approach, nor has it been fully "securitized" as an issue.

These different elements show a disconnect between rhetoric and reality in the EU policy in tackling threats to its security. The EU has to a large extent conceptualized its role as a security actor and the corresponding threats, yet remains marginally involved in policy implementation, which in the end cast some doubts about its status as a full-fledged security actor.

Europeanization and globalization: the EU as the problem or the solution?

The European integration and globalization processes have developed simultaneously and through a complex relationship.[54] What they have in common is that they both "provide external pressure to integrate and counter the nation states' desire to retain sovereignty."[55] The debate, then, is on whether Europeanization and globalization have taken place in parallel processes or whether the former is simply an illustration of the latter.[56] In fact, the European Union can be seen as both an expression of globalization and as a response to it. The EU reflects globalization in the sense that it promotes the circulation of people, goods, information and capital, and that it has thrived on the liberalization of markets. Both processes also challenge the centrality and relevance of the state, as well as call for a redefinition of the concept of state sovereignty. At the same time, the EU is a response to globalization insofar as it is protective of EU citizens and markets from the excesses of globalization. In the security arena, ESDP is supposed to provide the tools to better respond to the security challenges posed by globalization.

It follows that globalization is simultaneously an opportunity and a threat to the EU. The relationship between the EU and the globalization process is shaped by this dual characteristic. The European Commission's communication on "Europe in the World" states that "Europe has the potential to rise to the [new] challenges and to share in the new opportunities created by emerging markets and globalization."[57] At the same time, all EU documents on this theme also acknowledge that "Globalisation is accelerating shifts in power,"[58] and making the EU more vulnerable.[59] One of the key challenges for the EU in the coming decades will be to minimize the negative effects of globalization while maximizing the benefits it potentially brings. The EU is not ill-equipped for such a challenge, but the above-mentioned shifts in power go against the EU as a "center of global power."

The end of the Cold War and globalization brought peace and economic prosperity to Europe. This has enabled the EU to transform itself into a security provider, exporting security outside the European continent. However, a related and less positive consequence of these two phenomena is that Europe, as a region, has lost its centrality in world politics, and in the long run is likely to lose its predominance in economic terms as well.

The political and economic dynamics of change tend to work against the EU.[60] The emergence of China and India, global economic and demographic trends, and climate change are likely to make Europe more vulnerable, as opposed to less.[61] Two issues come into play: first there is the question of whether the EU will manage to maintain its economic clout in the face of rising China and India;[62] second is the issue of whether the EU will be able to translate such economic power into political influence. The prediction made by the US National Intelligence Council for 2025 is rather bleak:

> The EU will be in a position to bolster political stability and democratization on Europe's periphery by taking in additional new members in the Balkans, and perhaps Ukraine and Turkey. However, continued failure to convince skeptical publics of the benefits of deeper economic, political, and social integration and to grasp the nettle of a shrinking and aging population by

enacting painful reforms could leave the EU a hobbled giant distracted by internal bickering and competing national agendas, and less able to translate its economic clout into global influence.[63]

For the US, a consequence of a decrease in Europe's strategic importance is likely to be that Europe will benefit less from American attention and protection. But it will also make EU aspirations of becoming a worldwide political actor more acceptable, in contrast with the initial US reaction when ESDP was launched in the late-1990s. These two developments have indeed already taken place.

In a way, these trends and predictions reinforce the need for the EU to play a global role as the only way to exist on the international scene.[64] The entry into force of the Lisbon Treaty in December 2009 is an important first step. Yet, it is questionable whether European states, leaders and institutions have fully understood the scope of the shift and the risks that it carries. What is at stake is the ability of EU Member States to agree on what the EU should become and therefore rise to the challenge of making it happen. As noted above, the EU is not deprived of assets in this game. Relatively high scores in economic and social development, political stability and good governance, level of education and access to information, as well as military resources, undoubtedly make the EU a potential power. External perceptions of the EU also confirm that the EU is seen as a nascent global player.[65] Furthermore, the EU is relatively better protected than other potential poles from some of the threats emanating from globalization, such as climate change or even unsolicited migrations. Key questions here are whether the challenges brought by globalization will work toward Europe more or less; whether the EU will be strengthened as a result of an increasingly dangerous environment, or whether – on the contrary – it will pay the price of a re-nationalization of policies. In other words, is the EU a solution to, or a victim of, the negative dimension of globalization?

Conclusion

The notion of strategic culture or security culture is being constructed over time in a process that combines objective as well as subjective analysis relating to the identification of values, interests, how those values should be defended and under what conditions force could be used for this defense. The EU has achieved a lot in the process of developing a security culture for itself. It now exists as a security actor on the international scene that theoretically knows what threatens it and has put in place a wide range of instruments to enable it to respond to the identified threats.

On the other hand, what also characterizes the EU as an actor is the divide between potential and reality. The EU is potentially well-equipped and relatively strong, but in practice suffers from a number of key weaknesses that are true limitations to the expression of its potential. More worrying is the fact that the decades ahead will, in all likelihood, offer an international environment that will not work to Europe's advantage. The paradox is therefore that at the time when the EU is becoming a security actor, it is also becoming more vulnerable. At the policy level, a conclusion of this might be that it is this increased vulnerability that should justify the further strengthening of the EU foreign and security policy. As if the period of choice that characterized the 1990s would lead to a period of necessity.

Notes

1 The author thanks Léonard Graf for his research assistance on this chapter.
2 Barry Posen, "European Union Security and Defence Policy: Response to Unipolarity?," *Security Studies* 15, 2 (2006).
3 Robert Cooper, *The Breaking of Nations: Order and Chaos in the Twenty-First Century* (New York: Grove Press, 2003), p. 26.
4 F. Duchêne, "Europe's Role in World Peace," in *Europe Tomorrow: 16 Europeans Look Ahead*, ed. R. Mayne (London: Fontana, 1972).
5 Ian Manners, "Normative Power Europe Reconsidered: Beyond the Crossroads," *Journal of European Public Policy* 13, 2 (2006), Michelle Pace, "The Construction of EU Normative Power," *Journal of Common Market Studies* 45, 5 (2007).
6 Stanley Hoffmann, "Yugoslavia: Implications for Europe and for European Institutions," in *The World and Yugoslavia's Wars*, ed. Ullman Richard (New York: Council on Foreign Relations Books, 1996).
7 Jacques Chirac and Tony Blair, *Joint Declaration on European Defence* (Saint-Malo: Franco-British Summit, 1998).
8 Manners, "Normative Power Europe Reconsidered: Beyond the Crossroads."
9 Pace, "The Construction of EU Normative Power," 1042–1043.
10 European Council, "European Security Strategy, 'A Secure Europe in a Better World'" (EU High Representative, Dr. Javier Solana, 2003).
11 European Council, "European Security Strategy, 'A Secure Europe in a Better World'," p. 1.
12 European Council, "European Security Strategy, 'A Secure Europe in a Better World'," §19.
13 Council of the European Union, "EU Strategy Against Proliferation of Weapons of Mass Destruction" (2003), p. 8.
14 Robert Kagan, "Power and Weakness," *Policy Review* 113 (2002): p. 9.
15 Council of the European Union, "Report on the Implementation of the European Security Strategy: Providing Security in a Changing world" (2008).
16 Kagan, "Power and Weakness."
17 Anand Menon, Kalypso Nicolaidis and Jennifer Welsh, "In Defence of Europe: A Response to Kagan," *Journal of European Affairs* 2, 3 (2004).
18 European Union Institute for Security Studies (EUISS), *The EU's Strategic Objectives: Effective Multilateralism and Extended Security*, Discussion Paper (Paris 2003), pp. 1–2.
19 Nicole Gnesotto, "European Strategy as a model," *EUISS Newsletter No. 9*, 2004, p. 1.
20 Council of the European Union, "Report on the Implementation of the European Security Strategy: Providing Security in a Changing World."
21 High Representative for CFSP and European Commission, "Climate Change and International Security," *Paper to the European Council* S113/08 (2008).
22 B. Buzan, O. Waever and J. de Wilde, *Security: A New Framework of Analysis* (Boulder: Lynne Rienner, 1998).
23 Latvian National Security Council, *Report* (2008).
24 Council of the European Union, "Report on the Implementation of the European Security Strategy: Providing Security in a Changing World."

25 European Council, *Presidency Conclusions* (10–11 December 1999).
26 European Council, "European Security Strategy, 'A Secure Europe in a Better World'."
27 European Council, "European Security Strategy, 'A Secure Europe in a Better World'."
28 European Council of the European Union, "Treaty of Lisbon Amending the Treaty on European Union and the Treaty Establishing the European Community" (2007), art.28B §1.
29 European Council of the European Union, "Conceptual Framework on the ESDP Dimension of the Fight Against Terrorism" (2004), §10.
30 European Council of the European Union, "The EU Counter-Terrorism Strategy" (2005).
31 European Council, "European Security Strategy, 'A Secure Europe in a Better World'," p. 2.
32 European Council, "European Security Strategy, 'A Secure Europe in a Better World'," p. 11.
33 European Commission, "Towards an EU Response to Situations of Fragility – Engaging in Difficult Environments for Sustainable Development, Stability and Peace" (2007).
34 Catriona Gourlay, "Community Instruments for Civilian Crisis Management," in *Civilian Crisis Management: The EU Way (Chaillot Paper 90)*, ed. Agnieszka Nowak (Paris: EU Institute for Security Studies, 2006).
35 The APF budget is €300 million for 2008–2010; the EDF budget is €22,682 million for 2008–2013.
36 APF funds cannot be used to finance the purchase of weapons or military equipment, or to cover military expenditure.
37 The Instrument for Stability budget is €2,062 million for the period 2007–2013, with €260 million for 2009.
38 European Commission, "Europe in the World: Some Practical Proposals for Greater Coherence, Effectiveness and Visibility" (2006), p. 6.
39 Council of the European Union, "EU Concept for Comprehensive Planning" (2005), p. 5.
40 Council of the European Union, "The EU Counter-Terrorism Strategy."
41 Jörg Monar, "Common Threat and Common Response? The European Union's Counter-Terrorism Strategy and its Problems," *Government and Opposition* 42, 3 (2007).
42 Council of the European Union, "Report on the Implementation of the European Security Strategy: Providing Security in a Changing World."
43 Hugo Brady, "The EU and the Fight Against Organized Crime," in *Working Paper* (London: Centre for European Reform, 2007).
44 Council of the European Union, "EU Strategy Against Proliferation of Weapons of Mass Destruction."
45 By contrast, neither the ESS nor the EU strategy against WMD proliferation mentioned Iran.
46 Council of the European Union, "Report on the Implementation of the European Security Strategy: Providing Security in a Changing World."
47 Sten Rynning, "Peripheral or Powerful? The EU's Strategy to Combat the Proliferation of Nuclear Weapons," *European Security* 16, 3&4 (2007).
48 European Commission, "Strategy for a Secure Information Society. 'Dialogue, partnership and empowerment'" (2006), p. 3.
49 European Council, "Integrated Climate and Energy Policy – Presidency Conclusions" (2007).
50 High Representative for CFSP and European Commission, "Climate Change and International Security," p. 2.

51 James Kanter and Stephen Castle, "EU Leaders Dramatically Scale Back Their Ambition on Emissions," *International Herald Tribune*, 12 December 2008.
52 European Commission, "Second Strategic Energy Review: An EU Energy Security and Solidarity Action Plan" (2008), p. 3.
53 Charles Grant, "Is Europe Doomed to Fail as a Power?" (London: Centre for European Reform, 2009).
54 B. Rosamond, "Discourses of Globalisation and European Identities," in *The Social Construction of Europe*, eds. Christiansen *et al.* (London: Sage, 2001). Francis Snyder, "Globalization and Europeanization as Friends and Rivals: European Union Law in Global Economic Networks," *European University Institute Working Paper* 99/8 (1999).
55 Michael Longo, "European Integration: Between Micro-Regionalism and Globalism," *Journal of Common Market Studies* 41, 3 (2003): p. 468.
56 Longo, "European Integration: Between Micro-Regionalism and Globalism," p. 487.
57 European Commission, "Europe in the World: Some Practical Proposals for Greater Coherence, Effectiveness and Visibility," p. 2.
58 Council of the European Union, "Report on the Implementation of the European Security Strategy: Providing Security in a Changing World," p. 2.
59 European Council, "European Security Strategy, 'A Secure Europe in a Better World'," p. 2.
60 Thierry Tardy, ed. *European Security in a Global Context: Internal and External Dynamics* (London: Routledge, 2009).
61 N. Gnesotto and G. Grevi, eds. *The New Global Puzzle: What World for the EU in 2025?* (Paris: EU Institute for Security Studies, 2006). C. Grant and T. Valasek, *Preparing for the Multipolar World: European Foreign and Security Policy in 2020* (London: Centre for European Reform, 2007). High Representative for CFSP and European Commission, "Climate Change and International Security," Jolyon Howorth, *Security and Defence Policy in the European Union* (London and New York: Palgrave, 2007).
62 André Sapir, "Globalization and the Reform of European Social Models," *Journal of Common Market Studies* 44, 2 (2006).
63 National Intelligence Council, "Global Trends 2025: A Transformed World" (NIC, 2008), p. 32.
64 François Heisbourg, "The Unbearable Weight of Not Being," in *European Security in a Global Context: Internal and External Dynamics*, ed. Thierry Tardy (London: Routledge, 2009).
65 Bertelsmann Stiftung, "Who Rules the World?" (2007), Tardy, ed. *European Security in a Global Context: Internal and External Dynamics*.

Part IV
Conclusions
Cooperative and conflictual imperatives

11   Great Powers

Towards a "cooperative competitive" future world order paradigm?

Graeme P. Herd

It is almost axiomatic in international relations to argue that the current international system and power relations between states are shaped by two dynamic trends – the centrifugal force inherent in the move to a multipolar world and the centripetal impulse of interdependence. The first is generated by a shift in the relative balance of global power to East Asia and South Asia from the West, hitherto the center of gravity of political and economic activity and international affairs. The second is a deepening economic, environmental and energy interdependence as demand outstrips supply, leading to the convergence of national and global interests. Under such conditions, the previous durable, tolerable hegemony exercised by a single state – the US – is understood to be "decreasingly sustainable."[1] Past practice is challenged by present realities: emergent centers of global power may create an institutionalized directorate of Great Powers acting in concert or as a coalition-based hegemony. A US National Intelligence Council report, aptly entitled *Global Trends 2025 – A Transformed World*, predicts a revolutionized international system, as new players gain seats at the international high table to which they will bring new stakes and rules of the game.[2] In an era of growing complexity and dislocation, the emergence of China, India and the EU as new Great Powers – and the re-emergence of Russia as an old one – constitutes the central dynamic of the current and future global system.

Indeed, global financial crisis is understood to have powerfully reinforced – psychologically, politically and economically – this underlying global strategic paradigm shift. Javier Solana has observed that "the crisis is accelerating the power shift from the West to the East. This is true both in terms of material resources and ideological pull."[3] Niall Fergusson has characterized the crisis as an "axis of upheaval," with unpredictable and unintended geopolitical consequences, as it coincides with the depletion of non-renewable energy sources, a tipping point for global climate change and turbulence associated with a declining world hegemon – the US.[4] The crisis does indeed appear to have caused a realignment of influence of various countries and highlighted a structural change in the global economy, characterized by an accelerated power shift toward Asia and a multipolar global order. BRICs, especially China, enjoy a stronger relative global position to the US and Europe, whose standing as a credible model has been weakened. Creditor autocracies now enjoy greater influence over, and independence from, debtor democracies and are less constrained in their behavior. Protectionism, resource nationalism, the continued Balkanization of the Internet and the weakening of core alliances all testify to the reassertion of state control over economies and societies. Such policies risk creating an inward-looking "beggar-thy-neighbor" environment, in which zero-sum balance of power logic is the dominant force. If this becomes the predominant trend, challengers to US hegemony may well loosen ties with the political West, and emergent Great Powers could increase political, security and financial ties between each other, creating a parallel order.

Certainly, increasing power and status is the stated national strategic goal of all emergent Great Powers, as the authors who focused on the emergent Great Powers in Part III of this volume have observed. Bates Gill argues that China is as an emergent center of global power, with its growing diplomatic and economic weight in global affairs, deepening integration into a more globalized world, and its increasing ability to shape the future world order. Pavel Baev notes that Russia seeks a restoration of its Great Power status within a globalized multipolar rather than unipolar or non-polar world. Russia believes that the "post-Cold War model of globalization shaped by US domination and based on Western norms and values is breaking down" and interstate relations in the 2010s will be characterized by "tougher competition and less binding cooperation." Thierry Tardy argues that, with 27 states, the EU is one of a kind in the international system, a unique hybrid actor that has the potential to act as an independent pole within a multipolar system. In a globalizing world, it can maximize its soft power and translate its global economic role into global political influence, so consolidating its role as a nascent global player. Siddharth Varadarajan discusses India as an emerging economic and democratic Great Power, arguing that "since the end of the Cold War and especially after India tested a series of nuclear devices in May 1998 and openly proclaimed its nuclear weapons status, Indian strategic thinkers have argued that the world is 'multipolar' or 'polycentric.'"

Historically, with few exceptions, hegemonic transition has occurred as challengers accumulate political–ideological, military and economic power until a tipping point is reached and a paradigm shift enacted through violent overthrow. Hegemonic transition is therefore considered inherently destabilizing and turbulent. However, in an age of nuclear deterrence, military and coercive force-led hegemonic challenge is untenable. Such an approach would destroy the very object that the transition would seek to secure – the leadership of a viable and functional global system. Moreover, when we examine market-authoritarian Russia and China, there appears to be no ideational challenge from these emergent Great Powers and potential hegemonic challengers, with free-market capitalism the accepted global default system.[5] Pavel Baev characterizes Russia's governance model as a "quasi-democratic and hyper-centralized system of power based on a symbiosis between top bureaucracy and big business," which has proven vulnerable in the face of the global financial crisis. Indeed, in September 2009 President Medvedev himself, in a remarkably frank article, criticized Russia's "humiliating" dependence on raw materials, as well as its "inefficient economy, a semi-Soviet social sphere, an immature democracy, negative demographic trends, an unstable Caucasus."[6] Bates Gill emphasizes the importance China places on bilateral and multilateral cooperation within key international organizations and international law, as they are considered the most appropriate instruments to mediate challenges to global and regional stability within a "democratic world order."

When turning to India and the EU, we can also note qualifications and restraints that undercut Great Power hegemonic challenger considerations. Siddharth Varadarajan recognizes that India, as a rising power, "is not preoccupied with peer competitors and is wary of getting ensnared in rivalry between the Great Powers. The Indian conception of a stable world order, at the end of the day, is one that is based on cooperation driven by shared interests and common perceptions about where the principal threats and challenges to security lie. Such a framework will still allow for the pursuit of national interests by individual countries, so long as the temptation to think of power in zero-sum terms is kept firmly at bay." Thierry Tardy argues that the EU, while being "potentially well-equipped and relatively strong" in practice,

> suffers from a number of key weaknesses that are true limitations to the expression of its potential. More worrying is the fact that the decades ahead will in all likelihood offer an international environment that will not work to Europe's advantage.

In addition, Ikenberry has argued that China – as the greatest potential hegemonic challenger – is not only unwilling, but is also unable to challenge US primacy. It is unable because it is not just the US that would potentially be challenged but rather a Western-centered system of multilateral, regional and bilateral institutions and alliances, and the task is insurmountable. This system is characterized as a dense, encompassing, broadly endorsed system of rules, norms and institutions of non-discrimination and market-openness. Its leadership is coalition-based, the aggregate of all democratic–capitalist states that include, alongside the US, the EU at 27, India, Japan, South Korea, Canada, Australia, Brazil and South Africa amongst others. For this reason the system is deemed legitimate, accessible and durable, and its integrative nature – as well as its ability to engage and accommodate – renders it resistant to potential hegemonic challengers.[7] Not only does Chinese military power projection fall short of threatening US vital security interests and ability to deter, but, as Minxin Pei has observed:

> Those who think Asia's gains in hard power will inevitably lead to its geopolitical dominance might also want to look at another crucial ingredient of clout: ideas. *Pax Americana* was made possible not only by the overwhelming economic and military might of the United States, but also by a set of visionary ideas: free trade, Wilsonian liberalism, and multilateral institutions.

By contrast, "self confidence is not an ideology, and the much-touted Asian model of development does not seem to be an exportable product."[8] If India has the long-term political will to be a strategic player by balancing China, would not alignment with the US and Japan best serve that end?[9] Kishore Mahbubami suggests that India also seeks to be a bridging power between the rich and the poor (global North and South) and between the US and China.[10]

Both China and Russia benefit from the current status quo, both seek to modernize through deeper integration into the global system, and both therefore need to maintain access to US markets, technology and investments. Indeed, the global financial crisis has highlighted mutual economic interests and has drawn the US and China closer together. The US–China biannual bilateral Strategic Economic Dialogue (SED), for example, was upgraded. It is now a US–China Strategic and Economic Dialogue (S&ED), creating a framework and agenda on how to cooperate on a broad range of common issues, including the changing structure of world power. The Obama administration is in the process of abandoning the Bush Doctrine – which has been characterized as a "largely unilateral project of hegemonic renewal and global transformation"[11] and a "grand strategy aimed at preventing the emergence of new great powers that could challenge US hegemony."[12] As Matthew Rhodes notes, the emergent Obama approach appears to place a great emphasis on efforts to, in the words of Secretary of State Clinton: "lead by inducing greater cooperation among a greater number of actors ... tilting the balance away from a multi-polar to a multi-partner world."[13] In essence, the Obama administration is seeking to redefine hegemony as primacy based on material power (namely, the large military and economic resource-base necessary to lead), as realist international relations theory would suggest, but also embrace a new understanding of hegemony as "a status bestowed by others, and [one that] rests on recognition by them. This recognition is given in return for the bearing of special responsibilities."[14]

The US and the four other emergent centers of global power face a series of interlinked strategic threats, as outlined by Ekaterina Stepanova, Gustav Lindstrom, Caty Clément and Tapani Vaahtoranta in Part II of this volume. Ekaterina Stepanova defines terrorism as "the intentional use or threat to use violence against civilians and non-combatants by non-state actors, in order to achieve political goals in asymmetrical confrontation." She argues that conventional terrorist attacks on critical civilian infrastructure, such as transport, energy, water systems, information and communication networks, represent a more pressing and urgent threat than "WMD terrorism." Gustav Lindstrom focuses on the challenges WMD proliferation poses to international security, agreeing that a chemical, biological or radiological terrorist attack against a state is more likely than a nuclear one. Caty Clément examines fragile states, which constitute only 13 percent of states, with one-sixth of the world's population located within them, but account for 50 percent of civil wars, and 77 percent of all international crises of the post-Cold War era. Such states are contagious, with frequent overlap between poverty, conflict, criminality and state fragility in evidence. Tapani Vaahtoranta argues that climate change is potentially the greatest challenge to global stability and security and that "global trends in energy supply and consumption and the impact of our reliance on fossil fuels on the climate are unsustainable." Indeed, sophisticated climate-modeling suggests that climate-induced crises characterized by rising temperatures, surging seas and melting glaciers pose profound strategic and geopolitical challenges to Great Powers. This underscores the necessity of cooperative efforts to manage the effects of violent storms, food shortages, water crises, catastrophic flooding, drought, mass migration and pandemics in vulnerable regions, particularly sub-Saharan Africa, the Middle East and South and Southeast Asia.[15] As Henry Kissinger has observed in the US context, the Obama administration faces a set of strategic challenges that are closely related:

> For example, arms control negotiations with Russia will affect Russia's role in the non-proliferation effort with Iran. The strategic dialogue with China will help shape the Korean negotiations. The negotiations will also be affected by perceptions of regional balances of the key participants, for Russia, this applies especially to the former Soviet space in Central Asia; for China and the United States, to the political structure of Northeast Asia and the Pacific Rim.[16]

Alternative global orders?

Given the absence of immediate hegemonic challengers to the US (or a global strategic catastrophe that could trigger US precipitous decline), and the need to cooperate to address pressing strategic threats – the real question is what will be the nature of relations between these Great Powers? Will global order be characterized as a predictable interdependent one-world system, in which shared strategic threats create interest-based incentives and functional benefits which drive cooperation between Great Powers? This pathway would be evidenced by the emergence of a global security agenda based on nascent similarity across national policy agendas. In addition, Great Powers would seek to cooperate by strengthening multilateral partnerships in institutions (such as the UN, G20 and regional variants), regimes (e.g., arms control, climate and trade), and shared global norms, including international law. Alternatively, Great Powers may rely less on institutions, regimes and shared norms, and more on increasing their order-producing managerial role through geopolitical-bloc formation within their near neighborhoods. Under such circumstances, a re-division of the world into a competing mercantilist nineteenth-century regional order emerges.[17] World order would be characterized more by hierarchy and balance of power and zero-sum principles than by interdependence.

Relative power shifts that allow a return to multipolarity – with three or more evenly matched powers – occur gradually. The transition from a bipolar in the Cold War to a unipolar moment in the post-Cold War has been crowned, according to Haass, by an era of non-polarity, where power is diffuse – "a world dominated not by one or two or even several states but rather by dozens of actors possessing and exercising various kinds of power."[18] Multilateralism is on the rise, characterized by a combination of states and international organizations, both influential and talking shops, formal and informal ("multilateralism light"). A dual system of global governance has evolved. An embryonic division of labor emerges, as groups with no formal rules or permanent structures coordinate policies and immediate reactions to crises, while formal treaty-based institutions then legitimize the results.[19]

As powerfully advocated by Wolfgang Schäuble:

> Global cooperation is the only way to master the new, asymmetric global challenges of the twenty-first century. No nation can manage these tasks on its own, nor can the entire international community do so without the help of non-state, civil society actors. We must work together to find appropriate security policy responses to the realities of the twenty-first century.[20]

Highlighting the emergence of what he terms an "interpolar" world – defined as "multipolarity in an age of interdependence" – Grevi suggests that managing existential interdependence in an unstable multipolar world is the key.[21] Such complex interdependence generates shared interest in cooperative solutions, meanwhile driving convergence, consensus and accommodation between Great Powers.[22] As a result, the multilateral system is being adjusted to reflect the realities of a global age – the rise of emerging powers and relative decline of the West: "The new priority is to maintain a complex balance between multiple states."[23] The G20 meeting in London in April 2009 suggested that great and rising powers will reform global financial architecture so that it regulates and supervises global markets in a more participative, transparent and responsive manner: all countries have contributed to the crisis; all will be involved in the solution.[24]

However, when we turn to assessing the coherence of current generic responses to the management of these strategic threats, as addressed by the authors in Part II of this volume, it is clear that the evident need for greater cooperation does not always translate into practical pragmatic effect. While there is a clear conceptual need for greater cooperation between states to jointly manage sources of strategic threat, operational reality lags behind. Stepanova argues that efforts to manage the threats of terrorism and political extremism through intelligence, legal, judicial, military and police cooperation, as well as political coordination, can occur multilaterally but operates best at the bilateral level. Moreover, the global dynamics of terrorism are driven by major armed conflicts, particularly those characterized by external interventions. Lindstrom notes that the key challenge to managing proliferation is the increasing internal and external pressures facing the principal non-proliferation regimes, as well as strengthening non-proliferation tools, not least the Treaty on the Non-Proliferation of Nuclear Weapons, the Biological and Toxin Weapons Convention and the Chemical Weapons Convention. Caty Clément observes that when addressing the threat of state fragility and regional crises there is general agreement that integrated or the whole of national government approach is weak and that poor coordination between international actors and in different fields of activity is still prevalent.[25] In the words of Ramesh Thakur: "Unilateral and ad hoc interventions will sow and nourish the seeds of international discord. Multilateral and rules-based interventions will speak powerfully to the world's determination never again to return to institutionalized indifference to mass atrocities."[26] Rhodes argues that in the US under Obama, in an era of global financial crisis, the economy–energy nexus is the central security issue, and that strengthening fragile states primarily through an emphasis on good governance rather than the promotion of democracy is now the priority. Vaahtoranta notes that the US and China share an interest in supporting stable global energy production and transportation at an affordable price, and that shared interests generate cooperation and market-based approaches. Bates Gill reminds us that China's current focus is more on "domestic" or "internal" threats to Chinese statehood and it is through this prism that Chinese strategists prioritize the "global" challenges identified by the West. Nevertheless, common ground between China and the other four powers is expanded. In the words of Chinese Ambassador to the United Kingdom, Fu Ying:

> In terms of foreign policy, China has no intention of scrambling for hegemony or sharing hegemony with anyone. The major task of China's diplomacy is to create an external environment of peace and cooperation so that it can concentrate on building the country.[27]

Indeed, though the global financial crisis has increased the need for multilateral partnerships and made countries more selective by bringing greater focus to building partnerships and strategic relationships, which in turn should promote more effective international cooperation against a range of shared threats, the practical results are meagre:

> deadlines have been missed; financial commitments and promises have not been honored; execution has stalled; and international collective action has fallen far short of what was offered and, more importantly, needed. These failures represent not only the perpetual lack of international consensus, but also a flawed obsession with multilateralism as the panacea for all the world's ills.[28]

Multilateral institutions are not working and multilateralism is in fact in retreat. This is not because multilateral institutions lack representative legitimacy, but rather because "major states frequently do not agree on how to tackle shared challenges. Placing the priority on broader participation and inclusion will likely increase deadlock, thus weakening the architecture of cooperation, not strengthening it."[29] The UN Security Council (UNSC) does not function as the "management committee of our fledgling collective security system," in the words of Kofi Annan, or as a concert of the Great Powers – India and the EU are not present – but rather an important place for debate and argument.[30]

The BRICs hosted their first stand-alone summit in Yekaterinburg on 16 June 2009, but does what began as a Goldman Sachs marketing tool in 2003 now represent a genuine coalition, one with the potential to balance the US? This entity has yet to produce a coherent blueprint for international reform, while the US is taking the lead in reforming global institutions, so securing its primacy.[31] Its members exhibit more differences in power, approach and style than similarities.[32] In addition, the financial crisis has a more devastating potential impact on BRIC states than on the US and Europe. Established capitalist societies generally fall further but recover from such crises quicker than autocracies (which suffer less but for longer), with societies more prepared to suffer short-term pain for longer-term gain, and elites better able to establish effective regulation.[33] Moreover, the ability of BRICs and other potential global powers to balance the US is questioned – Brazil, Russia, India and China have distinctive cultural and historical trajectories, as well as domestic political systems. While they may share uncertainty over US hegemony, they band together to improve their negotiating position with the US rather than balance it.[34] Thus, despite the foreign and security policy rhetoric coming out of Beijing, Brasilia, New Delhi and Moscow, in reality multilateral global governance is only supported practically when it is in their interests. When analyzing Great Power involvement in, for example, the G8, G20 and UNSC, the status of their membership appears to be more important than their active participation leading to constructive outcomes. These emergent centers of global power privilege regional organizations above global bodies. Furthermore, zero-sum logic may be at work undermining BRIC coherence. Just as, for example, the Soviet Union's collapse removed one of China's key strategic rivals and therefore constituted a strategic gain for China, the further rise of China may imply the steady marginalization of Russia from regional and global decision-making.

Ethical and normative splits occur between the global North and South as well as between the Great Powers: while "no first use," "ecological responsibility," "distributive justice," "individual privacy," "democratic governance," "legitimacy," "responsible sovereignty" and "responsibility to protect" (R2P) are emergent norms, they are not universally espoused. When General Assembly president Miguel D'Escoto Brockmann of Nicaragua, for example, characterized "R2P" in terms of "redecorated colonialism," he reflected a sense of grievance, resentment and exclusion felt by many developing countries in that Assembly. Differing interpretations of Great Power global interventions – the accusation that the political West uses the language of virtue in pursuit of economic interests, for example – exacerbate the potential for Great Power regional entanglements leading to conflict between the Great Powers themselves. The assumed normative convergence that underpins so many contemporary global order paradigms is undercut as international norms are trumped by powerful domestic agendas and norms. This makes the challenge of effective, efficient and legitimate cooperation even more pressing.

2025: towards a globalized interdependent world order?

Global stability is a function of the ability of states, and Great Powers in particular (US, India, China, Russia and the EU), to manage increasingly interlinked strategic threats. In the early twenty-first century, following 9/11, the US National Security Strategy of 2002 stressed the nexus between terrorists, terrible weapons and tyrants/rogue and fragile states. While each constituted a distinct strategic threat, their sum impact was more than their parts. At the end of the first decade of the twenty-first century, and in the wake of the global financial crisis, a new and pressing nexus has received widespread attention, the relationship between the global economic system, the environment and climate change and energy resources. Today there are multiple challenges when attempting to conceive and execute efficient, effective and legitimate policy approaches and responses to manage these diverse strategic sources of insecurity.

The nature and nexus between these two sets of threats, and the dislocation this generates, must be understood. It is increasingly facile to suggest that the agenda of the post-financial crisis – a crisis that began in the US – is predominantly a function of Global North production and consumption patterns, while the Global South is the incubator of the post-9/11 agenda. The nature of contemporary transnational networks – whether they be proliferation, terrorism, cyber, finance, critical infrastructural, food-production or migration-based – integrate the boundaries of the Global North and South, both in time and functionally. Geographical proximity as well as shared network membership and connectivity render all states, but especially global powers, vulnerable to crisis, contingency and catastrophe. The greater frequency and impact of Black Swan-type events, with unintended consequences, spillovers and cascading second- and third-order effects, can be more devastating and the resultant disorder much harder to manage than the initial source of insecurity. Increasing synergy, inter-connectivity and coupling of complex systems generates unpredictable non-linear behavior and effects. It creates a power vacuum, raising questions of authority and control – who "owns" the crisis, who must manage it? The global financial crisis suggests that states do not yet exhibit the strength and solidarity to treat economic crisis management as a common endeavor.

The post-9/11 strategic agenda, focusing on known terror groups with global reach, fragile states and the proliferation of WMD, tends to dominate the headlines – al-Qaeda of Mesopotamia in Iraq, unannounced North Korean nuclear testing, state fragility in a nuclear Pakistan, the legitimacy of presidential elections in Afghanistan – and demands crisis-driven responses requiring immediate hard, soft or even smart power. The post-financial crisis agenda – with economic, energy and environmental security concerns gaining in visibility – is conceived of differently than the post-9/11 agenda. They are longer-term challenges, more structural and systemic-driven, requiring generational and holistic or comprehensive responses. Given that the post-9/11 agenda is partly the symptom of the structural and systemic impact of the intertwined economic, environmental and energy security nexus, what imperatives may shape Great Power efforts to conceive and execute security solutions?

Great Powers can utilize military force, regimes, international law, and a range of formal and informal institutions to jointly manage these threats. Potential equilibrium points between effective, efficient and legitimate responses can be imagined, though the interlinked nature of the threats and the need for constant adjustment of policy approaches and combinations of instruments deployed render this potential equilibrium the Holy Grail of a stable world order: a quest to be undertaken, if never ultimately achieved.

If a global governance system that is able to manage interlinked strategic threats effectively, efficiently and with legitimacy takes shape, then a world order characterized by cooperation rather than conflict between Great Powers will emerge. If such a globalized interdependent security governance system does unfold, then certain realities – which can be made explicit – must be in evidence. What are the embedded assumptions within this cooperative shared control-generating world order paradigm?

1   Great Powers share latent, potential and actual strategic sources of insecurity and so have a common interest and imperative to coordinate national policy responses within a collective effort to address these threats. This cooperative imperative is reinforced by the increasing realization that unilateral single-state responses (and, increasingly, even narrow ad hoc coalitions) to transnational and global sources of insecurity are demonstrably ineffective.

2   Great Powers need to optimize rather than maximize the role of the state through burden-sharing. To that end, consultative procedures in formal and informal institutional bodies constantly recalibrate an agreed equilibrium point between effectiveness (joint approach), efficiency (timeliness and cost) and legitimacy (moral and political) of responses.

3   Great Powers need a predictable rules-based global system and will make use of a set of shared tools (regimes, shared norms and institutions) appropriate to the nature of the strategic threat in the regional/global context – a global consensus emerges supporting the notion that there can no longer be a Western monopoly of operational responses.

4   Great Power cooperation under loose US hegemony to secure global commons/international public goods (e.g., policing international sea-lanes, species extinction, ocean fishery protection, greenhouse gases, Arctic resource exploitation) forges a shared recognition of global obligations, responsibilities and duties, and serves as a key driver in forging a shared ethical and normative base that, in turn, reinforces collective cooperative efforts.

5   Great Powers will rarely solve but rather manage the threats; the capacity and timeliness of global management will always be less than the magnitude and complexity of the threats to be addressed – the size of the gap defines "political" success.

6   Great Power success in these efforts enhances a cooperative imperative, reinforces interdependence and legitimizes Great Power leadership through multilateral partnerships, in whatever form it takes (singular, collective or coalition-based).

What's past is prologue?

Are these assumptions viable? Shared threats generate a process of convergence, fusion and synthesis leading to globalized interdependent security, according to liberalist international relations theory – but is this so in practice? Do shared threats generate a unifying collectivist and collaborative agenda for common action in international relations? Certainly, prescriptions, policies and strategies to manage strategic sources of insecurity lag behind both action to implement them and the unfolding of global trends themselves that generate the threats – but how far behind? Is the tragedy of the Great Power politics captured by the reality that effective cooperative efforts to manage shared threats will only occur when the possibility of effective management is no longer an option? If this is so, what are the global tipping points of no return? Can they even be identified to allow the possibility of coordinated and effective action? The Great Power ships-of-state may begin to change their rhetoric from the zero-sum realist narratives to interdependent cooperative liberalist visions, but is the time-lag between talk and policy action too slow to avoid redundancy? If an equilibrium or lowest common denominator agreed coordinated response between Great Powers can be achieved, might it have legitimacy but lack efficiency and effectives to be useful?

One set of early indicators of which pathway Great Powers might travel runs through the realm of global commons. In the stateless high seas, for example the maritime corridor in the Gulf of Aden off the Horn of Africa, all Great and Major Powers share a coincidence of economic and energy-based national interests in support of effective, efficient and legitimate collective action to uphold their national interests. UN Secretary-General Ban Ki-Moon characterized the Arctic as "our canary in the coal mine for climate impacts that will affect us all," arguing that

> Climate change is the preeminent geopolitical issue of our time. It rewrites the global equation for development, peace and prosperity. It threatens markets, economies and development gains. It can deplete food and water supplies, provoke conflict and migration, destabilize fragile societies and even topple governments.[35]

In 2008 the North West passage and Northern Sea routes were navigable for the first time in recorded history. With the increasingly visible impact of climate change, questions are raised over the management and exploitation of the energy and mineral resource-rich Arctic. The Arctic Council states – the US, Russia, Denmark, Canada, Finland, Iceland, Sweden and Norway – have declared interests, as have France, Germany, the Netherlands, Poland, Spain and the United Kingdom, which have secured permanent observer status on the Council, while China, Italy and South Korea have ad hoc status at the Council. It is uncertain whether states decide that there is more to be gained by cooperation, competition or conflict. Does the Arctic represent a new and frosty version of the Great

Game, in which security governance is characterized by low regulation, militarization and so the risks of escalation and military conflict?

Alternatively, might a benign Arctic emerge, characterized by the recognition of the need for international regulation, a concern for the environment, the joint management of fisheries, shared scientific exploration and search and rescue, with low levels of militarization? The need for shared technology, investment from the wider international community, and the lack of capacity of any single state to enforce asserted sovereignty combine to suggest cooperative impulses will coexist with competitive dynamics. Paradoxically, it is only by developing at least the rhetoric of common good preservation for the sake of humanity and planetary survival, rather than narrow state interest, that emergent Great Powers confirm their responsible stakeholder and Great Power status. Their power is reflected in their ability to organize and lead international cooperation for the common good. Is the Arctic a litmus test for Great Power relations, or in fact a barometer reflecting cooperative, competitive or conflictual tendencies elsewhere in the globe?

There currently exists only one region in which all Great Powers are present, albeit some more than others, and that is Eurasia and, in particular, the sub-region of Central Asia; the first meeting place of China, India, Russia, the US and the EU in history. Here the gaps between Great Power rhetoric and the reality of their policy approaches are all too evident. The challenge combines terrorism (real, instrumentalized and perceived), state fragility and authoritarian political systems alongside the environmental, energy and economic agenda, overlaid by Great Power interests. Regional stability in Central Asia is a necessary prerequisite for the effectiveness of the US's Northern Distribution Network that resupplies the counter-insurgency efforts in Afghanistan. Given that President Obama's entire foreign policy effectiveness revolves on the question of strategic success or failure in Afghanistan, US interest in promoting stability in this region is high. Although the "Putin doctrine" failed in Central Asia – full-scale economic integration with Central Asia has not led to political integration – basic Russian interests in the region have not changed under President Medvedev. The preservation of order, support for integration projections with Russia, extending Russian soft power influence (through language, cultural and educational programs) and minimizing Western influence are all dependent on stability in the region. Central Asian stability maximizes economic resource extraction, particularly gas exports, a factor of prime importance to the energy-hungry emergent centers of global power – China and India. For the EU, Central Asia poses self-identity questions and highlights tensions between normative and interests-based foreign-policy agendas. All Great Powers fear the emergence of a Talibanized nuclear Pakistan – a global swing state.

Successful patterns of cooperative practice – with the use of regimes, institutions and norms – may well prove self-sustaining demonstration models and so set the tone for intra-Great Power relations in this century. But how likely is this and what shape will it take? Former Council on Foreign Relations President Les Gelb argues that US power is what it always was – essentially the capacity to get people to do what they don't want to do, by pressure and coercion, using one's resources and position.... The world is not flat.... The shape of global power is decidedly pyramidal – with the United States alone at the top, a second tier of major countries (China, Japan, India, Russia, the United Kingdom, France, Germany and Brazil), and several tiers descending below.... Among all nations, only the United States is a true global power with global reach.[36]

The Obama administration promotes the US as first among equals and as an indispensably ally, rather than just another Great Power, by stressing "partnership," "engagement" and "common interests." It recognizes the indispensability of collaborating with others and repositions itself at the center of a web of global bilateral partnerships, which includes the G2 economic relationship with China, the strategic nuclear relationship with Russia and protecting global public goods with Europe. In this way the US has both convening power on all key strategic security-management initiatives and the capacity to create coalitions, networks and partnerships that ensure effective, efficient and legitimate management. Other Great Powers currently lack the capacity to fulfil this management role, and their ability "to adapt their grand strategies to a new American agenda is extremely limited, giving the United States a significant silver lining."[37]

Whether world order is to be driven by realist paradigms and embedded zerosum security dilemmas or liberalist pathways underscored by agreed regimes, shared norms and institutional interdependence will to a large extent depend on the malleable perceptions of Great and Major Power publics and the political will of their elites. Effective Great Power collective cooperation against shared threats has the potential to sustain internationalist, collaborative and collectivist behavior which becomes habituated and self-sustaining – nothing succeeds like success. But, as rising powers have ever-increasing domestic economic consumption imperatives, their acquisitive foreign and security policies can also be represented as threatening. Here, narratives, branding (which generates associations and expectations) and the framing of storylines that support and legitimize particular world views are all important. The role of academics and activists in civil society, practitioners and policy-makers in government, and especially opinion-shaping analysts in the media, will largely determine which "threats" are shared and what constitutes appropriate, affordable and acceptable responses. External shocks – such as the ending of the Cold War, the trauma of 9/11 or the global financial crisis – or the threat of future imminent catastrophe can trigger sudden strategic culture shifts, either toward continued collective cooperation or against. Sudden shocks focus attention and generate intense media-driven crisis learning that could support a process of convergence or divergence between Great Powers. Such a crisis could reinforce global confidence in US strategic competence; in the US as a responsible global guardian and custodian of a benign multilateral order; or exacerbate the perception of US strategic incompetence and arrogance. Historical narratives/memories, traditions, foundational myths, mind-sets, have a powerful pull and provide the most immediate prism through which crises are refracted and so interpreted. Could the "shadow of the future," the projected inevitability of rising centers of global power, promote hubris – the display of a premature arrogance of power? Conversely, might the lessons of history prove to be a trap, encouraging premature containment by the US? Either outcome would exacerbate latent competitive and conflictual tendencies.

Historically, cooperation and collective action against threats has been strongest when the hegemon takes a lead. The emergence of new Great Powers and global power shifts, as well as the complexity of common threats, the diversity of regional contexts, and the presence of cooperative, competitive and latent conflictual tendencies all suggest an organizational logic that promotes singular, collective and coalition-based hegemony appropriate to the region and functional threat to be managed. Rather than preventing Russia, India, China and the EU from emerging as independent "peer competitors" in a multipolar world, it appears that the operational concept of world order embraced by the Obama administration is a Concert of Great Powers, buttressed by a new institutional order, with shared norms and regimes whose combination and application is strategic threat-related and regionally sensitive. If this Global Concert is to avoid a dystopian future, accepting that utopia is not possible, it will need to enjoy broad mandates, be loosely organized, and be capable of accommodation and negotiation (the prerequisites for necessary constant recalibration of response to dynamic interrelated threats), in order to ensure policy coordination and effective collective action. Above all it must be inclusive of changing combinations of major states (not least Japan, Brazil, Turkey, South Africa and Indonesia) that unite for the purpose of joint management of international affairs. We will begin to witness clusters of cooperation and competitiveness in response to specific strategic threats, and the need to revitalize international institutions, regimes and norms to better address and manage these strategic sources of insecurity is a pressing challenge. With China not ready, India too emergent, Russia no longer resurgent and the EU lacking capability, variable hegemony – singular, collective or coalition-based – best encapsulates a mutually indispensable Great Powers "cooperative competitive" world order paradigm. This provides the framework for long-term strategic stability in the twenty-first century.

Notes

1 Ian Clark, "Bringing Hegemony Back In: The United States and International Order," *International Affairs* 85, 1 (2009): 23–36.
2 National Intelligence Council, "Global Trends 2025: A Transformed World" (NIC, 2008).
3 Javier Solana, "Discours du Haut Représentant de l'Union européenne pour la Politique étrangère et de sécurité commune," *Conférence annuelle de l'Institut d'Etudes de Sécurité de l'Union européenne*, 30 October 2008.
4 Niall Ferguson, "The Axis of Upheaval," *Foreign Policy* March/April (2009).
5 Jenny Clegg, *China's Global Strategy: Toward a Multipolar World* (London: Pluto Press, 2009), views China through the prism of consensus builder.
6 Medvedev, Dmitry. "Forward, Russia! [in Russian]." *Gazeta.ru*, 10 September 2009.

7 G. John Ikenberry, "The Rise of China and the Future of the West," *Foreign Affairs* 87, 1 (2008). To take a specific example, Japan's foreign policy is very much tied to the US and it can be considered a global ordinary power. See Takashi Inoguchi, "Japan as a Global Ordinary Power: Its Current Phase," *Japanese Studies* 28, 1 (2008).

8 Minxin Pei, "Think Again: Asia's Rise," *Foreign Policy* (2009), Thomas P.M. Barnett, *Great Powers: America and the World After Bush* (New York: G.P. Putnam's Sons, 2009).

9 The US offered India, a non-signatory to the Non-Proliferation Treaty, nuclear legitimacy. John Lee, "India Fast Becoming Asia's 'Swing State'," *The Straits Times*, 20 May 2009.

10 Kishore Mahbubami, *The New Asian Hemisphere: The Irresistible Shift of Global Power to the East* (New York: Public Affairs, 2008): "Asians are going from being passengers on the bus of globalization to being co-drivers."

11 Christian Reus-Smit, "The Misleading Mystique of America's Material Power," *Australian Journal of International Studies* 3 (2003): p. 423, cited by Clark, "Bringing Hegemony Back In," p. 26.

12 C. Layne, "The Unipolar Illusion Revisited: The Coming End of the United States' Unipolar Moment," *International Security* 21, 2 (2006): p. 12.

13 H. Clinton, "Address at the Council on Foreign Relations" (15 July 2009).

14 Clark, "Bringing Hegemony Back In," p. 24. The existential resilience of the US should not be underestimated; see George Friedman, *The Next 100 Years: A Forecast for the 21st Century* (New York: Doubleday, 2009). See also Josef Joffe, "The Default Power," *Foreign Affairs* 88, 5 (2009): 21–35.

15 John M. Border, "Climate Change Seen as Threat to U.S. Security," *New York Times*, 9 August 2009.

16 Henry A. Kissinger, "Obama's Foreign Policy Challenge," *Washington Post*, 22 April 2009.

17 Henry A. Kissinger, "The Chance of a New World Order," *New York Times*, 12 January 2009.

18 Richard N. Haass, "The Age of Nonpolarity: What Will Follow US Dominance?," *Foreign Affairs* 87, 3 (2008).

19 Risto Pettila, "Multilateralism Light: The Rise of Informal International Governance," in *EU2020 Essay* (London: Centre for European Reform, 2009).

20 Wolfgang Schäuble, "Speech at the 45th Munich Security Conference," *Munich Security Conference*, 2 July 2009; Lord Hurd, former British Foreign Secretary, points to the emergence of complex interdependence, in which democracies are tied to authoritarian states through overlapping, cross-cutting political networks. Douglas Hurd, "The Immoral Incompetents," *Guardian*, 15 June 2009.

21 Giovanni Grevi, "The Interpolar World: A New Scenario," *EU–ISS Occasional Paper No. 79* (2009).

22 Bruce D. Jones, Carlos Pascual and Stephen John Stedman, *Power and Responsibility: Building International Order in an Era of Transnational Threats* (Washington, DC: Brookings Institution Press, 2009), Jeffrey Sachs, *Common Wealth: Economics for a Crowded Planet* (London: Allen Lane, 2008), Michael Klare, *Rising Powers, Shrinking Planet: How Scarce Energy is Creating a New World Order* (Oxford: Oneworld Publications, 2008).

23 Fyodor Lukyanov, "Obama's Consensus Diplomacy Put To The Test," *Moscow Times*, 16 July 2009.

24 Mikhail Gorbachev reflected on the G20's location and role within the system of global institutions:

   What is this group: a "global politburo," a "club of the powerful," a prototype for a world government? How will it interact with the United Nations? I am convinced that no group of countries, even if they account for 90 per cent of the world economy, could supersede or substitute for the United Nations. But clearly, the G20 could claim collective leadership in world affairs if it acts with due respect for the opinions of non-members. The presence in the G20 of countries representing different geographic regions, different levels of development and different cultures is a hopeful sign.

(Mikhail Gorbachev, "What Role for the G-20?," *New York Times*, 27 April 2009)

25 It can also be noted that stateless, networked and resilient groups increasingly pose challenges to even Great and Major Powers. The diffusion of technologies and weapons makes such challenges more feasible and statelessness is itself a viable strategy for survival. See Jakub Grygiel, "The Power of Statelessness," *Policy Review* April and May (2009).

26 Ramesh Thakur, "Next Word on Intervention," *Japan Times*, 31 July 2009.

27 Li Peng and Wei Qun, "Chinese Ambassador to the United Kingdom Fu Ying: 'It is Time for the West To Understand China More'," *Zhongguo Xinwen She News Agency*, 15 June 2009.

28 As Moisés Naím has argued:

[the] last successful multilateral trade agreement dates back to 1994, when 123 countries gathered to negotiate the creation of the World Trade Organization and agreed on a new set of rules for international trade. Since then, all other attempts to reach a global trade deal have crashed. The same is true with multilateral efforts to curb nuclear proliferation; the last significant international nonproliferation agreement was in 1995, when 185 countries agreed to extend an existing nonproliferation treaty. ... On the environment, the Kyoto Protocol, a global deal aimed at reducing greenhouse gas emissions, has been ratified by 184 countries since it was adopted in 1997, but the United States, the world's second-largest air polluter after China, has not done so, and many of the signatories have missed their targets.

(Moisés Naím, "Minilateralism," *Foreign Policy* (2009))

29 Thomas Wright, "Multilateralism: Why Bigger May Not Be Better," *The Washington Quarterly* 32, 3 (2009), James Roberts, "Fold the G-8 into the G-20," *Heritage Foundation* Web Memo, 2538 (2009), Joseph Stiglitz, "One small Step Forward," *Guardian*, 28 June 2009.

30 Kenneth Anderson, "United Nations Collective Security and the United States Security Guarantee in a Multipolar World: The Security Council as the Talking Shop of the Nations," *Chicago International Law Journal* 1, 10 (2009).

31 Stephen and William Wohlforth Brooks, "Spearheading Reform of the World Order: How Washington Should Reform International Institutions," *Foreign Affairs* 88, 2 (2009).

32 Anders Aslund, "No Place in BRIC for Russia's Economic Mess," *Moscow Times*, 29 July 2009.

33 Walter Russell Mead, "Only Makes You Stronger," *The New Republic*, 4 February 2009.

34 Subhash Kapila points to the possibility of non-BRIC breakaway formations, arguing: "A possible Russia–India–Iran Strategic Triangle would be a formidable strategic combination to contend with, especially when no strategic cleavages exist between them. Such a combination could substantially alter the global balance of power and the Asian security landscape." Subhash Kapila, "Russia–India–Iran Triangle Strategically Possible," *South Asia Analysis Group*, 3363 (2009).

35 Ki-Moon, Ban. "The Ice Is Melting," *New York Times*, 17 September 2009.

36 L. Gelb, *Power Rules: How Common Sense Can Rescue American Foreign Policy* (New York: HarperCollins, 2009).

37 Patrick Doherty and Ben Katcher, "Time to Focus on Great Powers," *The Washington Note*, 7 August 2009.

Bibliography

The links contained in this bibliography refer to direct website sources that have been cited in the contents of the book. Additional website references, where they may be helpful to the reader, appear in the endnotes of the individual chapters, although online resources are often temporary by nature.

"2007 Global Trends: Refugees, Asylum-seekers, Returnees, Internally Displaced and Stateless Persons." Geneva: UNHCR, 2008.

Abebe, D. "Great Power Politics and the Structure of Foreign Relations Law." *Chicago Journal of International Law* 10, 1 (2009): 125–141.

Abraham, I. *The Making of the Indian Bomb: Science, Secrecy and the Post-Colonial State.* London: Zed Books, 1998.

Ackerman, S. "The Obama Doctrine." *American Prospect* 19, 4 (2008): 12–16.

Adomeit, H. "Inside or Outside? Russia's Policies Towards NATO." In *The Multilateral Dimension in Russian Foreign Policy,* edited by E.W. Rowe and S. Torjesen, 97–120. London: Routledge, 2008.

Alibek, K. and S. Handelman. *Biohazard.* New York: Random House, 1999.

Allison, G.T. *Nuclear Terrorism – The Ultimate Preventable Catastrophe.* New York: Times Books/Henry Holt, 2004.

Allison, R. "Russia Resurgent? Moscow's Campaign to 'Coerce Georgia to Peace'." *International Affairs* 84, 6 (2008): 1145–1171.

Altman, R. "The Great Crash 2008." *Foreign Affairs* 88, 1 (2009): 2–14.

Anderson, K. "United Nations Collective Security and the United States Security Guarantee in a Multipolar World: The Security Council as the Talking Shop of the Nations." *Chicago International Law Journal* 1, 10 (2009): 55–90.

Arbatov, A. "International Security After the Caucasian Crisis [in Russian]." *Polit.ru,* 17 October 2008.

Arbatov, A. and V. Dvorkin, eds. *Nuclear Weapons after the Cold War.* Moscow: Carnegie Center, 2008.

Arbatov, A. and R. Gottemoeller. "New Presidents, New Agreements? Advancing US–Russian Strategic Arms Control." *Arms Control Today* 38, 6 (2008): 6–14.

Arnson, C.J. and I.W. Zartman. *Rethinking the Economics of War: The Intersection of Need, Creed, and Greed.* Baltimore: John Hopkins University Press, 2005.

Arquilla, J. and D.F. Ronfeldt. *Networks and Netwars: The Future of Terror, Crime, and Militancy.* Santa Monica: Rand Corporation, 2001.

——. "Netwar Revisited: The Fight for the Future Continues." *Low Intensity Conflict & Law Enforcement* 11, 2 & 3 (2002): 178–189.

Art, R. *A Grand Strategy for America*. Ithaca: Cornell University Press, 2003.

Ashour, O. *The De-Radicalization of Jihadists: Transforming Armed Islamist Movements*. Abingdon: Taylor & Francis, 2009.

Åslund, A. "No Place in BRIC for Russia's Economic Mess." *Moscow Times*, 29 July 2009.

Åslund, A. and A. Kuchins. "Pressing 'Reset Button' on US–Russia Relations." In *Policy Brief*. Washington, DC: CSIS, 2009.

Baev, P. "Instrumentalizing Counter-Terrorism for Regime Consolidation in Putin's Russia." *Studies in Conflict & Terrorism* 27, 4 (2004): 337–352.

———. "Turning Counter-Terrorism into Counter-Revolution: Russia Focuses on Kazakhstan and Engages Turkmenistan." *European Security* 15, 1 (2006): 3–22.

———. "Infighting Among Putin's Siloviki Escalates to a 'Clan War'." *Eurasia Daily Monitor*, 11 October 2007.

———. "Leading in the Concert of Great Powers: Lessons from Russia's G8 Chairmanship." In *The Multilateral Dimension in Russian Foreign Policy*, edited by E.W. Rowe and S. Torjesen, 58–68. London: Routledge, 2008.

———. *Russian Energy Policy and Military Power: Putin's Quest for Greatness*. London: Routledge, 2008.

———. "Medvedev Fingers the "Reset Button" but Preaches Anti-Americanism." *Eurasia Daily Monitor*, 23 March 2009.

Bailes, A., P. Dunay, P. Guang and M. Troitsky. "The Shanghai Cooperation Organization." *SIPRI Policy Paper* 17 (2007): 1–29.

Bailey, K.C. "The Biological and Toxin Weapons Threat to the United States." Fairfax: National Institute for Public Policy, 2001.

Barnaby, F. *How to Build a Nuclear Bomb: And Other Weapons of Mass Destruction*. London: Granta Publications, 2003.

Barnett, T.P.M. *The Pentagon's New Map: War and Peace in the Twenty-First Century*. New York: G.P. Putnam's Sons, 2004.

———. *Great Powers: America and the World After Bush*. New York: G.P. Putnam's Sons, 2009.

Barysch, K., R. Cottrell, F. Frattini, P. Hare, P. Lamy, M. Medvedkov and Y. Yasin. *Russia and the WTO*. London: CER, 2002.

Bassin, M. "Civilizations and Their Discontents: Political Geography and Geopolitics in the Huntington Thesis." *Geopolitics* 12 (2007): 357–358.

Beam, A. "The Real Money's in Piracy." *International Herald Tribune*, 21 January 2009, 9.

Berger, S. "A Foreign Policy for the Global Age." *Foreign Affairs* 79 (2000): 22–39.

Bjørgo, T., ed. *Root Causes of Terrorism: Myths, Reality and Ways Forward*. Abingdon: Routledge, 2005.

Bjørgo, T. and J. Horgan, eds. *Leaving Terrorism Behind: Individual and Collective Disengagement*. Abingdon: Taylor & Francis, 2008.

Blair, D.C. "Annual Threat Assessment of the Intelligence Community for the Senate Select Committee on Intelligence." National Intelligence Council, 2009.

Boehme, P. "The Verification Regime of the Chemical Weapons Convention: An Overview." *Chemical Disarmament* 6, 4 (2008): 13–15.

Border, J.M. "Climate Change Seen as Threat to U.S. Security." *New York Times*, 9 August 2009.

Borgerson, S.G. "Arctic Meltdown: The Economic and Security Implications of Global Warming." *Foreign Affairs* 85, 2 (2008): 63–77.

Daalder, I. and J. Lindsay. *America Unbound: The Bush Revolution in Foreign Policy.* Washington, DC: Brookings Institution Press, 2003.

Dando, M. *The New Biological Weapons: Threat, Proliferation, and Control.* Boulder: Lynne Rienner Publishers, 2001.

Diakov, A. and E. Miasnikov. "Post-2009 SOA Control in Russia and the United States: Room for a Compromise?" *Security Index* 86, 1 (2008): 33–43.

Dixit, J.N. *India–Pakistan in War and Peace.* New Delhi: Books Today, 2002.

Djankov, S., J. Montalvo and M. Reynal-Querol. "The Curse of Aid." *Journal of Economic Growth* 13, 3 (2006): 169–194.

Dobbins, J. "Who Lost Iraq? Lessons from the Debacle." *Foreign Affairs* 86, 5 (2007): 61–74.

Doherty, P. and B. Katcher. "Time to Focus on Great Powers." *The Washington Note*, 7 August 2009.

Dormandy, X. "Is India, or Will It Be, a Responsible International Stakeholder?" *The Washington Quarterly* 30, 3 (2007): 117–130.

Duarte, S. *Luncheon Address: Making the 2010 NPT Review Conference a Success,* Arms Control Association Annual Meeting: The Nuclear Nonproliferation Treaty at Forty – Addressing Current and Future Challenges. Washington, DC, 2008.

Dubnov, A. "NATO Has No Trust in Russian Architects of European Security [in Russian]." *Vremya novostei,* 5 December 2008.

——. "OSCE as a Battlefield [in Russian]." *Russia in Global Affairs* 4 (2008): 93–105.

Duchêne, F. "Europe's Role in World Peace." In *Europe Tomorrow: 16 Europeans Look Ahead,* edited by R. Mayne, 32–47. London: Fontana, 1972.

Dunworth, T., R.J. Mathews and T. McCormack. "National Implementation of the Biological Weapons Convention." *Journal of Conflict and Security Law* 11, 1 (2006): 93–118.

Easterly, W. *The White Man's Burden: Why the West's Efforts to Aid the Rest Have Done So Much Ill and So Little Good.* New York: Penguin Books, 2006.

Eck, K. and L. Hultman. "One-Sided Violence Against Civilians in War: Insights from New Fatality Data." *Journal of Peace Research* 44, 2 (2007): 233–246.

Economy, E. "The Great Leap Backward?" *Foreign Affairs* September/October (2007): 38–59.

Economy, E. and K. Lieberthal. "Scorched Earth: Will Environmental Risks in China Overwhelm its Opportunities?" *Harvard Business Review* June (2007): 141–142.

Economy, E. and M. Oksenberg. *China Joins the World: Progress and Prospects.* New York: Council on Foreign Relations, 1998.

ElBaradei, Dr. Mohamed, IAEA Director General. "Statement to the Sixty-Third Regular Session of the United Nations General Assembly." (2008).

Ellingsen, T. and N.P. Gleditsch. "Democracy and Armed Conflict in the Third World." In *Causes of Conflict in the Third World,* edited by D. Smith and K. Volden, 69–81. Oslo: International Peace Research Institute (PRIO), 1997.

"Ensuring Fragile States Are Not Left Behind." Paris: OECD-DAC, 2007.

Esposito, J.L. *Unholy War: Terror in the Name of Islam.* Oxford: Oxford University Press, 2003.

European Commission. "Europe in the World: Some Practical Proposals for Greater Coherence, Effectiveness and Visibility." 2006.

——. "Strategy for a Secure Information Society. 'Dialogue, Partnership and Empowerment'." 2006.

——. "Towards an EU Response to Situations of Fragility – Engaging in Difficult Environments for Sustainable Development, Stability and Peace." 2007.

——. "Second Strategic Energy Review: An EU Energy Security and Solidarity Action Plan." 2008.

European Council. "European Security Strategy, 'A Secure Europe in a Better World'." EU High Representative Dr. Javier Solana, 2003.

——. "To Serve Europe in a Better World: European Security Strategy." Brussels, 2003.

——. "Integrated Climate and Energy Policy – Presidency Conclusions." 2007.

European Union Institute for Security Studies (EUISS). *The EU's Strategic Objectives: Effective Multilateralism and Extended Security*, Discussion Paper. Paris, 2003.

Evangelista, M. *The Chechen Wars: Will Russia Go the Way of the Soviet Union?* Washington, DC: Brookings Institution Press, 2002.

"The Failed States Index." *Foreign Policy* 167 (2008): 64–68.

"Failed States Index." *Foreign Policy* 173 (2009): 80–83.

Ferguson, C.D. and W.C. Potter. *The Four Faces of Nuclear Terrorism*. Monterey Institute of International Studies: Center for Nonproliferation Studies, 2004.

Ferguson, N. "A World Without Power." *Foreign Policy* 143 (2004): 32–39.

——. "The Axis of Upheaval." *Foreign Policy* 171 (2009): 56–58.

Finnemore, M. *National Interests in International Society*. Ithaca: Cornell University Press, 1996.

Focarelli, C. "The Responsibility to Protect Doctrine and Humanitarian Intervention: Too Many Ambiguities for a Working Doctrine." *Journal of Conflict and Security Law* 13, 2 (2008): 191–213.

"Foreign Student Quota to Expand." *China Daily*, 29 July 2008.

"Fragile States Strategy." Washington, DC: USAID, 2005.

Friedman, G. *The Next 100 Years: A Forecast for the 21st Century*. New York: Doubleday, 2009.

Friedman, T. "The First Law of Petropolitics." *Foreign Policy* May/June (2006): 28–36.

——. "Win, Win, Win, Win, Win …" *New York Times*, 27 December 2008.

Friedman, T.L. *Hot, Flat, and Crowded*. New York: Farrar, Straus & Giroux, 2008.

Fuerth, L. "Security Implications of Climate Scenario 2: Severe Climate Change Over the Next Thirty Years." In *Climatic Cataclysm: The Foreign Policy and National Security Implications of Climate Change*, edited by K.M. Campbell. Washington, DC: Brookings Institution Press, 2008.

Fukuyama, F. "The End of History?" *The National Interest* 16, Summer (1989): 3–18.

——. *The End of History and the Last Man*. Harmondsworth: Penguin, 1992.

——. *State-Building. Governance and World Order in the 21st Century*. Cornell: Cornell University Press, 2004.

Gaddis, J.L. "A Grand Strategy of Transformation." *Foreign Policy* (2002): 50–57.

——. *Surprise, Security, and the American Experience*. Cambridge: Harvard University Press, 2004.

Gates, R. "A Balanced Strategy." *Foreign Affairs* 88, 1 (2009): 28–40.

Gelb, L. *Power Rules: How Common Sense Can Rescue American Foreign Policy*. New York: HarperCollins, 2009.

Gellman, B. *Angler: The Cheney Vice-Presidency*. New York: Penguin, 2008.

Gerard, J. "The CWC at 10 Years – Partnership, Progress, and the Path Ahead, Statement by the CEO of the American Chemical Council." *OPCW Industry Protection Forum* (2007).

Gholz, E., D.G. Press and H.M. Sapolsky. "Come Home America: A Strategy of Restraint in the Face of Temptation." *International Security* 21, 4 (1997): 5–17.

Gill, B. *Rising Star: China's New Security Diplomacy*. Washington, DC: Brookings Institution Press, 2007.

Gill, B. and C.-h. Huang. "China's Expanding Role in Peacekeeping: Prospects and Policy Implications." In *SIPRI Policy Paper 25*. Stockholm: Stockholm International Peace Research Institute, 2009.

Gill, B. and M. Schiffer. "A Rising China's Rising Responsibilities." In *Powers and Principles: International Leadership in a Shrinking World*, edited by M. Schiffer and D. Shorr, 99–123. Lanham: Lexington Books, 2009.

Glaister, D. and J. Randerson. "Act on Climate Change, Top Scientists Warn US." *Guardian*, 30 May 2008.

Gleditsch, N.P. "Environmental Change, Security, and Conflict." In *Leashing the Dogs of War: Conflict Management in a Divided World*, edited by C.A. Crocker, F.O. Hampson and P.R. Aall. Washington, DC: US Institute of Peace Press, 2007.

"Global Report on Trafficking in Persons." Vienna: UNODC, 2009.

Gnesotto, N. "European Strategy as a Model." *EU-ISS Newsletter No. 9*, 2004.

Gnesotto, N. and G. Grevi, eds. *The New Global Puzzle: What World for the EU in 2025?* Paris: EU Institute for Security Studies, 2006.

Goldgeier, J.M. "NATO Expansion: The Anatomy of a Decision." In *The Domestic Sources of American Foreign Policy: Insights and Evidence*, edited by E.R. Wittkopf and J.M. McCormick. Lanham: Rowman and Littlefield, 2007.

Goldman, M. *Petrostate: Putin, Power, and the New Russia*. Oxford: Oxford University Press, 2008.

——. "The Russian Power Play On Oil, Natural Gas Reserves." *Boston Globe*, 23 August 2008.

Goldman Sachs. "Dreaming with BRICs: The Path to 2050." *Global Economics Paper* 99 (2003).

——. "The N-11: More Than an Acronym." *Global Economics Paper* 153 (2007).

Goldstein, A. *Rising to the Challenge: China's Grand Strategy and International Security*. Stanford: Stanford University Press, 2005.

Golts, A. "Landscape After the Battle [in Russian]." *Ezhednevny zhurnal*, 20 May 2009.

Gorbachev, M. "What Role for the G-20?" *New York Times*, 27 April 2009.

Gordon, M. and B. Trainor. *Cobra II: The Inside Story of the Invasion and Occupation of Iraq*. New York: Pantheon, 2006.

Gordon, P. *Winning the Right War: The Path to Security for America and the World*. New York: Times Books, 2007.

Gourlay, C. "Community Instruments for Civilian Crisis Management." In *Civilian Crisis Management: The EU Way (Chaillot Paper 90)*, edited by A. Nowak, pp. 49–67. Paris: EU Institute for Security Studies, 2006.

Grafova, L. "Migrants Must Become Legal! [in Russian]." *Novaya gazeta*, 13 November 2008.

Graham, B. "Bioterrorism: A Preventable Catastrophe." *Boston Globe*, 18 December 2008.

——. *By His Own Rules: The Ambitions, Successes, and Ultimate Failures of Donald Rumsfeld*. New York: Public Affairs, 2009.

Graham, B. and J. Talent. *World At Risk: The Report of the Commission on the Prevention of WMD Proliferation and Terrorism*. New York: Vintage Books, 2008.

Grant, C. "Is Europe Doomed to Fail as a Power?" London: Centre for European Reform, 2009.

Grant, C. and T. Valasek. *Preparing for the Multipolar World: European Foreign and Security Policy in 2020*. London: Centre for European Reform, 2007.

Graves, B. "Enjeux de Stabilité: Vers l'Emancipation Sécuritaire." Paper presented at the French Ministry of Defence Conference, Paris, 21 January 2009.

Greenpeace. "Bassin du Congo, Forets en Sursis." 2007.

Grevi, G. "The Interpolar World: A New Scenario." *EU-ISS Occasional Paper No. 79* (2009).

Grigoryev, E. "From Gorbachev to Obama; New US President Tries to Harvest Political Dividend from the Illusion of Nuclear-Free World [in Russian]." *Nezavisimaya gazeta,* 20 April 2009.

Grygiel, J. "The Power of Statelessness." *Policy Review* April & May (2009): 35–50.

Guriev, S. and O. Tsivinsky. "Ratio Economica: The Economics of Plague [in Russian]." *Vedomosti,* 12 May 2009.

Gurr, T.R. *Why Men Rebel.* 4th edn. Princeton: Center of International Studies, Princeton University Press, 1971.

Haass, R.N. "The Age of Nonpolarity: What will Follow US Dominance?" *Foreign Affairs* 87, 3 (2008): 44–56.

Heisbourg, F. "The Unbearable Weight of Not Being." In *European Security in a Global Context: Internal and External Dynamics,* edited by T. Tardy, pp. 210–217. London: Routledge, 2009.

Herbst, J. "Let Them Fail." In *When States Fail,* edited by R. Rotberg, 302–318. Princeton: Princeton University Press, 2004.

Herd, G. and G. Sargsyan. "Debating Russian Demographic Security: Current Trends and Future Trajectories." *Security Index* 82, 2 (2007): 51–68.

Herd, G.P. "International Relations Theory, Catastrophes and the Need for a New Paradigm." In *Potential Global Strategic Catastrophes: Balancing Transnational Responsibilities and Burden-Sharing with Sovereignty and Human Dignity,* edited by N.R.F. Al-Rodhan, 41–57. Berlin: LIT, 2009.

Herspring, D., ed. *Putin's Russia: Past Imperfect, Future Uncertain.* 3rd edn. London: Rowman & Littlefield, 2006.

Hewitt, J., J. Wikenfeld and T.R. Gurr. *Peace and Conflict 2008.* Boulder: Paradigm, 2008.

High Representative for CFSP and European Commission. "Climate Change and International Security." *Paper to the European Council* S113/08 (2008).

Hoffman, B. *Inside Terrorism: From the Iran Hostage Crisis to the World Trade Center Bombing.* New York: Columbia University Press, 1999.

Hoffmann, S. "Yugoslavia: Implications for Europe and for European Institutions." In *The World and Yugoslavia's Wars,* edited by U. Richard. New York: Council on Foreign Relations Books, 1996.

Holdren, J.P. "Science and Technology for Sustainable Well-Being." *Science* 319, 5862 (2008): 425–434.

Holmes, J.A. "Where are the Civilians?" *Foreign Affairs* 88, 1 (2009): 148–161.

Horgan, J. *The Psychology of Terrorism.* London, New York: Routledge, 2005.

Howorth, J. *Security and Defence Policy in the European Union.* London and New York: Palgrave, 2007.

Hughes, J. *Chechnya: From Nationalism to Jihad.* Philadelphia: University of Pennsylvania Press, 2007.

Human Security Report. "War and Peace in the 21st Century." University of British Columbia, 2005.

Huntington, S. "The Clash of Civilizations." *Foreign Affairs* 72, 3 (1993): 22–49.

——. *The Clash of Civilizations and the Remaking of World Order.* New York: Simon & Schuster, 1996.

Hurd, D. "The Immoral Incompetents." *Guardian*, 15 June 2009.

Hutchings, R. and F. Kempe. "The Global Grand Bargain." *Foreign Policy* webposting (2008).

Ikenberry, G.J. *After Victory: Institutions, Strategic Restraint, and the Rebuilding of Order after Major Wars*. Princeton: Princeton University Press, 2001.

——. "The Rise of China and the Future of the West." *Foreign Affairs* 87, 1 (2008): 23–37.

Ikenberry, G.J. and A.-M. Slaughter. *Forging a World of Liberty Under Law, U.S. National Security in the 21st Century*. Princeton Project on National Security Final Report. Princeton: Princeton University Press, 2008.

Illarionov, A. "Global Darkening: Absurd Goals, Expensive Decisions, Falsified Arguments in the Fight Against Climate Warming [in Russian]." *Izvestia*, 30 March 2005.

——. "On the Eve of the Summit: The Death of the G8 [in Russian]." *Vedomosti*, 18 April 2006.

"India Will Not Obstruct CTBT Coming To Force, Says Jaswant." *Rediff.com*, 9 February 1999.

Inoguchi, T. "Japan as a Global Ordinary Power: Its Current Phase." *Japanese Studies* 28, 1 (2008): 3–13.

Inozemtsev, V. "Dreams About a Multi-Polar World [in Russian]." *Nezavisimaya gazeta*, 18 September 2008.

International Energy Agency. "World Energy Outlook 2008: Executive Summary." Paris: OECD/IEA, 2008.

Ivanov, I. "What Could Be Offered to Tehran? [in Russian]." *Vremya novostei*, 29 May 2009.

Jaffrelot, C. and W.P.S. Sidhu. "Does Europe Matter to India?" In *European Security in a Global Context: Internal and External Dynamics*, edited by T. Tardy, 192–210. London and New York: Routledge, 2009.

Jervis, R. "Cooperation Under the Security Dilemma." *World Politics* 30, 2 (1977–1978): 167–214.

Joffe, J. "Who's Afraid of Mr. Big?" *National Interest* 64 (2001): 43–52.

——. "The Default Power." *Foreign Affairs* 88, 5 (2009): 21–35.

Johnston, A.I. *Social States: China in International Institutions*. Princeton: Princeton University Press, 2008.

Joint Forces Command. *The Joint Operating Environment: Challenges and Implications for the Future Force*. Norfolk, VA, 2008.

Jones, B.D., C. Pascual and S.J. Stedman. *Power and Responsibility: Building International Order in an Era of Transnational Threats*. Washington, DC: Brookings Institution Press, 2009.

Juergensmeyer, M. *Terror in the Mind of God: The Global Rise of Religious Violence*. Berkeley: University of California Press, 2000.

Kagan, R. "Power and Weakness." *Policy Review* 113 (2002): 3–28.

——. *Dangerous Nation: America's Place in the World from its Earliest Days to the Dawn of the Twentieth Century*. New York: Knopf, 2006.

——. "End of Dreams, Return of History: International Rivalry and American Leadership." *Policy Review* 143 (2007): 17–44.

Kan, S.A. "U.S.–China Counterterrorism Cooperation: Issues for U.S. Policy." *Congressional Research Service* 7 May (2009).

Kanter, J. and S. Castle. "EU Leaders Dramatically Scale Back Their Ambition on Emissions." *International Herald Tribune*, 12 December 2008.

Kapila, S. "Russia–India–Iran Triangle Strategically Possible." *South Asia Analysis Group* 3363 (2009).

Kaplan, R.D. "The Coming Anarchy: How Scarcity, Crime, Overpopulation, Tribalism, and Disease are Rapidly Destroying the Social Fabric of Our Planet." *Atlantic Monthly* 273, 2 (1994): 44–76.

——. *The Coming Anarchy: Shattering the Dreams of the Post Cold War.* New York: Random House, 2000.

——. "Center Stage for the 21st Century: Power Plays in the Indian Ocean." *Foreign Affairs* 88, 2 (2009): 16–32.

Kapur, A. *India's Nuclear Option: Atomic Diplomacy and Decision Making.* New York: Praeger, 1976.

Karaganov, S. "About Russia–NATO and More [in Russian]." *Rossiiskaya gazeta,* 26 March 2008.

Kearns Goodwin, D. *Team of Rivals: The Political Genius of Abraham Lincoln.* New York: Simon and Schuster, 2005.

Kennedy, J.F. "News Conference 52." *State Department Auditorium,* 21 March 1963.

Kent, A. *Beyond Compliance: China, International Organizations, and Global Security.* Stanford: Stanford University Press, 2007.

Keohane, R.O. *After Hegemony: Cooperation and Discord in the World Political Economy.* Princeton: Princeton University Press, 1984.

Kepel, G. *Jihad: The Trail of Political Islam.* London: I.B. Tauris, 2004.

Khanna, P. *The Second World: Empires and Influence in the New Global Order.* New York: Random House, 2008.

Khlopkov, A. "The Angarsk Project: Enrichment vs Proliferation." *Security Index* 85, 3 (2008): 27–44.

Ki-Moon, B. "The Ice Is Melting." *New York Times,* 17 September 2009.

King, L.J. "CDC Agroterrorism and Zoonotic Threat Preparedness Efforts, Statement Before the Committee on Homeland Security Subcommittee on Prevention of Nuclear and Biological Attack." US House of Representatives, 2006.

Kireeva, A. "Russia Spurs Ahead Environmental Overhaul of Decrepit Northern Fleet Bases." *Bellona News,* 12 January 2009.

Kissinger, H.A. "The Chance of a New World Order." *New York Times,* 12 January 2009.

——. "Obama's Foreign Policy Challenge." *Washington Post,* 22 April 2009.

Klare, M. *Rising Powers, Shrinking Planet: How Scarce Energy is Creating a New World Order.* Oxford: Oneworld Publications, 2008.

Kobrinskaya, I. "Russia: Facing the Facts." In *Enlarging NATO: The National Debates,* edited by G.A. Mattox and A.R. Rachwald, 169–186. Boulder: Lynne Rienner, 2001.

Kolesnikov, A. "Flying Pucks [in Russian]." *Kommersant,* 7 February 2009.

Konovalov, A. "The World Should Not Be Multi-Polar [in Russian]." *Nezavisimaya gazeta,* 16 September 2008.

Koshkina, A. "The Audit Chamber Evaluated the Waste [in Russian]." *Gazeta,* 22 May 2009.

Krauthammer, C. *The Unipolar Moment – Foreign Affairs: America and the World.* New York: Macmillan, 1990.

——. "The Unipolar Moment Revisited." *National Interest* 70 (2002): 5–17.

Krepon, M. "The US–India Nuclear Deal: Another Wrong Turn in the War on Terror." *The Henry L. Stimson Center* (2006). www.stimson.org/pub.cfm?ID=283.

Kristoff, N. "After Wars, Mass Rapes Persist." *New York Times,* 20 May 2009.

Krueger, A. and J. Maleckova. "Education, Poverty and Terrorism: Is There a Causal Connection?" *The Journal of Economic Perspectives* 17, 4 (2003): 119–144.

Kuznetsova, E. "Double Standards Russian-Style [in Russian]." *Nezavisimaya gazeta*, 17 March 2009.

LaFleur, V., N. Purvis and A. Jones. "Double Jeopardy: What the Climate Crisis Means for the Poor." *Brookings Blum Roundtable Report* 5 (2008).

Lake, D.A. "Regional Security Complexes: A Systems Approach." In *Regional Orders: Building Security in a New World*, edited by D. Lake and P.M. Morgan, pp. 45–67. University Park: Penn State University Press, 1997.

Lakshmi, R. "India Rejects Calls For Emission Cuts." *Washington Post*, 13 April 2009.

Lampton, D.M., ed. *The Making of Chinese Foreign and Security Policy in the Era of Reform*. Stanford: Stanford University Press, 2001.

Landler, M. "In China, Clinton Focuses on Climate Change." *New York Times*, 21 February 2009.

Laqueur, W. *A History of Terrorism*. 5th edn. New Brunswick: Transaction Publishers, 2007.

Latvian National Security Council. *Report*, 2008.

Lavoy, P.R., S.D. Sagan and J.J. Wirtz. *Planning the Unthinkable: How New Powers Will Use Nuclear, Biological, and Chemical Weapons*. Ithaca: Cornell University Press, 2000.

Lavrov, S. "Russia and the OECD." *Wall Street Journal*, 25 April 2007.

Layne, C. "The Unipolar Illusion: Why New Great Powers Will Rise." *International Security* 17, 4 (1993): 5–51.

——. "From Preponderance to Offshore Balancing: America's Future Grand Strategy." *International Security* 22, 1 (1997): 86–124.

——. "The Unipolar Illusion Revisited: The Coming End of the United States' Unipolar Moment." *International Security* 21, 2 (2006): 7–41.

Lee, H. and D. Shalmon. "Searching for Oil: China's Oil Strategies in Africa." In *China into Africa: Trade, Aid, and Influence*, edited by R.I. Rotberg, pp. 107–136. Washington, DC: Brookings Institution Press, 2008.

Lee, J. "India fast becoming Asia's 'swing state'." *Straits Times*, 20 May 2009.

Levine, V. and D. Dollar. "The Increasing Selectivity of Foreign Aid 1984–2003." Washington, DC: World Bank, 2004.

Levy, C.J. "In Siberia, the Death Knell of a Complex Holding a Deadly Stockpile." *International Herald Tribune*, 26 May 2009.

Lewis, B. *What Went Wrong? Western Impact and Middle Eastern Response*. New York: Oxford, 2002.

Lia, B. and K. Skolberg. "Causes of Terrorism: An Expanded and Updated Review of the Literature." Kjeller: Norwegian Defence Research Establishment (FFI), 2004.

Lieber, R.J. *The American Era: Power and Strategy for the 21st Century*. Cambridge: Cambridge University Press, 2005.

Lieven, A. *Chechnya: Tombstone of Russian Power*. New Haven: Yale University Press, 1998.

Lieven, D. *Empire: The Russian Empire and Its Rivals*. New Haven: Yale University Press, 2000.

Lindstrom, G. "Protecting the European homeland — the CBR dimension." *EU-ISS Chaillot Paper* 69 (2004).

Lingmin, Z. *Optimistic View of Sino-US Relations – Exclusive Interview With Professor Wang Jisi, Dean of the School of International Studies at Peking University*. Boston, 2008. http://hir.harvard.edu/index.php?page=article&id=1905&p=2.

Longo, M. "European Integration: Between Micro-Regionalism and Globalism." *Journal of Common Market Studies* 41, 3 (2003): 475–494.

Luft, G. and A. Korin. "Terrorism Goes to Sea." *Foreign Affairs* 83, 6 (2004): 61–71.

Lugar, R. "The New Energy Realists." *National Interest* 80 (2006): 30–33.

Lugar, R.G. "Raise the Gas Tax: A Revenue-Neutral Way to Treat Our Oil Addiction." *Washington Post*, 1 February 2009.

Lukyanov, F. "Sarcasm and Tiredness [in Russian]." *Gazeta.ru*, 1 November 2007.

———. "After the War of Ambitions [in Russian]." *Gazeta.ru*, 19 February 2009.

———. "The Legend About the Big Two [in Russian]." *Gazeta.ru*, 26 February 2009.

———. "Obama's Consensus Diplomacy Put to the Test." *Moscow Times*, 16 July 2009.

Luttwak, E. "Give War A Chance." *Foreign Affairs* 78, 4 (1999): 36–44.

Lynch, D. "Why Georgia Matters." *Chaillot Paper* 86 (2006).

Lynch, T. and R. Singh. *After Bush: The Case for Continuity in American Foreign Policy*. Cambridge: Cambridge University Press, 2008.

Lynn, J. and C. Bradford. "The Irrelevant G8 Summit in St. Petersburg." In *Global Economics Paper*, The Brookings Institution, 2006.

Mabey, N. "Delivering Climate Security: International Security Responses to a Climate Changed World." *The Royal United Services Institute for Defence and Security Studies, Whitehall Paper* 69 (2008).

Mack, A. and Z. Nielsen. *Human Security Brief 2007*. Vancouver: Human Security Report Project, 2008.

Mahbubami, K. *The New Asian Hemisphere: The Irresistible Shift of Global Power to the East*. New York: Public Affairs, 2008.

Mandelbaum, M. "Foreign Policy as Social Work." *Foreign Affairs* 75, 1 (1996): 16–32.

———. *The Case for Goliath: How America Acts as the World's Government in the Twenty-first Century*. New York: Public Affairs, 2005.

Mann, J. *Rise of the Vulcans: The History of Bush's War Cabinet*. New York: Penguin, 2004.

Manners, I. "Normative Power Europe Reconsidered: Beyond the Crossroads." *Journal of European Public Policy* 13, 2 (2006): 182–199.

Marshall, M. and B. Cole. *Global Report on Conflict, Governance and State Fragility 2008*. *Foreign Policy Bulletin*, Cambridge University Press, 2008.

Mastanduno, M. "Preserving the Unipolar Moment: Realist Theories and U.S. Grand Strategy After the Cold War." *International Security* 21, 4 (1997): 49–88.

Mayer, J. *The Dark Side: The Inside Story of How the War on Terror Turned Into a War on American Ideals*. New York: Doubleday, 2008.

Mayntz, R. "Organizational Forms of Terrorism: Hierarchy, Network, or a Type sui generis?" In *Max Planck Institute for the Study of Societies Discussion Papers*. Cologne: Max Planck Institute for the Study of Societies, 2004.

McMaster, H.R. "Learning from Contemporary Conflicts to Prepare for Future War." *Orbis* 52, 4 (2008): 564–584.

McNeill, J. *Something New Under the Sun: An Environmental History of the Twentieth-Century World*. London: Penguin Books, 2000.

Mearsheimer, J. *The Tragedy of Great Power Politics*. New York: W.W. Norton, 2001.

Medeiros, E.S. *Reluctant Restraint: The Evolution of China's Nonproliferation and Practices 1980–2004*. Stanford: Stanford University Press, 2007.

Medvedev, D. "Forward, Russia! [in Russian]." *Gazeta.ru*, 10 September 2009.

Menon, A., K. Nicolaidis and J. Welsh. "In Defence of Europe: A Response to Kagan." *Journal of European Affairs* 2, 3 (2004): 5–14.

Menon, S. *Maritime Imperatives of Indian Foreign Policy*. New Delhi: National Maritime Foundation, 2009.

Michta, A. "Double or Nothing." *National Interest* 93 (2008): 58–61.

Ministry of External Affairs. "The Road to Copenhagen: India's Position on Climate Change Issues." New Delhi: Public Diplomacy Division, 2009.

Monar, J. "Common Threat and Common Response? The European Union's Counter-Terrorism Strategy and its Problems." *Government and Opposition* 42, 3 (2007): 292–313.

"More Chinese students study abroad." *China.org*, 15 June 2009.

"Mortality in the Democratic Republic of the Congo: An Ongoing Crisis." International Rescue Committee, 2007.

Moshes, A. "EU–Russia Relations: Unfortunate Continuity." *European Issues (Foundation Robert Shuman)* 126 (2009).

Moyo, D. *Dead Aid*. London: Penguin, 2009.

Murdoch, J. and T. Sandler. "Civil Wars and Economic Growth: Spatial Dispersion." *American Journal of Political Science* 48 (2004): 138–151.

Naím, M. "Minilateralism." *Foreign Policy* 173, July/August (2009): 136–137.

Nakicenovic, N. *The Changing World: Energy, Climate and Social Futures*. Vienna, Austria: IIASA Conference '07 on Global Development, 2007. Podcast presentation.

Nathan, A. and R.S. Ross. *The Great Wall and the Empty Fortress: China's Search for Security*. New York: W.W. Norton and Co., 1997.

National Intelligence Council. "Global Trends 2025: A Transformed World." NIC, 2008.

"The National Security Strategy of the United Kingdom: Security in an Interdependent World." London: Cabinet Office, 2008.

Nemtsov, B. and V. Milov. "*Putin: Itogi (Putin: The Results)* – Independent Expert Report." *Novaya gazeta*, 2008.

Nodia, G. "The Wounds of Lost Empire." *Journal of Democracy* 20, 2 (2009): 34–38.

Nye, J. *Soft Power: The Means to Success in World Politics*. New York: Public Affairs, 2004.

Obama, B. *The Audacity of Hope: Thoughts on Reclaiming the American Dream*. New York: Three Rivers Press, 2006.

Olson, K.B. "Aum Shinrikyo: Once and Future Threat?" *Emerging Infectious Disease* 5, 4 (1999): 513–516.

O'Neil, Barry. "Speech by Barry O'Neil, President of the OIE International Committee." 76th General Session of the International Committee, World Organisation for Animal Health, 30 May 2008.

Orlov, V. and M. Fugfugosh. "The G8 Strelna Summit and Russia's National Power." *The Washington Quarterly* 29, 3 (2006): 35–48.

Ornstein, N. and T. Mann. "When Congress Checks Out." *Foreign Affairs* 85, 6 (2006): 67–82.

Orszag, P. "Estimated Costs of U.S. Operations in Iraq and Afghanistan and of Other Activities Related to the War on Terrorism." *Statement of the Director of the Congressional Budget Office*, 24 October 2007.

"Outbound Investment Unlikely to Outstrip FDI." *China Daily*, 2 July 2009.

Pace, M. "The Construction of EU Normative Power." *Journal of Common Market Studies* 45, 5 (2007): 1041–1064.

"Pakistan Must Tackle Terror at All Levels." *The Hindu*, 20 July 2009.

Papayoanou, P.A. "Great Powers and Regional Orders: Possibilities and Prospects After the Cold War." In *Regional Orders: Building Security in a New World*, edited by D. Lake and P.M. Morgan, pp. 125–139. University Park: Penn State University Press, 1997.

Pape, R. "Empire Falls." *National Interest* 99 (2009): 21–34.

Paper from the High Representative and the European Commission to the European Council. "Climate Change and International Security." S113/08, 2008.

Pedahzur, A. "Toward an Analytical Model of Suicide Terrorism – A Comment." *Terrorism and Political Violence*, 16, 4 (2004): 841–844.

Pei, M. "Think Again: Asia's Rise." *Foreign Policy* 173, July/August (2009): 32–38.

Peng, L. and W. Qun. "Chinese Ambassador to the United Kingdom Fu Ying: 'It is Time for the West To Understand China More'." *Zhongguo Xinwen She news agency*, 15 June 2009.

"Pentagon's Plan: 'Prevent the Re-Emergence of a New Rival'." *New York Times*, 8 March 1992.

Perkovich, G. *India's Nuclear Bomb*. Berkeley: University of California Press, 2002.

Pettila, R. "Multilateralism Light: The Rise of Informal International Governance." In *EU2020 essay*, pp. 2–3. London: Centre for European Reform, 2009.

Pfirter, Rogelio, OPCW Director-General. "Foreword to the Chemical Disarmament Quarterly." 6, 4 (2008).

Pilat, J.F. "The End of the NPT Regime?" *International Affairs* 83, 3 (2007): 469–482.

Podesta, J. and P. Ogden. "Security Implications of Climate Scenario 1: Expected Climate Change over the Next Thirty Years." In *Climatic Cataclysm: The Foreign Policy and National Security Implications of Climate Change*, edited by K.M. Campbell. Washington, DC: Brookings Institution Press, 2008.

Poe, M.T. *The Russian Moment in World History*. Princeton: Princeton University Press, 2003.

Polgreen, L. "As Chinese Investments in Africa Drop, Hope Sinks." *New York Times*, 25 March 2009.

"Poll, November." *NBC/Wall Street Journal*, 2007.

Posen, B. "Command of the Commons: The Military Foundations of U.S. Hegemony." *International Security* 28, 1 (2003): 5–46.

——. "European Union Security and Defence Policy: Response to Unipolarity?" *Security Studies* 15, 2 (2006): 149–186.

"Protocol Additional to the Geneva Conventions of 12 August 1949, and relating to the Protection of Victims of International Armed Conflicts (Protocol I) (1977)." 1949.

Qutb, S. "War, Peace, and Islamic Jihad." In *Contemporary Debates in Islam: An Anthology of Modernist and Fundamentalist Thought*, edited by M. Moaddel and K. Talattof, 240–242. London: Macmillan, 2000.

Rachman, G. "Europe Spurns the Beloved Obama." *Financial Times*, 30 March 2009.

——. "Obama and the Limits of Soft Power." *Financial Times*, 1 June 2009.

Rademaker, S.G. "U.S. Compliance With Article VI of the Non-Proliferation Treaty (NPT)." Paper presented at the Panel Discussion at the Arms Control Association, Carnegie Endowment Building, Washington, DC, February 2005.

Rajghatta, C. "No Difference with US on Iran: Manmohan." *Times of India*, 16 September 2005.

Ranstorp, M. and M. Normark, eds. *Unconventional Weapons and International Terrorism: Challenges and New Approaches*. London, New York: Routledge, 2009.

Rees, M.J. Our *Final Century: Will Civilisation Survive the Twenty-First Century?* London: Arrow, 2004.

"Reports of the TERRA (Terrorism and Asymmetric Warfare: Emerging Security Challenges after the Cold War) Project." Kjeller: Norwegian Defence Research Establishment (FFI).

"The return of Mr Nyet." *The Economist*, 17 July 2008.

Reus-Smit, C. "The Misleading Mystique of America's Material Power." *Australian Journal of International Studies* 57, 3 (2003): 423–430.

Revenkov, V.I. and V.I. Feigun. "'Gas OPEC' or Other Forms of Cooperation? [in Russian]." *Russia in Global Affairs* 4 (2007): 176–185.

Revkin, A.C. "Among Climate Scientists, A Dispute over 'Tipping Points'." *New York Times*, 28 March 2009.

Rice, C. "Promoting the National Interest." *Foreign Affairs* 76, 1 (2000): 45–62.

———. "The Promise of Democratic Peace." *Washington Post*, 11 December 2005.

———. "Transformational Diplomacy." Speech at Georgetown University, 18 January 2006.

Ricks, T. *Fiasco: The American Military Adventure in Iraq*. New York: Penguin, 2006.

Riedel, B. *American Diplomacy and the 1999 Kargil Summit at Blair House*. Philadelphia: Center for the Advanced Study of India, University of Pennsylvania, 2002.

Roberts, J. "Fold the G-8 into the G-20." *Heritage Foundation*. www.realclearworld.com/articles/2009/07/13/fold_the_g-8_into_the_g-20_96919.html, no. 2538 (2009).

Rodin, I. "The Government Contemplates the Rights of Migrants [in Russian]." *Nezavisimaya gazeta*, 2 February 2009.

Rodrik, D. *One Economics, Many Recipes: Globalization, Institutions and Economic Growth*. Princeton: Princeton University Press, 2007.

Rosamond, B. "Discourses of Globalisation and European Identities." In *The Social Construction of Europe*, edited by Thomas Christiansen, Knud Erik Jorgensen and Antje Wiener, pp. 158–173. London: Sage, 2001.

Rotberg, R. *When States Fail: Causes and Consequences*. Princeton: Princeton University Press, 2004.

Rothkopf, D. "A Thousand Envoys Bloom." *National Interest* 101 (2009): 15–26.

Rühle, M. "Enlightenment in the Second Nuclear Age." *International Affairs* 83, 3 (2007): 511–522.

Rumsfeld, D. "Transforming the Military." *Foreign Affairs* 85, 6 (2002): 20–32.

Russell Mead, W. "Only Makes You Stronger." *The New Republic*, 4 February 2009.

Russet, B. *Grasping the Democratic Peace: Principles for a Post-Cold War World*. Princeton: Princeton University Press, 1993.

Ryabushev, A. "Anti-Pirate Cruise of Neustrashimy [in Russian]." *Nezavisimoe voennoe obozrenie*, 13 February 2009.

Rynning, S. "Peripheral or Powerful? The EU's Strategy to Combat the Proliferation of Nuclear Weapons." *European Security* 16, 3 & 4 (2007): 267–288.

Sachs, J. *The End of Poverty*. New York: Penguin, 2005.

———. *Common Wealth: Economics for a Crowded Planet*. London: Allen Lane, 2008.

Sageman, M. *Understanding Terror Networks*. Philadelphia: University of Pennsylvania Press, 2004.

Saikia, J. and E. Stepanova, eds. *Terrorism: Patterns of Internationalization*. New Delhi, London: SAGE Publications Ltd, 2009.

Sakwa, R., ed. *Chechnya: From Past to Future*. London: Anthem Press, 2005.

———. *Putin: Russia's Choice*. 2nd edn. London: Routledge 2007.

Samarina, A. and A. Gorbacheva. "The Demographic Pit [in Russian]." *Nezavisimaya gazeta*, 6 March 2009.

Sample, I. "Climate Change: Carbon Capture from Power Stations Must Start Soon, Say Scientists." *Guardian*, 10 June 2008.

Santhanam, K. and A. Parthasarathi. "Pokhran-II Thermonuclear Test, a Failure." *The Hindu*, 17 September 2009.

Sapir, A. "Globalization and the Reform of European Social Models." *Journal of Common Market Studies* 44, 2 (2006): 369–390.

Saran, S. "Indo-US Civil Nuclear Agreement: Expectations and Consequences." *Address by Special Envoy to the Prime Minister*, 23 March 2009.

Schäuble, W. "Speech at the 45th Munich Security Conference." Munich Security Conference, 2 July 2009.

Schmid, A.P. and A.J. Jongman. *Political Terrorism: A New Guide to Actors, Authors, Concepts, Data Bases, Theories, and Literature*. 2nd edn. New Brunswick: Transaction Publishers, 2005.

Schwartz, P. and D. Randall. "An Abrupt Climate Change Scenario and Its Implications for United States National Security." Global Business Network, 2003.

Scowcroft, B. "The Dispensable Nation?" *National Interest* 90 (2007): 4–6.

Security Council. "UNSCR 1540." 2004.

Segal, G. "Does China Matter?" *Foreign Affairs* 78, 5 (1999): 24–36.

Sestanovich, S. "Cold War Leftovers." *International Herald Tribune*, 19 May 2009.

Sharavin, A. "Demonstrative Application of Allied Force [in Russian]." *Nezavisimoe voennoe obozrenie* (2009).

Shaw, M.N. *International Law*. 4th edn. Cambridge: Cambridge University Press, 1997.

Shelin, S. "The Bubble of Doubling the GDP [in Russian]." *Gazeta.ru*, 4 February 2009.

Shelley, L.I. "Methods and Motives: Exploring Links Between Transnational Organized Crime & International Terrorism." Washington, DC: US Department of Justice/National Criminal Justice Reference Service (NCJRS), 2005.

Shelley, L.I. and J.T. Picarelli. "Methods Not Motives: Implications of the Convergence of International Organized Crime and Terrorism." *Police Practice and Research* 3, 4 (2002): 305–318.

Shevtsova, L. *Russia – Lost in Transition: The Yeltsin and Putin Legacies*. Washington, DC: CEIP, 2007.

Sidhu, P. "Nuclear Proliferation." In *Security Studies: An Introduction*, edited by P. Williams, pp. 361–375. London: Taylor & Francis, 2008.

Small Arms Survey. *Small Arms Survey 2009: Shadows of War*. Cambridge: Cambridge University Press, 2009.

Smith, D. and J. Vivekananda. "A Climate of Conflict: The Links Between Climate Change, Peace and War." *International Alert* (2007).

Smith, G. "In Search of Sustainable Security." In *The Sustainable Security Series*. Washington, DC: Center for American Progress, 2008.

Smith, K.C. "Russia and European Security: Divide and Dominate." Center for Strategic and International Studies, 2008.

Snyder, F. "Globalization and Europeanization as Friends and Rivals: European Union Law in Global Economic Networks." *European University Institute Working Paper* 99/8 (1999).

Solana, J. "Discours du Haut Représentant de l'Union européenne pour la Politique étrangère et de sécurité commune." Conférence Annuelle de l'Institut d'Etudes de Sécurité de l'Union Européenne, 30 October 2008.

Solomon, J. and S. Gorman. "Pakistan, India and U.S. Begin Sharing Intelligence." *Wall Street Journal*, 22 May 2009.

Stent, A. "An Energy Superpower? Russia and Europe." In *The Global Politics of Energy*, edited by K.M. Campbell and J. Price, pp. 76–95. Washington, DC: The Aspen Institute, 2008.

Stepanova, E. *Terrorism in Asymmetrical Conflict: Ideological and Structural Aspects.* Oxford: Oxford University Press, 2008.

Steyn, B. "Understanding the Implications of UN Security Council Resolution 1540." *African Security Review* 14, 1 (2005): 85–91.

Stiglitz, J. "One Small Step Forward." *Guardian*, 28 June 2009.

Stiglitz, J. and L. Bilmes. *The Three Trillion Dollar War: The True Cost of the Iraq Conflict.* New York: Norton, 2008.

Stimson Center. "UN Peacebuilding Commission." www.stimson.org/fopo/pdf/UN_PBC_Fact_Sheet_Jun_07.pdf.

Subrahmanyam, K. *Shedding Shibboleths: India's Evolving Strategic Outlook.* New Delhi: Wordsmiths, 2005.

Sutherland, R.G. "Chemical and Biochemical Non-Lethal Weapons." *SIPRI Policy Paper* 23 (2008).

Sztompka, P. *The Sociology of Social Change.* Oxford: Wiley-Blackwell, 1994.

Tardy, T., ed. *European Security in a Global Context: Internal and External Dynamics.* London: Routledge, 2009.

"Terrorism Index." *Foreign Policy* 164, September/October (2007): 79–85.

Thakur, R. "Next Word on Intervention." *Japan Times*, 31 July 2009.

Thränert, O. "Would We Really Miss the Nuclear Nonproliferation Treaty?" *International Journal* (2008): 327–340.

Toft, M. "Peace Through Security: Making Negotiated Settlements Stick." *Discussion Paper*, Harvard University (2006).

Trenin, D. "Reading Russian Right." In *Policy Brief.* Washington, DC: CEIP, 2005.

Tucker, J. *War of Nerves: Chemical Warfare from World War I to al-Qaeda.* New York: Pantheon, 2006.

——. "The Body's Own Bioweapons." *Bulletin of the Atomic Scientists* 64, 1 (2008): 16–22.

UK Cabinet Office. "Investing in Prevention: An International Strategy to Manage Risks of Instability and Improve Crisis Response." Prime Minister's Strategy Unit Report to The Government, 2008.

UNEP. "From Conflict to Peacebuilding – the Role of Natural Resources and the Environment." United Nations Environment Program, 2009.

United Nations. "Report of the Secretary-General on Peacebuilding in the Immediate Aftermath of Conflict." UN Doc.: A/63/881–S/2009/304. New York, 2009.

Uppsala University Conflict Data Programme (UCDP). *Human Security Brief 2006.* Vancouver: Human Security Centre, 2006.

Varadarajan, S. "Ruses for War: Nato's New Strategic Concept." *Times of India*, 10 May 1999.

——. "America, India and the Outsourcing of Imperial Overreach." *The Hindu*, 13 July 2005.

——. "India Casting a Wide Net in its Hunt for Energy." *International Herald Tribune*, 25 January 2006.

——. "As Pakistan Hails 'Precedent,' Other IAEA Members Express Doubts, Fears." *The Hindu*, 2 August 2008.

——. "Fizzle Claim For Thermonuclear Test Refuted." *The Hindu*, 27 August 2009.

Victor, D.G. "What Resource Wars?" *The National Interest Online* November/December, 92 (2007).

Waldmann, P. *Terrorismus und Bürgerkrieg: der Staat in Bedrängnis.* München: Gerling Akademie Verlag, 2003.

Walker, I. and H.J. Smith. *Relative Deprivation: Specification, Development, and Integration.* Cambridge: Cambridge University Press, 2001.

Wallander, C. "The Politics of Russia's HIV/AIDS Policy." In *HIV/AIDS in Russia and Eurasia,* edited by J.L. Twigg, pp. 33–55. London: Palgrave Macmillan, 2007.

Walt, S.M. "International Relations: One World, Many Theories." *Foreign Policy* Spring, 110 (1998): 29–46.

Waltz, K. *Theory of International Relations.* Reading: Addison-Wesley, 1979.

Wein, L.M. and Y. Liu. "Analyzing a Bioterror Attack on the Food Supply: The Case of Botulinum Toxin in Milk." *Proceedings of the National Academy of Sciences (PNAS)* 102, 28 (2005).

Westing, A.M. "Environmental Factors in Strategic Policy and Action: An Overview." In *Global Resources and International Conflict: Environmental Factors in Strategic Policy and Action,* edited by A.M. Westing, pp. 3–20: Oxford University Press, 1986.

Wheeler, D. and K. Ummel. "Another Inconvenient Truth: A Carbon-Intensive South Faces Environmental Disaster, No Matter What the North Does." *Center for Global Development Working Paper* 134 (2007).

The White House. "The National Security Strategy of the United States of America." 2002.

——. "The National Security Strategy of the United States of America." 2006.

——. "Foreign Policy Agenda." www.cfr.org/publication/18307/obamabiden_foreign_policy_agenda_january_2009.html, 2009.

"Who Rules The World? The Results of the Second Representative Survey in Brazil, China, France, Germany, India, Japan, Russia, the United Kingdom, and the United States." Berlin: Bertelsmann Stiftung, 2007.

Williams, P. "Terrorism and Organized Crime: Convergence, Nexus or Transformation?" In *FOA Report on Terrorism,* edited by G. Jervas. Stockholm: Defence Research Establishment, 1998.

Wohlforth, W. "The Stability of a Unipolar World." *International Security* 24, 1 (1999): 5–41.

Woodward, B. *State of Denial: Bush at War, Part III.* New York: Simon and Schuster, 2006.

World Bank. "Frequently Asked Questions." http://web.worldbank.org/WBSITE/EXTERNAL/COUNTRIES/AFRICAEXT/CONGODEMOCRATICEXTN/0,content MDK:20779255~menuPK:2114031~pagePK:141137~piPK:141127~theSitePK:349466,00.html.

"World Drug Report." Vienna: UNODC, 2008.

Wright, T. "Multilateralism: Why Bigger May Not Be Better." *The Washington Quarterly* 32, 3 (2009): 163–180.

Xinbo, W. "Chinese Perspectives on Building an East Asian Community in the 21st Century." In *Asia's New Multilateralism: Cooperation, Conflict, and the Search for Community,* edited by M.J. Green and B. Gill, 55–77. New York: Columbia University Press, 2009.

Xinning, G. *Anti-Terrorism, Maritime Security, and ASEAN–China Cooperation: A Chinese Perspective.* Singapore: Institute of Southeast Asian Studies, 2005.

Yergin, D. "Ensuring Energy Security." *Foreign Affairs* 85, 2 (2006): 69–82.

——. "Energy Under Stress." In *The Global Politics of Energy,* edited by K.M. Campbell and J. Price, pp. 26–43. Washington, DC: The Aspen Institute, 2008.

Yost, D.S. "Introduction: Thinking About 'Enlightenment' and 'Counter-Enlightenment' in Nuclear Policies." *International Affairs* 83, 3 (2007): 427–430.

Zakaria, F. *The Post-American World.* New York: W.W. Norton, 2008.

Zanders, J.P. and K. Nixdorff. "Enforcing Non-Proliferation: The European Union and the 2006 BTWC Review Conference." *EU-ISS Chaillot Paper* 93 (2006).

Zartman, W. "Need, Creed, and Greed in Intrastate Conflict." In *Rethinking the Economics of War: The Intersection of Need, Creed, and Greed*, edited by C.J. Arnson and I.W. Zartman, 256–284. Baltimore: Johns Hopkins University Press, 2005.

Zhang, D.D., P. Brecke, H.F. Lee, Y.-Q. He and J. Zhang. "Global Climate Change, War, and Population Decline in Recent Human History." *Proceedings of the National Academy of Sciences (PNAS)* 104, 49 (2007): 19214–19219.

Zlobin, N. "The Window Is Open [in Russian]." *Rossiiskaya gazeta*, 18 March 2009.

Zoloth, L. and S. Maurer. "Synthesizing Biosecurity." *Bulletin of the Atomic Scientists* 63, 6 (2007): 16–18.

Zürcher, C. *The Post-Soviet Wars: Rebellion, Ethnic Conflict, and Nationhood in the Caucasus*. New York: New York University Press, 2007.

Index

"20–20–20 climate change commitments" 183–4
9/11: as asymmetrical violence 28; effect on US
    policy 103, 160; fatalities 23

A.Q. Khan network 105
Abilek, Ken 53
academic research, terrorism 30–2
affluence, and climate change 90–5
Afghanistan: China's investments in 147–8; as
    failing state 70–1, 160; US operations in 105,
    109
Africa: adaptation to climate change 92–3;
    failing states 66
African Union 180–1
aid, failing states 71–2, 74, 75–8
AIDS 67, 69, 130–1
al-Qaeda: and global terrorism 24, 33; Sanctions
    Committee 159; safe havens 67–8, 71; and
    trans-national extremist ideology 28–9; US
    policy on 160
Allison, Dr. Graham 46
Anglo-Saxon capitalism model 107
Annan, Kofi 73, 199
anthrax 53, 60
anti-Americanism 119
Anti-Ballistic Missile (ABM) Treaty (2001)
    127, 155
anti-system protest ideology 28–9; at national
    level 37–9
Arctic Council 203–4
Arctic ice cap 89
Asia-Pacific Economic Cooperation (APEC)
    121, 146, 149
Asia-Pacific Partnership for Clean Development
    and Climate 149
Asia, failing states 66
Association of South-East Asian Nations
    (ASEAN): Asian +3 process 146, 147, 149;
    Regional Forum (ARF) 145, 147
asymmetrical nature of terrorism 26–7
asymmetrical theory of conflict 31–2
Aum Shinrikyo cult 50, 54, 60
Australia Group 55
authoritarian regimes, support for 69

Baev, Pavel K. 18, 117–32, 194–5
Baku–Tblisi–Ceyhan pipeline 87
balance of power theory 7
Barnett, Thomas 15
"Battlegroup" concept 179
Berlin Congress (1878) 9
Bhagwam Shree Rajneesh sect 54
Bhopal chemical plant disaster 10, 57
bi-polar world order 12, 16
Biden, Joe 110, 112
Biohazard (Abilek) 53
biological proliferation 52–4; future trends
    59–60; management of 54–5
biological science, dual-use nature of 53, 55
Biological Weapons and Toxins Convention
    (BTWC) 51, 60, 198; adherence to 54–5;
    Implementation and Support Unit 55;
    verification and compliance regime 52–3
biological weapons, attacks with 46–7
bioregulators 59, 60
biosecurity/biosafety 55
biotechnology: advances in 59–60; dual-use
    nature of 53, 55
Bismarck, Otto von 114
Blackwill, Robert 161
book structure 17–18
botulinum toxin 53–4
Brennan, James 111
BRIC states: as fast-growing developing
    countries 4; and global financial crisis 16–17,
    121; Summit (2009) 78, 199–200
Brooks, Stephen 101
Bruntland Report 10
Brzezinski, Zbigniew 105
Bush administration, US 101, 102–7, 113,
    154–6, 196
Bushehr nuclear power plant 121, 127

capacity building programs 181
Carnegie Commission on Preventing Deadly
    Conflict (1997) 73, 74, 76
Carter, Jimmy 84
Center for Disease Control 54
Central Asia, stability in 204

Chad, as failing state 78–9
Chechnya, war in 126
chemical industry 56–7
chemical proliferation 55–7; future trends 60; management of 57–8
Chemical Weapons Convention (CWC) 51, 52, 60, 148, 198; adherence to 56–8; States Parties 57–8
chemical weapons, attacks with 46–7, 55–6
chemicals, dual-use applications 56
Cheney, Dick 106, 113
Chernoybl nuclear disaster 10
China: barter economy 78; benefits from status quo 196; current trends and trajectories 150–2; defense white paper 139–40; emergence as global power 137–8; energy policies 86, 88; Environmental Protection Agency 142; governance model 195–6; mitigation of climate change 93–4; relations with US 154–5; security priorities 138–44; response to security concerns 145–50; shared interests 199
Churchill, Winston 114
civilian nuclear programs 48
civilizational blocs 13–14
Clément, Caty 65–79, 196, 198
climate change: adaptation challenge of poor countries 92–3; consequences for failing states 67; EU response to 183–4; mitigation challenge of emerging economies 93–4; Russian stance on 128–9; as security threat 88–90; transition challenge of developed economies 94–5; visible impact of 203–4
Clinton, Bill 102, 104, 155, 157, 159
Clinton, Hillary 94, 108, 111, 113, 160, 196
Cold War: double standards in 68–9; legacies of 104; nuclear proliferation 45; superpower rivalry 7, 12
collective security 84, 85–6
Collective Security Treaty Organization (CSTO) 120
Collier, Paul 87–8
Commission on the Prevention of WMD Proliferation and Terrorism 46
common good, preservation of 204
Comprehensive Nuclear Test Ban Treaty (CTBT) 49, 148, 158, 162–3
confidence-building measure (CBM) forms 55
Congo Conference (1884–1885) 9
Congress of Vienna (1815) 9
constructivism 10
contagion effect 66–8
Container Security Initiative (CSI) 52, 147
Convention for the Suppression of Unlawful Acts Against the Safety of Maritime Navigation 163–4
Convention on the Prohibition of Development, Production, Stockpiling and Use of Chemical Weapons (1993) 128
Conventional Forces in Europe (CFE) Treaty 123

Cooper, R. 172
cooperative international management, aspiration for 4
Cooperative Threat Reduction (CTR) Program 52, 57, 128
counter-proliferation, bargaining 109–10
counter-terrorism: effective interaction on 40; at international level 39–41; at national level 37–9; revamping of 108–9
criminal networks: failing states 68, 71; EU 176, 182
criminological analysis of terrorism 32
crisis management focus 37; EU 173–5, 178–84
cyber security 176, 183
"czarism" 111, 113

D'Escoto Brockmann, Miguel 16, 200
"Dark Winter" exercise 52
debt servicing 75, 77
defense spending: Russia 119; US 11–12
defensive realism 8
democracy, spread of 104, 106
democratic principles, setting aside 112–13
Democratic Republic of Congo (DRC), as failing state 71, 76, 78
democratic universalism 13
developed economies, transition to low-carbon economies 94–5
"dirty bombs" 47, 51
Disarmament, Demobilization and Reintegration (DDR) 71, 76, 179, 181
domestic stability, China 139–40
domestic terrorism 35–6; China 142
donor agencies, failing states 71–2, 74, 75–8
Dunay, Pàl 3–18

E.coli 60
East Asia Summit 146
East Turkestan Liberation Organization 142
Eastern Turkestan Islamic Movement (ETIM) 142, 146, 147
Ebola virus 54, 67
Economic Community of Central African States (ECCAS) 180–1
economic development: and climate change 90–5; and security 180
economic fora, Russia's relations with 122–3
economic growth, China 140–2
economic independence, terrorists 35
economic instruments in conflict management 126
economic opportunity, lack of 104
economic power, EU 185–6
economy–energy nexus 108, 199
"effective multilateralism" 174–5
ElBaradei, Mohammed 59
emerging economies: mitigation of climate change 93–4; US ties with 112
energy challenges: China 140–2; EU 177

Energy Charter 149
energy security: China's response to 149–52;
  EU response to 183–4; India's response to
  165–7; Russia 128–9
energy strategy, Russia 119, 122–3
energy wealth 86–7
energy: as security threat 85–8; security trends
  84–5
energy–climate era 82–4
enrichment and reprocessing (ENR) technology
  158
environmental challenges, China 140–2
environmental Kuznets Curve 90–5
Environmental Protection Agency 108
environmental security: China's response to
  149–52; India's response to 165–7; Russia's
  response to 128–9
ethnic violence, China 142
European Arrest Warrant 182
European Commission: and climate change 92;
  communication on "Europe in the World"
  185; Energy Security and Solidarity Action
  Plan 184; role in security policy 180–1
European Common Foreign and Security Policy
  (CFSP) 173, 178–80
European Community 172, 173
European Council 183–4
European Defence Agency (EDA) 178
European institutions, Russian relations with
  123
European Neighbourhood Policy (ENP) 180
European Network and Information Security
  Agency (ENISA) 183
European Security and Defence Policy (ESDP)
  173, 178–80, 181, 185, 186
European Union (EU): African Peace Facility
  180–1; Civilian Planning and Conduct
  Capability (CPCC) 178; climate change
  policies 94–5; Counter-Terrorism Strategy
  (2005) 180, 181–2; Crisis Management
  Planning Directorate (CMPD) 178; energy
  supply 86–7; *European Security Strategy*
  (2003) 3, 45, 174–6, 177, 179, 180, 182;
  Europeanization and globalization 184–6;
  foreign and security policy 172–5;
  governance model 195; globalization process
  184–6; Headline Goals 173, 178–9; High
  Representative for Foreign Affairs and
  Security Policy 181; integration process 172,
  184–6; policy responses and instruments
  178–84; Secretariat of the Council 178;
  security ambitions 173–4; strategy against
  WMD proliferation 175, 182–3; threat
  assessment 175–7
Europeanization 184–6
EUROPOL 182
exclusive globalization 14–15
export controls, nuclear materials 50
external shocks 205–6
extremist ideologies, role of 27–9

failing states: challenges for China 144;
  China's response to 147–8; during Cold War
  68–9; identification of causes and remedies
  72–4; India's response to 164–5; late 1980s
  69–70; as new threat 68–72; peace-building/
  state-building 40; pitfalls of international
  action in 76; Russia's response to 118–19;
  solutions, future trends and trajectories
  77–9; as source of terrorism 110; strategic
  responses 74–6; as strategic threat 65–8,
  74–6; twenty-first century 70–2; US policy
  on 110
fatal discontinuities 11–12
Fergusson, Niall 16, 193
financial independence, terrorists 35
Fissile Material Cutoff Treaty (FMCT) 49, 163
foreign policy: EU 172–5; Russia 118–19
Freedom House 15
French Revolution 29
Friedman, Thomas 86, 108
Frontex system 67
Fukuyama, Francis 13, 14
funding, EU crisis-management operations
  180–1

G2 205
G7 120, 122
G8: Global Partnership Against the Spread of
  Weapons and Materials of Mass Destruction
  52, 57; Russian relations with 121–2
G14 5
G20 4, 17, 112, 113, 131, 198; Russian relations
  with 121–2
Gaddis, J.L. 155, 157
gas chromatograph–mass spectrometers (GC/
  MS) 58
Gates, Robert 111
Gazprom 119, 129
Gelb, Les 204–5
Georgia, Russian relations with 126
Gill, Bates 18, 137–8, 194, 195, 199
global financial architecture, reform of 198
global financial crisis: and G8/G20 121–2;
  impact on security 16–17; impact on US 107,
  108; and multilateralism 199–200; and power
  shifts 193–4, 196
Global Fund for Peace 74
Global Humanitarian Forum 90
global liberal actor, EU as 172–5
global orders, alternative 197–200
global powers: China as 137–8; EU as 172–5,
  186; need for concert of 154–7
globalization: EU 184–6; exclusive 14–15;
  "thick"/ "thin" 15
globalized interdependent world order 200–2
Gorbachev, Mikhail 17, 123
government appointments, US 111, 113
Great Power status, attainment of 3–4
greenhouse gases (GHGs) 88–9, 129, 165–6;
  emerging economies 93–4; US cuts in 108

Grevi, G. 198
Guantanamo Bay prison 104, 108, 112–13
Gulf War 86

Haass, R.N. 197–8
Hague Conventions 55
Hague Programme 182
Hamas 29, 106, 125, 160–1
hard power, EU 174
Hart, Liddell 167
health hazards: climate change 90; failing states 67; Russia 130–1
hegemony 157, 194–7
Herbst, Jeffrey 75
Herd, Graeme P. 3–18, 193–206
highly enriched uranium (HEU) 49–50
HIV 130–1
Hizbollah 29, 160–1
Holbrooke, Richard 109, 111
Hurricane Katrina 88
Hussein, Saddam 104, 105

ideological extremism 27–9, 38–9
Ikenberry, G.J. 195
India: environmental and energy security 165–7; governance model 195; mitigation of climate change 93; regional crises and fragile states 164–5; terrorism and political extremism 159–61; WMD proliferation 161–4
Indo-US nuclear agreement (2005) 158
institutions 5–6
integration process, EU 172, 184–6
intelligence gathering 103–4, 108–9, 160
interdependency 193–4, 198–9, 200–2
international action, failed states 76
international anti-terrorism measures 39–41
International Atomic Energy Agency (IAEA) 49, 121, 148, 157–8, 162; Additional Protocol 51
international contagion effect 66–8
International Court of Justice 162
International Criminal Court 157
International Energy Agency (IEA) 84, 122, 166–7
International Energy Forum 149
international humanitarian law (IHL) 26
international institutions: Russian relations with 120–3; trust and confidence-building in 9
International Labour Office 9
international law: China's recognition of 145; violation of 120
International Monetary Fund (IMF) 14, 75, 102, 110; HIPIC initiative 70
International Panel on Climate Change (IPCC) 88, 92
international relations, approaches to 6–12
International Rescue Committee 65
internationalization of terrorism 33, 35–6
IPAT equation 90–1

Iran: nuclear program 48, 49, 127–8, 143, 148, 156, 157–8, 164; US dialogue with 109–10
Iraq: sanctions against 154; war on 104, 105–6, 109, 155
Islamist terrorism 24–5, 28–9, 38–9

Jackson–Vanik Amendment (1974) 122
Jacobins 29
Jervis, Robert 8
jihad 28
Jones, James 111

Kadyrov, Ramzan 126
Kagan, Robert 15, 175
Kaplan, Robert D. 14, 168
Kennedy, John F. 45
Keohane, Robert 8
Khan, A.Q. 163
Khanna, Parag 16
Ki-Moon, Ban 203
Kissinger, Henry 197
Krauthammer, Charles 101
Kuznets Curve, groups of states on 90–5
Kyoto Protocol 103, 128–9, 149, 165

Lashkar-e-Tayyaba 160
Lavrov, Sergei 118
League of Nations 7, 9
left-wing terrorism 30, 33, 159
legal measures against terrorism 37–8, 39
legal norms 5–6
lethality of terrorism 32–3
Lewis, Bernard 104
liberalism 8–10, 172–5
Liberation Tigers of Tamil Eelam (LTTE) 164
Lincoln, Abraham 111
Lindstrom, Gustav 45–61, 196, 198
Lisbon Treaty 179, 181, 186
logistical conditions for terrorism 30
low-carbon economies, transition to 94–5
Lugar, Richard 128
Luttwak, Edward 75
Lynn, William 113

Maastricht Treaty 171, 173
McCain, John 111
McChrystal, General Stanley 109
maritime security 166–7
Mearsheimer, John 8
Medvedev, Dmitry 110, 118–19, 121–3, 129, 130, 194–5, 204
Menon, Shivshankar 166–7
Merkel, Angela 113
Middle East Peace Process 109, 156
Middle East, failing states 66
migration: and climate change 90, 92–3, 94; failing states 67; Russia 130–1
military capabilities, EU 173–4
Mitchell, George 109, 111
mixed-oxide (MOX) nuclear fuel 50

Monterrey Consensus (2000) 76
Moscow terrorist attacks 57, 124
multilateral institutions: China's engagement with
    145–6; engagement with failed states 69–72
multilateralism 112, 113, 174–5; in retreat 199
multipolarity 16–17, 107, 118–19, 157, 193–4,
    197–8
Munich Security Conference (2009) 110
Museveni, Yoweri 92

N-11 4
Nabucco pipeline 87
nanotechnology 60
national anti-terrorism measures 37–9
nationalist terrorism 29, 33
Natural Resources Defense Council 48
"natural resources trap" 87–8
Naxalite movement 35
neo-realism 8, 15
Netherlands Stability Fund 77
new social movements 10–11
new threats: EU responses to 175–7, 178–84;
    from fragile states 68–72; Indian discourse on
    158; use of crisis management 178–80; and
    EU 181–4
Nixon, Richard 84
non-interference principle, China 144, 147
Non-Proliferation Treaty (NPT): Additional
    Protocol 51; Article IV 59; challenges to
    47–9; and China 143, 148; inception 45; and
    India 161–2, 164; and Russia 126–7; State
    Parties 52; strengthening of 110, 198
non-state actors, rise of 9–10
Norilsk Nickel 129
norms 5–6, 200
North American Free Trade Agreement
    (NAFTA) 102
North Atlantic Treaty Organization (NATO): in
    Afghanistan 109, 112; and Europe 177;
    membership 110; re-tasking 154; and Russia
    123, 124–5, 126, 127; in Yugoslavia 120;
North Korea, nuclear program 48, 49, 127, 143,
    147, 148, 156
Northern Alliance 160
nuclear fuel banks 59
nuclear non-proliferation, Russian stance on
    126–8
nuclear power reactors 58–9, 166
nuclear proliferation 47–51; future trends 58–9;
    management of 51–2
Nuclear Suppliers Group 148, 155, 161–2
nuclear waste 128
nuclear weapons program: India 162–3; Iran 48,
    49, 127–8, 143, 148, 156, 157–8, 164; North
    Korea 48, 49, 127, 143, 147, 148, 156
nuclear weapons stockpiles 48, 128
Nunn, Sam 128

Obama, Barack 83; administration of 101,
    107–13, 122, 127, 156–7, 163, 196, 197, 205

offensive realism 8
oil crisis (1973) 10
oil imports, US 86–7
oil shortages 84–5
Oklahoma City bombing (1995) 35
Operation Desert Storm (1990) 154
Organization for Cooperation and Security in
    Europe (OSCE) 123
Organization for Economic Cooperation and
    Development (OECD) 66, 74, 76, 77, 84, 122
Organization for the Prohibition of Chemical
    Weapons (OPCW) 56, 58, 128
Organization of Petroleum Exporting Countries
    (OPEC) 122, 149

Pakistan: as threat to India 159–61, 163, 164;
    US focus on 109
Palestine Liberation Organisation (PLO) 38
Paris Declaration on Aid Effectiveness 77
Pax Americana 16
peace operations, Russia 125–6
peace-building, international support for 40
Pei, Minxin 195–6
Permanent Court of International Justice 9
Petersberg tasks 179
petropolitics thesis 86–7
plutonium (Pu) 49–50
policy instruments, EU 178–84
policy process, US 110–13
policy responses, EU 178–84
political assassinations 29–30
political extremism: China's response to 146–7;
    India's response to 159–61
political goals, terrorists 25–6
political influence, EU 185–6
political transformation, terrorists 38
political voice, lack of 104
poor countries: adaptation to climate change
    92–3; energy production in 87–8
population decline, Russia 130–1
population size, and climate change 90–5
poverty and terrorism 31
"pre-cursor" chemicals 56
preemptive action 103–4
Proliferation and Security Initiative (PSI) 52,
    163–4
Putin, Vladimir 118, 119, 120, 122, 124, 128–9,
    130, 155, 204

Qishan, Wang 107

R2P 200
radicalisation 28
radioactive materials, loss/theft of 49–50
realism 7–8, 119
Rees, Martin 12
regime type and terrorism 31
regimes 5–6
Regional Anti-Terrorism Structure, Tashkent/
    Uzbekistan 146

regional conflicts: China's response to 147–8; India's response to 164–5; Russia's response to 125–6
regional contagion effect 66
regional instability, China's challenges from 144
regional stability, Central Asia 204
religious terrorism 24–5, 28–9, 33
research sharing 53–4
resource dependency, China 141–2
resources: competition for 82–3, 89–90; scarcity in poor countries 92–3; shortages of 84–5
Rhodes, Matthew 18, 101–14, 196, 199
Rice, Condoleezza 103
risk management, Russia 124–9
Rodrik, Dani 79
Rome, Treaty of 172
Ross, Dennis 111
Rumsfeld, Donald 104, 106
Russia–Ukraine gas supply crisis (2009) 184
Russian Federation: benefits from status quo 196; biological weapons program 53; chemical weapons stocks 56, 57; energy resources 86–7; Federal Security Service (FSB) 125; Federal Service for Control over Trafficking of Narcotics 131; Foreign Policy Concept 124; foreign policy thinking and decision-making 118–19; governance model 194–5; National Antiterrorist Committee (NAK) 125; National Security Strategy 124, 128, 131; New National Security Strategy (2009) 3; relations with international institutions 120–3; relations with US 154–5; security challenges 130–1; threat assessment and risk management 124–9; threats from 177; US dialogue with 109–10; WMD stockpiles 51–2

Sachs, Jeffrey 75, 79
Saint-Malo Summit (1998) 173
Sakhalin-II project 129
Saran, Shyam 163
sarin attacks, Tokyo (1995) 46
SARS outbreak (2003) 47
security challenges: China 140–4; Russia 130–1
security policy, EU 172–5
security priorities, China 138–44
security sector reform (SSR) 179, 181
security trends, energy 84–5
security: climate change as threat 88–90; concept of 6–12; definition of 82–3; energy as threat to 85–8; terrorism as threat to 25–7
Shanghai Convention on the Fight against Terrorism, Separatism and Extremism 146
Shanghai Cooperation Organization (SCO) 120, 146; Regional Anti-Terrorist Structure 161
"Shanghai Five" 146
shared threats 203
Sharif, Nawaz 159
Small Arms Trade Transparency Barometer 71
smallpox 52

soft power, EU 174
Solana, Xavier 193
sovereignty, China 139–40
special operations 37
stability, energy-rich nations 85–6
state centrality 5
state power, Russia 119
state weakness *see* fragile states
state-building: failing states 78–9; international support for 40
Steinbrück, Peer 107
Stepanova, Ekaterina 18, 23–41, 196, 198
Stern Review 89
Strategic Arms Reduction Treaty (START-I) 110, 127
strategic culture, EU 175
Strategic Offensive Reductions Treaty (SORT) 48
strategic response: Bush administration 103–7; fragile states 74–6
strategic threat, from fragile states 65–8
Sudan: energy production 88; as failing state 78–9; Russian relations with 126
superpower rivalry 7, 12
sustainable futures 95
sustainable security 83–4
Swine Flu pandemic (2009) 11, 54, 130–1

Taliban 105, 109, 159, 160
Tardy, Thierry 171–87, 194, 195
technical conditions for terrorism 30
territorial integrity, China 139–40
terrorism challenges, China 142
terrorism: and biological weapons 54; challenges of combating 36–7; and chemicals weapons 57; China's response to 146–7, 150–2; current trends in 32–7; defining as security threat 25–7; EU responses to 181–4; evolution of understanding of 30–2; in failing states 67–8, 71; India's response to 159–61; origins and periodization of 29–30; role of extremist ideologies 27–9; Russia's response to 124–5; traditional forms of 24; US strategic response to 103–7; and WMD 45–52
terrorist networks 33–5, 41
Thakur, Ramesh 198–9
threat assessment: EU 175–7; Russia 124–9
threat perception, US 102–3
Topolanek, Miroslav 113
toxic industrial chemicals (TICs) 57
toxins, proliferation of 52–4
traditional forms of terrorism 24; India 158
traditional threats, EU 177
transnational actors, rise of 9–10
Transparency International 15
transport infrastructures, oil/gas 85–6
trinitrotoluene (TNT) 50
Truman, Harry 105

Uighur groups, China 142

UK: Department for International Development
(DFID) 74; National Security Strategy 82, 89
unipolarity 101–2, 154–5; rejection of 118–19
United Nations (UN) Security Council 75, 89,
121, 146–7, 154, 156, 157, 159, 164, 167,
199; Chapter VII resolution 174; Resolution
1267 146, 159; Resolution 1368 146, 147–8;
Resolution 1390 146; Resolution 1540 51,
58, 61, 146, 147–8, 183; Russian
Federation's relations with 120–1; seats on 4
United Nations (UN): Arab Development
Report (2002) 104; Charter 145, 183; climate
conference (2009) 93; Conference on the
Environment and Development (1992) 10;
Framework Climate Change Convention
(2009) 150; General Assembly 89, 156–7,
162; High Level Panel on Threats,
Challenges and Change (2004) 76, 174–5;
Human Development Index 15; interventions
73, 77, 147, 148, 165, 173; Millennium
Development Goals 93; Peacebuilding
Commission 77; Report on Peacebuilding
(2009) 76; sanctions on Iran 143
US Intelligence Community threat assessments
89
US Millennium Challenge Accounts 70
US: Bush administration 102–7; challenges to
hegemony of 193–200; chemical weapons
stocks 56; dialogue and diplomacy 154–6;
energy policies/oil imports 86, 87; Freedom
Agenda 104, 106; *Global Trends 2005 – A
Transformed World* report 193; National
Intelligence Council 185–6, 193; National
Security Strategy (2002/2006) 3, 45, 66, 103,
154–5, 201; Northern Distribution Network
204; nuclear deal with India 49; Obama
administration 107–13; policy on Pakistan
159–61; power of 204–5; ratification of
CTBT 162–3; shared interests 199; State
Department 77; unipolarity 101–2
US–China Strategic and Economic Dialogue
(S&ED) 112, 196
use of force: capacity to authorise 120; EU
reluctance for 175

Vaahtoranta, Tapani 18, 82–95, 196–7, 199
Varadarajan, Siddharth 18, 154–68, 194, 195
vertical weapons proliferation 48
violence, targets of 26

Waltz, Kenneth 8
war on terror: and EU 182; failure of 101; nature
of 25; pre-emption/intelligence gathering
103–4, 108–9; targets of 23
Warsaw Treaty Organization 12
weapons of mass destruction (WMDs):
challenge of managing proliferation 47–58;
challenges for China 142–3; China's
response to 148–9, 150–2; EU response to
182–3; future trends in proliferation 58–60;
India's response to 161–4; link with terrorism
108; Russia's response to 126–8; threat level
32; threat of proliferation 45–7
Westphalia, Treaty of (1648) 7
Westphalian international system 5, 172
Wohlforth, William 101
World Bank 14, 70, 76; LICUS team 74; World
Development Report 78
World Commission on Environment and
Development (1987) 10
World Energy Conference 149
World Health Organization (WHO) 90
world order paradigms 12–17
world order (2025) 200–2; operational concept
of 4–5
World Trade Organization (WTO) 14, 102, 110,
122, 129
World Uighar Youth Congress 142
World War II 9, 55
world-view, US 102–3

Yeltsin, Boris 123
Yergin, Daniel 85
Ying, Fu 199
Yugoslavia, NATO operations in 120

Zakaria, Fareed 16
Zangger Committee 148
Zartman, William 72

what makes GP?
   capacity all about power
   reg recognition.

                    Capacity / recognition
                    ─────────────────────
                    Power   external
                               status

   great power

, - economic & poli political stability.

2 -   recognition -
          external

    GP = united nat UNSC.
       great power: needs to
    have nuclear weapon.!

       UNSC ⇄ EU
       WTO ⇄ EU

                        are
                    GP usually regional
                    hegemons.

Lightning Source UK Ltd.
Milton Keynes UK
UKOW05f1312060215

245807UK00003B/56/P